Self-Destruction

Self-Destruction

THE DISINTEGRATION AND DECAY OF THE UNITED STATES ARMY DURING THE VIETNAM ERA

by Cincinnatus

W·W·Norton & Company
New York London

LIBRARY
The University of Texas
At San Antonio

ALL RIGHTS RESERVED

Library of Congress Cataloging in Publication Data
Cincinnatus.
Self-destruction, the disintegration and decay of the
United States Army during the Vietnam Era.
    Bibliography: p.
    Includes index.
    1. United States. Army. 2. Vietnamese Conflict,
1961–1975—United States. I. Title.
UA23.C547 1981   355.4′8′09597   80–15803
ISBN 0–393–01346–4

W. W. Norton & Company, Inc. 500 Fifth Avenue, New York, N.Y. 10110
W. W. Norton & Company Ltd. 25 New Street Square, London EC4A3NT

2 3 4 5 6 7 8 9 0

To the
46,616 combat dead
and the
10,386 noncombat dead

57,002

Contents

Introduction

Since 1973, the standard explanation given by the military for the defeat of the United States Army in Vietnam is that the politicians were to blame. Had they given United States forces a free hand to do what needed to be done, the war would have been won. Without that freedom and unable to do what was necessary, the theory goes, the army was compromised and the battle was lost.

The author of this book is persuaded of the following propositions: The Vietnamese conflict, like all wars, was indeed a political war. Politicians did place certain limitations upon the United States Army's freedom of action. All armies face such restrictions. Within the bounds of those political restraints, America's military had wide latitude of action and a clear opportunity to win in Vietnam. It met defeat because it failed to "know the enemy" and therefore could not adopt the strategy and tactics that were specific to the particular enemy it faced, and because it forgot vital lessons learned in its own history. Vietnam showed clearly that our strategic and tactical military thought can be shamefully shallow and palpably wrong. It further demonstrated that as the war dragged on, the army acted as though it was more interested in self-perpetuation and self-aggrandizement than in the efficient fulfillment of its mission.

The defeat in Vietnam is behind us, but its nature poses queries about the future. Having been wrong in Vietnam, is the army's approach to conflict still wrong? Has the army begun an internal reassessment in order to identify and cure its ills? It is a question on which the future of the nation may hang.

The army chose not to adapt to the unique environment of Vietnam. It conducted big-unit operations against bands of guerrillas. It sought to achieve victory through attrition. It was uninterested in providing greater security for the people of the countryside and cities. It repeatedly relied on tactics already proven inadequate. It seemed not to understand the need for pacification and when it belatedly tried out that approach, it combined pacification with combat operations, thus negating both. It relied too heavily on technology and the lavish use of firepower. It refused to adopt more primitive tactics that could have dealt effectively with the sort of enemy it faced. It ignored calls for change that came from within. It continued to function as if it was pursuing enemy units of the Warsaw Pact nations across the plains of central Europe.

Stated simply, the army made too many mistakes in its years in Vietnam. If those same errors are not to be repeated in some future conflict, their sources must be identified, understood, and corrected. At some point, for reasons then believed good, America's army will once again be sent into battle. It will be unfortunate if it has closed its eyes to the lessons of Vietnam and again faces a débacle.

America's military must remain healthy and innovative. It must encourage the original thinkers within its ranks if it is to meet diverse challenges from diverse foes. It must learn to encourage suggestions and criticisms from within its own ranks and listen to challenges to its doctrines of battle. For too long, innovative thought on strategy and tactics has come not from within the army but from civilian contract consultants. Unlike in the earlier days of Sherman and Lee, McArthur and Patton, Thayer and Mahan, Washington and Greene, officers today offer infrequent and usually low-level "suggestions."

The army's view of its military mission has been out of focus. It thoroughly misunderstood the appropriate ways to fight limited wars or wars of national liberation within the Third World. Past mistakes are unacknowledged. The old, old refrain that the army failed because of political softness and social unrest at home is still the theme song of the upper ranks. The fact is that the military disaster in Vietnam grew out of ineptitude at the top.

The pages that follow narrate the manifestations and explore the causes of that ineptitude. It is to be hoped that this document will engender comment and debate. There are many within the military hierarchy who still believe in old ways and who will dispute what follows. Such debate is essential if from the Vietnam crucible is to come improvement in the flexibility of thinking and tactical adaptability of this nation's military forces.

The material set forth here may seem obvious. In one sense, at least, it is, for all the information set down here long has been available to the army's leaders. Had they been persuaded of its validity, they would have instigated changes. They should be aware that the ideas here are not the author's alone but that they enjoy consensus among countless hundreds of his associates within the military who are Vietnam veterans. Attention paid to problems now might save a new generation of American soldiers from another disaster.

*   *   *

As its title indicates, this study deals with troubles encountered by the United States Army during the years of the Vietnam conflict. It is not a history either of Vietnam during those years or of America's involvement there. Numerous chronologies exist, many of which are cited herein.

Although the pages that follow center upon the years of United States activity in Vietnam and use illustrative material from that conflict, their focus is on the United States Army (and occasionally on its sister services) during that war. More specifically, it is a discussion of the difficulties that arose within that branch of the military as a result of its participation in combat in Southeast Asia. The focus is on the army rather than upon the totality of United States forces, not because other branches had no problems, but in order to make this study manageable in size and because the author knows the army more intimately. Furthermore, the war was mainly an army war. That branch provided the most men and the military commanders, and established the parameters of the war. Although their members might disagree, the navy, the air force, the marines, and the Coast Guard all fought as auxiliaries to the main effort on the ground.

The insights of those who actually served and fought in Vietnam are basic to a document such as this. Too little effort has been made to record those impressions and convictions while they remain fresh. Thus, in addition to studying available written sources (published and unpublished, private and public, civilian and military, classified and unclassified), it seemed valuable to interview as many persons as possible who had been there. The author gathered opinions and reactions from veterans who ranged from generals to privates, from military wives to National Guardsmen, from the cautious to the bold, from the optimistic to the cynical, from those still on active duty to those who have resigned or been retired.

The bulk of the conversations were taped and were held with men in grades from captain to colonel, most of whom are still in active service. By and large they showed a real willingness to help and expressed hope that reforms might come about as a result of this work. Some of those interviewed were contacted a second or third time for additional discussions. The analysis developed here has resulted from careful study of as much of the writing about Vietnam as the author could master and from extensive consideration of the remarks made to him by officers and enlisted men over a period of many months of travel and interviewing.

In many cases, those interviewed wished to remain anonymous. Many feared that their careers would be jeopardized if their comments were publicly attributed to them. Several refused to have their words tape recorded, and one or two did not even want notes to be taken during the conversations. Since so many desired anonymity, this treatment was extended to all who are quoted herein.

Eventually it was decided to extend the cloak of anonymity beyond those who were interviewed and to cover the author's own identity. In certain churches, ministers wear dark clerical garb to obscure as much as possible of themselves in order to allow their listeners to concentrate exclusively upon what is being said rather than upon who is saying it. That is my hope here as well.

*   *   *

It is difficult, in a project that by necessity takes this form, to give thanks in any appropriate way to all those who have offered me so much counsel and support. Without their aid, this book could not have been written. As always, there have been some who have been of particular help, and to them I offer special thanks. Perhaps they will be able to recognize themselves within the list below.

LTC J.D.A.
COL. R.F.E.
LTC R.S.L.
MAJ J.L.Y.
CPT H.R.C.
LTC ....V.
COL B.E.J.
MAJ S.E.H.
COL T.B.W.
GEN ....A.
LTC T.A.S.
MAJ ....E.
LTC ....S.
MAJ L.B.C
SSGT J.S.
LTC ....D.
LTC W...F.
LTC ....G.
LTC A.B.J.
LTC ....M.
LTC B...M.
LTC H.A.S.
LTC L.G.W
MAJ L.J.S.

They come from many branches: Artillery, Infantry, the Chaplaincy, Medical Corps, Intelligence, Adjutant General's Corps, Armor, Engineers, Signal, Quartermaster, Transportation, and Military Police.

Most hold regular-army commissions, although one is a navy officer and two are officers in the United States Air Force, while four others serve in the Army National Guard.

With but one exception, they all served in Vietnam. They were stationed in places from Nam Can to Con Thien, on assignments ranging from a LRRP member to brigade commander to divisional staffs, from Saigon posts to senior province advisers in "eye" corps, from Special Forces units to ARVN-counterpart advisers.

They served. They offered their help on this manuscript.

They have my thanks.

COL E.R.S.
COL A.W.G.
COL R...M.
LTC T.D.C.
LTC B.K.W.

Prof. L.A.P. Prof. R.P.I. Prof. T.P.D.	My academic advisers: men knowledgeable in their fields who saved me from many pitfalls and who proferred much help.
Mrs. A.B.E.	My able and invaluable assistant.
Mr. W.E.H. Mrs. J.J.A. Mrs. L.G.C.	My readers and critics of my writing style who enabled me to set this forth in English.
. . . G.	My consort.
and, of course,	My editor, Eric P. Swenson

Observations and conclusions throughout are my own. Errors of any kind that persist into print do so in spite of those listed above.

CINCINNATUS

July 1979

Glossary

AID (USAID) United States Agency for International Development

American decade The years of greatest U.S. involvement in Vietnam, 1964–1973

Aerial Observer (AO) An observer, often for an artillery unit, who makes his terrain surveillance from a helicopter

Army Regulation (AR) Rules established by the army to govern actions and activities in the several areas of military endeavor

Army of the Republic of Vietnam (ARVN) The South Vietnamese army

Body counts The practice by the United States and its allies in Vietnam of tallying enemy dead and using such figures as "statistical indicators of military success"

Combined Action Program (Platoon) (CAP) A marines program for integrating U.S. and Vietnamese troops into coherent units for purposes of local security operations

Cherim A Hebrew word meaning "holy war of destruction"

Chieu Hoi A program in effect for a time during the Vietnamese conflict in which enemy soldiers were encouraged to defect to friendly forces; the term is a Vietnamese word meaning "open arms"

Civilian Irregular Defense Group(s) (CIDG) A Vietnamese defense force

CINCPAC Commander-in-Chief, Pacific

COMUSMACV Commander, U.S. Military Assistance Command, Vietnam

CORDS Civil Operations and Revolutionary Development Support

CP Command Post

Enclave strategy A program espoused by Gen. James Gavin in which U.S. forces would clear and hold certain areas—or enclaves—along the Vietnamese coast

FM Field Manual

FO Forward observer for an artillery unit

Fodding A term current within the U.S. Air Force and Navy referring to damage of machinery: foreign-object damage

Fragging The term used to describe efforts at harassment and assassination of career enlisted men and officers by disgruntled draftees

Free Fire Zone An area of terrain in which artillery could target and fire without restriction

Friendly fires The volume of fire, usually artillery, fired by U.S. forces against the enemy

Friendly wounds An injury suffered by an American soldier from friendly fires

FSB Fire-support base

Geneva Accords Signed on 20 July 1954, following the Vietminh victory at Dienbienphu, in order to put an end to the French Indochinese war by ordering a cessation of hostilities in all Vietnam. These accords established a temporary demarcation line at the 17th Parallel, north of which Communist forces were to regroup, while forces allied with the French were to do so in the south. General elections, which were to have been scheduled within a short time, were never held.

Gook Derogatory term used by U.S. soldiers to refer to Vietnamese nationals

Green Machine A term used by draftees to refer to the institutional army

H and I Harassing-and-interdiction artillery fires

Hoc tap A Vietnamese word meaning "reeducation"

IDAD Internal defense and development—a term referring to efforts at pacification of the countryside population of Vietnam; synonomous with stability operations, revolutionary development, internal security, pacification, the other war, rural construction, neutralization operations, nation building

Infantry-heavy forces American division weighted to give it more infantrymen than it would normally have

Internal Security See IDAD

JCS Joint Chiefs of Staff

LRRP Long-range reconnaissance patrol(s)

LZ A landing zone for helicopter use

MAAG Military Assistance Advisory Group

MACV Military Assistance Command, Vietnam; the general headquarters and staff of the American expeditionary forces in Vietnam

MASSTER Mobile Army Sensor Systems Test and Evaluation Resources

MTOE Modified table of organization

Nation building See IDAD

Navarre Plan The program of GEN Paul Henri Navarre, which he devised to defeat the Vietminh insurrection in French Indochina

Neutralization Operations See IDAD

NLF National Liberation Front; the political organization for South Vietnamese guerrilla forces

NVA North Vietnamese army

OPLAN CEDAR FALLS Operation Cedar Falls—a division-sized search-and-destroy mission in Vietnam

OPLAN JUNCTION CITY Operation Junction City—a division-sized search-and-destroy mission in Vietnam

OPLAN ROLLING THUNDER The U.S. Air Force's operation calling for the massive and continuous bombing of North Vietnam

"Other War" See IDAD

Pacification See IDAD

Phuong Hoang A Vietnamese word meaning "phoenix"; the program of disruption and assassination of the VCI

PRG Provisional Revolutionary Government for the VC National Liberation Front, constituted on 6 June 1969

PIO Public Information Office of the United States Army; now usually referred to as Public Affairs Office

Punji stakes Sharpened bamboo stakes, usually smeared with feces, located within cover and concealment, on which unwary American soldiers might step or fall

Revolutionary Development   See IDAD

RF/PF   Regional Forces/Popular Forces

ROAD   Reorganization of Army Divisions—a periodic shuffling of the military fighting structure

Rural Construction   See IDAD

Sapper   An infiltrator who makes his way through enemy defenses in order to set charges and blow holes in those defenses

Shekina   A Hebrew word meaning "the visible presence of JHWH"

Stability Operations   See IDAD

TAADS   The Army Authorization Document System—a record-keeping method used by the U.S. Army

Tailoring   The name used for the shuffling of combat forces to provide for more or less of one type of unit as the need arises

TAOR   Tactical Area of Responsibility

TOE   Table of organization and equipment

VCI   Vietcong infrastructure; that is, the leadership organization of the guer- rilla movement within South Vietnam

Viet Cong   A Vietnamese term signifying the "Communist" guerrillas within the south

Viet Minh   The name of the guerrillas during the anti-French resistance

Vietnamization   The term used to describe the American attempt to turn the main role in the Vietnam War over to the government and army of the south

ZI   A military term for the U.S.—the zone of the interior

Self-Destruction

One

The last United States military unit was withdrawn from Vietnam on March 29, 1973. As late as 1978, General William C. Westmoreland, a central figure during the United States intervention in Vietnam, speaking before the student body at the United States Army Command and General Staff College at Fort Leavenworth, Kansas, observed that "the handling of the Vietnam affair was a shameful national blunder." Although few could disagree at that point, he went on to make clear what he meant. America's military forces in Vietnam had been hamstrung by the home front's politicization of the war. The army had been prevented from doing what needed to be done. Political controls of various kinds had been imposed, which doomed the military enterprise to ultimate failure.

According to Westmoreland, the war dragged on indefinitely because of political considerations. "It is lamentable," said the retired general, "that so many did all possible to erode support for a policy associated with six presidents and endorsed by nine Congresses." Betrayal of America's goals and national will, however, was accompanied, he said, by a "sterling performance of the military" as it fought the forces and wily minions of Hanoi. General Westmoreland insisted that "in our national interest, that unhappy experience should not be swept under the rug and forgotten," for "there are lessons to be learned."[1] On that point only should there be any widespread agreement with the general.

Wrong in his assessments during his time as commander in Vietnam, Westmoreland remains an unreconstructed advocate of the proposition that America's politicians and populace betrayed its own military during those difficult days. He believes that United States fighting men, had they been freed from restrictions and properly supported, could have achieved victory in Vietnam.

Westmoreland's comments are typical of those of many of his peers.

Throughout the Vietnam era, our military leaders were the ones who briefed the politicians, who planned the operations, who developed the tactics, and who ordered the assaults. They were not only consistently wrong in their assessments; they were ineffective in execution of their own concepts. Time and again, new and "flawless" proposals were set forth by our military leaders that would theoretically allow for real advance to be made militarily against the Viet Cong and North Vietnamese regular soldiers. Repeatedly these proposals had to be abandoned in the face of unforeseen difficulties. Failures mounted year upon year.

Despite a nearly unlimited supply of airplanes and artillery, M-16s and mortars, napalm and night scopes, draft levies and deficit-swollen defense budgets, the richest nation on earth was unable to impose a military solution upon one of the poorer countries of Asia. Successive war plans emanated from the highest levels of our military leadership, which then was unable to carry them out. In all, the Vietnam war revealed a shockingly low caliber of military leadership, which in turn was an indictment of the selection and promotion process within the United States armed forces.

It is not surprising that Westmoreland should have sought to pin responsibility for such failures upon segments of the population outside the military. However, the fact is that America's military establishment had a very free hand in the prosecution of the war.

Except insofar as all wars have political limitations and consequences and all generals have certain restraints laid upon them by the political structure within which they operate, the United States military forces during the Vietnam era had political support for their efforts until the very end. America did suffer a political defeat in Southeast Asia but even more basically it suffered a military defeat brought about by the ineptness of its soldier leaders. Most of them quite naturally sought to lay the blame for failure elsewhere.

Some time in the future, for reasons that at the time will be believed to be good, American soldiers will again fight on hostile and foreign soil. It would seem essential that this nation learn the lessons taught by our military failure in Vietnam.

*   *   *

The land of Vietnam consists of the eastern portion of a long peninsula at the southeastern tip of Asia, shaped like a giant letter *S*, jutting south out of China into the South China Sea. The northern part of this land consists of the heavily populated, highly cultivated, and very productive delta of the Red River. As one moves south, these northern flatlands give way to a long, undulating coast pocketed by small, fertile plains, occasionally challenged by rocky promontories reaching out into the sea. This thin coastal strip widens, further south, eventually falling toward the rich alluvial loam of the delta country around the Mekong River. The inland mountains of the north slope into the Annamite chain, which merges with a group of western plateaux. From north to south, the high country follows a line parallel with that of the coast.[2]

Chinese and European names came to be fixed upon this land; thus in modern times it has been known as Cochinchina (South Vietnam), Annam (Central Vietnam), and Tonkin (North Vietnam). In the Vietnamese language, those names are Trung Viet, Bac Viet, and Nam Viet, respectively. The Vietnamese derived the name Nam Viet, the earliest of the lands they eventually inhabited, from the Chinese *Yueh-nan,* an ancient term for the South Chinese province of Kwangtung. Written in Vietnamese characters, it meant "south of Yueh," and later simply "Land of the South" or "distant south."

While under Chinese control, the Vietnamese drank deeply of the wisdom of Confucius. They based much of their society upon his doctrines and from them developed well-ordered patterns of living, which continued largely unchanged for dozens of generations. Custom and law molded everyone into the place in life that was rightful and proper. One's primary and basic loyalty was to the family, which included not only the living but also the dead. Ancestors were neither really dead nor forgotten. They played an important role in family affairs and were consulted periodically by the father, who believed that they could offer both protection and helpful advice. All family obligations were respected, extending even to remote cousins. Respect prevailed at all levels—brother to elder brother, wife to husband, son to father, all to those who had become ancestors. Loyalty, obedience, and status were bywords for Vietnamese families.

Almost everywhere throughout the land, people labored as rice farmers, and the land they tilled was sacred to them. It cradled the graves of their ancestors, the hut in which the family lived, the hamlet of several nearby families, and the village, which was made up of two or more hamlets. Life was very rural, and the Vietnamese people drew their strength from the soil on which they lived.

Social classes and status grew out of broad-based support from these rice farmers. Above them were landowners, merchants and artisans, priests, mandarin scholars, and nobles. At the top was the emperor as head of state. Separate from the rest were those men who had failed at all other livelihoods and were thus forced to become soldiers. Such men were the least respected class in society. They might, from time to time, have power but never respect.[3]

The basic governmental organization was the village, consisting of a cluster of hamlets, each of which might better be described as a neighborhood, divided along geographic or residential lines. The population of such a village might range from several hundred to several thousand families who were thus enabled to share a common leadership, a community center house, and usually a market. Modern Vietnam had some seventeen thousand such hamlets, which composed roughly eight thousand villages.

The people of such settlements looked to one another and within themselves for guidance and direction rather than outward toward some "higher" government. Here were their families and the spirits of their ancestors—all associated with home and village—and so they remained on the same land through successive generations, spiritually linked in a continuity with the past. So tied were these people to their native villages that they seldom traveled more than a short walk from their homes throughout their entire lives. And those villages survived the vagaries of war, the idiosyncrasies of successive emperors, and the destruction of the Vietnamese empire.

Government within such villages was exercised by the fathers, who were heads of households, by teachers, who were given great respect because of their learning, and by elected village elders. Resistance was inevitably fierce over the years when any ruler endeavored to tamper with this village autonomy, for to do so ran counter to the force behind an old saying: "The law of the sovereign gives way before the custom of the village." The system of villages embraced nearly 95 percent of the Vietnamese population, and except at tax time the people had little contact with any higher echelon of government. As they said, "The authority of the emperor stops at the village gate."[4]

Immediately above the village was the canton, roughly equivalent to an American county. Here again the village played a role, for canton leaders were elected by village elders. Above the canton was the province, its overseers appointed by the emperor or his representatives. These administrators of the state were mandarins who for at least a thousand years played a fixed and important role in government. Steeped in the lore of Confucius, they held authority based on their knowledge of the wisdom of the past. Their primary task was to insure that little changed, that society looked to old answers rather than to new ideas. In this way they guided the conventional behavior of the Vietnamese.

Mandarins perpetuated a static world view, which provided an internal order based on obedience, loyalty, hierarchy, and respect. Social change was to be avoided; one's duty was to follow the way of the past. They thus maintained a collective society in which the interests of individuals would always voluntarily be subordinated to those of the group: the family, the land, the hamlet, the village, teachers, elders, mandarins, nobles, emperor. From this structure grew a situation strange to Western eyes. Acceptance of such authority meant that individuals never thought of themselves as occupying a position where they could control or even affect their own environment. They never developed any clear notion of the idea of free will that has been so important in the lives of Europeans.

At the apex of society was the emperor, a father figure and chief religious leader, who was believed to be able to communicate directly with heavenly powers as he acted out his role of intermediary between the gods and the people. His was not a necessarily hereditary throne, for his subjects believed that national misfortune was an indication that he had lost heaven's mandate and therefore should be replaced by someone else. It is little wonder that when Vietnam was ravaged by war, first by the French and then by their American successors, the people believed that the puppets who represented those nations had lost the mandate of heaven, particularly when neither nation was able either to destroy the guerrilla infrastructure or to block North Vietnamese troop infiltration into the south.

As a result of repeated invasions, expansion, and the passage of time, the Vietnamese developed regional differences. These should not, however, obscure the recognition of a strong sense of unity within the Vietnamese nation—north, central, and south. Political turbulence has never been able to limit the nationalism the people feel. Those who lived in the south during the American intervention did not, for example, regard Ho Chi Minh as a northern foreigner, but simply as another Vietnamese like themselves. Many, whether they lived north or south of the 17th Parallel, shared one common hope: they looked forward to a day of liberation when their country would be free from foreign domination, for Vietnam had been a captive of European colonization since the nineteenth century. Dismemberment of Vietnam began on 31 August 1857 and lasted twenty-six years, by which time the French controlled the entire country.[5]

For a time shortly after World War II it looked to proponents of Vietnamese independence as if they had secured their goal. On 29 August 1945, the Viet Minh founded their "Provisional Government of the Democratic Republic of Vietnam," and on 2 September, Ho Chi Minh formally proclaimed the independence of his nation. His words ring familiar to American ears:

> All men are created equal. They are endowed by their Creator with certain inalienable rights, among these are Life, Liberty, and the pursuit of Happiness.
>
> This immortal statement was made in the Declaration of Independence of the United States of America in 1776. In a broader sense, this means: All the peoples on the earth are equal from birth, all the peoples have a right to live, to be happy and free.[6]

An independent Vietnam did not last long, for the French were adamant about reinstating their colonial rule there. They made the most of Mao Tse-tung's Communist takeover of mainland China at the end of 1949, parading themselves as the West's front-line troops, bravely combating the minions of Asiatic communism by standing firm in the path of Mao Tse-tung's hordes, who surely would move into Indochina at the earliest opportunity. If Europeans proved faint at such a moment, all of Asia would quickly fall under Communist control. Only France stood in the gap. A sullied colonial military venture thus began to take on the overtones of a "holy war" with the French *shekina* leading the Western chosen peoples on a *cherim* against the "Reds."

Prior to this time, the United States had taken little interest in the struggles in Indochina, other than to suggest occasionally to its European ally that it might do well to grant independence there, or at least a fuller measure of self-rule. This changed after the fall of China and the recognition by China and the Soviet Union of Ho Chi Minh's government on 18 and 31 January 1950, respectively. "Communist" was a fearful word in America's lexicon.

The United States actually knew almost nothing about Vietnam except what it was told by the French. Certainly it was difficult for the government in Washington to consult on the issues at stake with the Vietnamese, for there were few American experts in Vietnamese linguistics or studies upon whom the American government could call for advice.[7] John T. McAlister, Jr., writes that it was not until his senior year in college at Yale in 1957 that he prevailed upon the faculty there to institute the nation's first university-level course in the Vietnamese language—seven years after America's opening moves into Vietnam. That introductory course in the Vietnamese language had three students.[8] Whatever "expertise" America had in the Vietnamese language, culture, and history came after, rather than prior to, our involvement there. The United States military had to assign selected officers to become "familiar" with the customs and language of Vietnam. Men so chosen had to divide their time and effort between school and military duties, study and service in various tasks. There was never time to reflect quietly, to study at leisure, to become versed in the alien ways of that country in order to prepare plans based upon thorough knowledge. The result was disastrous.

By 1954 America was subsidizing much of the cost of France's colonial war. Despite massive injections of money and matériel, French military efforts in Vietnam were in disarray. It had lost all but a small portion of the country.[9] The French consistently made mistakes from which they did not learn and which the United States would repeat a decade and more later. What Westmoreland would describe as "search and destroy" was known to the French as "hit and run." The French referred to indiscriminate artillery fires as "raking over" the countryside. American batteries used the nomenclature of "free-fire zones," on which they dropped "harassing and interdicting" shells. The French cleared an area of enemy troops in "mopping up" actions; American

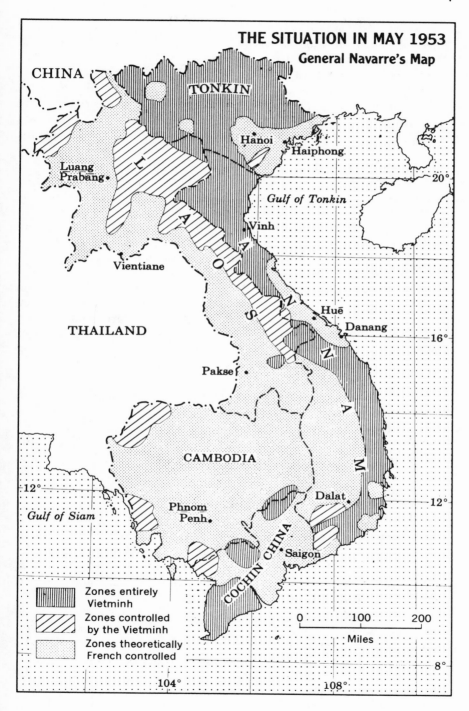

THE SITUATION IN MAY 1953
General Navarre's Map

CHINA

TONKIN

Hanoi
Haiphong

Luang
Prabang

20°

Gulf of Tonkin

Vinh

L
A
O
S

Vientiane

Hué

THAILAND

Danang

16°

Pakse

N
A
M

CAMBODIA

Dalat

12°
12°

Phnom
Penh.

Gulf of Siam

COCHIN CHINA

Saigon

Zones entirely
Vietminh
Zones controlled
by the Vietminh
Zones theoretically
French controlled

0   100   200

Miles

8°

104°
108°

and South Vietnamese commands called such operations "seize and hold" or "clear and hold." French commanders made use of falsified "body counts," freely admitting that the way to find a Viet Minh soldier was to look for any dead Vietnamese.

The United States would later imitate, also unsuccessfully, France's earlier effort to bind military operations and civil-action programs into one combined thrust toward pacification, thus "winning the hearts and minds of the people." Both nations used Vietnamese troops against other Vietnamese soldiers, and both were repeatedly appalled at the unwillingness of southerners to fight their northern cousins.

"Vietnamization" of the war was still another idea developed by the French. Paul Reynaud, vice-premier of France, proclaimed in June 1953: "This war must stop being a French war supported by Vietnam and become a Vietnamese war supported by France." In his turn, General Creighton Abrams could not have phrased it more aptly.[10]

In the midst of French disaster, the renowned General Henri-Eugène Navarre arrived in Indochina to take command of the war effort and recoup French losses. Counseled by Lieutenant General John ("Iron Mike") O'Daniel, head of a special American advisory mission, Navarre came up with a concept known as the "Navarre Plan." Other Americans also gave the French general the benefit of their ideas, including the members of the Military Assistance Advisory Group (MAAG) in Saigon and a ubiquitous CIA agent who usually wore an Air Force uniform, Colonel Edward Lansdale.[11]

Under the Navarre Plan, the French would tempt the Viet Minh forces into the open by offering their own army as attractive bait. When the Viet Minh struck, they would be crushed by French forces. As he activated the Navarre Plan in the fall of 1953, Navarre commanded a huge army of over five hundred thousand men—only a few thousand short of what the American force would be at its height a decade and a half later. Eighty thousand French officers, noncommissioned officers, and specialists controlled 48,000 troops from French colonies in North Africa, 20,000 soldiers from mixed backgrounds serving with the foreign legion, and nearly 370,000 Indochinese fighting men. All of this had cost America a great deal of money and materiel. Since 1950, America had sent hundreds of tons of war supplies, including planes, boats, tanks, thousands of heavy weapons, small arms without number, and millions of rounds of ammunition.

Dien Bien Phu, which in the Vietnamese language meant "seat of the border-county prefecture," was a fortress in northwest Vietnam only eight miles from Laos, named for a small village of 112 houses, the main crops of which were rice and opium. Positioned in a valley twelve miles long and four miles wide, ringed with jungle and surrounded by hills, the fortress was impregnable against all types of attack except artillery. That was what made it such an attractive location for Navarre, for he knew that the Viet Minh would find it impossible to transport what few field pieces they had along the narrow jungle trails and over the mountains on a 350-mile-long supply line.

Beginning 20 November 1953, French planes carried thousands of parachute troops to the fortress. Thousands of soldiers and vast quantities of matériel were dropped onto the site. Ultimately, 10,814 men-at-arms waited there for a Viet Minh attack. They dug bunkers, extended trenches, emplaced claymore mines, unrolled concertina wire, and endured the hot, muggy climate.

The troops were French, but the battle would be fought according to American ideas and with American equipment, the cost of which, for this one battle alone, totaled more than $10 million. Americans suggested where the French should emplace their field pieces and where automatic weapons should be sited. Nothing in the records suggests that any of the high-ranking American visitors who came to the fortress were concerned about the nearby hills or suggested that if the Viet Minh had artillery, the French would find themselves in a hopeless situation. On the contrary, they were elated at the prospect of victory. Their optimism was duly reported at home. *U.S. News and World Report* informed its readers that "victory in Indochina, in short, is within . . . grasp . . . in the opinion of most American experts."[12] An ecstatic General Navarre spoke of his coming success: "A year ago none of us could see victory. There wasn't a prayer. Now we see it clearly—like light at the end of a tunnel."[13] The analogy would be used later, again and again.

The jungle and hills around Dien Bien Phu began to fill with Viet Minh troops. A few opening shots sounded on 12 March 1954. Their piercing whistle must have horrified the French defenders, for they were *artillery* rounds. That which had been adjudged impossible by the best minds of the French and American armies had occurred. Using coolie labor and human backs, the Viet Minh troops had hauled heavy artillery pieces through savage terrain into the hills overlooking Dien Bien Phu. Those tubes were well laid and pinpointed on precise targets. The French suffered casualties almost immediately as the enemy artillery "walked" rounds toward their bunkers and redoubts. The enemy had not only field pieces but also some forty thousand combat troops— all dedicated to overwhelming and annihilating the eleven thousand French defenders.

On 17 April, while the battle still raged, President Dwight D. Eisenhower spoke of Indochina and of falling dominoes. The loss of Vietnam would topple Burma, then Thailand, the peninsula, and finally, Indonesia. The consequences would be "just incalculable." Dominoes would become one of his favorite analogies, one that would long outlive him.

For over fifty days French troops fought bravely at Dien Bien Phu against superior odds. On the fifty-fifth day, 7 May 1954, they surrendered, having suffered the worst defeat ever administered to a French colonial army. All across Vietnam the tricolor began to come down as France faced the prospect of forced withdrawal from Indochina. The French had lost their colony through stubbornness and pedantic thinking, refusing to admit to the potential strength of their enemy. That same attitude would later become a pervasive one among Americans as well.

When on 4 June 1954 France gave Vietnam its independence, only one man in that country seemed prominent enough and sufficiently untainted by either French or Viet Minh to be worthy of United States support. His name was Ngo Dinh Diem. He took office as premier on 7 July. Aware of these developments in Saigon, Ho Chi Minh installed himself in Hanoi, renaming the Viet Minh the North Vietnamese People's Army, and the temporary demarcation line of the 17th Parallel became a political and geographical boundary line, separating the region controlled by the Viet Minh from that supervised by Diem's government in the south. For approximately two years there was a lull in military conflict in now divided Vietnam, while governments of north and south consolidated themselves and the population shifted back and forth as people sought to move to the region with which they felt the most sympathy. The result was a massive and confused *hegira.*

After an election in which he established himself as president of the Republic of Vietnam (carrying the 450,000 registered voters of Saigon by some 605,025 votes), Diem dramatically increased his hold on the south, using aid offered by the United States, which was swiftly building an overseas civil-military bureaucracy in Vietnam. Personnel of the United States Operations Mission (USOM) tendered technical advice. The American Agency for International Development (USAID) provided money and a great many experts, who offered answers to immediate problems. The Central Intelligence Agency (CIA) honed in on problems of security for the new nation, and its agents moved among the people, recruiting and training them for possible counterguerrilla activities. Early in February 1955, the first three hundred United States Army advisers arrived in Saigon under the auspices of the United States Military Assistance and Advisory Group (USMAAG) to train Diem's new Army of the Republic of Vietnam (ARVN). That army would soon be put to the test.

Members of the Viet Minh who had remained in place in the south became active again in 1956. They formed small cadres, which moved through villages, teaching that Diem and his government were traitors to Vietnam: he was a dictator, a puppet of the United States. Bands of guerrillas kidnapped and occasionally murdered village and hamlet officials who were too openly sympathetic to the Saigon government.[14] Diem reacted to this threat by sneering at it, contemptuously dismissing the dissidents as Vietnamese Communists—Viet Cong. In September 1959, Viet Cong guerrillas first tested themselves against regular South Vietnamese troops. They had previously shown that they could succeed against local police in skirmishes and raids on hamlets. Now it was time to see what they could do against supposedly better-trained and -equipped troops. In that one month they engaged and defeated two ARVN companies, which performed so poorly that they cast real doubts upon the abilities of the Diem government to field an adequate army and upon the American advisers who had trained ARVN troops. In January 1960, the Viet Cong struck again, destroying another ARVN unit. From that point on, they increased the frequency of attack on South Vietnamese forces.

The stage was set for a conflict that would ravage Vietnam, kill hundreds of thousands, make millions homeless, destroy vital resources, drag the United States government and its people into an undeclared war, and besmirch the reputation and bring into question the ability of the United States Army.[15]

* * *

The United States Army faced a guerrilla war in Vietnam, a small Southeast Asian country of some 65,000 square miles with a population of about 16,000,000 people. That nation fought to a standstill the United States of America, with over 200,000,000 citizens—one of the largest nations on earth and, surely, one of the most powerful.

America's fighting men won every major battle, including such crucial conflicts as Ap Bia (called "Hamburger Hill" by those who fought there) in the Au Shau Valley, Khe Sanh, and Tet 1968, yet they lost the war. Maneuver battalions of the United States Army, equipped with the latest weapons that Western technology could provide, struggled through the brush and jungle never knowing the kind of war they were fighting and seldom seeing the enemy unless he chose to let them. United States Army officers served as "expert" advisers to every level of Vietnam's civil and military hierarchy and succeeded not in furthering the war effort but in compounding confusion and in creating a mirror image of the American military system with all its blindnesses. As Edward Lansdale once observed: "The harsh fact . . . is that, despite the use of overwhelming amounts of men, money and materiel, despite the quantity of well-meant American advice and despite the impressive statistics of casualties inflicted on the Viet Cong, the Communist subversive insurgents . . . still retain the initiative to act at their will in the very areas of Viet Nam where Vietnamese and American efforts have been most concentrated."[16]

From beginning to end the United States Army faced a guerrilla war in Vietnam. It should have been capable of a more appropriate reaction to such an enemy, for it had had vast experience in facing such foes. Americans first encountered enemies who used guerrilla methods while they remained colonial subjects of Great Britain. Various Indian tribes, experts at hit-and-run tactics, at ambush, at cover and conceal-ment, at forest fighting, at harassment of superior forces, bitterly re-sisted their displacement from ancestral lands by white settlers. Out of necessity, American colonists living in the wilderness studied such tac-tics and adopted and adapted to them. From the uprising in Virginia colony in 1622 through Braddock's Defeat in 1754 to the Seminole Wars from 1835 to 1842 to Wounded Knee in 1890, Indian tribal warri-ors gave lessons to American soldiers in the inherent nature of guerrilla warfare.

During the French and Indian (or Seven Years) War (1754–1763), an American, Major Robert Rogers, formed a fighting corps six hundred strong called "Rogers' Rangers," which, using guerrilla tactics with dash and courage, clashed repeatedly with French forces and their Indian allies. Those Rangers were not only skilled in Indian-style fighting but, when the need arose, could also engage enemy main-force units in "set piece" battles, as they proved in their capture of Ft. Ponchartrain in 1760. Today's American Ranger units trace their heraldry back to Ro-gers' Rangers of colonial times. Their mission is to be as skilled as was Rogers in raiding and close combat behind enemy lines.

During the American Revolution, Lieutenant Colonel Francis Mar-ion, a native of South Carolina, gathered a raiding force to harass the British regular army in the South. The Redcoats were never able to close with this legendary will-o'-the-wisp who knew the terrain so well that time after time he escaped from pursuers into the sanctuary of Carolina's marshes. Thence, rested and restored, Marion would again lead his men forth to fall upon unsuspecting British units. An assault completed, Marion, the "Swamp Fox," would once more vanish.

A contemporary of the "Swamp Fox" was the commander in chief of the American army, George Washington. Writers have too often underestimated or belittled his military skills, for his actions during the Revolution indicate that he was familiar with principles basic to uncon-ventional warfare. General Washington knew the great value of dedica-tion to revolutionary principles: the ideals, motivation, and commit-ment of leaders must be beyond question, and he became a living symbol of dedication to the American cause. He was wise enough to know that he could not survive if he pitted his troops in pitched battle against the British except in unusual circumstances. Thus he harassed supply lines. When his troops were cornered, he led them as they slipped away during the night while their campfires still burned, mov-ing through British lines to launch a surprise attack in the enemy's rear area.

Washington seldom attacked an objective save when he felt confi-dent that his troops outnumbered the British, thus increasing the odds for a victory. Washington knew the value of "public" and "world" opinion and skillfully manipulated it through use of volunteers from several nations, who were given high rank and position. Through most of the maneuver terrain of America, Washington could be certain of support from the civilian population, while the British were everywhere confronted by stolid, suspicious, and angry faces. Perhaps most important of all, Washington recognized that to endure long enough was to win. His gainsayers aside, it is no accident that both Mao and Ho studied Washington's military career seeking to gain insights that they could adapt for use in their own revolutionary struggles. More emphasis needs to be given to and more studies need to be made of Washington as a role model for later leaders of revolutionary warfare.

Both North and South employed guerrillas during the savage years of the American Civil War, but the outstanding example was the Confederate officer Colonel John S. Mosby, the "Gray Ghost." An adept at guerrilla tactics, Mosby led his mounted Raiders in numerous forays behind Union lines. They blew bridges, seized supplies, cut communications lines, ambushed Northern units (and occasionally fought head-on against Union cavalry forces), and in one spectacularly successful adventure kidnapped a Union general and thirty-three men of his command. For several years the elusive Mosby spread confusion and havoc among his foes by his use of guerrilla tactics.

The years following Appomattox brought no diminution of the army's opportunities to remain acquainted with guerrilla warfare. Those were the decades when Indian tribes made their last stands for independence and freedom. Sioux, Comanche, Kiowa, Arapahoe, and Apache all gave constant evidence to the conventional forces of the United States Army of the value of skirmishes fought from cover, of carefully laid ambushes in territory where no ambush seemed possible, of sudden strikes and hit-and-run tactics. Indians were superb at patrolling, whether in forest, plain, or desert country. They had few peers in the use of cover and concealment, in sniping, or in small-unit tactics that depended upon surprise for their success. They were predisposed to such battle by their cultures, which called for the development of qualities that are great assets in guerrilla warfare: individual action, self-reliance, improvisation, ingenuity, and integrated small-unit teamwork.

Perhaps the most graphic lessons learned by the United States Army in those waning years of Indian conflict were taught by a Bedonkohe Apache whose Indian name, Goyahkla, meant "He Who Yawns." He is more familiarly known as Geronimo. From May 1885 until September 1886, Geronimo and his army terrorized the American Southwest, leaving in their trail murdered settlers, demolished homesteads, slaughtered ranch animals, burning wagons, and the stiffening bodies of soldiers unfortunate enough to be caught unawares. Geronimo was pursued successively by generals Oliver ("Bible") Howard, George Crook, and Nelson Miles. The latter commanded one-fourth of the entire American army in his pursuit of the "renegade" Indian. Until the end, all those soldiers were able neither to capture nor to kill a single one of Geronimo's *nineteen* warriors, although one, Masai, did voluntarily surrender.[17]

The importance of guerrilla war as a means of tying up large numbers of troops was demonstrated once again to the United States Army in the opening years of the twentieth century. Following the close of the Spanish-American War, America laid claim to the Philippine Islands, only to find that the people there had other ideas. They sought independence. Once again, in swamps, sloughs, and jungles, Emilio Aguinaldo, leader of the Philippine "Insurrection," provided American soldiers with ample opportunity to refresh their minds on the subject of guerrilla and counter guerrilla warfare.

During World War II, the army selected COL William O. Darby to head up an elite force of shock troops, Darby's Rangers, which used many of the tactics of guerrillas, including silent hand-to-hand night fighting. Brigadier General Frank Merrill commanded a specially trained select team of infantry known as "Merrill's Marauders." Skilled and toughened jungle fighters, they served in the Burma-India theater of war, cutting Japanese supply lines and ambushing enemy troops, living always in danger of sudden annihilation from the numerous forces of their foes. They were capable of seemingly impossible activities, such as hundred-mile marches through enemy territory, all the while remaining undetected. One might also count the mixed troops of General "Vinegar Joe" Stilwell, which often fought guerrilla style during battles in Burma against the Japanese. And there were members of the Office of Strategic Services, on specific assignments, who fought alongside native guerrilla forces, and who trained their companions in the manner and art of irregular warfare.

Thus it can fairly be said that the United States Army—at the beginning of the Vietnamese involvement—had had and should have learned by as much experience in the tactics of guerrilla warfare and counterinsurgency as the soldiery of any other modern nation. The army should have known the importance of "winning the hearts and minds of the people." It should have been aware of the difficulties inherent in locating and destroying small, mobile bands of irregular troops. The lessons of history should have taught it that superior firepower affords little protection against sniping or hit-and-run raids. It should have remembered from the years of Indian warfare on the High Plains that cannon fire is no great threat against an enemy that has no forts or emplacements. The experience of members of state militias during the American Revolution should have shown for all time how men soldier during a campaign or an emergency and then fade indistinguishably into the civilian population, all but immune to enemy detection. Governmental policies that strove to drive all members of Indian tribes onto supervised reservations should have demonstrated to U.S. generals of the 1960s the implausibility of establishing "agrovilles" and using other measures that uprooted Vietnamese peasants from their ancestral soil. Mosby's kidnapping raids should have reminded a later generation that irregular troops can strike swiftly, taking quick reprisal against opposition leaders.

The Upper Delta region in Vietnam is densely populated, flat, and swampy, with a dense network of waterways offering limited cover and concealment in its level, open terrain. There are but two seasons: wet and dry. The American army should have remembered that it had fought in similar terrain in the past—during the Seminole Indian War and at times during World War II in the Southwest Pacific.[18]

Despite its own history and experience with guerrilla warfare, the American army entered upon the Vietnam scene *de novo,* like a New World Athena, lacking experience and without a past. There was little or no excuse for the army's higher generals—its "war managers," to use Douglas Kinnard's phrase[19]—to allow the situation to develop as it did. Their blindness to earlier lessons learned (which, after all, are the purpose of every After Action Report ever submitted) was little short of criminal negligence. Our military leaders were both recipients and keepers of the collective experience—good and bad—of the United States Army since its inception in 1775. The Mosaic tradition had the Law of *JHWH,* explicit down to the last jot and tittle of ritual and moral prescription, with an "on the one hand" and an "on the other hand," and a wise rabbi to interpret how a man could walk wisely and justly between them. Just so, the war managers had history books, libraries and archives, the Principles of War, army regulations, and field manuals incorporating the wisdom of the centuries. They furthermore had a plethora of high-ranking staff officers to study every problem and brief each general on available options so that he might decide how to walk boldly between the "on the one hand" of military defeat and the "on the other hand" of total war. Yet somehow, in the process, doctrines learned in the past and taught at all service schools were forgotten. Called sometimes one thing and at other times something else, at Ft. Leavenworth those basic principles were known as METTW: Mission, Enemy, Terrain, Tactics, Weather. These have been crucial factors in every military engagement since the time of Cain.

In Vietnam, the mission was often obscure. The army forgot the old dictum "Know your enemy." The terrain was found to be impossible to master. Tactics varied from commander to commander. Only the weather forecast was certain—it was going to rain. Yet there was no need for the army to have suffered under the disabilities that limited it in Vietnam. Perhaps it may be forgiven for having forgotten the

lessons of its own history. It is more difficult to overlook the fact that it
seemed unable to read. It would not have been difficult, had anyone
been interested, for military analysts to have found statements such as
the following:

> There is only one means of defeating an insurgent people who will not
> surrender, and that is extermination. There is only one way to control a
> territory that harbours resistance, and that is to turn it into a desert. Where
> these means cannot, for whatever reason, be used, the war is lost.[20]

Those words were Robert Taber's, set forth in his book *The War of the
Flea,* published in 1965, just at the time that President Lyndon B.
Johnson was beginning to order the American military buildup in Viet-
nam.

Taber was not, however, alone in his exposition of the nature of
revolutionary warfare. In forming his thoughts, he drew freely from
other authors whose writings were generally available to anyone desiring to read them: Fidel Castro, Che Guevara, Régis Debray, Mao Tse-
tung, Ho Chi Minh, Vo Nguyên Giap—even Sun Tzu, who about 650
B.C. composed *The Art of War,* one of the oldest existing writings on
the subject of guerrilla warfare.[21]

Sun Tzu foresaw some two thousand years ago what the military
nature of twentieth-century revolutionary warfare would be like. Except for some technological innovations that have not changed basic
principles, very little that is new has been developed in the years since
he wrote. Consider a few of Sun Tzu's strictures:

> If I am able to determine the enemy's disposition while at the same time
> I conceal my own, then I can concentrate and he must divide. And if I
> concentrate while he divides, I can use my entire strength to attack a
> fraction of his.
>
> The enemy must not know where I intend to give battle. For if he does
> not know where I intend to give battle, he must prepare in a great many
> places. And when he prepares in a great many places, those I have to fight
> in any one place will be few. . . . And when he prepares everywhere, he
> will be weak everywhere.
>
> All warfare is based on deception. Therefore, when capable, feign in-
> capacity; when active, inactivity. When near, make it appear that you are
> far away; when far away, that you are near. Offer the enemy a bait to lure
> him; feign disorder and strike him. When he concentrates, prepare against
> him; where he is strong, avoid him. Anger his general and confuse him.
> Pretend inferiority and encourage his arrogance. Keep him under a strain
> and wear him down. When he is united, divide him. Attack where he is
> unprepared; sally out when he does not expect you.

Readers who know the military axioms of Mao Tse-tung will see close
parallels with Sun Tzu that are not coincidental, for Mao carefully
studied the words of his ancient countryman as he developed his own

views on revolutionary warfare. Compare Mao: "The enemy advances, we retreat; the enemy camps, we harass; the enemy tires, we attack; the enemy retreats, we pursue." Many of Mao's famous principles were simply paraphrases of Sun Tzu. Not only Mao but such theoreticians as Ho Chi Minh and Vo Nguyên Giap also adapted Sun Tzu's writings to their own circumstances. Their axioms sound like a historical description of what happened in Vietnam to the American army.

Taber is again worth listening to. Modern warfare is, in his opinion,

> a cant phrase, indicative of the confusion of journalists, and politicians [and one might, here, also add military men] who mistake technology for science. For despite the impressive technological innovations of the twentieth century, the principles of warfare are not modern but ancient; they were well established when Caesar marched out on his first campaign. And what is true of war in general is even more true, if possible, of guerrilla warfare in particular. . . . If there is anything new about guerrilla war . . . it is only in its modern, political application. To put it another way, the specifically modern aspect of guerrilla warfare is in its use as a tool of political revolution—the single sure method by which an unarmed population can overcome mechanized armies, or, failing to overcome them, can stalemate them and make them irrelevant.[22]

The army purchased large quantities of Taber's book for internal distribution, yet its leaders paid scant heed to what he had to say. Taber's exposition was not the only one available. Yet having forgotten its own history, the modern military managers seemed intent on remaining blissfully ignorant of available works in print that dealt with the art and craft of guerrilla warfare.[23]

Upper management refused even to harken to the voices of its own lower-level specialists. One such was Jeffrey Race. Race went to Vietnam initially in the mid-1960s as an army officer assigned as adviser to a district chief in Phuoc Tuy province. Having learned Vietnamese on his own, he returned to that country after his release from active service. His purpose was to study the nature of revolutionary warfare in microcosm by concentrating on one province, Long An. He hoped to learn why the guerrilla infrastructure there had succeeded, and why the Saigon government and its American ally had been defeated so ignominiously. Perhaps it was his choice of topic that caused his Department of State Vietnam-study grant to be "unilaterally rescinded" immediately after his arrival in Vietnam. Although the results of his studies were not published in book form until 1972, the attitudes that informed and gave birth to them were established in earlier years.

Race comments that while serving in the army in Vietnam

> my fellow officers and I frequently had to make decisions affecting people's lives with an insufficient understanding both of actual conditions and of the nature of the conflict itself of which we were a part . . . . [O]perational

doctrines seemed inadequate to account for the events around us, just as
the programs we were charged with executing seemed an inadequate
response to those events. . . . [T]his widespread failure of understanding
permitted a belief at higher levels of government in possibilities that did
not actually exist, in turn leading to increased intervention and to the high
costs which the failure of that intervention has subsequently entailed.[24]

That was not his only condemnation. Race saw clearly that there was
a "generally poor American preparation for dealing with Southeast Asia
and the types of conflicts likely to arise there." Even worse, there was
a severe shortage of researchers qualified "in the understanding of
revolutionary social movements," and the army seemed not to care.[25]

Another man experienced in the nature of revolutionary warfare
in general and its application to Vietnam in particular once spent much
time on active duty there. Some jokingly said of him that he spent more
years in Vietnam than many prisoners of war spent there in internment,
for he extended his tour time after time. He learned to speak Vietnamese like a native. After arriving in Vietnam in August 1964, he was
assigned to several duties, among which were those of interpreter and
adviser to a district chief. Many of his jobs brought him into intimate
contact with the Vietnamese people, and he often dressed in the land's
traditional garb of black pajamas.

Since he also spoke French, many in rural areas assumed that that
was his nationality. "I never volunteered to people that I was a French
citizen. I never said 'I'm a Frenchman.' I only let them feel that by
giving them indirect indicators. I let them assume that and then at the
most I only confirmed their misconceptions." His linguistic skills and his
manner of approach gave him an opportunity to tap what he believed
were some of the real feelings of the Vietnamese with whom he talked
and worked. He wrote dozens of reports that went through channels to
higher headquarters. He remembers that one recommendation "was
received intially with enthusiasm by General Westmoreland when I
briefed him on it. At the general's request, I also briefed the Vietnamese general staff on the matter. Then my report was turned over
to Westmoreland's staff for a staff study. They staffed it and that's the
last I ever heard of it. I can't tell you why it was not regarded with much
favor after staffing.[26] I just know that I went back to my assignment and
never heard another thing about it."[27]

Taber, Race, Ted Robert Gurr,[28] Bill Corson,[29] and a myriad of
other names—all had ideas about more effective ways to approach
revolutionary warfare. In the last analysis, all were ignored. Even one
of the army's own, on whom stars were destined to fall, had little effect.
George S. Patton (the one in Vietnam who sent out Christmas cards
bearing the picture of dead Vietnamese and the words "Peace on
Earth," not the fighting soldier-general of World War II), while still a
lieutenant colonel on the way to his first star and a student at the Army

War College, chose to investigate the nature of revolutionary warfare as the subject of his thesis. In a not very incisive analysis written in 1965 (which still remains classified), Patton suggested certain changes in approach that were generally ignored.[30]

Not only was the command structure of the army generally unaware of the nature of revolutionary warfare; it was abysmally lacking in trained linguists knowledgeable in the Vietnamese language. John T. McAlister, Jr., asserts that

> during my senior year in college in the autumn of 1957, after persuading the faculty at Yale to inaugurate the country's first university course in Vietnamese, I began studying the language with an able teacher, Huynh Sanh Thong, who had come to New Haven to teach three students.[31]

Eleven years later, at a time in 1968 when the buildup of the United States Army in Vietnam had assumed monumental proportions, the military still had no real linguistic capability. Despite thousands of officers and enlisted men who had suffered through Vietnamese-language courses, giving them a capability to "order a meal in a restaurant or tell somebody where to carry a bundle," there were only a precious few able to "discuss the nuances of politics and security with the peasants, let alone the generals." Nor did the army have intelligence officers sufficiently proficient to interrogate North Vietnamese or Viet Cong prisoners. Those who were captured were turned over to the South Vietnamese interrogators, who "squeezed" them dry of whatever they knew through techniques that often included torture. As late as 1968, in America's colleges and universities, there were only some thirty individuals who could be considered Vietnam specialists, and only a dozen of those had real language proficiency.[32] In Vietnam we were as mute as Balaam's ass.

Contrast that situation with the capabilities enjoyed by the United States Army during World War II. In the European Theater of Operations, the high command had available thousands of American ethnics of German, French, Italian, Flemish, and Dutch descent. Civil-affairs units could draw upon hundreds of academicians knowledgeable in the religious, cultural, and political affinities of those in areas through which the fighting raged. A similar situation existed in the Pacific Theater of Operations. After the initial military refusal to use American Nisei waned, plenty of interpreters proficient in Japanese were found and used throughout the remainder of the war. And then there was Vietnam, where we fought the longest war in our nation's history. Lieutenant General James M. Gavin has made it abundantly clear both in speeches and writings that cultural limitations of the American army in Vietnam received no recognition whatsoever.[33] Similar views were expressed by Major General Charles J. Timmes, who served in Vietnam as deputy and then chief of the USMAAGV from 1961 to 1964 and as special adviser to the United States Embassy in Saigon from 1967 to 1975. He has decried the lack of emphasis given by the army to cultural considerations in the decision-making process.[34] Almost no one knew the first thing about the Vietnamese language, the country's nationalism or its politics, its culture, or the special problems existing there as a result of guerrilla activity. Thus there were only a few able to give advice on how best to help the South Vietnamese.

It made no difference. Ignorant of the nature and culture of our enemy, oblivious to the realities of revolutionary warfare, unable to talk either to South Vietnamese friend or North Vietnamese and Viet Cong foe, the United States Army forged ahead, certain that it knew the best way to secure a quick resolution of the military situation in Vietnam. The result was a débacle of its own making.[35]

*   *   *

Although the aspects of insurgency are complex, at base it is primarily a political conflict, waged to win people's allegiance. The Viet Cong sought to weaken Saigon's control over the cities, villages, hamlets, and farms of the south. Toward that end, the VC employed propaganda, subversion, persuasion, and violence. When necessary, VC cadres used techniques of kidnapping, torture, and assassination. But at all times, the Viet Cong concentrated on its ultimate goal, gaining the support of the people, for the VC knew beyond contention that if they won the allegiance of the population, they would win the war. This was the political face of the Vietnam conflict. But like Janus, the Roman two-faced god, it had another aspect, that of guerrilla warfare against the military forces of the "duly constituted" government of the south.

While the practice of "political insurgency" may have been new (although there are some experts who would vehemently disagree with that proposition), guerrilla warfare itself is very old. The term derives from the Spanish *guerra*, or war, and means "little war." It is, in basic terms, the practice of combat by small units of armed men against the better-equipped forces of a larger, more powerful army. Because the United States Army saw fit to remain ignorant of the theory and oblivious to the practice of guerrilla warfare, its reward was an internal chaos of AWOLs, fraggings, drug problems, combat refusals, and resignation of its best and brightest. Morale and dedication and ethical behavior disintegrated within the officer corps of the army and deteriorated throughout the structure. Disillusionment became epidemic. Its ultimate reward was discord of unparalleled ferocity and defeat "with honor."

*   *   *

In all, the Vietnam conflict cost the American taxpayers many billions of dollars. The United States was willing to spend some $250,000 to kill each guerrilla fighter it could locate in the jungles of Vietnam. So profligate was the U.S. that in only one year, it provided the army with one million rounds of artillery shells, at $100-plus per round, to be fired just in harassing and interdiction missions. There were, of course, numerous other fire missions that expended millions of additional artillery rounds.[36]

Spendthrift with the weaponry of war, the army reacted in niggardly fashion toward requests for funds that would be spent in other ways. One writer charged in 1968 that

> for the price of ten airplanes, $25 million, we could train a thousand people to be fluent in Vietnamese. It could be done in two years. If we had a thousand men and women who were bilingual in Vietnamese, perhaps eventually the presence of the planes and their bombs would not be necessary. . . . However, the Department of Defense and the Department of State refused. Their reasons were that there was neither time nor funds.[37]

The war South Vietnam waged against its Viet Cong enemies began in 1957, gradually, without battles between armies, marked only by raids, murders, and kidnappings.[38] It was not slowed by efforts of the ARVN, the police, the Civil Guards, or the Self-Defense Corps; they were barely able to defend themselves, much less anyone else. American advisers reported that VC terrorists would fade away as soon as they were curbed by firm police actions, for the insurgents were only "bandit remnants."[39] American ambassadors, military advisers in Vietnam, even high-level Pentagon officials, concurred. The real threat to South Vietnam, they indicated, lay not in local terrorism but in invasion from the north by Hanoi's 350,000-man army. So the south waited for an invasion that did not come, while the VC termites destroyed its structure. The latter were seldom perceived as much of a threat, because they "operated with a collection of handmade and homemade weapons and arms taken from Government troops."[40]

Since no real threat was recognized, there was time for fun and games. At one point, the United States Information Agency sponsored a contest "for a new name for the Vietcong guerrillas," offering a cash prize for a "colloquial peasant term implying disgust or ridicule." Agency officials were chagrined to learn that in South Vietnam, the only terms that met the criteria were the words for "French" and "American."[41]

The American government was told by top-level army officers that guerrilla warfare "had ceased to be a menace to the government," which was "now able to maintain internal security." The Viet Cong, however,[42] was busy using the Ho Chi Minh Trail to bring in weapons more sophisticated than handmade ones. Trained by specialists from the north who were expert in propaganda, weapons, communications, and small-unit tactics, the VC continued to disrupt life in the south.

Between 1957 and 1959, South Vietnamese military raids unearthed more than 3,500 insurgent arms cachés, containing matériel ranging from mortars to bazookas, from rifles to electric generators. On 20 December 1960, such dissidents formed the National Front for the Liberation of South Vietnam (NLF).[43]

Hopes of easy victory continued to appear in print, the result of "assessments" by top military men. One such promise came from General Paul Harkins, commander of the U.S. forces in Vietnam, who in August 1963 predicted confidently "that the war will be over in December."[44] Some men, with less rank, did not feel as certain of the outcome. They commented that if they were winning the war, they would hate to serve in a losing one. A cynical song, sung to the tune of "Twinkle, Twinkle, Little Star," made the rounds of Saigon's watering holes, where lower-level American military advisers hung out:

> We are winning, this we know;
> General Harkins tells us so,
> In the delta, things are rough;
> In the mountains, mighty tough.
> But we're winning, this we know;
> General Harkins tells us so.
> If you doubt that this is true,
> McNamara says so, too.[45]

As early as the end of 1961, America suffered its first recorded Vietnam battle death: Specialist Fourth Class James T. Davis, killed in a VC ambush a few miles outside Saigon. Within a year, forty-one other American soldiers had joined Davis in death, and twenty-two American generals had found berths for themselves in Vietnam.[46]

During that early period, in an effort to make the struggle against guerrillas easier, American military forces in Vietnam launched Operation Hades. (The name was later softened to Operation Ranch Hand.) This program initiated jungle defoliation to remove cover where insurgents might hide and was described as "improvement of visibility in jungle areas." Crops that were believed to be for use by VC were systematically poisoned in efforts at "resources control," and villages that were deliberately or inadvertently destroyed to deny them to VC troops were euphemistically portrayed as having suffered "collateral civilian damage."[47]

It was not enough. The VC had come a long way. In 1961 there may have been as many as five thousand Viet Cong guerrillas active in the south. By January 1962 that number had mushroomed to more than 16,000, assisted by some 100,000 sympathizers, supporters, and part-time warriors. The insurgents divided themselves into two categories —full-time soldiers who were hard-core regulars and those who for the most part lived civilian lives and who occasionally took up arms. They developed, by 1962, an efficient chain of command reaching all the way to Hanoi. Practically every village in the south had a Viet Cong cell; they were present even in those villages that they did not control. Early in that year, the VC could claim that it was the *de facto* government in some 80 percent of the Vietnamese countryside. Its influence was felt and feared in the remaining districts that it did not dominate. Only the cities remained firmly under the control of the government of the south, and even there, bomb-throwing terrorists kept the people nervous.[48]

Despite this, the United States Army, emphasizing its "can do" attitude, continued to insist that its warriors and their leaders could bring the insurgency in Vietnam to a rapid defeat. Disengagement was still possible. Only a few American lives had been lost. Just a pinch of her treasure had been expended. There was still time. But it was not to be.

Two

Occasionally in the late 1960s and early 1970s there were GIs in Vietnam with the legend UUUU chalked on their helmets: "The unwilling, led by the unqualified, doing the unnecessary for the ungrateful." That they were unwilling could easily be noted by any observer on the scene. Many of them were undisciplined and surly, making it through their year "in-country" by shirking, loafing, playing, going AWOL, and refusing to enter combat. That millions of Americans at home were ungrateful was obvious to every watcher of the nightly news or reader of the daily newspapers. American society in those years savagely rejected the United States effort in Vietnam, declaring its displeasure by means of pickets, marches, sit- and stand-ins, letter-writing campaigns, bumper stickers, arson, mass gatherings, and bombings. Hardly a segment of American society was untouched by the violent reaction against the war.

Many GIs further claimed that they were "led by the unqualified, doing the unnecessary." They could mean by those phrases only that they believed that those who gave them orders lacked the requisite talents, training, and character to be respected leaders. They could mean only that the tactics of war they followed were irrelevant and meaningless, given the nature of the people and the conflict. UUUU. What could have brought American soldiers to a pass as sorry as that slogan indicated? The answer lies in events that began several years earlier, shortly after the close of World War II.

Today's military jargon might describe what happened by claiming that the Department of the Army "massaged" the structure so thoroughly that it produced "turbulence" in America's military organization. The army entered World War II still organized under the old "square division" concept of World War I, wherein each division consisted of four regiments. During the Second World War, the square divisions that Pershing would have found familiar eventually were reorganized after a successful modification first used by armored units. They had structured themselves into "combat commands" that were divided into three strike forces (Combat Command A, Combat Command B, and Combat Command C), enabling them to use two elements for combat while holding a third in reserve, to be thrown into the fray wherever and whenever necessary. The idea was picked up by infantry outfits, which organized a similar formation called "regimental combat teams."

The new units, known as "triangular divisions," became the framework within which the entire army ordered itself as the war progressed. The result is easily described. In each division were three regiments, two for combat and one in reserve. In each regiment were three battalions, two up and one back. Each battalion was composed of three rifle companies, each company had three rifle platoons, and each platoon had three rifle squads. All the way up and down it was a three-three-three pattern of progression. There were exceptions: battalions had an additional heavy-weapons support *company;* companies had an extra heavy-weapons *platoon;* a heavy-weapons *squad* belonged to every platoon. But the regularized dependence upon the three-three-three system allowed for great flexibility. It grew out of combat experience, and it worked. One advantage lay in the fact that various levels of the chain of command were only a little ahead of or behind the next. Lieutenants commanded platoons, captains commanded companies, lieutenant colonels commanded battalions (with majors as executive officers), colonels normally commanded regiments (although some brigadier generals occasionally received such a posting), and major generals commanded divisions (with brigadiers as their assistant division commanders). It was a natural progression of command. The triangular division did not, however, long endure after the close of World War II.

Shortly after the destruction of the Axis powers, a conflict started to grow between the United States and the Soviet Union—the beginning of the Cold War. America saw the menace of communism everywhere, instigated and controlled by the USSR. Pentagon military-contingency planners had to regard a new factor: the specter of atomic warfare, with the chief threat believed to be the USSR. The logical battlefield would be the European continent. The battlefield environment of the future would be an atomic one. General Maxwell Taylor, one of the chief architects of the army of the future, saw clearly, while he served as chief of staff, that the structure of the army would have to be changed if it was to survive atomic warfare still capable of functioning as a fighting force.

Thus the pentomic-division concept came into being in the late 1950s. Under this doctrine, the army's traditional reliance upon a regimental organization came to an end. No longer would three battalions form a regiment while three regiments composed a division. In place of regiments came "battle groups." Each division would have five (thus the name "pentomic") battle groups, each group composed of five companies made up of five rifle platoons. This, the planners insisted, was a necessary step toward providing proper troop dispersal over a wider area, increasing the chances of survival ("survivability," as the jargon had it) in nuclear conflict. Dispersal of units would also assure strength and maneuverability sufficient to drive enemy forces onto preselected "killing zones." Nuclear fires would then be directed onto such zones, destroying the enemy with minimal risk to soldiers of the United States Army.

There was a very real problem with the pentomic concept. It so widened the rank differential between existing unit commanders that they were isolated from one another. It is not too difficult for a second lieutenant platoon leader to bring a problem to a first lieutenant company executive officer, or even to the captain company commander. A captain can usually talk freely with a battalion executive officer who holds the rank of major, or with the battalion commander, a lieutenant colonel. Yet the pentomic organization ignored this fact and forced very junior and very senior officers to work closely with one another. There were only two command slots in battle groups: a captain for companies and a colonel commanding the group. It was difficult for company-grade officers to bring their problems to the attention of a senior field-grade officer. Consequently, problems proliferated.

An organization providing only two command positions also created too long a wait between the time a man might head up a company and the point at which he would finally become eligible to command a battle group. To progress from captain to colonel took fifteen or more years, during which time a man had no opportunity for command leadership. All his duties revolved around staff functions, a poor training ground for excellence in leadership.

As important, the battle-group reorganization ended the army's reliance upon regiments, a tradition dating back to the Revolutionary War. As a retired artillery officer put it: *"Esprit de corps* is a much overused expression, but it's damn hard to have *esprit* when there ain't any *corps.* And the regiment was a 'corps' both officers and men could identify with and be proud of."[1]

These problems, and objections made by qualified officers at the time of the battle-group reorganization, were considered by military planners to be an unfortunate by-product of the changing system, "fall-out" from malcontents who did not wish to face the more efficient wave of the future.

Fortunately, the pentomic organization was not a factor in Vietnam. It was never tested in combat, for it came into being after Korea and was phased out prior to American involvement in Vietnam. Suddenly those who had been so enthusiastic about pentomic divisions became vociferous proponents of a still newer concept spun off the drawing boards of army technocrats. This was the plan for the Reorganization of Army Divisions (ROAD). The new doctrine came about because Pentagon planners finally recognized that all battlefield environments are not alike. To meet changing circumstances, it would be advantageous to have units that could be adapted to the actual situations divisional commanders might face. Now the brigade-sized unit came into its own. Divisional headquarters would remain fixed, but its character and makeup could be changed by "tailoring" the nature and number of brigades assigned to it. In heavily forested terrain, a division might be made up of "infantry-heavy forces"—two battalions of infantry augmented by a company of tanks. In open, rolling country the division might consist of two battalions of tanks and a battalion of infantry. Of course, in all cases, a division would retain such elements as signal, supply, engineers, and so forth. Planners thus greatly improved army structure with the "tailoring" design of the ROAD system.

The term ROAD is not used today and has not been for some years, yet the army structure by the time of the Vietnam buildup was essentially a ROAD one. Further reorganizations occurred periodically, but the army has remained faithful to an intentionally streamlined ROAD concept of mixed forces and tailored brigades under a fixed divisional headquarters and base. Changes have been made in the fleshing of the force, rather than in the skeletal structure. Enduring in singular fashion through all post-World War II army reorganizations, however, has been the notion that when "the balloon goes up" it will do so in Europe, with Soviet hordes pouring through the Fulda and Hof gaps, while the United States Army buys time, slowly retreating as it destroys Russian tanks on something like a ten-to-one ratio, breaking out of a bottleneck at Bad Orb, falling back toward the Rhine while awaiting reinforcements. Whether or not the United States Army could actually play out such a scenario in Europe is beyond the scope of this essay to speculate on; it need only be emphasized here that the army was repeatedly reorganized in efforts to make it more fully capable of doing what might be necessary in the face of an attack by Warsaw Pact powers. In the process, lessons learned from other kinds of battle, and the ability to function in other types of combat, were excised from its Tables of Organization and Equipment (TOE). Its force structure was shaped into one of massive response (including nuclear) to a conventional thrust into Western Europe by the Soviets. Its capability to react to any other kind of threat became minuscule.

The army was not totally unaware of the possibility that limited wars might occur in underdeveloped countries around the world with which we had treaties. Doctrines were developed for "brushfire" conflicts in such nations. The military in the early 1960s discussed and planned possible intervention in such places. Actions would be surgically precise, using, for the most part, air-mobile or paratroop forces, airlifted to the source of trouble. Arriving in preponderant strength, continually resupplied by air from the United States (which the army describes as the "zone of the interior" [ZI]), these troops would quickly achieve specific tactical objectives. Soon, the Communist-inspired local force that had sought by whatever means to overthrow the existing government (treaty bound to the United States) would find itself out-fought, overpowered, and destroyed. Once again, Communist aggression's ugly head would find itself crushed. For this task, the army turned to the new XVIII Airborne Corps, formed from the 82nd Airborne at Fort Bragg and the 101st Air Mobile at Fort Campbell. (Later, under *Caber Warrior* contingency plans for the Mideast, XVIII Corps' capacity would be augmented by the assigning to it of infantry units from Fort Lewis and armored elements from Fort Hood). For a time, XVIII Corps' commander was Lieutenant General William C. Westmoreland, who thus had opportunity to gain invaluable insights into limited warfare. His troops were in a constant-readiness status, prepared to move anyplace at any time to douse Communist-inspired brushfire wars.

Another problem the army faced was the need for a response to guerrilla movements that had not yet escalated to "brushfire" levels. To that end the army established at Fort Bragg, in the late 1950s the army Special Forces, an organization designed specifically to engage in counterguerrilla fighting. Known today as the Military Assistance Institute, it was named the John F. Kennedy School for Special Warfare after the president became captivated by the idea of counterinsurgency.

Housed in a magnificent edifice just the throw of a shot glass away from the club in Moon Hall's bachelor-officers' quarters, the "Green Berets" have had an up-and-down roller-coaster ride since their inception. They were the forgotten offspring of the army in the early days, and it took seemingly endless hours of work by dedicated officers to keep the Special Forces intact. Entrance requirements were tough and performance standards high. Initial requirements included graduation from Ranger and Airborne schools. Physical fitness was an obsession, as indeed it had to be. The continual training was an accepted part of everyday life. The outfit was enthusiastic about education and was one of the first army units to require a college degree of its officers. Intellectual proficiency was important in the effort to know the potential enemies. It was expected that *all* soldiers of the Special Forces be multilingual, for only with such facility could teams build the capacity to operate in countries around the world. Special Forces believed its mission to be unique; it abandoned the old battalion organization in favor of a team concept, using A and B teams capable of operating independently or reinforcing one another. The smallest teams were composed of eight men (a fallback to the old army belief that such a number is the largest group one man can satisfactorily command).

Within eight days after his swearing in, President Kennedy approved a counterinsurgency plan that would use Special Forces soldiers in Vietnam (National Security Action Memorandum #52, approved by the National Security Council), and recommended deployment in Vietnam of four hundred Special Forces troops for counterinsurgency efforts, including initiation of a covert-warfare campaign against North Vietnam. Counterinsurgency and how to cope with it became the "in thing" in both the civilian and military sectors of the government. The two groups were in agreement that all revolutions that they might have to face would be struggles between Communist forces on the one hand and the United States on the other. Special Forces seemed to be one particularly effective answer to such threats.

Even the founders of Special Forces, however, much less those in the rest of the army, held to the old-fashioned notion that guerrilla warfare was entirely a matter of techniques and tactics. They did not perceive the importance of ideology and so thought that counterguerrilla efforts could play a crucial role in any irregular-warfare situation. Although they were wrong and the portion of the military effort and planning devoted to it was minor, the men of the Special Forces became the finest commandos America's military had ever had. Crosstrained in half a dozen techniques from radio to simple surgery, from special weapons to survival without reinforcement or resupply, they were elite troops able to track, patrol, raid, kill, and ambush with efficiency.

They were not guerrillas, for wearing a spotted-tiger camouflage suit did not make a soldier into a guerrilla. But the skills behind the wearing of that uniform did make them exemplary commandos. Yet, in a real sense, the Special Forces were unsuccessful in covert activities, for they knew only how to *kill* guerrillas. They had no effect on the sources that were supplying new guerrillas faster than they could be killed. For that, nation building and pacification were the answers, and neither Special Forces nor XVIII Corps nor army NATO troops were capable of, interested in, or trained for accomplishing those ends.

In the early days of its service in Vietnam the Special Forces was funded out of money in the hidden budget of the Central Intelligence Agency. Later, after the massive buildup of arms and matériel in Vietnam under Johnson, Special Forces became simply another of the several military elements there. Then, under pressure from the Department of the Army, Special Forces began to lower its standards. For a time it was the ambition of many up-and-coming young officers to serve with the Special Forces so that they, too, might "style around" in a green beret. By the end of the Vietnam era, the army was concerned about those who despite career incentives chose to continue serving in the Special Forces. To combat such stubbornness, the Department of the Army repeatedly downgraded the Special Forces. For a time, until it broadened its mission from special warfare to military assistance, it was—as it had been at the beginning—a dogged remnant, hanging on in the face of rigorous opposition to something it believed to be of value. The ride on the roller coaster had gone through a complete cycle.

America's army faced growing involvement in a war in Southeast Asia with its new structure untested by battle. Its larger focus was not on Asia but on Europe. It was honed for a large-scale, conventional conflict on the plains of Europe with only a secondary, limited, "brushfire" capability. Its counterinsurgency capacity was limited to a single commando group able to fight only in counterguerrilla style. The army had no training, and worse, no trainers, for the war into which it was racing pell-mell.

*   *   *

Throughout the Vietnam conflict, most of the army's research was directed toward studies of general, rather than limited, conflicts.[2] For all these reasons the military hierarchy resisted effective reorganization as an unnecessary and undesirable step. Even the common reference to "unconventional warfare" indicated the attitude of army brass toward wars of national liberation. Much of the army tended to pay as little attention as possible to guerrilla warfare, paying it only lip service. (Each basic-training center, for example, had a mock "Vietnam village" set up in a maneuver area, where recruits received a brief orientation on the hazards of warfare in the jungle.)

So long as the Vietnam involvement remained small, the army largely ignored it and the special problems it generated. When the war there grew larger, they claimed that counterinsurgency efforts were no longer relevant because the army there now faced enemy main-force units and such confrontations could be dealt with in traditional ways. Theories, doctrines, and tactics regarding counterinsurgency efforts, unconventional-war approaches, and studies of psychological operations continued to be of only peripheral concern to the bureaucratic army. This attitude was perfectly illustrated by the phrase used to describe nation-building efforts: "the Other War." The other war was not to be confused with the *real* one, dedicated to killing the enemy wherever he might be found. "More often than others, military men make mistaken predictions because of a gross inability to emphathize realistically with their enemies. . . . My own conversations with several military men in Vietnam (mainly those ranked between sergeant and colonel) support this characterization of the public statements of officers of ranks higher than colonel. Their one most striking common characteristic seemed to be inhibition of curiosity, both about the viewpoint of the enemy and about the background of the war. . . . The military record of understanding what the political war actually calls for has been meager, to say the least."[3]

Most of America's manpower, materiel, and resources were assigned to the "real" war, while those whose duty it was to work with Vietnamese civil projects regularly had to beg and plead for what they needed.[4] As one officer involved in that effort noted: "It would be instructive, but depressing, to contrast the total cost of resources devoted to programs to eliminate the VCI [Viet Cong infrastructure] and improve the RF/PF [Regional Forces/Popular Forces] with the cost to support *one* U.S. Division. We may recognize the importance—but we still deny the priority."[5]

The author of those words, Lieutenant Colonel Carl Bernard, had been assigned as a senior province advisor. He made other enlightening observations. "Ominous and far reaching is the cavalier disregard of . . . US commanders for the dictates of the 'pacification' program, in their headlong rush to 'kill VC'—still touted as the objective." He complained that only a "minor fraction" of America's resources went into programs of pacification, while "almost all" efforts were being expended in traditional methods of warfare that sought nothing more than the killing of enemy troops.

> The tools of the Viet Cong are primarily *non*-military—political subversion by use of persuasion, explanations to the foreign and domestic press, propaganda, and terror—all calculated to gain control over people. The tools [of the United States] overwhelmingly are military—bombs, artillery and infantry battalions . . . .
>
> This basic failure in . . . US . . . perception of the war has insured that the enemy becomes stronger each year, despite heroic lists of KIA, weapons captured, VCI eliminated, and kill ratios. The . . . US continues to concentrate the bulk of . . . resources and military might on controlling the terrain and looking for massed enemy formations. The VC continues to concentrate its talents on controlling the people. Each succeeds.

Bernard believed that the very presence of the United States in Vietnam was a mistake.

> It *hasn't* been a success because it *couldn't be!* We went soberly about making a rabbit stew without the guest of honor. The beast in the bag is not a rabbit. And it's been a pretty odd dish ever since. We hire a new chef from time to time, and we buy a new potion and mix it in and tell the folks who are paying the bill that "it's almost ready!" But, it still is not what we think it should be—because the ingredients are not what we have labeled them.

The senior province adviser was not at all sure that United States military efforts were relevant or were even focused on the war's pertinent issues. We had, he charged, plenty of programs to deal with various perceptions of the situation. "We do *not* have a very complete intelligence on the size and qualities of the beast itself—and some of our programs may be so inappropriate as to be nourishing the insurgency."

Perceptions of the war, he believed, "vary with each observer; we have built programs to fit the views most commonly held. There is little doubt that we are moving lustily forward on our programs; there is much doubt that the programs are relevant."

Bernard recalled for his readers a common occurrence that was a sore point with all involved in the advisory program at whatever level.

> The precipitate departures in mid 1969 of two gifted officers from their assignments as Province Senior Advisors has been well noted by US Army officers fulfilling the same post elsewhere. Both PSAs were dumped unceremoniously at the insistence of the US Division Commander resident in the province. Both had made the US commanders aware of the misbehavior of their troops, and the malcomprehension of pacification by their subordinate commanders and staffs. Their comments—designed to limit the bad effects of some counter-productive measures taken by the division's units—were not acceptable. The lack of knowledge displayed by the US Divisions' officers has survived these incidents intact.

This astute officer ended his comments with a warning. "We can continue our present management methods and lose the war, or make a massive reevaluation and take action with some brighter hopes!"[6] Bernard has been quoted here at some length not because his warnings were unique, but rather because he had the talent to express with clarity what was a constant sentiment of literally hundreds of other officers who were assigned to similar positions. No one heeded their clarion call. "Business as usual" was the watchword of the day.

*   *   *

General William C. Westmoreland formally took command of the United States Military Assistance Command, Vietnam (USMACV), on 20 June 1964, and later said: "I believed from the beginning that the key to the effectiveness of the Vietnamese Army lay in improving leadership at all levels, and in improving the training of the small infantry units, and in providing them with adequate weapons and equipment. Advisors were instructed to concentrate on these basic matters and also to do their utmost to encourage commanders of Vietnamese forces to move back into the countryside to patrol, to attack, and to regain the initiative."[7] On the basis of his comment it would seem that from the beginning Westmoreland had little insight into the nature of the war he was now commanding. Pacification never had a real chance to get out of the backseat of the U.S. war machine.[8] Westmoreland's attitude was bolstered by advice from his nominal boss, Admiral U.S.G. Sharp, commander in chief, Pacific. Sharp said that as far as he could determine from contact with the Joint Chiefs of Staff, "Westy" 's job was to get on "with killing Cong."[9] Westmoreland intended to do precisely that. He was supported in his devotion to duty by President Lyndon Johnson, who, reelected to office in November 1964, had already instituted an air war against North Vietnam that was enthusiastically supported by the air force.

The first phase of the air war was known as Operation Plan Flaming Dart—developed to carry out retaliatory air strikes in the North.[10] It was later succeeded by OPLAN Rolling Thunder, the extended and regular bombing of selected North Vietnamese targets.[11] At the outset of the war over the north, the Joint Chiefs of Staff recommended that ninety-four targets be hit in sixteen days. The plan was disapproved, the President instead opting for a doctrine of "gradualism," allowing the air force to hit a much smaller number of targets.[12] General Curtis LeMay, ex-commander of the air force's Strategic Air Command, had a simpler view. Rather than advocating gradualism, he wanted to go north in force and bomb North Vietnam "back to the Stone Age."

Unfortunately for air-power advocates, North Vietnam was insufficiently advanced technologically to provide rewarding and worthwhile targets. Thus, as Kendrick puts it, "The B-52 bombers, built as the ultimate weapon of their time to carry nuclear devastation to the homeland of an equally armed and powerful adversary, were used in Vietnam to destroy the barnyards, as well as the bridges, supply trucks and military emplacements of a small, largely agricultural and, until the war itself changed things, obscure state."[13]

The air war went through several rationales. It was begun as retaliation against the north for "attacking" two United States Navy destroyers, the *Maddox* and the *C. Turner Joy,* with patrol boats in the Gulf of Tonkin off North Vietnam on 4 August 1964.[14] It was broadened following the blowing up of an American military cantonment in Pleiku early in February 1965. To justify continuation of the bombing, its defenders then pointed to the necessity for its use to stop the southward flow of supplies. Later, some argued that it was necessary in order to force the North Vietnamese to the peace table. A cynic might say that it was the means by which the United States Air Force, the United States Navy, and the United States Marine Corps could play "crucial" roles in Vietnam, thus enhancing their own relative positions vis-à-vis other services.[15]

Since, by definition, an insurgent group has no air force, bombing in the south was unopposed. Yet whether it was north or south, both tactically and strategically, bombing was indefensible, for it did not contribute to military success, and certainly it played havoc with nation building when sticks of bombs went astray. Politically, the bombing produced a catastrophe, the result perhaps of too much credence in the far-reaching claims of air-power proponents.[16] As a result of their claims, millions of tons of bombs were dropped on such strategic targets as enemy water buffalo, treetops, and rice paddies. In spite of stops and starts in the continuation of the air war and despite restrictions placed on hitting certain targets in the north, "Rolling Thunder" continued year after year.

During the process, North Vietnam improved its air-defense capability from about 1100 light-to-medium antiaircraft guns to perhaps one of the heaviest defensive concentrations in the world. It emplaced some eight thousand guns, over two hundred surface-to-air missile (SAM) launchers, a highly complex radar-detection system, and central control centers. By November 1967, the U.S. Air Force had lost over 730 planes on missions to the north. That year, testimony before the United States Congress indicated that the air force had successfully destroyed some $320 million of North Vietnamese facilities during "Rolling Thunder" at a cost *three times as great as that of the targets destroyed.* USAF aircraft losses alone totaled more than $911 million.[17]

Air-power advocates insisted that such inconclusive results were the fault of the policy of gradualism, which kept the air force from unleashing its fury in the way it had wanted. Maxwell D. Taylor, for example, believed that the policy of gradualism "violated the military principles of surprise and mass as a means to gain prompt success with minimum loss."[18] There were, of course, other opinions. An English newspaperman, allowed to observe the air war from the north, wrote:

> So far from terrorising and disrupting the people, the bombings seemed to me to have stimulated and consolidated them. By the nature of the attacks so far [1966], civilian casualties had not been very great, but they had been great enough to provide the government of the Vietnam Republic with the most totally unchallengeable propaganda they could ever have dreamed of. A nation of peasants and manual workers who might have felt restive or dissatisfied under the stress of totalitarian conditions had been obliged to forget all their differences in the common sense of resistance and self-defence. From the moment the United States dropped its first bomb on the North of Vietnam, she welded the nation together unshakably.[19]

While jet planes were warming their engines to mount OPLAN Rolling Thunder, the escalation of the war on the ground continued. In March 1965, President Johnson ordered into Vietnam the first American ground troops: two battalions of marines from the 9th Expeditionary Brigade at Okinawa. Soon augmented by two additional battalions, an air squadron, and an army military-police battalion, the marines established defensive perimeters around their bases, called "enclaves." In April they were permitted to expand their operations and enlarge their enclaves, marking the beginning of a much argued about but short-lived "enclave strategy," under which U.S. troops would move into selected areas and clean out the VC there in a demonstration of American resolve. This would free ARVN soldiers for killing operations against the VC, despite the fact that ARVN had displayed no evident readiness to begin such operations.

The chief defender of the enclave strategy was General James Gavin, the paratroop hero of World War II. He believed it was better for U.S. troops to hold enclaves along the coast, clearing them of enemy forces and pursuing pacification measures within those areas, than for America's efforts to be spread across the entire countryside, dissipating strength the farther they were extended. American-occupied enclaves grew rapidly. Between March 1965 and March 1966, the marine enclave at Danang expanded from seven to 675 square miles.[20] A similar growth could be seen in army-occupied areas. But Gavin's concept had been designed to deny the enemy victory, and that was not enough. The army had to be the aggressor and bring total defeat to the enemy. So the enclave strategy was shelved in its infancy.

In one sense, even after Gavin's proposal was replaced, American troops in Vietnam continued to live in and occupy enclaves. Units lived in defensive bases surrounded by barbed wire, mine fields, and other protective measures. Ironically, the army discarded Gavin's coastal enclaves and then, of necessity, opted for enclaves everywhere.[21]

One reason given for the need to introduce soldiers of the United States Army into Vietnam was the purported infiltration into the south of regular forces of the army of North Vietnam. By August 1965, American troops numbered about 75,000, and by the end of the year some two hundred thousand U.S. soldiers were stationed there. By that date the government of North Vietnam had infiltrated only 14,000 troops. A year later, the end of 1966, America had 360,000 soldiers in 'Nam; the number of North Vietnamese infiltrators had grown from 14,000 to 50,000. In 1967, the United States added another 140,000 men, but the North Vietnamese maintained their troop strength in the south at 50,-000—totaling nearly 500,000 against 50,000. (All told, between 1964 and 1968, the American military rotated some 2,500,000 volunteers and draftees through the jungles of Vietnam.)[22] At the same time, between the introduction of American combat troops in March 1965 and the end of 1967, *locally* recruited Viet Cong increased from 140,000 to nearly 300,000. The threat was not from the north but from within the south.[23]

As soldiers of the United States Army came "in-country," they found themselves ill equipped to deal with the enemy they were supposed to "find, fix, and finish." Infantry battalions deployed to Vietnam during the early years of the buildup were organized, manned, and equipped to fight either a conventional or a nuclear war in the European theater, not a war of counterinsurgency in Asia.[24]

Battalions, the army's basic maneuver and combat element, typically comprise about eight hundred soldiers led by some thirty-five officers. The commander is a lieutenant colonel; his executive officer is a major. They supervise four companies (or, in the case of an artillery battalion, five batteries), each of which is commanded by a captain. Of the four companies, three are combat units and one is a headquarters organization. Infantry companies are armed basically with rifles, augmented by an independent platoon or two that provide heavier firepower—automatic weapons, mortars, antitank weapons. Additionally, a battalion often has attached to it a reconnaissance platoon.

The staff of a battalion commander is a small version of the staff of all larger units, such as brigades and divisions, and four men advise him on the many separate activities common to all outfits: *(a)* a captain, known as the S1, advises the commander on personnel functions and is responsible for orders, awards, assignment of new replacements, pay, maintenance of personnel records, and various other administrative matters; *(b)* a captain, designated as S2, advises the commandant on matters of intelligence, ranging from POW interrogation to weather reports and map and terrain studies; *(c)* a major, the S3, advises the commander on all matters involving training and operations, and inasmuch as he is always deeply involved in the planning and execution of operations, he runs the battalion during the commander's absence; *(d)* a captain, the S4, counsels the commander on all aspects of supply and logistics; and *(e)* a position not authorized during peacetime for a battalion is that of the S5, another captain, whose function it is to advise the commander on matters of importance in the area of civil affairs. In the modern army, this staff function is nearly defunct at every level of command. The Civil Affairs School, long located at Ft. Gordon, Georgia, has been phased out, and its responsibilities are now carried out by the army reserve.

Adaptations had to be made in such battalions in order to fit them for combat in 'Nam. The "operational environment" there was characterized by Colonel Y. Y. Philipps as "predominantly an infantry war. More than this, it is a light infantry war. What you can take to the fight is what counts."[25]

Learning what weapons and equipment to "take to the fight" came through trial and error. Conditioned by their Tables of Organization and Equipment (TOE) for a fight in Europe, battalions found their enemies were irregular soldiers, the terrain heavily foliated and frequently mountainous, jungle, or both, and the climate inevitably hot and humid. Philipps categorized the TOE weapons and equipment that battalions took to Vietnam as "rarely, if ever, used, sometimes used, and habitually used."[26] The "rarely, if ever, used" weapons included the Davy Crockett and the ENTAC in the antitank platoon. Antitank weapons were not taken with units headed for combat, except for very rare use against VC-fortified positions. Occasional battalions did find a use for their 106mm recoilless rifles mounted on ¼ ton M151A1s, using them in convoy-protection roles.

The fact that such heavy weapons were sent with infantry battalions was a glaring and flagrant misuse of finances and space, for not only did the Viet Cong have no armor with which to threaten American units, but the bulk and weight of antitank weapons and ammunition seriously hindered infantry mobility, as foot soldiers slogged through rice paddies and struggled through jungle. As a result, antitank weapons were usually returned to the military supply system to be stored, or returned to the United States for use elsewhere. Occasionally they were kept for base-camp defense, convoy security, or some other field purpose.

The "sometimes used" category of weapons and equipment included the battalion ground-surveillance radar and the 4.2 inch mortar (called a four-deuce). Ground-surveillance radar could seldom be used, for it could not penetrate the triple-canopy cover of 'Nam's jungle foliage. Four-deuce mortars were used in combat, but only when helicopters were available to lift them and their ammunition into position. Too heavy to manhandle, at other times they just sat, metal monuments to another kind of war.

Infantry battalions modified and adapted some "habitually used" weapons for uses other than those for which they were originally intended, in an effort to lighten the "field load." (A "field load" is the weapons a unit takes with it into combat—the field.) Although rifle companies, for example, had three 81mm mortars, they rarely took more than one on operations, since "three of them with full complements of ammunition would crucify foot mobility in the hot, humid Vietnamese climate and jungle."[27] Put simply, the necessary reaction of infantry battalions that were armed for Europe but found themselves in Vietnam was to carry with them on field operations only those weapons and equipment that could be man packed over difficult terrain in a highly debilitating climate. All other weapons and equipment, including most of their ground-transport vehicles, were left at base camps or returned to the military supply system.

Not only were such uniits faced with making adaptations in the equipment they used; they also had to make organizational adjustments. There were at least two types of changes in structure: those that combined combat-support elements into new arrangements within the organizations, and those that added fourth-maneuver elements to battalions and rifle companies.

One of the earliest of such changes placed battalion antitank squads —which were normally housed in the weapons platoon of rifle companies—under battalion control at the base camp.[28] Likewise, 81mm mortar squads, originally housed in weapons platoons of rifle companies, were often withdrawn and also placed under the control of the battalion weapons platoon.[29] This was done informally; authorization did not come down from higher up. This change came about because it was a logical way of preparing for hostile combat in an environment different from that for which the unit had been organized by TOE. Most units that made such changes did not submit through channels a request for a new, Modified Table of Organization and Equipment (MTOE), since they assumed such changes were temporary, operational ones, necessitated by local conditions of climate and the type of enemy they faced.

The army bureaucracy did, however, have a Table of Organization and Equipment revision underway that would alter the way infantry battalions structured their combat-support elements. This was the G-Series TOE revision, which included the formation of the combat-support company. Stripped of the administrative and logistic elements of a battalion headquarters company, the new combat-support company became the controlling force for combat platoons and sections, including the heavy mortar, antitank, and scout platoons and the air-defense section.[30]

The second structural change implemented by many infantry battalions was the creation of additional maneuver elements. By drawing down the strength of other rifle companies in a battalion, by converting the combat-support company to a rifle company, or by combining the scout and antitank platoons, many battalion commanders created a fourth rifle company within each of their commands. This "square" configuration allowed commanders to deploy more firepower in combat while still maintaining route and fire-base security forces.[31]

One unfortunate result of such reorganizations was that they were not adequately recorded in the institutional memory of the army. Such a memory bank does exist. It is known as the Army Authorization Document System (TAADS), and its use is an established procedure for initiating and authorizing organizational changes. Presumably no one thought the *ad hoc* changes occurring in Vietnam were sufficiently important to record within the TAADS system. As a result, after the first units deployed in Vietnam finally learned how to adapt to the environment there, later units had no opportunity to profit from previous experiences and had to start from the beginning. Newly deployed units had to go through the same process, time and again—a time-wasting, costly, and dangerous procedure. Had the TAADS system been used, or if a more efficient system had existed, predeploying planning would have insured that standard TOE weapons, equipment, and personnel inappropriate to Vietnam would not have been deployed. It was like history—those ignorant of it are inevitably "condemned to repeat it."

*   *   *

The *only* function of an army in a democratic society such as the United States is to serve constituted power, that is, the power that the citizens themselves have created and in which they participate through constitutional channels. An army's function is not to serve itself, but its society. Its leaders must remember at least two fundamental duties: when it is strong and is called upon, it must sally forth, banners flying, to meet and destroy the enemy. When it is weak, or unprepared for the type of combat it faces, it must be brave enough to say so and to urge the resolution of issues facing a nation by means other than military ones. To fight when unprepared is an invitation to defeat and disaster.

A retired general of the U.S. Army recently reflected on the fundamental duties of an army. General Hamilton Howze reminded his readers of a former general of the German *Reichswehr,* Hans von Seeckt, who "had a simple way of describing the relationship which should exist between the politician and soldier when war becomes a possibility." Von Seeckt believed that the soldier should determine precisely what he was being asked to do. He should ask the politician, "What do *you* want? What do *they* want?" In similar vein, the politician should be aware of the soldier's capabilities and limitations. He should ask the soldier, "What do *you* have? What do *they* have? What can *you* do? What can *they* do?" Howze suggested that two additional questions should be added to Von Seeckt's list, addressed by the soldier to the politician: "What level of effort and punishment will *our* people stand for? What will *their* people stand for?" General Howze concluded that "on the answers to these eight questions must the basic decisions be made."

The general made these points in order to address the American war that had been fought in Vietnam. At all times, he wrote, a fundamental privilege of government is that of telling "the professional military what it wants it to accomplish and to impose any limitations in the way the military may go about it." But, he warned, just as government has fundamental privileges, so also does the army, for "if the military leadership judges that given the imposed limitations, the means available, and the size and nature of the problem, it cannot expect to accomplish the mission, then it is the soldier's privilege and duty *to tell the politician so, in the plainest terms.* "[32]

Presumably the sentiments expressed by Howze are ones with which General William C. Westmoreland would have agreed, for that USMACV Commander kept a quotation, supposedly first written by Napoleon, under a sheet of glass on his desk:

A commander-in-chief cannot take as an excuse for his mistakes in warfare an order given by his sovereign or his minister, when the person giving the order is absent from the field of operations and is imperfectly aware or wholly unaware of the latest state of affairs. It follows that any commander-in-chief who undertakes to carry out a plan which he considers defective is at fault; he must put forward his reasons, insist on the plan being changed, and finally tender his resignation rather than be the instrument of his army's downfall.

Since one seldom keeps quotations close at hand unless they are mean-
ingful, it is safe to assume that Westmoreland thought Napoleon's words
were sage advice. That he truly believed the military to be responsible
for giving counsel to politicians may also be seen from an address he
delivered early in 1970 at Lincoln Academy of Illinois: "Military leaders, however, are singularly qualified by education, experience, and
profession as a group to addressmilitary aspects of national security
problems thoroughly, competently, and without equivocation. And that
is their responsibility under law."[33]

Thus, for Westmoreland, a "commander in chief" must be willing to "put forward his reasons" if he thinks a plan is faulty; he must
"insist" on its being changed, and if politicians are unwilling to do so,
then that military leader must "tender his resignation rather than be
the instrument of his army's downfall." Westmoreland believed
generals to be uniquely qualified to give such advice to politicians,
because of their "education, experience, and profession." Furthermore, it was mandatory that they do so, for it "is their responsibility
under law."

Such a general, believing a plan to be faulty, having advised against
it, aware that his counsel had not been accepted, just might explode,
as did an actual senior American general during Vietnam: "I will
be damned if I will permit the U.S. Army, its institutions, its doctrine,
and its tradition to be destroyed just to win this lousy war!"[34] At that
point, an honorable man would resign, as Napoleon had counseled
(but there is no indication that the above-quoted individual did so).
Where, in his memoirs,[35] his press conferences, his public speeches
or his private comments is there any evidence suggesting that
General William C. Westmoreland ever contemplated resigning in
protest over the situation into which the American army was thrust
in Vietnam?

There is no indication that *any* American general resigned in protest over *any* issue raised by Vietnam: no full generals, no lieutenant
generals, no major generals, no brigadier generals.[36] The name of only
one full colonel, David Hackworth, comes to mind. One has to drop
down to the rank of lieutenant colonel before names of resigned pro-
testers begin to appear: Anthony Herbert, William R. Corson, Edward
L. King—they were the famous ones; they wrote books. A good many
majors left the service, as did thousands of captains and lieutenants of
both grades. These latter men, too low in the rank structure to effect
changes, simply clamped their mouths shut, served in bitter silence,
and got out of the service at the first opportunity.

Others have also noted the curious reluctance on the part of the
military managers to submit resignations, or, short of that, even to
protest. Kinnard, who served in Vietnam, has wondered: "Why didn't
the military leaders at the top speak out?"[37] The immediate reaction is

"Why didn't *he*?" There is an answer, suggested by familiarity with such men, an answer picked up by Maureen Mylander. She has written that "most generals keep their dissent private and take what the Army offers for as long as possible. To become a general, and particularly to become a high-ranking one, an officer must conform, avoid error, shun controversy, and forego dissent."[38] These leaders had a ready aptitude for rationalization and self-deception.

According to Kinnard, almost 70 percent of the army generals who led the war in Vietnam were uncertain what the objectives of that combat were. Over 50 percent of those generals believed that the United States Army should not have participated in the Vietnam war. An even 61 percent were aware at the time that "indicators of progress" such as body counts, kill ratios, weapons captured, and so forth, were inflated and invalid. Where were their voices when they were needed? Kinnard suggests that they kept quiet because "their careers were at stake and they could not afford to make waves."[39] If generals could not do so in order to call attention to problems needing redress, how could anyone of lower rank be expected to step forth? What sort of training and selection system allowed such men to rise to the top echelon?

There is almost an Alice-in-Pentagonland quality about generals in the middle and late 1970s who claim, now that it is safe to do so, that they were really opposed to the war in Vietnam from an early date. King speaks to this proposition so clearly that he is worth quoting at some length. It may be so, he wrote, that many high brass in the army questioned the war privately, yet "all of these Army leaders formerly publicly supported the war." He criticizes such men for their silence. "If Army leaders were aware that things were not going right in the war and were concerned about what was being done to the Army, why didn't they speak out and voice their concerns *before* so many soldiers died?" Officers below the highest command levels are now, King asserts, "alibying their failure to question policies and tactics that were inimical to the best interests of the country and the Army by claiming they didn't have 'sufficient information' to make a judgment." In his view, such a claim will not "wash."

> The officer corps has been satisfied to hide behind duty and the old adage of "Mine not to reason why, mine but to do or die" as a rationale for lack of concern for what was happening to the men of the Army in Vietnam. In return for more rapid promotions, increased high-command slots, larger forces, more weapons systems, and other benefits of wartime activity, the officer corps closed its conscience to any question of what it was doing in the name of freedom. It accepted the mind of the institution and ignored its own responsibilities to the American people and the men of the Army. By so doing it broke the long-standing public trust in the integrity of the officer corps. This trust will be difficult to restore.[40]

A possible explanation for the behavior of such men is that they desperately wanted to believe that what they were doing was worthwhile. After a time, believing it made it so. If that is correct, then they had ignored a warning given by Clausewitz:

> The first, the grandest, the most decisive act of judgment which the . . . General exercises is rightly to understand the War in which he engages, not to take it for something, to wish to make of it something, which by the nature of its relations it is impossible for it to be.

Another possibility is that such leaders were simply "organization men," military technicians and soldier bureaucrats—war managers, in Kinnard's phrase—owing their loyalty to the institution and to nothing else. General Maxwell Taylor had been one of the first such men who, as chief of staff for the army, introduced the corporate structure, image, and attitude to the service. "Ambition, promotion, organization and expansion were the computerized elements of a military conglomerate" that came into being under his direction.[41] Technocrats like Taylor supplied the army with such concepts, but others moved quickly to implement them. Precepts of modernization and constant growth were extolled, as was the "modern army" itself.

Loyalty to the army became a good in itself, whereas in earlier years that concept had always been tempered by dedication to the nation and to the public good. Fewer and fewer austere old troop leaders could be found in the halls of the Pentagon, since they, together with their horses, were put out to pasture as rapidly as possible. "During General Taylor's tenure as Chief of Staff, service with troops became less important for officers than speaking a foreign language and holding at least one advanced degree. The pursuit of the good staff life, rather than troop command, became the goal of nearly every aspiring young career officer."[42]

General William C. Westmoreland, a "moderately intelligent product of the Army system,"[43] came out of such a background. He was a manager, a technician, a bureaucrat, rather than a troop leader. He was a "Big Corporate Military Executive, geared to large-scale, fast-moving modern operations supported by maximum firepower."[44] Vietnam was an ideal milieu for him, for it afforded the opportunity to manage a war by statistics and computer and to institute "indicators of progress" to gauge success in the war. At first he was portrayed as just the right man for the job. Enthusiasm was high. In a three-part series in the mid 1960s, *Newsday* described "Westy" as a "super-soldier." In 1965 *Time* magazine named him "Man of the Year." He was given, in 1967, the unusual distinction of addressing a joint session of Congress. His name was on the lips of soldiers of all ranks, those at higher levels preening themselves as they proclaimed how in accord they were with the thinking of Westy. He was a confidant of the mighty and received academic honors and military decorations from the grateful. But then came Tet 1968, and, having led the army to that pass, he fell from the favor of the mighty. The military looked to new leadership, and within the Pentagon, his former haven, junior officers formed a society known as GROWN: "Get rid of Westmoreland now."[45]

But all that was still in the future. He had replaced General Paul C. Harkins as commander in Vietnam, and that country was a challenging place for a manager to be. The American presence was quickly changing the land. In earlier years, Saigon had been a beautiful city. It was a pleasure to live in one of its terraced apartments, to stroll through its parks, to drive down its wide streets overhung with flowering trees. Now it had become more "efficient." Trees were cut systematically so they would not impede the flow of military truck traffic. Landlords raised the rent on apartments and did nothing with them but watch them become slums. Garbage and waste piled up on sidewalks and overflowed into streets. Rivers became open sewers. Everywhere prices skyrocketed to take advantage of GIs whose pockets were full of dollars. The beautiful Tu Do Street, previously a respectable area of shops, reincarnated itself as a sex supermarket catering to the desires of the American soldier.

These things happened because of "military necessity." In the countryside, Viet Cong had made roads unusable. The only major railroad had long since ceased to operate. Saigon was the south's only major port, and it was already clogged. Thus not only that French city but the rest of the nation had to be remade overnight in order to handle the American presence. Ports, warehouses, cantonments, air bases, communications centers and systems, repair facilities, drydocks, maintenance depots—all had to be built from scratch, immediately.

Either new or vastly expanded port facilities were brought into operation within months at Qui Nhon Nha Trang, Cam Ranh Bay, Vung Tau, Saigon, and Danang. Four million square yards of earth were covered over by army engineers to provide facilities for air bases and heliports. The army said it needed twenty million square feet of either covered or open storage facilities, plus 500,000 cubic feet of refrigerated storage—and lo, it was done. General-support and direct-support units could be found behind nearly every tree. If an island was needed and God had not seen fit to provide one, the engineers were willing to act as his servants. At Dong Tam, in the delta of the Mekong, they dredged millions of cubic yards of sand to create a six-hundred-acre island.

By 1967, transport brought 850,000 tons of supplies every month to Vietnam to feed the American military, its indigenous allies, and token bodies of foreign troops. GIs alone ate some ten million field rations every month, shot up eighty thousand tons of ammunition, and burned eighty million gallons of petroleum, oil, and other lubricants.

Ninety-six pounds of supplies arrived in Vietnam every day for every American in the theater. It was an immense logistical effort that spewed forth America's plenty to those of her children who had to be away from home to defend democracy, to stop Communist aggression, and to save the territorial integrity of South Vietnam.[46] With a war machine like that supplying him, Westmoreland knew he could do nothing but win. Overwhelming firepower,[47] consummate supply, superior troops—all were his.

Supported by his hand-picked assistant, Brigadier General William E. Depuy, Westmoreland worked out the basics of the American approach to "finding, fixing, and finishing" the VC. They developed three types of tactical operations: search and destroy, clearing, and securing. Field commanders of American units quickly picked up Westmoreland's enthusiasm. Like him, they were confident that the solution to Vietnam's problems lay in aggressive conventional-force action with the objective of destroying Viet Cong units in the field. Their attitude toward ARVN seemed to be "Step aside, little boys, we're going to take care of this."[48] One observer spoke of Westmoreland's "brilliantly successful" operations against the enemy, "proving that insurgent heavy units can be found, and when they are, almost always destroyed."[49] The fortunes of war seemed to be improving for the United States Army. Yet the gloom was not being dissipated by the light at the end of the tunnel, but rather by a false dawn.

Three

On 30 April 1978, commemorating the third anniversary of the fall of Vietnam, the Associated Press wires carried Vietnam war correspondent George Esper's interview with retired general William C. Westmoreland. The headline proclaimed, "Westmoreland Hasn't Changed Views on War." Westy insisted that "militarily we were successful" inasmuch as "we didn't lose a single battle above company level." In other comments, he indicated that the United States had involved itself in Vietnam as "champions of liberty" in order to "resist the aggressive actions by a belligerent, aggressive power." The reason for America's defeat there, said Westmoreland, was that although "we had the power," the United States "in the final analysis" simply "didn't have the will." The nation's military adventure in Southeast Asia was "highly idealistic, and, I would say, moralistic." The general reflected that "the military were given a job to do by political authority and we put our heart and soul into it. We did our best." Throughout the conversation there was no hint of the besetting problems that then faced the army, caused, in large part, by that general's own direction of the war. The news story made plain that Westmoreland had not learned much from his Vietnamese experience.

Reading that story, one would never suspect the *internal* problems the army faced in Vietnam. Heroes were awarded high medals for acts of "valor" performed while they were so spaced out on drugs that they had no idea what they were doing. Use of marijuana and harder drugs became so common that NCOs and officers simply turned their backs, officially ignoring what their men were doing. In many units, tension, and even hatred, between conscripts and "lifers" grew so strong that they fought not only with the enemy but among themselves. The term "fragging" came into the language, describing assaults, sometimes ending in death or mutilation, on NCOs and company-grade officers, initiated by the men they led. According to some reports, troops of the 101st

Air Mobile Division offered a reward of $10,000 for the assassination of the officer who gave them the order to attack the meat grinder in the Au Shau valley, Ap Bia, known to the soldiers as Hamburger Hill. For the year 1969, the army admitted to at least two hundred documented fraggings. In 1970, it announced, there were 363 such actions.

Incredible in the eyes of older soldiers was the impunity with which conscripts, in Vietnam for a year's tour of duty, declared their attitudes toward both the war and the army. Penciled on helmet camouflage bands and chalked elsewhere were such graffiti as peace symbols, slogans such as "Re-up? I'd rather throw up," "Power to the People," "Kill a noncom for Christ," "No gook ever called me 'nigger,' " and "The army [or Westmoreland, or some other selected person or outfit] sucks."

Vietnam became the laboratory in which professional soldiers could gain practical experience, an important rung on the promotion ladder. As the words of the old army song stated, "There's no promotion this side of the ocean," and so Vietnamese service became the *sine qua non* for rapid upward mobility.

Generals used the war for testing tactical theories and new weapons. Army Research and Development (R & D) worked on armaments that would have made Buck Rogers swoon with jealousy. R & D produced one-thousand-pound parcel bombs that opened while still airborne to strew a hundred antipersonnel bombs over as many yards. It developed amphibious gun carriers capable of penetrating dense swamps and marshes. It created infrared, heat-sensitive sniper scopes capable of detecting guerrillas during the darkest of night hours. Later models were so sensitive that users could determine whether or not men wore facial hair and could read identification numbers painted on vehicles. To complement infrared scopes were those that operated by intensifying available light 70,000 times and more, thus allowing helicopters, jeeps, and other vehicles to be operated during night hours. Mobile radar units could spot infiltrators on the ground at a thousand and more yards. Mobile Army Sensor Systems Test and Evaluation Resources (MASSTER) projects at Ft. Hood, Texas, developed "people-sniffing devices" capable of tracking columns of men and indicating whether or not they carried weapons. A variety of such detectors, relying on chemical, sound, heat, light, and magnetic means were tested, and some approved for field use. Had the war in Vietnam lasted longer, automatic data-processing equipment would have appeared on the battlefield to turn command posts into computerized models of efficiency (except when the computers were down).

Normal war objectives lost their significance as generals created missions that fitted American units to the new machinery of the "electronic battlefield" instead of providing weaponry suitable for Vietnamese realities. No scheme was so far-fetched that it was rejected out of hand. As one NCO, a sergeant first class, commented: "The damn generals do nothing but experiment. They don't give a damn about our lives. Why should they as long as they think of us as laboratory rats to be used to prove their theories?"[1] One such experiment was the effort, begun about 1967, to erect an electronic barrier fence across Vietnam along the 17th Parallel to keep infiltrators and supplies from reaching the insurgents in the south.

Major General Tran Do, deputy commander of Communist forces in South Vietnam, ridiculed the idea of such a barrier. "What is the use of barbed-wire fences," he scoffed, "when we can penetrate even Tan Son Nhut Air Base outside Saigon?"[2] Wilman D. Barnes summed up the project: "At best, it is a costly undertaking which could impede some infiltration; at worst, it is an unwise, costly scheme fraught with severe political and military disadvantages, and one whose potential value is greatly outweighed by its cost and its inherent disadvantages."[3] General Alfred Starbird was placed in charge of the fence's construction, but, after the expenditure of millions of dollars, the project was finally abandoned when the brass were finally persuaded that the idea was unreliable. Had it been completed, infiltrators and elements of the NVA would simply have detoured a few miles through Laos to avoid detection by the "fence."

No casual reader of Westmoreland's newspaper interview would have been reminded, or informed, of the immensity of the corruption that riddled the American effort in Vietnam. Time after time, when this author interviewed those who served in Southeast Asia and asked them what stood out most in their minds about that experience, they responded, "The corruption." William Lederer, writing years ago, commented upon the same point. He quoted an American serving in 'Nam: "The only way to keep a stable government here is let the generals make a few bucks on the side. The peasants will get along somehow. It's the power structure we have to support."[4] The CIA supported that power structure by protecting Vietnamese officials' poppy fields and flying their heroin out of the country on Air America planes.

Traditional war objectives (hills, rivers, cities, targets to be seized and held) lost their meaning under the doctrine of search and destroy. American soldiers fought over the same terrain time and again, only to relinquish it after capturing it. Skeptics were increasingly harsh in their criticism of the casualties suffered at places such as Khe Sanh when "key" tactical and strategic sites were evacuated after withstanding VC assaults. Another frequently heard criticism dealt with the military policies that called for use of CS gas and herbicides. All this, of course, changed the landscape into a vicious, twisted parody of its former beauty.

Jonathan Schell, a writer for the *New Yorker,* described the land as follows:

In 1967, I spent a month in Quang Ngai province [frequently flying] in forward air control planes. . . . I saw that the land below me had been completely devastated. It looked like a scene from World War II . . . and I decided that I would attempt to survey Quang Ngai province from the air and on the ground to discover what the results of our bombing and our military presence had been, at least for this one province.

I flew for several weeks with military maps, shading the areas that were destroyed. Since the inhabited parts of Quang Ngai province are quite small—about forty miles long and five to ten miles wide—I was able to produce quite accurate statistics, which were later confirmed by checks on the ground and interviews with the three main ground commanders. . . . The destruction of society in Quang Ngai province was not something we were in danger of doing; it was a process we had almost completed. About 70% of the villages in the province had been destroyed.[5]

Military problems continued to proliferate. Debilitation of morale among the ranks was felt, not only because of increased involvement with drugs, but through growing racial hatred. Black soldiers created an enclave within the city of Saigon, where they lived and relaxed during off-duty hours. Estrangement of the races became so grave that white military policemen refused to enter that area of the city except when accompanied by armed convoys.[6]

There was also the indiscriminate killing of Vietnamese civilians, done deliberately at My Lai and probably elsewhere, and accidentally at other places. Records repeatedly reflected that civilians had died from "friendly wounds" caused by "friendly fires." And there was the bombing and shelling by artillery. Kinnard claims that "total munitions employed by the United States in Vietnam was greater than tonnages employed world-wide in the 1941–1945 war. . . ."[7] Such an expenditure in a nation as small as Vietnam is mind boggling. It is no wonder that Vietnamese civilians were alienated from us.

There were the PX scandals and the NCO-club scandals and the sergeants-major scandals. And there was the black market. Present everywhere, but especially noticeable along Le Loi, a main east-west street in downtown Saigon, sidewalk vendors openly hawked Ameri-can-made goods to which they had no legal access.

Simple theft, by PX employees, construction workers, and GIs as-signed to warehouses and supply depots, ran into millions of dollars annually. Illegal profit by various individuals who sought to take advan-tage of the war-racked economy of Vietnam was bad enough. Worse, however, was the fact that the Viet Cong received a large percentage of their supplies *from the United States* via the underground routes of the black market: kerosene, sheet metal, oil, gasoline engines, claymore mines, hand grenades, rifles, bags of cement. The variety of goods and their quantity was seemingly endless. At Nha Trang, at Cam Ranh Bay, at the large Central Market in Danang, as well as at Saigon, American goods were funneled through the black market to the VC. Often members of the Viet Cong did not even need to deal through the black market in order to obtain what they needed: they simply appeared openly—since they bore no identifying marks proclaiming them to be members of the insurgency—and bought what they wanted.

Such occurrences backfired against morale in two ways. Opportunity for quick and easy profit tempted many—American and Vietnamese—to deal in the black market as the expense of the jobs they were supposed to be concentrating on. Second, when GIs found American-made materials used against them by their enemies, they could not help wondering whether they were fighting in vain. Among enlisted men who had been forced into the military by way of the draft, such cynicism eroded confidence in the honor and purpose of those who led them. It is little wonder that GIs came to the point where they no longer believed the rhetoric of American generals who asked them to risk their lives to achieve the noble goals of the United States in Vietnam.

The "bottom line" in all this, it must be remembered, is that this stench of corruption rose to unprecedented levels during William C. Westmoreland's command of the American effort in Vietnam. Had he been more interested in, or capable of, controlling such things, he might have had a more solid backing from his troops for the military effort against the VC and NVA.

The blame for the corruption in Vietnam must be shared by hundreds of individuals, Vietnamese and Americans, who put personal profit above duty. The fault for instituting such military tactics and doctrines as "search and destroy," "reconnaissance in force," "body counts," "harassing and interdicting fires"—and other such woefully inadequate approaches to combat—must be borne by Westmoreland alone. Emblazoned and articulated in Army Regulations (ARs) and Field Manuals (FMs), hallowed and enshrined by tradition down the course of years, and enjoined and inculcated in military schools from preparatory academies to the War College is the notion that always, without exception, a commander is ultimately responsible for everything that goes on within his command. Every victory belongs to him, for it was his judgment that set in train the events that propelled the enemy to defeat. If an intelligence-staff officer fails in getting information about an enemy unit to the operations officer for inclusion in Paragraph 5 of an Operations Order, the fault is attributable, in the final analysis, not to the intelligence officer but to the commander.

Should a G-4 supply officer neglect to procure equipment necessary for a battle, he may well be relieved of his position. His incompetence may affect the outcome of a battle, but to the degree that it does so, to that extent it is the commander who must bear the burden. In military classrooms, instructors ask the rhetorical question "Who has

the responsibility?" And students respond in chorus, "The commander." It is a sacrosanct, inviolable, and appropriate doctrine within the
military.

In Vietnam, the responsibility for what occurred within the army
belonged to Westmoreland. Brigadier General Theodore Mataxis, commander of the American Division in Vietnam for a time, once said that
the experience of the United States in Vietnam was "the opposite of
Korea. There we went in with a bad army and came out with a good
one. In Vietnam we went in with a good army and came out with a bad
one."[8] Bernard Fall, the insightful student of Southeast Asian conflict,
wrote that the American army had gone about its task in the wrong
way, "at the price of which Tacitus spoke when he said of the Romans
in Britain, 'You have made this a desolation and you call it peace.' "[9]
Some of the brightest field-grade officers who served in Vietnam came
home disheartened and discouraged. One colonel related that he came
to the point where "under no circumstances would I return for another
tour of duty there. The best thing that all of us could have done was
simply to go home. With faulty leadership at the top there was no way
we could ever accomplish our mission."[10]

Colonel David Hackworth, one of the most decorated officers of the
Vietnam era, put it pointedly. "We had all the assets to win this war.
We had half a million troops, unlimited amounts of money and the
backing of the administration. No doubt we could have won if we'd had
commanders who knew how to use these assets, instead of these amateurs, these ticket punchers, who run in for six months, a year, and don't
even know what the hell it's all about."[11]

Then there was Major General John H. Cushman, for a time the
ranking officer in the Mekong Delta, later the commandant of the
Command and General Staff College at Ft. Leavenworth. Later, given
a third star, he replaced Major General John K. Singlaub (relieved,
much later, of his command of American forces in Korea for criticizing
President Carter's proposed drawdown of troops there). While still in
Vietnam, Cushman commented: "You've got to be worried. If you're
not, you don't understand the situation."[12]

We know the conclusions of such writers as Mylander, Loory, King,
Lederer, and even Kinnard. Vietnam hurt the army badly. Indeed, no
writers have dared to suggest that the Vietnam experience was good
for, or improved upon the performance of, the army. At the time,
officers gravely wondered what would happen to their units if the chips
were down. Would their outfits still be able to fight, to function? Too
often they came to negative conclusions. The reason was plain. For a
military unit to be able to function effectively it has to have excellent
discipline and capable leadership. By the late 1960s, the U.S. Army in
Vietnam had neither.

An instructor in the Department of Tactics at the Command and

General Staff College graphically described the situation. "My God, man, in the latter years of the Vietnamese experience the army was almost unusuable. You had a fantastic breakdown in cohesion. Discipline was shot, absolutely shot. There were internal doubts, self-doubts, about those working and fighting beside you. Things like this had developed to the point where we didn't have a unit in the U.S. Army by late 1972 or early 1973 that really was at all usable, except perhaps for some in technical activities. It was a case of double deterioration—from the top down and from the bottom up—as the officer corps became more engaged in matters of promotion and ticket punching rather than in concentrating on doing their jobs and staying with their people."[13]

Or consider the words of Lieutenant General DeWitt C. Smith, Jr., commandant of the Army War College. Although he does not mention Westmoreland, the criticism of him is direct enough. "We study . . . the body count as a measure of 'success.' " Shaking his head sadly, the small-stature general, commander of the army's highest school, wonders, "How did we ever come to use such an odious phrase? How did it come to be that some people allegedly changed statistics so they looked advantageous?" What, he asks, "are the ethical implications of sending young men . . . to fight . . . and putting them in a climate where, while dying horrible deaths, we have a giant PX importing French perfume and nylons right behind them?" As a result of intense feelings about such ethical implications, Smith introduced courses and seminars on ethics within the military shortly after he arrived at the Army War College in Carlisle, Pennsylvania.[14]

Shortly after taking over in Vietnam, Westmoreland instituted three tactical measures that he declared would bring victory: search-and-destroy, clearing, and holding operations. Were these tactical methods the result of study committees, of military-school doctrines, of think-tank concepts? A spokesman at the Center for Military History comments that such was not the case. Like Topsy, they just grew. And Westmoreland, turning to his trusted associate General William E. Depuy would say: "Bill, what should we call this?" And Bill responded, "How about 'search and destroy'?" In such a way was a tactic born.[15]

Clearing and holding operations, while often spectacularly successful, failed to have lasting results, because the army, while strong enough to clear any given area in a sweep through the countryside, could not thereafter hold on to such regions without dangerously scattering its troops. Nor did such operations often weaken the Viet Cong in any significant way. Faced with such a clearing sweep, guerrillas simply withdrew to other, safer, areas and redoubled their activities there.

Another spokesman at the Center for Military History (CMH) further elaborated upon the tactical situation in Vietnam. Many of the army's various tactics were developed in *ad hoc* fashion depending upon our abilities at any given time, i.e., the number of troops we had in-country. He stressed that "it is wrong to think we fought a guerrilla war, except at the very first. After the buildup, which occurred under Westmoreland, we fought a very conventional war."[16] Somehow that makes it even worse. To lose a guerrilla war for which we were unprepared would have been one thing. To lose a conventional war against a rag-tag, bobtail collection of ill-equipped soldiers is quite another. If Vietnam *was* primarily an insurgency, we had no business trying to fight it in a conventional way. If it was primarily an aggression from the north fought along generally conventional lines, as the CMH spokesman has insisted, then our troops had no justification for doing as poorly as they did, nor in being instructed to use tactics such as search and destroy.

This was the concept of Westmoreland's which eventually became the most controversial. We know that the air-force chief of staff and the commandant of the Marine Corps opposed it, although it was favored by General Earle Wheeler, army chief of staff and chairman of the Joint Chiefs.[17] The heads of the air force and the marines favored rather the enclave strategy espoused by Gavin.

Although Westmoreland would later deny that search and destroy was a specific tactic, it was certainly the dominant one followed by American fighting units of all sizes in Vietnam. He emphasized its potential for carrying the war to the enemy rather than sitting back and waiting for their probes. He spoke of its ability to use the mobility and firepower of the American army in such a way as to inflict heavy and decisive casualties upon the enemy. In brief, search and destroy emphasized attacking the enemy rather than acquiring territory. Troopers struck into areas of supposed enemy strength to "find, fix, and finish" them, and, mission accomplished, they would be withdrawn to their home base until ordered out on the next such operation. Applied cleanly, with surgical precision, the objective of search and destroy was to weaken and ultimately destroy VC and NVA units while keeping American losses to a minimum. It did not, however, always work that way.

Komer faults Westmoreland's tactics. Our search-and-destroy policy was brought about, he states, because we had equipped and prepared the army to fight in Europe and nowhere else. The army's purpose and *raison d'être* was to fight Russians on the plains of the European continent. Suddenly, faced with Vietnam, we brought the whole military force intact to Southeast Asia, and fought the only way we knew, "at horrendous cost and with tragic side effects—because we lacked the incentive and . . . capability to do otherwise." Relying on unrivaled firepower and mobility—which would have been crucial in Europe—search and destroy was, Komer writes, "a natural response of American commanders deploying forces hugely superior in mobility and firepower against an elusive enemy who could not be brought to decisive battle. But his ability to control his own losses by evading contact and using sanctuaries frustrated our aims."[18]

It was, Komer suggests, a policy of attrition. He is not the only such critic. Sir Robert Thompson comments that the best thing about search and destroy was that it achieved "commendable results on the casualty graphs" with which Westmoreland was infatuated. Unfortunately, however, "it permitted Hanoi to hold the strategic initiative by accepting the casualties in order to achieve her political aim."[19]

Even Westmoreland saw it as a policy of attrition. In a speech delivered at the Waldorf in New York City in April 1967, Westmoreland stated that "the end is not in sight. . . . We will have to grind him down. In effect we are fighting a war of attrition. The only alternative is a war of annihilation."[20] One wonders why his imagination and talents were so limited that he could see only two alternatives, attrition or annihilation. Lieutenant Colonel Dave Richard Palmer, in a military-history textbook used at West Point, took the general to task for his limited imagination.

> But one thing should be made absolutely clear: attrition is not a strategy. It is irrefutable proof of the absence of any strategy. A commander who resorts to attrition admits his failure to conceive of an alternative. He turns from warfare as an art and accepts it on the most nonprofessional terms imaginable. He uses blood instead of brains. Saying that political considerations forced the employment of attrition [in Vietnam] does not alter the hard truth that the United States [army] was strategically bankrupt in Vietnam.[21]

On the tactical level, the thrust of the VC insurgent effort clung to the doctrine that the purpose of a battle is not necessarily to win it, but simply to fight it. Every strike that levels a village or cuts a road or kills innocent civilians contributes to the ultimate victory even if the military engagement is lost—even if the guerrillas lose both ground and men. For all such military operations, by their very nature and destructiveness, alienate the people among whom they occur. Kinnard speaks to this point.

> One of the problems with the search-and-destroy strategy was the open-ended nature of the commitment. If the objective is to defeat an enemy force rather than denying it victory, then the eventual cost depends as much on the enemy as on one's own plans. It in effect depends upon what price the enemy—in this case, North Vietnam—is willing to pay. The more he is willing to pay in terms of manpower, the more one must increase one's own units.[22]

As late as Tet 1968, the VC and NVA attacked when and where they wished. The important fact is not that the United States ultimately pushed them back into the jungle, but that they were able to launch such a massive attack at all. Tet demonstrated that for all of America's

search-and-destroy efforts, VC and NVA units still operated with impunity.[23] If it was to be a war of attrition, they had more time than did
the United States and were willing to expend more men than were the
mothers of America. And nowhere in Vietnam were American soldiers
safe if the enemy chose to bring the war to them. Search and destroy
was a born loser, first, because North Vietnam was willing to accept
staggering military losses in order to achieve its political aims, and
second, because all of our battlefield firepower and methods of attrition
alienated even those citizens of the south who might initially have been
willing to side with us.

There were those, however, who sang the praises of search and
destroy and who explained why such a tactic was necessary. Bradford
explained how obvious it was "that the US Army is inherently ill-suited
for producing substantial numbers of soldiers" capable of counterguerrilla fighting. "As an Army, we are broadly representative of the general
population—technically inclined, conditioned to a high standard of living, and, of greater significance, Western, largely white, and English-
speaking. Only with great difficulty can many of our soldiers who are
drawn from that population be given more than superficial training of
the type needed to make them effective" in a guerrilla war.[24] Fortunately, he believed, the "Army does not need to adopt guerrilla measures. Rather the helicopter can be used, once the enemy is found, to
resupply U.S. forces so rapidly that 20 men can be landed every minute"; the combat elements of a battalion could be brought into action
within thirty minutes. Helicopters could emplace troops in blocking
and encirclement positions around enemy units, preventing their retreat and allowing the "massive application of firepower from aircraft
and artillery" to provide the *coup de grace*. [25] Heliborne tactics of search
and destroy thus allowed for defeat of the enemy with fewer U.S.
casualties. Bradford's analysis lacked real insight.

Search-and-destroy missions were, theoretically, a very effective
way to conduct combat. Aimed at enemy forces in Vietnam's jungles
and mountains, they were designed to hit bases and supply areas, keeping enemy maneuver battalions on the defensive, unable to move into
populated areas and mount attacks against either U.S. or ARVN units.
The first such operations began in the central highlands in October
1965, when the 1st Air Cavalry Division was committed to the Ia Drang
Valley. Its task was first to search for the enemy and, when it found him,
to destroy him.[26]

Units conducting search-and-destroy operations were assigned a
specific area to cover. Borrowing from the Marine Corps, the army
assigned units to Tactical Areas of Responsibility (TAORs). Corps assigned TAORs to divisions, divisions to brigades, brigades to battalions,
and, sometimes, battalions to companies. The size of a TAOR depended
upon the unit assigned to it, the mission designated, the enemy situa-

tion, the terrain, the weather, and similar factors.

While engaged in search-and-destroy missions, units made no effort to seize or hold terrain. Once they had searched an area and eliminated enemy forces there, they would be pulled out to conduct similar missions elsewhere. It was not uncommon for American units to conduct repeated search-and-destroy missions in the same area. Such missions numbered in the thousands before publicity at home became too negative and they were renamed "reconnaissance in force" operations and then, finally, discontinued altogether in the last years of the American drawdown in Vietnam. Throughout the years of their existence, search-and-destroy missions depended heavily upon the use of helicopters to support airborne assaults, to provide logistical support and communications, and to bring in reserve troops if and when they were needed.

Entry into a battle area was normally accomplished by American infantry battalions making a heliborne approach. Successful assaults required considerable planning and depended upon a controlled execution. In the planning phase, a battalion commander developed his operational plan in close coordination with the brigade aviation-support commander. In their command and control helicopters, usually UH 1Ds (equipped with a console radio and capable of carrying a four- or five-man command group) they made a joint aerial reconnaissance of the proposed battle area to select primary and alternate landing zones (LZs). In much of Vietnam, choices of LZs were extremely limited, causing many operational plans to be altered according to their availability and the realities of the terrain. Experience demonstrated that an LZ, in order to be adequate, had to be large enough to accommodate the simultaneous landings of at least six assault helicopters. It was also desirable to have at least two LZs in order to conduct simultaneous landings in two locations. Once the LZs were selected, the commander turned to his fire-support commanders to plan artillery and air preparatory fires on the LZs and to work out touchdown times for the assault elements.

Some commanders seemed not to have recognized that from the air, one gets an idealized, oversimplified picture of the ground. Distances look shorter, the terrain smoother, and the situation simpler to the airborne observer than to the soldier on the ground. Once a battle began, from his aerial perch a commander could reconnoiter, direct supporting fires, observe and direct a battle unfolding below, and communicate directly with superior and subordinate commanders. This was possible because of the monitoring of two and sometimes three command radio nets from aboard the bird, using PRC-25 radios. On board the command and control chopper rode the battalion commander, his aviation-support commander, the artillery-liaison officer, the battalion S-3, and the battalion sergeant major. They circled above the LZ at a low-enough level to give good visual observation but high enough to escape random small-arms fire. An operation began with a thirty- to forty-five-minute artillery and air bombardment, known as the "preparation" of the LZ. As those heavy fires lifted, incoming choppers landed assault troops on the LZ.[27]

Normally, the battalion fire-support base (FSB) was established first. The first rifle company on the ground secured the LZ, protecting it from enemy fire and attack while choppers brought in the necessary men and equipment to set up the FSB. In the FSB were located the battalion command and control elements, a 105mm artillery battery, a 4.2" mortar platoon, a reconnaissance platoon, and the rifle company that had initially secured the area. After offering penetration support, that company was used as area security for the combat-support elements. The other two rifle companies of the battalion operated as strike forces searching for the enemy within the assigned TAOR. Within the FSB were located all the administrative, logistical, and combat-support units required to support the battalion while it was on its search-and-destroy mission.

An FSB was normally about three hundred yards in diameter. Within that area, soldiers dug three-man foxholes with overhead cover for protection against enemy mortar rounds, recoilless rifles, or rockets. Mortar and artillery positions were dug in, and ammunition storage pits were provided with overhead cover. The battalion command post (CP) was bunkered in, while logs and sandbags provided protection for communications vehicles. The security rifle company conducted extensive patrolling around the FSB during the day and at night established ambushes and listening posts along likely enemy routes into the FSB perimeter. Early concentration on setting up the FSB permitted the 105mm artillery battery and, occasionally, the 4.2 mortar platoon, to support subsequent incoming helicopter landings of the other two rifle companies of the battalion.

As a precaution against an enemy strike, close-in defensive fires were registered around the FSB as soon as possible after closing on the LZ. Artillery units within range agreed to provide defensive fires if called upon. Mortar units armed with 81mm and 4.2" weapons provided additional support. An air-force noncommissioned officer in a communications jeep accompanied the battalion headquarters troops into the FSB to provide instant communication with supporting air power, should the need arise for help from the air force.

Established by helicopter, FSBs were also resupplied by them. Normally the UH-1D transported personnel and supplies while the Chinook CH-47 carried in heavy loads, such as one-quarter- and three-quarter-ton trucks, artillery pieces, and heavy mortars. Once all units had closed on their LZs and the FSB was in operation, the battalion was in position to commence its search-and-destroy mission.

With one rifle company providing FSB security, the actual burden of the mission fell to the battalion's two remaining rifle companies. Each one might be assigned a TAOR within the battalion operational area, or perhaps they would be given a specific route to follow as they searched for the enemy. This latter course of action was often followed when the battalion commander needed tight control over his companies in order to keep them within mutually supporting or reinforcing distance. Since they could move only on foot, they could not afford to become too far separated. Assault companies seldom operated beyond the range of their supporting artillery.

Assault companies usually conducted searches during daylight hours and then moved into night locations about two hours before the onset of darkness. This gave them time while it was still light to establish company perimeters, to prepare defensive positions with overhead cover, to receive helicopter resupply, to register defensive fires around their positions, and to establish ambushes and listening posts. They avoided night moves and night combat because of their strong conviction that "the hours of dark belong to the enemy." If dusk or late afternoon found them in a location with no existing or natural LZ, they cut a minimum-one-ship-sized LZ to allow resupply and for dust-off medical evacuation flights, in case it became necessary to airlift wounded comrades from the area.

Some units made it a standing operating procedure (SOP) to airlift one 81mm mortar into position for immediate fire support in case of ambush or attack. In each three-man foxhole, one soldier was always supposed to be awake during night hours to provide security for his sleeping buddies. While in such a defensive position, company situation reports were radioed hourly to battalion headquarters. At dawn, all personnel were on "stand-to," that is, they were awake, fully dressed, and ready either to fight or to move out for further searches. Just before breaking camp, they made a perimeter sweep to a distance of about two hundred yards to determine if an ambush had been prepared for them during the night by enemy soldiers. While on the move, companies kept a fire-team-sized security element scouting 150 to 200 yards in front of them. Simultaneously, flank-security units moved seventy-five yards out from the main body along both sides of a route. If such assault companies were lucky, and if the intelligence reports upon which they acted had been correct, and if the VC units for which they hunted had not been alerted and thus vanished into their jungle fastnesses, then the American search unit found, fought, and finished some Viet Cong or North Vietnamese Regular Army unit. After the skirmish, the American force checked the number of enemy dead, returned to its FSB, packed up its gear, and was moved by helicopter back to its permanent base.

That was the theory. In actual practice there were probably as many divergences from this pattern as there were maneuver battalions and battalion commanders. Much depended upon the enemy. The most difficult problem—and one that the army never resolved—was finding him. For the most part, search-and-destroy missions were fruitless. Plans would be laid for days or weeks. Penetration would be made. An FSB would be established. Assault companies would comb the terrain and come back emptyhanded. The enemy had disappeared. Or, having found nothing, an American unit would suddenly be ambushed in an area that it had already searched and found to be clear of enemy troops. Hit when they least expected a fire fight, American soldiers could only huddle down into some semblance of a defensive formation and return fire while they called in Cobra gunships or protective artillery fires. Too frequently those fires had to be called down upon their own positions in order to make the enemy break contact. Then came the dust-off choppers to evacuate American wounded, and after that, if possible, the rest of the strike force would be airlifted out. Another search-and-destroy mission was over.[28]

In this way the enemy demonstrated his ability to remain hidden until he was ready to fight on terms he believed to be favorable to himself. American units time and again found themselves suddenly engaged in close-in combat at a time and place of the enemy's choosing. Thus U.S. troop commanders violated an important principle of war, one that states that a successful campaign is one in which a strike force surprises its foe. Surprise all too often lay with the opponents rather than with those engaged in search and destroy.

The reason for these repeated American failures was twofold: the speed with which Hanoi learned to deal with search-and-destroy missions, and the clumsiness of the American operations themselves. To learn how to cope with this new military problem they faced—heliborne mobility, massive artillery, and air support—Hanoi conducted a costly experiment very early, during the Ia Drang campaign. The NVA high command ordered its military leaders in the Ia Drang Valley to accept battles they could not possibly win. They were further instructed to maintain fighting contact for a longer period of time than any guerrilla army should. A high-ranking defector later explained: "We had to learn how the Americans fought."[29] From this and subsequent battles, the North Vietnamese learned by their mistakes how to modify their military tactics and techniques to counter U.S. superiority in fire-power, airborne mobility, and communications.

Evidence of the North Vietnamese ability to cope was soon reflected in American newspaper headlines:

G.I.s Pay Dearly in 7-Hour Battle of Equal Forces—Enemy Death Toll Is Set at 166 after Battalion Is Surprised in Highlands.[30]

Trapped Americans Fought 400 North Vietnamese Today in a 4-Hour Battle in the Central Highlands. They Called in Artillery Fire on Their Own Positions before Being Overrun.[31]

40 G.I.s Stand Off Ia Drang Attackers: 102 Foe Killed—the United States Unit, a Reconnaissance Platoon from the First Cavalry Division (Airmobile), Suffered Heavy Casualties, with Most of Its Members Either Wounded or Killed.[32]

Dozens of similar headlines over the following years could be cited.

American ineptitude was also an important factor. As Lieutenant Colonel James R. Lay observed: "We tip our hand prior to our heliborne assaults." This was done in several ways. In order to shoot

preparatory artillery fires into the LZ, it is necessary to register the supporting batteries. This is normally accomplished twenty to thirty minutes prior to the beginning of the preparation. This registration begins with a high smoke streamer or smoke round, both of which are easily recognizable in the jungle. Should the enemy be in the vicinity of the LZ, he immediately knows that we are likely to enter the area. He then has a choice of disappearing into the jungle or defending the LZ.[33]

The helicopters that provided easy jungle access for American troops were also a problem. They regularly gave away to the enemy the information that a search-and-destroy mission was beginning. Aerial-reconnaissance flights, sweeping back and forth across a particular grid of terrain in ever narrowing arcs, were a dead giveaway to hidden observers in the jungle below that an operation was about to be launched in the vicinity. They could often pinpoint the LZ selected by the Americans and, if they wished, be there waiting to ambush the G.I.s as they offloaded from their choppers. Thompson has written that the helicopter "exaggerated the two great weaknesses of the American character —impatience and aggressiveness. . . . It is probable that without the helicopter 'search and destroy' would not have been possible and in this sense, the helicopter was one of the major contributions to the failure of strategy."[34]

If the enemy had not located a proposed LZ prior to the beginning of a mission, observation of choppers as they brought in men and matériel to erect an FSB clearly revealed its location. VC and NVA troops could watch 105mm howitzers being lifted into an LZ from miles away. A minimum of actual ground reconnaissance then led them to the perimeter of the new LZ. Without making contact, an experienced NVA commander could deduce the area through which U.S. troops would conduct their sweep. He could determine how far out from the FSB the G.I.s would move, for he knew that such units inevitably stayed within supporting range of their 105mm howitzers. By drawing a 10,000-meter-radius circle around the location of an FSB, he could plot where the noisy, jangling, littering American troops would be conducting operations.

Having now defined an American unit's area of operations (AO), the North Vietnamese commander's task of finding its rifle companies was relatively easy. Experience had proved that strike forces started preparing their night locations in midafternoon. They usually selected an open area for easy helicopter resupply. It was easy for enemy main-force soldiers to locate such companies: they listened for sounds of digging and for trees being cut for use in defensive cover; they watched for bursting artillery shells as far-away batteries fired defensive registration patterns around the area. Incoming resupply helicopters gave additional evidence, if any was still needed. All this—yet the North Vietnamese or Viet Cong unit had thus far masked its own presence. There had been no contact. No American had yet learned of their positions. No shots had been fired. With all their mobility, fire superiority, and communications, the Americans were deaf and blind in the double- or triple-canopied jungle that overhung their positions. They had not yet heard or seen the poised-and-waiting enemy.

If it was easy for North Vietnamese units to detect American battalion-sized LZs and FSBs, it was even simpler for them to locate brigade forward-command posts and medium-artillery positions. These tended to be almost permanent and were generally situated near roads, for purposes of easy access. In some instances, the enemy may have known their whereabouts more exactly than did the maneuver battalions that were under the operational control of those brigade CPs.

The choices the enemy could make in such situations were manifold. They could engage American units in full-scale set-piece battles, and occasionally they did so. From secure locations, they could shell brigade forward CPs or supply installations, stopping the shelling before counterfire could be brought to bear against them. They could conduct harassing ground attacks against unit locations, or spring ambushes, or plant booby traps, or use sniper fire. Using mortars, recoilless rockets, and other medium weapons, they could bring firepower to bear on battalion FSBs or company night-defensive positions. Or they could slip away undetected, avoiding contact and engagement with American troops.

The choices the Americans could make were fewer. They could launch mission after mission, searching and researching the jungles for enemy installations, caches, and units. Sometimes army efforts paid off, and they found what they looked for. It can be truthfully said that Americans searched for enemy troops until those soldiers allowed themselves to be found.[35]

It need not have been that way. Enemy avoidance of search-and-destroy operations could have been made much more difficult by the use of a few simple devices. Some commanders used all of them. Others never used any. Why all were not mandated for strict compliance by every commander is inconceivable. The measures were not difficult. Units could have deviated more often from routine practices—always a good idea for keeping an enemy off his guard. Instead of occupying prepared defensive night locations while on operations, assault companies could have moved into alternate positions after dark. Battalions could and should have conducted their operations without resupply for a period of from three to five days. In this way they could have moved without letting helicopters constantly give away their new locations. An important step would have been to prohibit all helicopter traffic over unit locations, except for dust-off evacuations of wounded personnel. At that point the enemy would already have been found, in any case, and cautionary use of choppers would not have been so crucial. There should have been minimum aerial reconnaissance of battle areas and proposed LZs by battalion commanders and their staffs. The army had available a number of Long Range Reconnaissance Patrols (LRRPs) capable of moving out into disputed territory and, relying upon their own resources, operating for many days without the need to touch home base. Such LRRP groups were used occasionally to locate suitable LZs for search-and-destroy missions. Regular reliance upon them would have been wise.

Too often battalion commanders supervised battle progress from the air rather than with their troops on the ground, using their command and control helicopters as aerial observation posts. Such a platform gave them speed, mobility, and, occasionally, an excellent opportunity to see troops below them in relationship to the terrain in which they fought. A senior captain who served in 'Nam as a forward observer (FO), an aerial observer (AO), and an artillery-battery executive officer admitted the shortcomings of such aerial command. "The eye in the sky might be fine for traffic direction in the U.S., but it's lousy direction of a war. It was too high up and too removed from the scheme of things." Asked if it did not provide a commander with good visual command of his troops, the captain replied, "Not in double- or triple-canopy jungle! It might be a good auxiliary tool, but commanders in 'Nam relied on it all too exclusively. With cover like that it was no help to commanders as they tried to determine how fast, and in which direction, their men should be moving. The real situation can't be determined from three or four—or even a thousand—feet."[36]

Another man, who had served as an infantry captain in Vietnam, recalled that another problem with "eye in the sky" control was that "every higher level of commander, on arriving at the scene, had to request an update on what was happening on the ground. He would request you to change to his frequency and tell him what was going on. This got very inconvenient after about the second time we had to change frequencies so we could inform other people who really ought to have been informed by an after-action report. They had no *need* to know right on the spot. And insisting on knowing simply complicated matters for us on the ground when we were supposed to be concentrating on the firefight going on."[37]

A third veteran of such tactics remarked that "we always had a horror that one day things would come to a standstill. Overhead would be circling our battalion commander. Above him would be his brigade commander. Higher than both would be the division commander and hovering over him would be his corps commander. All circling in their 'charlie-charlie' choppers, all demanding to know what was going on down on the ground. So much command and control would be present that those with their 'ass in the grass' would no longer be able to function at all. It never happened, but it came close."[38]

Almost everyone interviewed had incisive comments about this particular phenomenom. "Pity the new, inexperienced platoon leader who had to try to conduct ground operations while trying to satisfy simultaneous demands for information from several levels of command choppers insistently talking to him from above."[39] "They gave us advice we didn't want or need. They left no chance for a man to do things on his own."[40] "What business does a division commander have directing the assault of a company? Whatever happened to the chain of command?"[41] "It's easy to be omniscient when you're sitting 1,500 feet up in the air. I wonder how those bastards with their free advice would have fared had they been down there with me!"[42]

Mylander also noted this phenomenom. She observes that "colonels commanding brigades monitored platoon activities in detail, while major generals commanding divisions supervised companies . . . functioning more as emotionally involved participants than as detached directors of the action below."[43]

For the man on the ground such oversupervision presented a problem of another kind—the cluttering of the airwaves. American soldiers use communications equipment all too freely. No one is anyone without a radio and a call sign of his own. Commo traffic regularly consists of conversation, much of which is trivial and a great deal of which should never have been broadcast. A few years ago, while driving in convoy during a night move under blackout conditions and commo security, I heard someone make the following transmission: "Be careful. As you make the right turn, watch out for the big pothole." In a "respectable" war, two such transmissions would have been enough for an enemy listening post to triangulate the location of that convoy and call in artillery fire upon it.

As one forward observer in Vietnam put it, "When you updated your commander, you updated everybody, since both Viet Cong and NVA monitored our frequencies. It was very convenient for everyone concerned except for the grunts on the ground. For example, when a helicopter pilot would ask you to mark your location with smoke, you couldn't tell him what color you would use. If you did, identically colored smokes would appear in three or four places. Instead you would simply say, 'I pop smoke now.' He would call back and say, for example,

'I identify green.' And as soon as the identification of color was heard, you could count on having two or three other green smokes pop in the vicinity, within a grid square of you. That's how well we were monitored."[44]

Then there was the overabundance of artillery fires, which the army used as a matter of course in Vietnam. Kinnard reports that "one of the more expensive and least effective techniques of employing artillery fires was what was known as harassing and interdiction (H and I) fires."[45] This was the name given to artillery rounds dropped on preselected targets outside the perimeters of friendly installations. They were generally fired at night in the hope of preventing attacks upon those bases. Other targets were also selected at random and included trails, areas where someone suspected enemy troops might be concentrating, and sites that might possibly be enemy base camps.

HI fires, like search-and-destroy missions, came in for criticism within the army and without. Ward Just, author of *Military Men*, concluded that "in one year, the Army fired more than one million rounds of artillery in HI (at $100-plus per round); surely somewhere there is a classified document reporting on their effectiveness."[46] They were not all that effective. Enemy soldiers were trained to disappear into foxholes or tunnels when they heard the fluttering whistle of the first incoming round. The victims who suffered and died were often Vietnamese civilians who had no place to hide. Kinnard quotes one general who served in Vietnam who described HI fires as "madness."[47] Just as search and destroy was renamed "reconnaissance in force" when it received a bad press, so HI fires came to be called by a new term, "targets of intelligence." This was done, says Kinnard, "to give the impression that they were based on much better information . . . than the previous HI fires. That they were is questionable."

Kinnard relates how on the day after he became commanding general of II Field Force Artillery, in May 1969, "I asked to have the intelligence targets plotted on my map. Afterward, I asked to see the person who selected the targets, together with the data on which he based his selections. A first lieutenant appeared with a coordinate square; inspecting a map, he selected, at random, points in the areas where nighttime firing was authorized, and then measured off the coordinates for firing. This had been the method of choosing intelligence targets in that zone for the preceding several months."[48] My own research supports the general's observation. An artillery captain reported that during his year as service battery commander for a 105mm-howitzer battalion, the unit shot some five hundred to one thousand rounds each day. "We had a real trucking problem in hauling that ammo to our firing batteries. But the ammo kept coming whether or not we had targets for it, so the batteries fired their allotments every opportunity they had, whether there was actually anything to shoot at or not."[49] Part of that huge allotment could be consumed through SLAM firepower exercises: "seeking, locating, annihilating, and monitoring" coordinating efforts, in which artillery firepower was centered upon a concentrated attack on some preselected target.

An artillery-battalion commander remembered that "no matter how cautious a man might try to be, artillery is not a pinpoint effective weapon. Rounds fall short, or coordinates are off. Sooner or later you drop rounds where they're not supposed to fall and civilians die."[50] Another artilleryman, since retired, stated that "we were supposed to shoot it just because we had it. Maybe artillery was the answer in World War II, when there were real targets to aim at—enemy artillery or fortresses or fortified positions or massed enemy-troop formations or even bridges. In Vietnam there were none of those things, and for the most part, artillery fires were a waste. They did nothing but kill a lot of innocents and alienate us from those we were supposedly trying to help."[51]

Artillery fires may not have stopped either VC or NVA attacks—obviously they did not, for the enemy continued to confront American units when and where they chose—but such weapons did destroy a lot of villages, piling up corpses in the streets, sending terror-stricken survivors in screaming dashes for safety. Thus, despite its superiority in manpower, firepower, communications, and mobility, the American army came to depend upon such tactical measures as search and destroy and HI fires. In its hundreds of confrontations with the enemy, it was inevitably the VC or NVA units that broke contact and withdrew during a firefight. Many American leaders mistakenly concluded that such withdrawals were equivalent to an acknowledgement of defeat. In this way a myth developed that America's forces were doing better than was actually the case. In retrospect, some of Kinnard's generals could conclude that "Giap could have gone on indefinitely. It was unwinnable the way we played it." Another admitted that "there was a tendency to underestimate the enemy. They were in fact the best enemy we have faced in our history."[52] No military voices raised such cries at the time.

Since progress could not be measured by such traditional yardsticks as miles gained or cities won or armies destroyed, both Secretary of Defense McNamara and the upper echelon of his military followers sought other ways to compute the relative advantage of America over its adversaries, for there was no question that the United States was winning. The "light at the end of the tunnel" was coming ever closer —so they all said.

The "solution," acclaimed by both military and civilian parties, was to apply statistics to the battlefield: search for significant factors that would lend themselves to statistical manipulation; tabulate relative position semiannually, or monthly, or weekly, or daily, or hourly, then do it again and compare results with those previously determined. In this way one could provide ample demonstration of America's progress. No one would quarrel with figures, for figures do not lie (although, as the old adage claims, liars do sometimes figure). "Statistical indicators of military progress" became the watchword from the battlements.[53]

Staff officers could supply ever eager and inevitably receptive commanders with a number of such statistical indicators; they could be found on every hand. How many actions had been instituted last month by ARVN units? How many by U.S. troop units? How many by corps, by division, brigade, battalion, battery, or company? Were there more such actions this month than last? How many VC had been killed? How many captured? How many wounded? How many NVA in the same categories? What was the ratio of VC to U.S. killed? Of NVA to U.S.? Were VC desertions up? By how much? Was the American AWOL rate down? By what percentage? How many enemy weapons were captured last week? What types of weapons were they? How many army-gunship sorties had been flown last month? How many enemy trucks destroyed? How many miles of roads were now open for traffic?

Our mania for data that could be statistically plotted became so feverish and so well known that a Vietnamese army officer was heard to exclaim: "Ah, *les statistiques.* Your Secretary of Defense loves statistics. We Vietnamese can give him all he wants. If you want them to go up, they will go up. If you want them to go down, they will go down."[54] And the Vietnamese were not the only ones willing to manipulate data. In this regard, American officers had no peers. As Kinnard has written, "When higher commanders rode lower ones for better statistical results, it was evident that they were going to get either the statistics or the results, and on fortunate occasions, both."[55]

However, reports from different units seldom agreed. Results were often faked entirely, or skewed by addition or elimination of certain information. One officer, who for a time served as a brigade historian, testified that "the result is that the battle news is edited and revised until it's acceptable to higher-ups. I've even been ordered to write open lies on our civil-aid programs, such as increasing fifteen English classes to three hundred to make it look good to the politicians and the people back home. I've been ordered to raise the figures for food distribution in refugee villages. I've also had to retype battle reports . . . where the whole time sequence was destroyed in the wording of the report and vital facts omitted by the commanding general . . . thereby turning an NVA victory over superior American forces into a U.S. victory."[56]

Lowry asserts that "duplicity became so automatic that lower headquarters began to believe the things they were forwarding to higher headquarters. It was on paper, therefore, no matter what might have actually occurred, the paper graphs and charts became the ultimate reality."[57] In time, statistics were everywhere the only important factor, and nearly everyone juggled figures in order to look good, or to impress his superior, or to avoid punishment of some kind. All the "figurers" had become liars.

*   *   *

The entire syndrome of Vietnam-era statistical reporting by the United States Army came to be summed up in the epithet "body count." As early as 1968, one military writer suggested that "one of the leading candidates" for worthless practices that should be relegated to the dustbin of history was "that unique contribution the war has made to the annals of U.S. warfare—the 'body count.' "[58] The body count was not something totally new. It has been around, in one form or another, since Samson "found a fresh jawbone of an ass, and put out his hand and seized it, and with it he slew a thousand men."[59] One wonders whether the number slain was a swollen count.

It has always been natural for one side in an armed conflict to estimate the number of casualties it has inflicted upon the other side. Not until Vietnam, however, did "estimated enemy casualties" become an all-encompassing obsession of the army. The feverish pursuit of this talisman actually led to increased American losses, brought dishonor upon those who espoused the practice, and generally lessened the stature of the army within American opinion. The "credibility gap" operated with a vengeance when outside observers began to double-check military "body count" lists and found discrepancies, contradictions, and exaggerations. (If it were possible to add up all the "body count" claims made throughout the years of war by the army, one wonders, what would they total?)

A small sampling of quotations taken from a few months in 1968 indicates how widespread disbelief had become about the truthfulness of military-casualty lists. Look at Tet, 1968:

> Official estimates of enemy casualties last week should be viewed with the utmost skepticism. Body counts of enemy dead are at best always open to doubt; almost every reporter in Vietnam has his own personal example of inflated reports of enemy dead in battles that he himself has observed. To think that in the midst of last week's chaos and breakdown of communications, a careful tabulation of such an enormous number of bodies was actually made defies logic and contributes further to the credibility gap . . . .[60]

Or again:

> There is considerable doubt about the accuracy of the Allied claim of thirty-six thousand Communists killed between January 29th and February 18th.[61]

Reporters cynically observed that

the intelligence men say that the Saigon command "grossly overstated" enemy deaths during the Tet and follow-up offensives.[62]

With his tongue firmly placed in his cheek, Douglas Robinson observed in the *New York Times* that

> military observers here tended to look askance at the estimated total of 7,500 killed over the last eight days, since both the South Vietnamese and American military commands have been found at times to exaggerate enemy casualties. This morning, for example, the U.S. command said that 92 enemy had been killed in a sharp clash . . . which . . . ended at 7 P.M. The casualty announcement was ready at 8:30 this morning, indicating that American soldiers apparently had stayed up all night counting enemy bodies by flashlight in an area that was probably within sniper range and certainly exposed to possible mortar or rocket fire. "It does sound incredible, doesn't it?" the high-ranking spokesman said this afternoon. "I didn't check that one out."[63]

And David Duncan, in the old *Life* magazine, concluded that "every press conference reeks with these two words [body count]. It is unescapable, insidious, corrosive. . . . Someone decided there must be a way to keep score in a war where there are no victories."[64]

Perhaps Public Information Officers (PIO) had given out inflated body-count figures from the beginning of the American buildup in Vietnam. That can be checked some day, should someone be interested, when the requisite military records are catalogued and opened to researchers. The first well-publicized lie in which the army found itself caught, however, was when a company of the 173d Airborne Brigade was ambushed near Dak To on 22 June 1967. In that one action, eighty Americans were killed and thirty-four more wounded, a result that effectively wiped out the company as a fighting unit. The first figures released by the army admitted heavy American casualties but insisted that although it had suffered severe losses, the company inflicted 457 casualties on the enemy attackers. This figure was picked up and carried by some news media.[65] Then came a report that an on-the-scene search of the terrain had located only ten dead enemy soldiers. The army began to waffle. "Well, maybe we killed only 450 rather than 475."

A little later, army spokesmen readjusted their sights and fired again. "In any case," they claimed, "we killed over four hundred." The final count, below which the army would not admit having fallen, was 106 enemy dead, although no military spokesman ever publicly disputed the claim that only ten enemy bodies had ever been located at the scene.[66] Presumably those foes who survived the ambush of the American company carried off their fallen dead—a ploy the army would repeatedly and increasingly insist upon whenever the specific number of enemy dead varied from PIO claims for total body-count casualties.

Officially, it was U.S. policy to claim as enemy dead only those bodies that had actually fallen on a battleground and had been physically counted by an American commander. Any man who has ever been to war, particularly anyone who ever fought in Vietnam, knows that such a policy was impossible to implement or enforce and, consequently, was conducive to "estimates" which could easily be falsified. Yet once entered upon a report form, such estimates took on a reality of their own, transcending anything that might have actually happened. No matter how arrived at, the figures themselves became real. And such dubious statistics were used to measure American "progress" in the war effort.

Perhaps it was no wonder that even within the military, many believed that the war was going better than it actually was. The higher up the ladder of rank a man went, the more detached he became from what went on "in the field." He forgot, if he ever knew, that a platoon leader, responsible for the lives of those in his unit, trying to maneuver his platoon under fire, fighting for his own life as well, simply did not have the time or energy to count fallen enemies even had he the interest in doing so. At the same time it is also certain that there were numbers of high-ranking general officers in Saigon and elsewhere who, if they did not actually believe it to be the case, still personally insisted that all body counts were compiled by responsible individuals who had literally counted enemy corpses.[67]

In some instances this was actually done. Many of those interviewed for this study reported that they had personally inspected battle sites and had physically walked the terrain, counting fallen enemy dead. A few related how they had insisted upon having photographs of every corpse that would be used for compilation of statistical data. Others told of collecting gruesome tokens, such as ears or fingers. Positive evidence for some was the testimony of subordinates that they had fired a bullet round into the face or chest of each enemy soldier. Others were satisfied with less rigorous evidence. A few included in the body counts those corpses that could clearly be seen from the air and that obviously were not moving. Occasionally no physical evidence remained, but witnesses could testify that they had shot an enemy soldier whose body had then fallen into a stream or river and was unrecoverable. Such testimony came from those who, in their own minds at least, endeavored to report their kills with strict accuracy.

Even such men as these, however, were under pressure to exploit the firefights of their units by inflating the number of enemy casualties they reported. Among those interviewed, many reported that they were under constant pressure from their command headquarters to report higher body counts. Some resisted. Most shrugged and went along with the demands, for it could only make the battalion look better and, after all, others were doing it. Some men became defensive. "The people who challenge the accuracy of the body count are usually liars themselves. They do business that way, and they expect everyone else to."[68] As pressure for higher body counts intensified, it made itself felt all the way up and down the line. "My brigade commander constantly insisted upon a high body count from all his combat units. If one company fell very far behind the others, he'd begin to squeeze that commander until his figures got back in line."[69] Another man commented that "it ended up a real competition between the companies, as if it were a basketball game or something."[70]

To satisfy the demands of their superiors, American officers began using presumptive evidence to swell their totals. No bodies might be found after an engagement, but three trails of blood could be seen leading off into the jungle. Quite a lot of blood had been lost by someone. Therefore, those blood trails could be used as "evidence" that three enemy soldiers had been so grievously wounded that they had undoubtedly died as a result of their injuries. Blood trails became a standard method for computing total body count.

Suppose an assault company on a search-and-destroy mission engaged an enemy unit. When quiet returned to the jungle, eight dead soldiers sprawled on the ground. Their bodies were tallied: In addition, however, three enemy rifles were recovered from elsewhere in the area. Now, no soldier drops his weapon unless he is dead or badly injured. No bodies were found near the weapons, proving that the withdrawing force had carried its dead away. VC units were often poorly armed, with many members going into combat unarmed, ready to catch up a rifle from the twitching fingers of a wounded or killed comrade. Therefore, finding three abandoned weapons had to be proof positive that in addition to the enemy bodies still on the ground, three others had been carried away. Total enemy dead? Eleven. Weapons found on a battle site became another indicator for the ravenous body counters.

There was also the "partial-body" count. Particularly after an artillery barrage had ranged through an enemy camp, advancing American units frequently found pieces of bodies—blown-off arms or legs or even worse. Was the arm part of a blown-apart body, the rest of which was scattered over the area, or had it belonged to a man who had then run or been carried elsewhere? As often as not, the scattered limbs were tallied as having come from separate enemy soldiers. One man tells the gory tale

> of an experience where he almost had to get in a fist fight with an ARVN adviser over an arm, to see who would get the credit for the body, because they were sorting out pieces. . . . it just made him sick to the stomach that he was put in such a position that a body was so important to the next higher headquarters or to the division, that he had to go down and argue over pieces of a body to get credit for it.

He concluded that "nobody out there believes the body count. They couldn't possibly believe it. This is probably the most damning thing the Army has used recently."[71]

And there was the overlapping count. Although American units did operate within assigned tactical areas of responsibility (TAORs), it was common for more than one outfit to make sweeps through the same area. When enemy dead lay quietly in an area, to whom did they "belong"? The result was that more than one unit often counted those slain as part of their own "score." Cases were reported where the same body was counted by a Vietnamese outfit, a Korean force, and one or more American units.

One of the more macabre results of the emphasis on high body counts was the occasional practice of some commanders, who sent units into areas where earlier battles had been fought. These soldiers searched for enemy graves, then dug up decaying corpses and carted the grisly remains to a central location where they could be counted and computed for the Saigon statisticians. Why go to such lengths?

> The demand from higher headquarters to get a body count was almost unreal. Once I established contact with the enemy, within minutes I would receive a message asking me for a body count. This would usually come when I was still in the middle of my maneuver, or attempting to develop contact. Thus, I usually made an estimate of the "body count" to please higher headquarters. Afterwards, this estimate would be confirmed by an accurate count when time permitted.[72]

When enemy casualty figures are requested of a commander before battle has begun, something has gone awry.

Unfortunately for the statisticians, sometimes the VC or NVA won a firefight. "Sometimes the score was in the enemy's favor, and this is when the cry came in from higher headquarters for another count."[73] No matter what was true, by hook or crook correct statistics must be arrived at, because it would be figures that told the story.

> I know some commanders who put so damn much pressure on subordinates, that exaggeration was inevitable.

> Some commanders were *told* to come up with a higher body count. In such a situation, the commander is under considerable pressure to report a body count of such a nature that his contact [with the enemy] won't look bad.

> The Division Commander told me I should be more lenient in accepting body count figures from my subordinate units. He said that my body count was too low.

> Body count figures in my unit were accurate . . . until General ____ ____ took command of the division. After that, there was so much emphasis on getting a high body count and getting it reported quickly, that

I was no longer able to personally check the reports originating at the company and platoon level.

I know one unit that lost 18 men killed in an ambush and reported 131 enemy body count. I was on the ground at the tail end of the battle and I saw five enemy bodies. I doubt if there were any more.

Exaggeration did not always originate with personnel at battalion. One of the ADC's [assistant division commander] got a report from a company commander of 30 enemy killed. When the ADC got back to division, he turned in a report of sixty. I don't know whether he forgot the figure the company gave him or if he just felt the company's estimate was too low.

At one point seven battalions of artillery fired a barrage onto the site of a supposed heavy enemy-troop concentration.

A sweep through the area later failed to reveal one body, although pools of blood and equipment were all over the place. In this instance, the commander reported what he thought was a reasonable estimate of the enemy dead.

Some individuals acted from motives they believed to be honorable when they gave inflated body counts. In one instance, an assistant division commander told the officers of a unit that had just sustained very heavy casualties that inasmuch as most of a company-sized unit had been lost, the officers should "have a good body count so we can tell the survivors they did well."[74]

From such a shoddy base grew the spate of statistics that army spokesmen spewed forth as they gave routine briefings to U.S. officials visiting Vietnam, to newsmen, and to the general public. Body-count tallies based on such practices had no validity whatsoever, yet PIO personnel continued to provide "the latest list of enemy casualties" to bored and waiting newsmen and to do so with straight faces. Since as early as 1968 the supposed enemy losses had already reached a total of more than 250,000 dead, with the army claiming that it had killed another 100,000 VC and NVA troops in the seven months immediately following the Tet offensive of that year, one wonders out of what bottomless pit welled forth the continuing stream of fresh enemy troops.

Even if those figures had been reliable, which they were not, the North Vietnamese and their Viet Cong allies could still have continued to fight indefinitely. Phil G. Goulding, an assistant secretary of defense, acknowledged that fact.

Some analysts and some optimists cite those tremendous casualty figures and predict that the North Vietnamese cannot stand such losses very much longer. I offer no such assurance. North Vietnam is a nation of more than 18 million persons. The armed forces still at home number about 350,000 and their militia and security forces are that size or larger. The country has nearly three million men between 17 and 35 years old. Additionally, some

200,000 more males reach 17 each year—and more than half of these men are physically fit for military service. Statistically, then, there are men enough for the North Vietnamese to continue high infiltration rates into South Vietnam and to absorb high casualties.[75]

The conclusion was clear. At the rate of attrition then being exacted by the United States, the NLF and the North Vietnamese could have long continued to replace their losses. Furthermore, as Hanson W. Baldwin suggested, "the Communists do not measure victory or defeat by body counts,"[76] which were so important to the American high command, but by whether or not their interests were furthered through their sacrifices.

What, then, was the point of the American emphasis upon body counts? It could not have the same function as did the earlier Malaysian check-off of enemy dead when the British fought Chinese insurgents to a standstill. Because the number of those revolutionaries was known, British counting of enemy casualties gave definite information as to the progress of their campaign there. The same was simply not true in Vietnam, where the NLF and NVA had the capability of replacing their losses indefinitely.

Even in a war of attrition, such as General Westmoreland believed he had to fight and was fighting, a body count was a valueless tool. Lessons from the past should have taught him that it was not always the side that lost the most men that suffered defeat. If such had been the case, the Union would have lost the Civil War. The Allies would have lost World War I and World War II. In both of those global conflicts, Germany lost only about 4 percent of its total population before surrendering. North Vietnam would have had to have suffered over 1,500,000 casualties before reaching that proportional loss. Even then, Westmoreland could not have been certain of victory. In the Lopez War of 1865–1870, Paraguay lost 84 percent of its male population before admitting defeat.[77] Long before Vietnam had suffered that kind of destruction, America would have been rent by internal discord of a kind never seen in the late sixties and early seventies; Chinese "volunteers" would have poured across the border as they had done twenty years earlier in Korea; and nations everywhere would have looked with dismay at an America capable of inflicting such misery upon another nation.

But body counts as an indicator of military progress were not only meaningless; they were also counterproductive. The army's official position was based on lies, and no institution that builds on that kind of sand can long endure in a free society. Honorable officers were placed in situations where they had to compromise their word, their honor, and their oaths of office in order to satisfy their superiors.

Perhaps the gravest problem produced by this sort of statistical frenzy was the brutalization of American fighting men. It is one thing to kill an enemy during battle. It is quite another to kill indiscriminately in order to swell a tally sheet in some higher headquarters. Army sergeants knew the pressures their officers were under. They knew how to relieve such strains. The learning began at home, in the United States, at camps and forts that provided draftees with their basic training. One enlisted man wrote that his training sergeants made it clear what would be expected of them in a combat situation "right at the start of A.I.T. [Advanced Individual Training]. 'When you come into an enemy village,' we were told, 'you come in opening fire. You kill everything that's living—women, children, and animals.' And when we asked how to tell an enemy village from a friendly one, we were instructed that an enemy village was any village from which you were fired upon. Even if only one round was shot by only one person—that village was an enemy village as far as the army was concerned. And that meant you killed everyone. You destroyed everything."[78]

This man had been in Vietnam only a few days when his platoon leader lined up the men to explain how body count worked. "For the benefit of the new men . . . let me remind all of you that it's possible for you to pick up a three-day pass out here if you're on the ball. Every dead Vietnamese body earns three days off for the soldier responsible for it. So, stay on the alert, and when the time comes to use your weapon, make it count!"[79]

His later experiences confirmed what he had learned in training in the States and what he had been told upon his arrival in 'Nam. "In the field, the rule to follow was a simple one. Shoot anything that runs. And the army couldn't be bothered worrying about why somebody might be running away. Like maybe he was scared, or just a kid who didn't know better. In this area, to be Vietnamese was to be the enemy."[80]

Another Vietnam veteran recalled that "we had a kind of unwritten order" so far as body counts were concerned: "for every dead one make it three."[81] The same man told how things sometimes got out of hand. He observed a unit cresting a hill, below which was a hamlet nestled in a hollow. The commander "just didn't like the looks of the place—women and children were down below in the village—and he just had his thirty-five gunners lob down a couple of 'Willie Peters'—white-phosphorus rounds—and wiped out the whole village. For no reason at all."[82]

The same man told how "we'd get orders to leave the people alone, not to harm them or their property, but so what? I saw Americans bothering the people all the time. We'd ask for their identification cards, start a firefight, and accidentally kill a son or a mother. In all the hamlets and villages I visited as a medic . . . I saw hate in their eyes. . . . At the beginning of my tour I thought it funny that the first Vietnamese words I learned were 'Beat it,' 'Get out of here,' and 'Your identification card?' Only after I left the country did I understand why."[83]

GIs became infected by the "gook syndrome." The people within whose country they operated, and for whom they supposedly were fighting, were seldom thought of as Vietnamese. All of them—north or south, NVA or VC, ARVN or villager, Saigon bar girl or Hué business- man—were "slopes," or "dinks," or "slants," or "zips," or "gooks," and not fellow human beings. One lieutenant colonel put the matter suc- cinctly. "The GI isn't tolerant. Never has been. His job is to kill. I've never seen the place where GIs could get along with the local populace. Our boys are full of fighting spirit, whiskey, women. They'll think more often about the cars they left back home than about the rules of warfare. Indeed they disrupt civilian communities, here in the States and wher- ever they're assigned overseas. To find this to have been the case in Vietnam and to say it was wrong is true, but irrelevant. It has always been that way."[84]

The "gook syndrome" was pervasive in Vietnam. "The Americans don't want to be there and don't know why in hell they are there. The result is, the Vietnamese become their only visible enemy, and accord- ing to the syndrome, all Vietnamese are equally bad."[85] It was not long before "everyone I knew was saying, 'I'd just as soon shoot a South Vietnamese as a VC.' "[86] Either way, the individual became suddenly dead, and thus grist for the body-count mill. As Anthony Herbert put it: "Regardless of what a person might have been before he was killed, afterwards he was a dink. Very damned few people ever reported killing a civilian, regardless of how unavoidable the death might have been, and very damned few dead civilians failed to be included in the body counts."[87] Herbert registered utter disgust with the policy of rewarding troopers with an in-country R and R for their "kills." When he took charge of his battalion,

> I also stressed that we were changing the body count policy. There would be no more in-country R and Rs for "dead dinks." From now on, I said, the R and Rs would be for live prisoners and only for live prisoners. We needed intelligence badly, and you only get intelligence from live people. The trooper would get five days for a legitimate POW, with one day subtracted for each cut, bruise, or contusion on the prisoner. The better the condition of the merchandise, the more we were willing to pay for it.[88]

Some individual commanders resisted the practice. Yet the army's atti- tude toward the VC and soldiers of the NVA—and thus ultimately toward all Vietnamese—brought about a brutalization of the war and a lessening of the careful distinctions that should have been made meticulously between combatants and noncombatants, soldiers and civilians.

"Kill them even if they try to surrender—we need the body count."[89] One of many rules of thumb often followed by helicopter gunners was simply "If they look up, they're VC. Shoot 'em." Troopers on the ground followed the rule, "If they run, they're VC. Shoot 'em." Shoot with artillery, with napalm, with rockets, with mortars, and with small-arms fire. Spread herbicides indiscriminately across their country. In such an atmosphere, there were bound to be incidents.

In Detroit, Michigan, for the three days between 31 January and 2 February 1971, the Vietnam Veterans against the War held a series of public meetings, which they called the "Winter Soldier" investigation. Over one hundred ex-servicemen, from the lowest enlisted ranks to midrange officer grades, testified to violations of the rules of warfare that they had either seen or participated in while serving in Vietnam —acts of savagery, rape, brutality, torture, humiliation, massacre.[90]

One witness said that "I'm here because my conscience will not let me forget what I want to forget. . . . So I'm here, not as a member of any political group, not as a member of any lobbying group. I'm just here as myself, you know, saying to other people, to other human beings, something that I just have to say."[91] He spoke for many who attended that meeting in Detroit. Were they all lying? Unfortunately, no civilian or military investigation resulted from these public confessions, so it is likely that we will never know.

We do, however, know about one case with certainty, for it received the widest-possible publicity. In early March 1968, army intelligence identified an experienced and hardened unit of the NLF, operating on the Batangan peninsula, as the Forty-Eighth Local Force Battalion. That portion of the peninsula was referred to by the army as "Pinkville," because of its color on the maps. The guerrillas were supposedly concentrated at Son My hamlet, Son Tinh District, Quang Ngai Province. From 16 to 19 March, Task Force Barker, the First Battalion, Twentieth Infantry Brigade of the Twenty-Third, or "Americal" Division, conducted a tactical operation into the area, to ferret out and to destroy the NLF enemy.

Army maps designated Son My as My Lai (4) and this hamlet became the assigned objective of Charlie Company, Ernest Medina commanding. Presumably there were no written operational plans (at least none were ever found), so Captain Medina briefed the platoon leaders of his company by drawing upon past experience. He anticipated heavy casualties and ordered his officers to conduct themselves in a manner that would minimize such losses. As the operation began, Second Lieutenant William L. Calley, Jr., led his platoon into the southern part of the hamlet. Soon his field radio crackled with questions. "What is wrong with your platoon? Why aren't you shooting anybody?"

Lieutenant Colonel Frank Barker, leader of the task force, later told the story of the battle—of snipers firing from the village, of encountering devilish booby traps, of firefights within the confines of the hamlet. Task Force Barker had accounted for 128 VC KIAs and had captured 13 VC sympathizers. Three American rifles had been seized from the village and recovered. The army reported the action as a significant victory.

A year later, Ron Ridenhour had become a civilian. A Vietnam veteran, he had become interested in stories he had heard about Son My. In March 1969, he wrote letters to the White House, the State Department, the Pentagon, and several congressmen, claiming that there was more to the action at My Lai (4) than had been revealed. Something "dark and bloody" had happened there. Supposedly, when Charlie Company moved out from the hamlet on 16 March, the community had been devastated. All four to five hundred inhabitants were dead, the huts burned, the animals slaughtered, the wells polluted.

The army finally opened an investigation of the operation, but it was another year before Lieutenant General William R. Peers, the man chosen by the army to head the inquiry, announced his findings.[92] In the meantime, Barker had changed his account of the battle, insisting that the residents of My Lai had died as a result of artillery or gunship activity. No one would ever be able to change his story, for he had since been killed in an air crash.

The courts-martial began. Staff Sergeant David Mitchell, squad leader in Charlie Company, explained that he had only been doing his duty. He was acquitted. Sergeant Charles Hutto explained that he had been carrying out orders and would not have thought of questioning them. He was acquitted. At that point, charges against all other enlisted men were dropped. Captain Ernest Medina was tried and acquitted. Colonel Oran K. Henderson, the brigade commander, was tried and acquitted. The division commander, Major General Samuel W. Koster, was censured rather than tried. His Distinguished Service Medal was taken from him. He lost one star, retiring from the service as a brigadier. Only one man, First Lieutenant (later Captain) William Calley, was ever found guilty of having been responsible for the murder of at least 102 "Oriental human beings." The figure was probably more nearly 347 or more: civilians, mostly women and children, systematically gunned down in cold blood.

Summary of Actions Taken against Individuals Listed in Peers Report—"Omissions and Commissions"

Number listed:	30
Number against whom charges were preferred:	16
Number brought to trial:	4
Number acquitted:	3
Number convicted:	1

Number against whom charges were dismissed	12
Number against whom administrative action was taken:	8*
Number against whom no action was taken:	14
Number deceased:	4
Number civilians:	7
Chaplains:	1
Others:	2**
Additional personnel not listed in Peers Report against whom charges were preferred:	9
Number against whom charges were dismissed:	7
Number acquitted:	2

* These 8 personnel had charges preferred; charges against 7 were dismissed and 1 was tried by court-martial and acquitted

** The two individuals were accused primarily of "failing to report" whatever knowledge they had of the incident to higher authority. One was the supporting aviation-battalion commander and the other was assigned duty as senior adviser, 2d ARVN Division. Neither was in the chain of command of the maneuver elements involved.[93]

The record of the various army headquarters charged with court-martialing those involved in My Lai was not a particularly brilliant one, as the above chart indicates. Their efforts were a whitewash. Boards had been convened. Reports had been issued. Press conferences had been held. A guilty man had been found, and the army could now press forward, its sins forgotten—but this time not quite.

Most people believed that the army was far guiltier than it had found itself to be. Herbert Kelman spoke for civilians when he wrote that "the My Lai massacre, however, was not an isolated, aberrant event. Similar actions were not uncommon in Vietnam; in fact they were an inevitable by-product of the very nature of the war."[94] Edward L. King's view expressed the way in which many within the army looked at the incident. "My Lai represented to the average professional soldier nothing more than being caught in a cover-up of something which he knew had been going on for a long time on a smaller scale."[95] An army captain put it more bluntly: "It's necessary today, to lie, cheat, and steal to meet the impossible demands of higher officers or continue to meet the statistical requirements."[96]

How had the war come to be fought in such a way that it bred savagery among GIs? Kinnard claims that it could not have been West-moreland's fault. "Westy" had "published more than forty directives of his own which contained explicit guidance on proper treatment of

civilians and their property as well as on a discriminating use of firepower."[97] Elsewhere he reminded his readers that in late August 1966,
Westmoreland had announced that "it is extremely important that we
do all we can to use our fires with discrimination and avoid noncombatant battle casualties. Kinnard had forgotten that policy statements are
one thing, policy enforcement quite another. He further failed to recall
that basic question within the military "Who is responsible?" The commander is responsible. Kinnard, an ex-general, does admit that while
there may have been a "command emphasis" upon following the rules
of warfare, no system existed to ensure compliance.[98]

It well may be that one of the officers interviewed for this study
uncovered the root of the problem when he said simply: "There used
to be a regulation in Vietnam covering everything. At the battery level,
I ignored most of them. No one ever cared at battery level. Now, if
something had gone wrong, they would probably have hung me because of the regulations I was violating. But as long as things went
smoothly, no one cared what I did."[99]

There was a time in American history when even those in the army
could become shocked and angered at clear violations of the rules of
engagement. The slaughter of Polish officers in the Katyn Forest (by
either Nazis or Russians), the Malmédy massacre of American POWs
during the German Ardennes offensive of late 1944—both aroused
anguished protest. Americans righteously scolded other nations for
committing such atrocities, secure in their belief that they would themselves never do such a thing.

Vietnam brought home a different kind of truth to Americans. The
"Green Machine," geared to attritional slaughter in order to satisfy
statistical requirements of those who sought ever greater "indicators of
military progress" could indeed lash out in frenzy when provoked.
American boys from cities and farms found themselves halfway around
the world, living in an alien culture, fighting and dying in a cause they
at best only half-understood. They saw their buddies "blown away" or
"wasted" or maimed. They were repeatedly told they could trust no
one—not the bar girl, nor the sidewalk peddler, nor the farmer. They
must be on guard against six-year-old children, for some of that age had
been known to be armed and ready to kill. The people lived in rude
shelters in which animals wouldn't be housed at home. Weather was a
constant enemy, rotting, mildewing, raining, seeping into jungle boots
and pelting against ponchos.

Danger was always at hand. Booby traps exploded with mindless
violence. Sniper bullets found men quietly taking their ease. Enemy
rockets blasted at sandbagged emplacements. Ambush caught the unwary and the watchful alike.

Nor could they rely on their ARVN "allies." Those men weren't fit
to be called soldiers. Cowardly, lazy, moving slowly out on search-and-

avoid missions, they seemed to do their best ṅot to trigger the tempers of the VC.

Anyone would sell anything. A boy would quickly quote a price for his mother or sister. Drugs were easily procured and quickly consumed in order to quell the terror always lurking just below the surface of consciousness, in some secret corner of the mind. Facing them all was the threat of imminent extinction. They knew the stories of "human wave" attacks by shrieking, indestructible enemies lusting to slice off testicles, ears, and noses, or to disembowel with the curving thrust of a knife. Only subhumans would attack with such goals in mind—only gooks. When GIs couldn't tell friend from foe, they came to hate and despise them all. All slopes are dirt. Viewing all Vietnamese as less than human released American boys from their own humanity. Now, suddenly, it became possible to squeeze off M-16 rounds at a boy herding two water buffalo, not really with the intention of hitting him, just of frightening him and making him run. It wasn't really anybody's fault that one shot was a little high and the kid fell and lay kicking in the dust. He was, after all, only a dink. All dinks bred like lice anyway. In the time it took to kill the boy a dozen more had been conceived in furtive, sweaty embraces in some rice paddy.

And so the process went, until in the minds of some observers Vietnam had been turned into a gigantic My Lai. No longer was it a case of one massacre amidst a long war; the war itself was a massacre of an entire people. One hundred million pounds of 24D and 245T compounds sprayed over one-seventh of South Vietnam's land area between 1962 and 1971 during Project Agent Orange. By 1972, out of a population of eighteen million in South Vietnam, more than five million were homeless refugees. Gabriel Kolko once wrote that "any objective and carefully prepared account of the history of Vietnam must conclude with the fact that the United States must bear the responsibility for the torture of an entire nation since the end of the Second World War."[100]

And the words of Alexander Kendrick strengthened that argument. Suppose, Kendrick posited, that the motives and methods used in the Vietnam War had been "applied to Europe rather than to the small southeastern corner of Asia. Imagine then what would have been done to the people and terrain of the 'Mother Continent' by the unrestricted bombardment of undefended populations, the massive destruction of crops and forests, the forcible removal of whole villages and provinces of civilians, search-and-destroy missions under 'Free Fire Zone' rules, and the Phoenix program to destroy by kidnapping and murder the political leadership and cadres of insurgent organizations. In truth such things have been done in Europe, which has known bloody war for centuries, but those who did them in World War II were brought to book at Nuremberg."[101]

Four

Putting the best face possible on affairs is part of the soldier's craft and an essential aspect of the art of warfare. It is a practice as old as conflict itself. Did not Cain respond to the Almighty One's query as to the whereabouts of Abel with the rejoinder "Am I my brother's keeper?"[1] In order to function efficiently, however, it has always been necessary for those within the military to remember the difference between reality and their own public description of it. In Vietnam, the United States Army unaccountably lost sight of that *caveat* as upper echelons of the military establishment began to believe their own propaganda statements indicating that the war was progressing according to expectations. Consequently, army brass cut themselves off from any corrective analyses, even from those within the system who tried to make alternative suggestions.

Public-affairs spokesmen inevitably insisted that both faces of the war were proceeding as planned. Military actions and nation-building efforts appeared on briefing charts, reduced to bar graphs. Briefing officers could point to weekly improvements in both areas as they stood before their tripod-mounted graphics, regaling enchanted audiences with crisply enunciated descriptions of battles won by some army elements while other units simultaneously hacked away at the root causes of the conflict from which had grown the weeds of war. They pretended that nation building—"the other face of war"—was as important to the army as were successful search-and-destroy missions. They lied.

That was the myth in Vietnam. The reality was far uglier. The United States Army faced a conflict in a country where the enemy was expected to be a pushover. It found instead that the enemy was tough, persistent, ingenious, and aggressive. The years lengthened. Before victory could be grasped, it was essential for the army to institute an emphasis upon nation building. Unfortunately, the military did not address the problem in any appropriate way.

The military in the past *has* been active in ways that, during the Vietnam era, were described as nation building. In Cuba, following the Spanish American War, the United States established a military government. Under army direction, progress was made in education, public works, and health. On the other side of the world, while the army fought the Philippine patriot Emilio Aguinaldo, it simultaneously made great strides in nation building in areas of public health, transportation, and education. After World War II, the United States Army was deeply involved in nation building throughout the war-devastated nation of Germany. In the Far East, it was General Douglas MacArthur, the military commander, who not only supervised the restoration of the Japanese islands but also personally steered its new government into more democratic ways. Indeed, *any* general war fought by the United States Army should, of necessity, involve such nation-building activities. Eisenhower and MacArthur were well aware of this need. Their military successors were less insightful when faced with the needs of Vietnam.[2]

In Vietnam, the American army almost exclusively emphasized combat power rather than dealing with social, religious, economic, educational, and political needs that cried out to be met. This need not have been. There were many with negative attitudes toward American policy in Vietnam, and not all of them were held by civilians. In addition to civilian observers, many individuals within the army structure set forth their evaluations. Some wrote books arguing with military actions. A great number spoke from within the school system of the army, either as faculty or students. Others resigned from the military and then spoke out. Inevitably, the army gave lip service to the fact that it listened to such divergent views. In fact, it did not.

The army has long maintained that military education, at least in its higher service schools, involves a two-way learning process. Faculty learn from students at the same time that those attending the school receive new views from their instructors. This is even ritualized in AR 623-1, a regulation that allows school staff members to write up official "academic evaluation reports" on some 10 percent of the best students in any given class. At Ft. Leavenworth, that report is entered on DA Form 1059 (CGSC), and an evaluation written on a major not too long ago stated in part: "His participation [in a contingency FTX] and the observations he submitted in his after-action report called attention to some real and vital problems which have existed in contingency plans. His suggestions have been forwarded to appropriate authority and the adoption of his suggestions will enhance the resolution of such problems confronting commanders."[3] This, then, is one supposed route allowing suggestions to be introduced and considered within the army system.

There is a second method. This consists of the various reports that emanate from faculty committees and student study groups at Ft. Leav-

enworth's Command and General Staff College and at senior service
schools such as the Army War College. At CGSC during the school year
1975–1976, a number of faculty and students developed an interest in
the army's involvement in Vietnam. They subsequently decided to
pursue their interest and to conduct extensive research into various
areas of the Vietnam effort.

So far as was possible, they looked at the records of the various
headquarters responsible for conduct of the war—command units
known by such acronyms as MAAG—VN, USARV, MACV, PACOM,
DA, DEF, and JCS. They conducted interviews with high-level participants, reviewed written efforts of former students, and searched files in
both the classified library and the college library. They corresponded
with personnel in the History Office of the Training and Doctrine Command (TRADOC), the Army War College Library, and the Department
of Army Military History Office. Ultimately they wrote a number of
reports based upon what they had learned, many of their observations
leavened in some measure by their own Vietnamese experiences.[4]
Those reports now gather dust in a file in the classified section of the
CGSC library, placed in that forgotten location by a since retired faculty
member who had been involved in directing the Vietnam Special Study
Project. The information gathered by that group was, at least, available
to CGSC faculty for their own use. They had the opportunity to abstract
information from those reports to include in their own briefs, filed
upward through channels. Whether or not this was done is unknown.

There is a third method by which higher commanders can be
informed of views differing from their own. These are the student
essays and theses written by officers attending such schools as the Army
War College. From the earliest days of the army's participation in the
Vietnam War, officer students evaluated various army doctrines as a
part of their assigned work. Lieutenant Colonel Maurice D. Roush, an
officer in the Corps of Engineers, gave excellent advice late in 1967
when he wrote:

> Combat strategy in Vietnam is pacification [one of several terms used at
> one time or another for nation building], for in no other way can the
> breeding ground of insurgency be eliminated. The root goal of our strategy
> is Nation Building, and it must be sought with skills and weapons that take
> a soldier out of the purely military sphere and require that he understand
> the fields of the technician, administrator, and reformer. No longer can we
> neatly categorize actions as either "civil" or "military"; the integral nature
> of our operations in Vietnam requires the soldier to consider his actions in
> terms of their consequences in the civilian sphere and dictates that the
> civilian plan his programs within the context of military realities.
>
> All of our efforts must be directed toward elimination of the causes of
> insurgency. . . . military strategy must be subordinate and responsive to
> pacification strategy.[5]

Barely a month later, a Quartermaster officer, Colonel Robert E. Huber, turned in an essay, the words of which should have been engraved in stone for General Westmoreland and his deputies. Huber wrote that in spite of our much vaunted search-and-destroy policy "most of the battles are at a place and time determined by the enemy." He further inquired how was it possible to convince a mother that American troops were there to help her

> when her child is burned by napalm? And how can we expect a young man to fight for us when his aged father was killed by artillery fire? Indeed, how can we claim to be with the people when we burn their homes simply because those homes happen to be in the Viet Cong–controlled territory?

Huber quoted from another writer who had asked, "Why are we not winning in Vietnam? My answer is simple. The misplacement of the order of importance. The Magsaysay way is: Winning the people first, winning the war second. I am afraid in Viet Nam today, the order is reversed."[6]

Huber's insight was clear. He stated present military policy, contrasting it with his own proposed course of action.

Present Policy	Proposed Policy
Bomb selected targets in North Vietnam.	Halt bombing for one month.
Search and destroy the enemy in South Vietnam.	Decrease open warfare and give first priority to nation building.
Gradual escalation of the war.	Deemphasize open warfare and increase the use of unconventional forces (guerrilla-type special-forces teams).
Heavy commitment to battle of US troops.	Greater use of SVN troops in open combat and guerrilla roles with a gradual phase-down of US armed forces.
No persistent demand for United Nations action.	Pursue with great vigor UN action in Vietnam.

The Quartermaster officer insisted that the United States "must exploit the power which we have and which the enemy cannot match . . . economic power. Fewer military campaigns would permit concentration on a combined military-civilian effort toward developing a progressive economy and improving the life of peasant workers and refugees." Why should such a change be made? "It would give the war a new dimension . . . directed toward a peaceful effort . . . signifying that the US purpose is not total destruction. . . . We must win the support and loyalty of the bewildered South Vietnamese peasants, overcoming their widespread suspicion of foreigners. This cannot be done by bombing, scorching the earth and driving them from their homes." For Huber, such a new approach "must be founded on actions which clearly demonstrate the basic principles of freedom, justice and goodwill, along with effective military techniques to thwart the enemy whenever peaceful objectives are threatened." Beyond everything else, he warned, "All military efforts must be in support of nationbuilding."[8] Few high-level advisers at the presidential, state, or JCS staffs ever saw the problems in Vietnam as clearly as had Huber. There is, unfortunately, not the slightest evidence that anyone with real "clout" ever read his work or heard of his ideas. In any case, what would he know? He was in quartermaster, not even an officer in one of the combat arms.

James H. Chapman, a field-artillery major at CGSC, came to conclusions similar to those of Huber in his study *The US Army and Pacification in Vietnam: An Assessment of the Army's Ability to Cope with an Insurgency* (1976).[9] Another critic, a RAND consultant, spoke out in 1970 to tell of his convictions that "the Army's doctrine, its tactics, its organization, its weapons—its entire repertoire of warfare—was designed for conventional war in Europe. In Vietnam, the Army simply performed its repertoire even though it was frequently irrelevant to the situation. . . . Our Army seemed to be prevented by its own doctrinal and organizational rigidity from making any changes in the way in which it has fought this war."[10]

A lieutenant colonel of military intelligence, Richard McMahon, argued late in 1968 that the army should cease its reliance upon such statistical indicators as "body counts."[10] V. H. Lipsey questioned the validity of the American approach to Vietnamization of the war.[11] Officers high and low criticized the buildup in Vietnam and the way troops were utilized there.[12]

Reacting shortly after the debacle itself, an officer student at the War College studied the incident and wrote *The Battle of Khe Sanh: Sound Strategy or Costly Miscalculation?*[13] The army's reaction was a traditional one; it slapped a "secret" classification on the report, precluding wide distribution, and continued unchanged with its policies, still referring to Khe Sanh as a necessary tactical and strategic action. With this as with many other studies, contributions that might have brought about changes in army doctrine and tactics were lost in dead-end corridors, committee baskets, or hidden under security blankets. They should not have been discarded in such a manner.

There was still another route by which information from the field could have been brought to the attention of the war managers, producing change for the better. This was the "in-house" procedure of year-end statistical studies and end-of-action lessons-learned reports, filed regularly within army channels. Such communications varied from loss and expenditure data derived from statistics on combat operations[14] and unit after-action reports to end-of-tour officer-debriefing programs.

The air force conducted a magnificently methodical debriefing program for its officers, known as "Project Corona Harvest." Those reports are now housed at the Albert F. Simpson Historical Research Center, Maxwell Air Force Base, Alabama. There are some 2,500 such transcripts of debriefing sessions, some of which are declassified, although the bulk remain under a security classification of one sort or another.[15]

The army's program, similar in nature, was known as the Senior Officer Debriefing Report Program (SODR),[16] in which each senior officer leaving Vietnam was to file a report detailing his actions and attitudes for the period of time covering his service in 'Nam.[17] For the most part, however, as one would expect, such observations tended to be self-serving, pointing up accomplishments and downgrading difficulties of any kind. There was little in them that was critical of policy or strategy or tactics. Almost without exception, the content focused on military activities to the neglect of nation-building efforts.

A review of documents at Ft. Leavenworth (including debriefing reports of four corps, ten divisional, and two brigade commanders) made it clear that such men placed almost exclusive emphasis upon conventional aspects of the Vietnam War. Generally no more than one short paragraph in an otherwise lengthy report was devoted to nation building. (The report of Lieutenant General Melvin Zais, for a time commanding general of XVIII Corps, was an exception.)

Four paragraphs out of a 31-page report, written by Lieutenant General Fred C. Weyand, commanding general of II Field Force Vietnam from 29 March 1966 to 1 August 1968, emphasized pacification efforts.[18] Brigadier General Carleton Peer, Jr., deputy senior adviser for III Corps, dedicated only *seven* lines of a 107-page report to civic action for the period 1 May to 30 November 1969. Three of those seven lines dealt with the laundry contract for the unit widows' association.[19] Brigadier General D. P. McAuliffe mentioned neither pacification nor any related subject.[20] Reports submitted throughout 1969–1970 indicate that professional soldiers of high rank had learned little since 1955–1956.

Perhaps the best example of a military manager's lack of appreciation for the significance of nation building comes from the debriefing report of Major General S. H. Matheson, CG, 1st Brigade, 101st Airmobile Division.

On 10 June 1967 the brigade began the evacuation of people and livestock from Song Ve Valley. There were approximately 8465 people and 1149

animals. The people were told that they could take what they could carry.
. . . ARVN was to have driven the livestock, however, they considered the
job degrading and began to shoot the cattle so they had to be replaced by
Americans. . . . On leaving the village, crops were burned to prevent
enemy use and to discourage the return of the villagers. The Song Ve
Valley was the largest civil affairs project ever undertaken by the 1st
Brigade. *It was an overwhelming success and a model for future opera-
tions.* [21]

Matheson had followed a model indeed, but it was a faulty one, having
failed the earlier French army, the South Vietnamese government and
its military forces, and his own predecessors in command. In a rational
world, any manager who so adamantly refused to profit from the mistakes of the past would have been peremptorily relieved from his position on the spot. Yet Matheson was typical of all too many, an example
of those who persuade themselves that they can function in any situation and environment without adaptation. Convinced that they are
right, they think only of applying their own earlier experiences to new
situations. Utterly convinced of their own rectitude, opinions to the
contrary by others they disregard without hesitation. It was too often
the story of senior military men in Vietnam. Halberstam discussed how
it worked with one individual, Bill Depuy. That general

> was also one of those most confident about the capacity of American troops
> to fight there. John Vann would later recall that when Depuy took over
> the 1st Division, Vann and a few senior Vietnamese officers tried to advise
> him a little about the background of the fighting and the Vietcong. But
> Depuy was not interested, no one who had been associated with the past,
> flawed as it was, could teach him anything. He told the old-timers in effect,
> Just stay out of my way and I'll show you how it's done. He believed that
> massive fire power and American mobility were the answer, that the
> enemy simply could not stand up in the face of it.[22]

Such attitudes show up regularly in the pages of the Senior Officer
Debriefing Reports. The American military seemed to learn very little,
as the years passed, about either Vietnam or wars of national liberation.
Even worse, as Vietnam recedes into the background, the army's institutional memory is quickly being purged of what little knowledge was
acquired. Those few lessons that were learned will soon disappear as
officers leave the system for retirement or are assigned to other pur-
suits. Yet unless that war is carefully analysed and its lessons truly
learned, it may well be that, faced with any similar situation in the
future, the army will once more react as it did then—*and we will lose
again.*

Our generals succeeded only in doing what they knew how to do
best, that is, to act like generals. In so doing, they reacted as Giap hoped.
He once said: "Protect the people by keeping their enemies well away
from them. The only reason VC main force units exist is to give

GVN/MACV an excuse to waste money and attention on ARVN; our real antagonists are the local organizers."[23] Thus the generals from Westmoreland down focused on VC and NVA main-force units when the objective should have been the pacification the people in unstinting efforts at nation building.

This obtuseness in the dry pages of the *Senior Officer Debriefing Reports* is surprising in light of Kinnard's later survey of such men. In polls of general officers, taken after 1974, Kinnard found that throughout the war they had been "acutely" aware of tactical and strategic problems in the way the war was conducted. He learned that nearly 70 percent of general officers had been uncertain of the objectives of the war and complained that the Pentagon allowed a "play-it-by-ear gradual escalation."[24] Some 56 percent believed that the will and determination of the enemy to continue the war was not sufficiently considered before 1968 (to say nothing of the period that followed).[25]

Search and destroy, Kinnard claims, was described by 32 percent as never having been a sound method of approach; 51 percent believed that execution of search and destroy was less than adequate; 42 percent believed that large-scale operations based on that tactic, such as OPLAN JUNCTION CITY or OPLAN CEDAR FALLS or DENVER or MARAUDER or CRIMP or DAVY CROCKETT or HOOKER I or MOSBY I, and all the rest, were overdone from the very beginning.[26] Thirty percent considered there to have been too much use of artillery, and 28 percent believed that too much air support had been used.[27] A total of 51 percent believed that B-52 strikes against North Vietnam had been either unessential or not worth the effort.[28] Forty-one percent had serious reservations about the use of herbicides for defoliation purposes.[29] Over one-third, 35 percent, thought that there had been overcontrol of units by higher commanders.[30] A surprising 94 percent agreed that there were real problems with statistical measurements of the war, out of which came those famous indicators of military progress.[31] Only 3 percent claimed that body counts were underestimated, while 61 percent indicated that, conversely, it was regularly inflated out of proportion to reality.[32] Eighty-seven percent believed careerism, lack of professionalism, and ticket punching to have been problems for the Vietnam-era army.[33] Thirty-two percent perceived leadership qualities of junior officers to have deteriorated as the war continued.[34] They did not comment on the leadership exhibited by senior officers, but one is inclined to believe they would have found it to have been of superb quality throughout the war.

Seventy-three percent of the generals who served in the combat zone believed that the Vietnamization program should have begun years earlier than it actually did.[35] As late as 1974, only 8 percent indicated that ARVN constituted an acceptable fighting force.[36] Sadly, a majority believed that the army had been wrong to insert combat troops into 'Nam, 25 percent holding that the military should have insisted only upon an advisory role, 28 percent that none of it was "worth the effort."[37]

Kinnard's findings reveal what must have been vast turbulence and turmoil in the hearts and minds of the Vietnam-era war managers. They eagerly spoke of their earlier misgivings when, in 1974, Kinnard had queried them. Why, then, had they not resigned in previous years when they supposedly so opposed various command-level policies? Why are the *Senior Officer Debriefing Reports* devoid of criticism of army tactics and doctrines, save for a few very carefully guarded remarks? Where, when it was needed, was the moral courage of those dedicated warriors who had reached the apex of their careers, built upon the qualities of "duty, honor, country"? Where was the much vaunted "professionalism" of these men?

And then, as still a further possibility for self-correction of army policies, there were the "unit-lessons learned" after-action reports consistently filed by outfits ranging in size from platoons to divisions. Surveying such observations brings both amusement and disquiet to a researcher. Such a one can only shake his head in despair at the low level of the lessons supposedly learned. As one man put it: "My God, Moses knew some of these things when he wrote the book of Deuteronomy!"[38]

A check through the files in the classified section of the library at Ft. Leavenworth reveals drawers full of entries under the category of "lessons learned." The information they reveal, however, goes far toward explaining the outburst of the infantry officer just quoted. The reports advise, with deadpan seriousness, that units should keep their radio and electronic gear dry and protected from the weather. Men on patrol should carry two canteens rather than one so that they will not risk running short of water.

Someone had had to relearn the lesson that patrols should not be kept out in the field more than five or six days at the maximum, and two or three days only were better for troop morale. Fire-support bases grow large and cumbersome if their commanders do not keep a close watch on base development. In a night-defensive position, each man should have overhead cover and a cleared field of fire. Artillery fires may be called in for positional defense and protection if such rounds will not jeopardize the security of the American unit involved. For unit security against ambush or sudden assault, trip flares and claymore mines should be in position covering all likely avenues of approach. Members of a unit must be thoroughly briefed on the location of friendly protective devices so that they will not accidentally stumble across them.

Furthermore, claymores should be brought in from their night locations every morning for checking to insure that no one has tampered with them. The more protective wire that is used around a defense position, the more difficult it will be for enemy sappers to crawl through it. Communications checks are important for determining whether equipment is operating. Proper fundamentals of defense include correct use of terrain, efficient security, appropriate barrier planning, effective use of available time, and all-around (or perimeter) fire cover. It is better for outfits to keep active patrols operating in their tactical area of responsibility (TAOR) than not. The position of listening posts should be changed frequently. Deception plans ought to be used whenever possible. If sophisticated equipment is unavailable, C-ration cans tied to protective wire can be used as anti-intrusion devices. Troops should be alert whenever possible. Base camps should have alert systems to notify everyone in case of attack. Adequate protection should be provided for men both in living quarters and in working areas. All supporting fires should be coordinated. Commanders should endeavor to see that their men practice good field sanitation and personal hygiene.[39]

The words of an actual such report are revealing.

We learned that the commander must not overlook any detail of the individual soldier's equipment. The overladen soldier was prone to overheating and stayed prone under fire. For example, careful planning for individual military loads was often frustrated by a soldier's tendency to carry ration supplements, cameras, and other impediments, or white insect repellent bottles or cigarette packs in his helmet band which violated otherwise good camouflage discipline.

We discovered that . . . ammunition packaging was especially critical. . . . Overloaded, poorly protected rifle magazines invite stoppages. Machine gun belts carried around necks are no good! They cause stoppages.

Contact with an enemy in the jungle will usually occur at point blank range.[40]

During an interview conducted while this study was being researched, one man commented that an "important" lesson learned had been the importance "of establishing a fire base and operating within its ranges, which is the antithesis of what we had done in earlier years, when the artillery was supposed to keep up with advancing infantry. In 'Nam, of course, the infantry went in after the artillery was in place in a fire-support base."[41] One wonders how many of the above comments could have been offered without embarrassment, yet they came from supposedly seasoned soldiers or troop units hardened in battle. Such observations are not appropriate "lessons learned" for a unit in the field. If soldiers do not go into battle with such information burned into the very fibers of their being, they are not likely long to survive in combat.

The very filing of such fundamentals under the rubric of "lessons learned" bespeaks volumes about the training and preparedness of Americans who fought in Southeast Asia. Officers should have become familiar with such precepts in Officer Candidate School (OCS) and in their basic branch schools. Enlisted men should have been drilled into familiarity with such measures in Basic Combat Training (BCT) and Advanced Individual Training (AIT). Without such training, men go into battle—as ours did too often in Vietnam—overconfident and underprepared.

Far from being the "best-trained soldiers in the world," as GIs were often called, they were, in many ways, mediocre at best. They were beset by racial problems and drugs. Rarely were they well enough trained to practice either noise or light discipline. They smoked in situations where even a whiff of tobacco, scented by an enemy, could produce tragic consequences. Their officer platoon leaders were themselves often incompetent owing to lack of sufficient training. GIs were regularly commanded by officers more interested in their own career progression than they were in the well-being of those they commanded. American troops faced a war the nature of which they seldom understood and that often was not thoroughly explained to them. Troubled by all these problems, the GI in Vietnam was very often an ineffective fighting man who felt he might be sacrificed in a cause he neither understood nor sympathized with. No wonder some adopted the slogan "UUUU."

The soldiers GIs found themselves pitted against were also very often of top caliber, well-trained, inured to hardship, dedicated to a cause. One of Kinnard's generals described VC and NVA soldiers as "the best enemy we have faced in our history. Tenacious and physically fit."[42] This view was clearly corroborated by an officer interviewed for this study. An infantry lieutenant colonel during his last tour in Vietnam and a battalion commander, he recalled how "man for man, any comparison of our soldiers with theirs would have brought ours off second-best."[43]

Unfortunately, however, very few officers could have submitted reports to higher headquarters through channels charging that the troops coming to them were undertrained and underprepared. To have tried to do so would have accomplished no more than to end their own careers without upgrading the quality of troops coming into Vietnam. The "Green Machine" was not ready to accept that kind of criticism about the training it was offering to its draftees. Komer recognized this problem when he stated that "there was a notable dearth of systematic analysis of performance . . . mainly because of the inherent reluctance of organizations to indulge in self-examination."[44]

Komer wrote that despite the "cumulatively enormous U.S. input —550,000 troops at peak . . . and $150 billion. . . . our actual performance . . . does indeed seem marked more by ignorance, misjudgment, and muddle than by foresight, awareness and calculation."[45] He continued with the following words:

> We imported into a small, undeveloped country all the enormous array of sophisticated technological means that the world's most advanced industrial nation thought might be useful, and used them to oppose an army that walked, that used mortars as its chief form of artillery, that used almost no armor until 1972, and that was near-totally lacking in air support. At the least, many of our military techniques were not very cost-effective.[46]

John M. Collins, a retired army colonel, is a senior national defense specialist for the Congressional Research Service. Writing recently in *Parameters*, the journal of the Army War College, and quoted in *Army Times*, Collins said that "we overrated ourselves and underrated our opponents." He further concluded that "we oriented on opposing armed forces, not opposing strategies, a fatal *faux pas* in that war. . . . Finally we forgot that armies are not the only weapons in the counterinsurgent's arsenal, nor even the most important."[47]

Somehow, army managers failed to get vitally needed information that the war was not progressing as they so desperately wanted to believe. Komer concurs. "To read the rhetoric enshrined in official statements you might think that those who drafted them were often talking about a different war from the one we know. We now know enough of the classified documents and message traffic to realize that we meant what we said."[48] This, of course, makes that situation even sadder. For those military leaders to have tried deliberately to mislead the nation would have been one thing. That they were so lacking in insight that they believed their own propaganda, and really did not know how out of touch with reality they actually were is quite another, and can only make one weep.

If the military managers were wrong in Vietnam, how right can one expect them to be in understanding any other conflict in which the United States might find itself involved? How adaptable are those who lead our army? How keen is their insight? How applicable are tactical doctrines to situations other than the ones for which they were developed? The "lessons learned" from Vietnam give cause for disquiet as one ponders such questions.

Comments by our military leaders from that era indicate how truly blind they must have been to the circumstances facing them. "The war is being properly managed. . . . We must keep doing what we are doing," said General Paul C. Harkins, one-time commander of U.S. forces in Vietnam, after his being relieved from that position.[49] "I would say that our strategy today is that which I have been recommending. . . . As we get greater forces we can always move toward some objective which is so valuable to the Viet Cong that they must stand and fight." So spoke General Maxwell Taylor in 1965.[50] Chairman of the Joint

Chiefs of Staff General Earle G. Wheeler commented the same year: "I believe, then, that our U.S. forces . . . should be able to defeat the Viet Cong and to re-establish this favorable balance that we had a couple of years ago. . . . No, we are not turning it into an American war. . . . General Westmoreland understands this clearly."[51] Late in 1965, Admiral Sharp announced that "we have stopped losing the war."[52]

The next year, Major General H. W. O. Kinnard could report that "we are winning the war militarily and can keep on winning it militarily."[53] Whether on active duty or retired, military men were optimistic. Retired brigadier general and military author S. L. A. Marshall claimed that "I think we can bring the war to a conclusion within the next year, possibly within the next six months."[54]

Nothing changed in 1967. Westmoreland boasted that "we're going to out-guerrilla the guerrilla and out-ambush the ambush. . . . because we're smarter, we have greater mobility and firepower, we have more endurance and more to fight for. . . . And we've got more guts."[55] The commander of OPLAN JUNCTION CITY asserted: "I would hate to be a VC and know that I have no safe haven in South Viet Nam any more."[56] General Harold K. Johnson reported that "we are very definitely winning in Vietnam."[57] He was echoed by Sharp, another perennial optimist: "The war is going along quite steadily in our favor."[58]

Robert Komer, whose hindsight was excellent and who has frequently been quoted in this study, stood at the time foursquare behind conventional army wisdom. As civilian deputy for Westmoreland, he announced in 1968 that "I see not a single unfavorable trend."[59] Nothing seemed able to dampen the spirits of the war managers. In the days following TET 1968, Westmoreland announced that "militarily, we have never been in a better relative position in South Vietnam."[60]

Sharp's successor, Admiral John S. McCain, Jr., announced in 1969 that "we have the enemy licked now. He is beaten."[61] A lower-ranking officer, the next year, indicated his agreement. Colonel William Pietsch exulted that "Charlie is on the run everywhere. He's whipped."[62] Westmoreland never did seem able to admit the difficulties the army faced. Long after his relief from command in 'Nam, he was capable of believing that "the Army has 'bottomed out' of its problems. . . . We're on our way up . . . the pendulum is beginning to swing."[63]

Perhaps the problem with such men was that they were unable to hear contrary opinions. During the course of research for this book many lower- and mid-ranked officers who served in Vietnam complained that their superiors acted in two ways. They spoke about their interest in hearing evaluations "from those in the field." Yet juniors who tried to take advantage of such invitations found themselves reprimanded by those in a general's entourage, warned against ever again offering unsolicited views. Staff officers in this way successfully insulated even the most open general from hearing anything that might "upset" him. The *Study on Military Professionalism* includes a comment by a colonel who remarked that "in some cases the upper levels of command are actually unaware that they are unapproachable."[64] The *Study on Military Professionalism* also listed a major's statement. "Only when a commander establishes an atmosphere of freedom of expression will he get accurate information and be believed when he gives his reasons. Training in really listening should be given to all commanders at every echelon. They have to hear what is being said and also what is not being said—which may be more important in the long run."[65] Still another major was quoted as saying that "more emphasis must be placed on pressing ranking officers to listen as well as speak."[66]

In the *Study on Military Professionalism* company-grade officers repeatedly "made the point that they didn't think that they could talk to the senior officers. First of all they said they don't dare to bring any problems to the next senior officer because if you bring him a problem you might get your head cut off because he doesn't want to hear problems. . . ."[67] As a result of such isolation, the free flow of information was cut off; commanders at many levels were prohibited from having the give-and-take that might have better informed them.

Even the *Study on Military Professionalism* with its many cogent analyses, recommendations, and observations seems not to have been widely read or taken to heart by those who manage the "Green Machine." Throughout the Vietnam years, the army stressed procedures and reports of statistical indicators in lieu of substantive confrontations with the real nature of the conflict. The officer corps knew how to conform but was wary of creativity. It could interpret but was fearful of innovation. And widespread dissatisfaction grew to overwhelming proportions.[68]

*   *   *

In general terms, the army ignored those who sought to modify or change its behavior in Vietnam. It reacted defensively or with hostility or allowed to pass in silence comments from those within and without the system who desired alterations or modifications in its approach to the Southeast Asian conflict. Many voices spoke. Retired officers wrote books and articles of criticism and analysis. Occasional civilian authors also sounded alarms or made suggestions. Reports entered the system from staff officers and instructors at various service schools.[69] Student analyses at those same schools became available in the form of reports, essays, and theses. (Someone read such papers, for many were slapped with security classifications.) The army drew from regular compilations of statistical data and from after-action reports submitted by field units —many of which pointed toward existing difficulties.

The high command of the army had available hundreds of *Senior Officer Debriefing Reports* from those who had held top leadership positions in Vietnam. "Lessons learned" from field experience, submitted by combat units, moved upward through channels, only somewhere to be dead-ended. Private conversations among general officers, who later claimed to have had serious misgivings about the system while they commanded in Vietnam, might easily have engendered substantive modifications of doctrine and tactics had they seriously attempted to do anything about it.

Official reports, authorized at the highest levels, such as the *Study on Military Professionalism*, became available to pinpoint clearly many of the personnel problems facing the army. Military scandals, such as the My Lai massacre, surfaced, affording the army the opportunity to clean its own house, demonstrating to critics its dedication to policing its own ranks.

With some few possible exceptions, the army did not do *any* of these things. Its initial inability to understand the nature of guerrilla warfare continued intact until the American evacuation. Its search for a time and place in which to force Vietnamese irregular soldiers into a "set-piece" battle lasted throughout the war. Its neglect of pacification, or nation building, persisted through all the years of the conflict. Its insistence upon bombing, and overwhelming use of firepower against dubious targets never lessened. Its eternal optimism never flagged or faded, despite much evidence to the contrary. Perhaps most damning, the army inevitably tended to look elsewhere to find fault and regularly tried to blame all the troubles besetting it on its civilian supervisors or upon the "permissive society" out of which its draftee manpower came.

Kinnard quotes several who placed the blame for army difficulties on the civilian sector. "The enemy's will to continue varied directly in proportion to the dissidents and the uproar back home about continuing the war." "Criticism of the type voiced by Mansfield, Kennedy, Fulbright, et al., probably strengthened the enemy's resolve to do what he did subsequent to 1968." "His will was particularly bolstered by appearances of divisiveness and antiwar sentiment in the United States." "Impossible to fight with imposed constraints." "Too much civilian interference in military matters—too many constraints. We were in essence handcuffed and not allowed to win."[70] Comments of a similar nature could be extended indefinitely.

Certainly the army's own studies of its performance during the Vietnam conflict did not dwell unduly on perceived or real difficulties. Rather, they were a set of studies, self-congratulatory in tone, that dwelt on major topics within its repertoire. The names themselves indicate the tone set within the covers: *CEDAR FALLS—JUNCTION CITY: A Turning Point; Training and Buildup of ARVN; Tactical and Materiel*

Innovations; Sharpening the Combat Edge; Law at War—Vietnam.[71]

Each study opens with a foreword proclaiming, "The United States Army has met an unusually complex challenge in Southeast Asia . . . has fought in support of a national policy of assisting an emerging nation to develop governmental processes of its own choosing, free of outside coercion." Quaint phrases appear that disguise the eventual U.S. failure in Vietnam. One such example is the words "during the buildup of forces and beyond."[72] The same source concluded its essay on Vietnam by stating:

> In spite of restraints in manpower, finance, management, and materials, the Army engineers have added new laurels to their history of support. All Americans can again take pride in the flexibility of thought, the responsiveness to need, the ingenuity, the diligence, and the adaptability of their engineer soldiers and units.[73]

The work on logistics suggests that "at no time was logistic support a constraint on a major tactical operation."[74] Logistics people learned as a result of Vietnam such surprising lessons as the following: A twelve-month tour is too short if a logistic system is to operate at near-peak efficiency. A need existed to improve driver-training programs in the United States, since poor drivers frequently had wrecks. Cross-country petroleum, oil, and other lubricants (POL) pipelines can be used despite the fact that they are subject to interdiction. Fresh foods can be provided to the combat soldier on a regular and routine basis. This requires a lot of refrigeration equipment. Preventive-maintenance programs are basic to achieving high operational rates on vehicles. Abandoned equipment should be destroyed to prevent its falling into enemy hands and being used by them.[75]

It is fortunate for logistics people that the Vietnam War came along. Otherwise they might never have had a chance to learn such valuable lessons. Surely the experiences of World War II and Korea would never have taught soldiers about the need for careful driving, or that fresh foods spoil without refrigeration, that preventive maintenance of vehicles is a wise course of action, or that enemy troops often make use of captured weapons and stockpiles.

The War in the Northern Provinces, 1966–1968 is divided into chapters with such upbeat headings as "U.S. Response to the Tet Offensive," "The Free World Counteroffensive," and "Analysis of North Vietnamese Goals and Failures." We can read therein news revealing that "the success of the Free World Forces can be attributed to their flexibility in organizations and tactics to meet the ever changing enemy situation and their mutual co-operation in conducting combined operations against the foe. . . . The establishment of programs to win the allegiance of the people to their government by eliminating the social, political, and economic injustices which provided a fertile environment for insurgency also furthered success."[76] A reader wonders what country is being described.

Allied Participation in Vietnam, written by Lieutenant General Stanley R. Larsen and Brigadier General James L. Collins, Jr. (presently serving as chief, Center for Military History; a pleasant man who walks with the aid of a cane), carries the above theme into greater detail. Neither author saw fit to mention that "free-world forces" served in Vietnam, for the most part, only because of pressure put on them by the United States or because America handsomely underwrote all their expenses. Within such parameters, some 50,000 soldiers from the Republic of Korea and 12,000 from Thailand, plus token presence of other nations' military units, served "alongside" U.S. outfits in Vietnam.

It is little wonder that civilian historians tend to disbelieve purported historical treatments issued by the military. And so go the booklets. They are packed with much information. Perhaps inevitably, however, one reads them with the growing conviction that the United States won in Vietnam after all. That is their major weakness. None of them is able to grasp the nettles of the failure of America's goals in Vietnam and ask "Why"?

*   *   *

The military did, from time to time, publish studies and issue directives on the subject of nation building. It even created a definition, as early as 1965, of what it meant when it spoke of pacification, or nation building. Owing to the whim of some bureaucrat in the long-defunct MACV headquarters, however, that early definition remains classified "confidential." A later statement that is almost identical to the one set forth in 1965 was included within the Combined Campaign Plan of 1970, which is unclassified. It reads as follows:

> The military, political, economic and social progress of establishing local government responsive to and involving the participation of the people. It includes the provision of sustained, credible territorial security, the destruction of the enemy's underground government, the assertion of political control and involvement of the people in government, and the initiation of economic and social activity capable of self-sustenance and expansion. The economic element of pacification includes the opening, securing and improving of lines of communication important to economic and military activity.[77]

The definition was an acceptable one. It was too bad the army never saw fit to emphasize such activities in any significant manner. Occasional good intentions, erratic sincerity, and enthusiasm shown only by a dedicated few served the United States poorly in Vietnam. Frustrated because the Vietnamese seemed uninterested in following American norms, acting regularly in irrelevant and counterproductive fashion, devoted to its own ethnocentrism, inefficient and vacillating, the army could never seem to make headway in its efforts at nation building. It provided only a program that was hopelessly flawed.

The buzzword, of course, was WHAM: "winning the hearts and minds" of the people. There were high hopes during the "American decade," between 1960 and 1970. Doctrine proudly proclaimed that

> Internal Defense and Development is defined as "the full range of measures taken by a government and its allies to free and protect its society from subversion, lawlessness and insurgency. . . . to promote its balanced growth by building viable institutions—political, economic and social—that respond to the needs of its society."[78]

Unfortunately, American doctrinaires could not even agree on what to call whatever it was they wanted to do in Vietnam. It has been referred to variously as nation building, internal defense and development, pacification, internal security, counterinsurgency, civil support for revolutionary development, revolutionary development, rural construction, internal-defense operations, and stability operations. These terminological differences cut deep. "Proponents of what is called so loosely in this paper 'pacification' were often in such violent disagreement as to what pacification meant that they quarreled publicly among themselves and overlooked their common interests."[79]

Each proponent agency, from USOM to USAID to CORDS to US-MACV, had its own experts, its own ideas, its own program, its own goals. Nor was there any central coordination. The differences among the programs of those agencies stand out clearly as one peruses the mass of information available in official publications, directives, standard operating procedures, briefings for incoming personnel, end-of-tour debriefings, end-of-year reports on specific programs, individual research reports, theses and dissertations, and government-contract evaluations. It began early.

In the summer of 1960, Lieutenant General Lionel C. McGarr, armed with a study on internal security prepared for him by the staff of the Command and General Staff College, arrived in Saigon to assume command of USMAAG. His "Counterinsurgency Plan for Vietnam" was a blueprint for reorganization of South Vietnam's military and paramilitary forces into an effective force under a single chain of command in order to combat internal subversion in its conventional and unconventional forms. The United States would quickly foil the insurgents padding on bare feet through the jungles of a backward nation.[80] This plan was generated and proposed by the United States military.

Brigadier, later Major, General Edward Lansdale proposed an alternative. Sometime CIA agent, veteran of the Huk rebellion in the Philippines, he suggested that it would make more sense if an attitude of mind, rather than a specific program, permeated American actions in Vietnam. The military should select dedicated Americans, capable of feeling empathy toward Vietnamese with whom they might work. They should be people who would advise their counterparts with understanding and wisdom. Such advisers would not be tied down with bureaucratic red tape but would be free to pursue tasks and goals generated by their understanding of the Vietnamese scene. They would be supported in their work by USOM in every practical way it could. Advisers would earn the trust of their counterparts and would not force their own ideas through coercion or threats. They would live in the field, seeing problems at first hand, rather than being quartered in secure rear areas far from the scene of conflict. Lansdale thus proposed an extrabureaucratic, uninhibited advisory system in which participants would have lengthy tours, giving continuity to programs and policies. He sought to unfetter advisers, to give them an unstructured and and unprogrammed nonorganization.

> The real decisions will be made in little daily actions in Vietnam, not in Washington. This is why the best are needed on the spot. Leverage should be the product of persuasion and trust, not the result of control over funds and materiel. Perhaps we should help those who help themselves.[81]

Despite some interest in his program by President Kennedy, nothing ever came of Lansdale's suggestions.

In November 1961, General Sir Robert Thompson, head of the newly arrived British Advisory Mission, presented the South Vietnamese government with his "strategic program" calling for pacification of the Delta. The U.S. quickly adopted it as its own. American military men saw the new concept as one that could provide security. Saigon saw it as one to give it control over the people. Social, economic, and political needs of the countryside were ignored in favor of barbed wire, sandbags, mine fields, and punji stakes. People were herded from ancestral lands into new settlements.

Little, if anything, was effectively done toward identification of Viet Cong leaders and destruction of the base from which they operated. Although there was much talk about winning the hearts and minds of the people during the period 1964–1965, after the collapse of Diem's Strategic Hamlet Program in late 1963, thoroughgoing pacification efforts were practically nonexistent. Only one abortive program seemed to offer any hope at all. That was an effort at cooperation, or *hop tac*, among the multiple agencies involved in nation-building programs. *Hop Tac* was a plan whereby a special council would be established to coordinate all agencies to secure the region around Saigon by concentrating on four concentric-circular zones extending out from the city. The purpose was to clear the seven provinces surrounding Saigon of VC once and for all. *Hop Tac* was publicized as a major feature of the American military effort in Vietnam, but it also failed. Its goals were

unrealistic, probably because once again the program was U.S. conceived and planned, while implementation was to be accomplished by
Vietnamese who did not identify with it. They refused to give high
priority to *Hop Tac*, despite the high-level council they established to
supervise it. Their cooperation was motivated primarily to appease
their American allies.[82]

Pacification stumbled along as everyone's poor cousin. Both Vietnamese and Americans continued to talk of WHAM, to state goals, and
to institute short-lived programs. Inevitably, however, goals were
stated in terms of roads, bridges, dams and canals, hamlets and villages
fenced or ditched, new identification cards issued, curfews established.
Never did anyone seem to see a need to talk in terms of leaders trained,
of determining village needs and meeting them.

Concurrently the Viet Cong strength grew. The VC saw and seized
opportunities. They provided activities based on immediate needs,
which also fit in with their long-range goals. They propagandized people face to face rather than through poorly printed propaganda leaflets.
They stressed to their cadre the need to remain credible with their
countrymen.

On the other hand, U.S. and Saigon efforts at nation building were
characterized by laborious planning, complicated execution, insistence
upon statistical indicators, reliance on advanced technology, and inordinate efforts at documentation and description of what they accomplished (or claimed to have completed.)[83]

American military leaders naively accepted guerrilla military units
as the real problem they had to combat. They concentrated on identification and location of VC troop units and mounted operations to destroy them when found. While dissipating American men, matériel, and
money in such efforts, the generals failed to recognize that the prime
force behind those enemy troops remained intact. Viet Cong organizational, administrative, leadership, and control elements could thus continue to refill, refit, retrain, and resupply the units decimated by American military actions.

American generals further tended to urge upon the government of
Vietnam plans and programs that were American in concept and design. Neither the GVN nor its people could identify with those programs or feel much dedication in carrying them out. During the entire
"American decade," the overwhelming assumption of the generals of
the United States Army was that willpower, buttressed by American
brains and technology, could defeat the Communist insurgency.

Furthermore, the officers of ARVN were of a caste and class that
set them apart from the rural people they were supposedly helping.
ARVN officers, for the most part, came from the upper class. Educated
in an urban environment, insulated from social problems of the countryside, isolated by the caste system within which they moved, and

commissioned and promoted all too often because of social status or for
political considerations, ARVN officers generally found little common
ground with the peasants in districts and provinces outside Saigon.

To make matters more difficult, the conventional military tactics
they had been taught by American advisers left ARVN commanders ill
equipped to deal with VC forces and their shadow government. ARVN
troops usually did not serve in the region in which they had been born
and raised. They were strangers among their own people. They were
not imbued with a spirit of victory but rather beset with homesickness
for their own villages and families. Desertion rates skyrocketed disas-
trously. Inevitably such circumstances combined to cause ugly incidents, troop retaliation, exploitation of civilians, and unnecessary casualties among both ARVN troops and civilian populations among which
they moved. All of this was quickly and adroitly exploited by the VC,
who emphasized local recruitment along with training and returning
workers to their home areas to live and work among their friends and
relatives. Unlike ARVN, VC field promotions tended to be based strictly
upon merit.

Most Americans who went to Vietnam as advisers were not prepared for the language barriers and cultural shock involved in living
with and fighting alongside the Vietnamese.[84] They tended to be impa-
tient and direct in their speech and approach. They valued Western
cultural systems and norms above those of their counterparts. And the
U.S. military constantly rotated its advisers in- and out-of-country. The
standard tour was just a few days less than a year. It came to be known
as the "revolving door" concept. Each new adviser came fresh from the
States, often directly from a branch school, full of enthusiasm and highly
motivated. He planned to "get things done" immediately and with a
minimum of "fuss," in order to show that it could be done and to
establish a good record for himself. This could usually be accomplished
only by scrapping the plans and programs of his predecessor and starting afresh with new ideas and different policies. The Vietnamese found
themselves faced with a highly accelerated, unstable, adviser-counter-
part relationships and were forced into a situation of having to establish
rapport with one new adviser after another, most of whom had little
real experience and less wisdom. By the time a new adviser began to
know what was happening, his tour was half over.

In such situations, counterparts regularly knew more about conditions than did those who were supposed to advise them. Vietnamese
officers, after all, had hardly known a day within their lives when war
had not beset their land. Resolution of difficulties seemed to have less
urgency for them than for their "friends" from across the sea. It was not
uncommon to find a young, aggressive army captain, arms akimbo,
demanding, in a loud, heated voice, to know why some project or other
could not be completed within some reasonable time. His Vietnamese

counterpart could only reply in a quiet, tired voice: *"Dai uy,* I have been doing this for thirty years. I did it before you came here. In six months you will go away and a new *Co van my* will take your place. But I will still be here, still faced with the same problems. I cannot go away. I have no other place to go."

American advisers and personnel at all echelons wanted immediate action with significant statistical feedback on their impact on the situation to which they had been assigned. Yet penetration and subsequent "roll up" of the Viet Cong infrastructure was an incredibly long, brutally slow and painstaking task. Most Americans had neither the training nor the stomach, let alone the patience, for such operations. They often advised abandoning neutralization operations rather than spending the time necessary to solve significant problems inherent in searching out and destroying the enemy infrastructure.

Without ever having really tried effective nation-building operations, the United States Army shifted its emphasis to conventional tactics, operations that would target large American units against VC military forces. Time and again, such enemy forces were destroyed. Yet the prime infrastructure behind those enemy activities continued unimpaired, capable of reinforcing and renewing any losses incurred.

Not only could the American army not destroy the Viet Cong insurgency; it could not cope well with its host country. Americans isolated themselves from the Vietnamese by building compounds and installations, effectively severing themselves from contact with Vietnam's nationals except when they chose to leave the "safety" of those enclave compounds for official business or recreation. Simultaneously came a conscious or unconscious subhumanizing of the Vietnamese people. American soldiers too often lumped all Vietnamese—friend or foe—into the same category. Major General Charles Timmes, as observer of the "American decade" in Vietnam, commented:

> In retrospect, I am appalled at how little we understood the Vietnamese people . . . how little we understood the Viet Cong and how little we knew about guerrilla warfare. We didn't know what the VCI [Viet Cong Infrastructure] was. We didn't speak the language. I felt we were absolutely ineffective against the VCI.[85]

The very forms in which American activity cloaked itself were determined by the means already available rather than being rationally selected to accomplish specific goals. Ready availability of large-scale destructive weapons brought on the use of Operation Rolling Thunder, Operations Cedar Falls and Junction City, and the many other divisional-level search-and-destroy missions.

Heavy bombers made the bombing of North Vietnam possible— and therefore inevitable—despite mixed evidence of any benefit to be wrought from it. Flocks of helicopters gave the American army the capability to mount search-and-destroy missions at whatever level, from division down to battalion. Even psychological operations tended to reflect what the U.S. Army had rather than what was needed.[86] Such efforts in support of pacification and rural development tended to emphasize leaflets, posters, canned loudspeaker broadcasts, and other forms dependent upon mass media in an attempt to make up for American inability to talk directly with the Vietnamese.

Americans could not talk with those of the countryside, and the Saigon government would not. In turn, owing to American pressure, the GVN adopted the same procedures, causing the Vietnamese Information Service to become overmechanized with our machinery. Face-to-face contacts would have been infinitely superior. The VC used this latter method routinely and effectively. American technology could not be brought to bear efficiently in small-unit operations against the VC. (The army looked upon the Marine Corps' Combined Action Platoons [CAP] as an aberration rather than as a model to be emulated. CAP activities involved meeting people and establishing personal relationships with rural Vietnamese over an extended period of time, allowing trust to build up. Despite obvious successes in the CAP program, the army shunned its adoption. It may well be that the army's inability to use its sophisticated equipment and technology in such programs dampened any enthusiasm among the war managers for such nation-building operations.[88])

Army generals, however, gave the nod to such programs as *Chieu Hoi* (Open Arms) and *Phuong Hoang* (Phoenix). As with so many ideas, *Chieu Hoi* was not conceived by the Vietnamese but was foisted upon the Saigon government by American and British advisers (including the ubiquitous Sir Robert Thompson). They persuaded a reluctant Diem to undertake this new program. It offered amnesty and a return to "normal" life to VC members if they would defect and turn themselves in to GVN.[89] The number of those willing to do so varied from time to time and the results were never as great as originally hoped.

Cynics believed—with some evidence for their position supplied by VC defectors—that insurgents surrendered whenever they had been in the jungle long enough to warrant a time of rest and recuperation. Since the VC had no facilities of their own, they simply rallied to the GVN under the terms of the *Chieu Hoi* program, got out of the fighting long enough to eat good food and rebuild their endurance. When they had restored themselves, they once more disappeared into the jungle fronds to rejoin their old comrades.[89] There were indications that with decent and circumspect intervals, some VC changed sides as many as five times.

Throughout the live of *Chieu Hoi*, those who "rallied" tended to belong to the lower levels of the VC apparatus. Its greatest failure was "its apparent inability to attract more than a small number of the high-ranking VC military and political cadres."[90] Furthermore, "its administration by the GVN over the years has often been inefficient, ineffectual, indifferent, corrupt, and hamstrung by bureaucratic red tape and interests."[91]

And then there was *Phuong Hoang,* the Phoenix program. Carl Bernard has written that *"Phuong Hoang* is the most important program you have, and if it is not properly attended will assure the ruin of everything."[92] *Phuong Hoang* was designed as a program aimed at the "neutralization" of the Viet Cong infrastructure. Westmoreland believed that thereby the army would be able "to identify and excise" the enemy leadership.[93]

Once again, it was a concept conceived by the American army and foisted upon GVN and ARVN. Those agencies regarded it as another bit of American patchwork, to be tolerated but not taken seriously. Worse, the advisers chosen to head up the Phoenix program were all too often inadequate. Second lieutenants, fresh from the United States, and completely innocent of the least understanding of the Vietnamese and their culture, were assigned to on-the-job training and directed to make order out of the *Phuong Hoang* campaign. Perhaps this confirmed GVN in its original impression that this was not an effort to be taken seriously.

As Westmoreland indicated, the formal purpose of *Phuong Hoang* was to identify and eliminate individuals of stature within the Viet Cong infrastructure.[94] This could be done through means as varied as friendly persuasion, convincing people to rally to the side of GVN, all the way to assassination. All too often those involved in the program believed that membership therein made them honorary participants in Murder, Inc. With such wide discretionary powers, it was easy to arrest, imprison, or assassinate the wrong people, for reasons ranging from petty dislike to bureaucratic snafus.

> Often "Viet Cong" are arrested on the basis of anonymous denunciations received by the police from those who bear personal grudges against the "suspect." Of greater concern, however, are the large numbers of persons arrested in connection with the efforts of each provincial security agency to fulfill the quota assigned to it, regardless of a suspect's political affiliation, and it has not been unknown for province or police chiefs to seek each month to exceed their quotas in order to demonstrate their competence. With large numbers of helpless persons detained . . . opportunities for corruption have proliferated. . . . The Phoenix program has been turned into a money-making scheme through which a villager's release can be obtained for the payment of a bribe, usually about $25 to $50.[95]

Like so many other programs, Phoenix was ineffective because it was poorly managed and because those in charge subverted it to personal profit rather than using it for the national welfare. As with so many other American-conceived programs, Phoenix failed to appreciate the complexities of Vietnamese village life and culture, and thus its results were poor.[96]

The Phoenix adviser program was beset by constant rotation of personnel, a factor the army describes as "turbulence." Accurate records were seldom kept. Efficiency seemed to be something honored in the breach, for prisoners captured at district level would be transferred to higher authorities for interrogation. By the time information filtered back to local areas, if it ever did, such intelligence was long out of date and consequently nearly worthless.[97]

One of the more lasting results for those who participated in *Phuong Hoang* was that of a troubled conscience. Several individuals interviewed for this study indicated remorse, feelings of enduring guilt, and a sense of personal anomie in their lives today as a result of their work in Phoenix.[98] In the end, Phoenix failed to achieve those things hoped for by its creators. The VCI was *not* eliminated or neutralized. Vietnamese nationals felt more estranged from their government because of their fears that at any moment, someone might target them as an enemy of the state, with consequent arrest, torture, imprisonment, or death. *Phuong Hoang,* like many other American ideas, passed through the traditional six phases that old sergeants claim happen with all army projects: (1) great expectations, (2) disillusionment, (3) panic, (4) search for the guilty, (5) punishment of the innocent, and (6) reward of the nonparticipants.

Having created successive unworkable and unrealistic programs in an effort to "win the hearts and minds" of the people, and having seen so many of them fail, one after another, junior-level officers of the American army in 'Nam became increasingly cynical, both toward the results of their own efforts and promises of generals. There was no light drawing near. There was only an endless, dark-filled tunnel. Nothing seemed to work, save actual firefights where one could see bodies fall and notice civilians cowering in fear. Perhaps that was the key.

Someone, somewhere, finally came up with a slogan that seemed to fit the situation. It became standard within Special Forces units in 'Nam and was also regularly quoted by others. There was a way, after all, to control the situation and gain the sympathies of the Vietnamese peasantry:

> *Grab them by the balls, and their hearts and minds will automatically follow.*

It was a cynic's solution, but there seemed to be few alternatives.[99]

At least there were few alternatives for the rigid, conformist, tradition-bound army managers of the war. Notoriously resistant to change, unable or unwilling to perceive a realistic way through the morass of Southeast Asia, such men—from Wheeler to Westmoreland to Abrams to the end—continued to insist on the complete rectitude of their own obviously faulty strategy and tactics. They did not wish to be instructed as to their errors.[100]

It did not help matters when on 1 July 1968 Westmoreland relinquished his command in Vietnam to General Creighton Abrams, who thus became the new commander, United States Military Assistance Command, Vietnam (COMUSMACV). Although Abrams made some small modifications in the American effort, the main thrust continued unabated. The major shift was from large-unit missions in remote areas to small-unit operations in more populated sectors, with closer liaison with ARVN. Unfortunately for the American war effort, however, was the fact that Abrams had served as Westmoreland's deputy.

Much of Abrams's conceptual framework of the war had been provided by his experiences under Westmoreland, and he shared many of his old commander's perceptions of what was appropriate and what the best ways were to route NVA and VC forces. It may even be that Abrams's changes were motivated less by arguments with Westmoreland over tactics than by the orders he received to hold down the number of American casualties, coupled with the later emphasis upon "Vietnamization" of the war. For whatever reason, despite some changing orders from Abrams at the top, the actual course of army participation in the war continued largely unchanged and unchecked. Jenkins concluded that "General Abrams has only partly succeeded in making his own ideas prevail over the traditional [i.e., Westmoreland's] doctrine." He added that "our military institution seems to be prevented by its own doctrinal and organizational rigidity from understanding the nature of this war and from making the necessary modifications to apply its power more intelligently, more economically, and above all, more relevantly."[101] What Jenkins saw was an unabated military effort to win in Vietnam by applying men and firepower in the hope of wearing down the insurgency by exacting an unacceptable number of casualties. Throughout the American experience in Vietnam, the army leopard refused even to consider changing its spots.

There was never any other official solution. Resistant to change whether suggested from lower levels within its structure, or by counterpart officials from other governmental institutions, the army continued to insist that its own course of action would prevail. Traditional doctrines, slightly modified, could readily be used in a guerrilla situation to destroy insurgents.

Sir Robert Thompson tells a story that supports this view. At one point he found himself at the Air Force Academy at Colorado Springs watching a film on the training of army and air force cadets. "It was really quite revealing and at the end of the programme I turned to my wife and said: 'My God, they could be Russians!' The training and indoctrination seem to have led to a view of strategy which at best is getting there 'firstest with the mostest,' which makes a little sense, and

at worst is 'find 'em and fight 'em,' which makes no sense at all."
Thompson summed up his reaction with the comment that "while
there have been plenty of younger Americans, both military and civil,
who have had a good understanding of the war, they have made no
impression at all on the system. . . . The lessons of the past in Vietnam
and elsewhere have just not been learnt."[102]

Insisting on its own rectitude, the army could only condemn critics
of whatever variety, suggesting they spoke from lack of information, or
experience, or for personal gain, or from jealousy. The army tended to
mount its defenses by relying on the logically fallacious *argumentum ad
hominem.* That is, it attacked the motives of those who put forth objections rather than examining the suggestions themselves. Used since
ancient times, it has always been a good device for dismissing one's
opponents and for ignoring arguments for which one does not have a
ready answer.

Three and one-half million tons of bombs were dropped. Jungles
were defoliated. Harassing and interdicting fires fell on combatant and
noncombatant alike. Search-and-destroy sweeps killed thousands and
generated literally millions of refugees. And we lost. There is no other
way to describe the result. As we withdrew from the war zone, the
insurgents and their northern allies waited. Following the army's evacuation, the American-trained and -equipped ARVN took over the task
of internal defense. When the Communist push began, the South Vietnamese army, upon which America had expended billions of dollars,
55,000 lives, and two decades of time, simply came apart like a house
of cards. As Kinnard said: "The light at the end of the tunnel had been
reached, and it was red."[103]

Not the least of the anomalies involved in that disintegration was
the fact that South Vietnam had the third-largest army in Asia, behind
only those of the People's Republic of China and the Republic of Korea.
The Army of the Republic of Vietnam was 350,000 strong. The "Ruff-
Puffs" (Regional Force/Popular Force) added another 320,000; the Civilian Irregular Defense Guard (CIDG) contained another 40,000.
There were 30,000 males in the Armed Combat Youth (ACY) and 75,-
000 in the National Police. There were, in all, over 800,000 troops
available to GVN. Despite their numbers, they utterly failed to stand
firm, after American troops had been withdrawn, in the face of the final
VC/NVA offensive.

Perhaps part of the explanation for the crumbling of that GVN
military structure may have been provided by Colonel Amos A. Jordan.
ARVN, he claimed, while under the leadership and direction of the U.S.
Army, became a laboratory for almost every half-baked idea espoused
by the American military from MAAG days to the end of MACV. Each
new proposal supposedly furthered the building of ARVN into a modern strike force patterned after American models. Jordan called the

process "mirror-imaging," and it proceeded until ARVN had become a grotesque copy of a United States Army field force, totally incapable of meeting either a conventional or unconventional challenge from the VC or NVA. It had surrendered any capacity it might ever have had for the absolutely essential "dig 'em out one by one" tactics required to fight a guerrilla force. Equipped with aircraft, naval vessels, and sophisticated antipersonnel detection devices; composed of heavy divisions with cumbersome staffs; restricted to road movements; unwieldy, over-centralized, and riven with tensions, ARVN *might* have been capable of repelling a Korean-type invasion, but little else. Kinnard may have said it best. "We invented a form of war which only we could fight and which was irrelevant to long-term political objectives. . . . Our heritage to our ally was a form of warfare he could not sustain."[104]

Despite some lower-level discontent at the time, no high military managers voiced concern with the state of ARVN's readiness, nor did the American army predict how suddenly ARVN would collapse when faced with a contentious foe.[105] Certainly no army leader took upon himself or his institution any blame for what occurred. Neither then nor since has any official military spokesman or any army school publicly admitted that its training program, its strategy, or its tactics in Vietnam were in error. No one has publicly suggested that the army fought the wrong war in the wrong way, thus making the results there a foregone conclusion.

There is a worse problem. Those who once had some expertise in counterinsurgency activities and who taught its theory and practice to others within the army have now gone on to other assignments or into retirement. One officer, interviewed during the course of research for this study, put it this way:

> There is not one school in the whole of the United States army that is seriously teaching students about real low-intensity [counterinsurgent] warfare—except Ft. Bragg, which has such a course which they teach primarily to members of the reserve components rather than to those in the active army. And even they are teaching it to perhaps no more than 30 to 40 people a year. Even Bragg is almost out of business.
>
> The army wants to make sure that we don't lose what precious little bit of expertise that is still residual from our experience in Vietnam. Yet this is a laugh a minute, for the army talks one thing and means another. For most of the people who are dealing with this are talking not about low-intensity warfare but a much higher-intensive activity.
>
> For despite what the army officially claims, the lessons learned and the expertise gained in Vietnam all took place at a higher level of intensity. So today they talk about how to use helicopters, how to use armor, how communications are employed, how to resupply in the jungle, and so forth and so on. Unfortunately, none of these things have any relevance in a real low-intensive situation. They fought a mid-intensity war and called it a

low-intensive one.[106] So of course, when they speak of lessons learned, then that's where the goddamned lessons learned came from. So what the army doesn't understand even yet is that it lost the war at a level it doesn't even *see*. What we did and what we learned from it may not be invalid—it may even be useful, but it sure as hell won't help us win another Vietnam-type conflict. And the army doesn't recognize this. The worst problem is that it will only be another couple of years before anybody with real insight into what went wrong in Vietnam will be out of business.[107]

The training programs on counterinsurgency at the various military centers are nearly gone. Those capable individuals who do remain are scattered throughout the system. They are the ones who might still be able to point out (were anyone interested in listening) that it would not necessarily be wise to rely solely on General Nathan Bedford Forrest's dictum of "gitting thar fustest with the mostest."

The path chosen in Vietnam was no solution at all. It insured defeat for America's military by a tenth-rate "power," and, in the process, allowed the army to adopt policies that came close to destroying it as a viable institution.

Five

Front-page headlines informed the nation about the ugliness of My Lai. The United States Army later launched an official investigation of that incident. William R. Peers, a three-star general headed the inquiry. His final report,[1] dated 14 March 1970 (but not released to the public until 13 November 1974[2]), was turned over to General William C. Westmoreland, army chief of staff, on 15 March. At the same time, Peers submitted a little-known, long-classified memorandum to the chief of staff. That memo reputedly had almost as much impact on General Westmoreland (who had been rewarded for his sterling leadership in Vietnam by being named to the army's top job) as did the report on My Lai itself.

Peers's secret memorandum suggested that there was something deeply and basically wrong with the moral and professional climate of the Army Officer Corps, that a problem existed that desperately needed to be studied and resolved.[3] Peers set forth his thoughts on those factors that make an effective combat leader. He touched upon points as fundamental as honesty, integrity, interest in and care for one's troops, ultimate command responsibility for all actions within a unit, the need for careful supervision and occasional corrective action, and the ineffective nature of leadership when conducted on any basis other than personal contact.

Peers indicated his belief that any officer in violation of such precepts profaned his own commission. He wrote of the need to be discriminating in use of firepower and of a commander's responsibility to protect private property, to safeguard processing of suspects and prisoners of war, and to provide humane treatment of refugees, noncombatants, and enemy wounded. He stressed the importance of discerning the difference between tough pursuit of the enemy and illegal activities leading to disasters such as the ones that brought about My Lai.

Thus, in the same mail, Westmoreland received two disturbing documents. Ever the good staff officer, Westmoreland decided that the best way to handle Peers's communications was to call for a staff study. Only three days later, on 18 April 1970, he turned to the Army War College, directing it to conduct a study of the leadership and professional attitudes of army officers and to plumb the moral climate of the corps. The assignment was as momentous as any given within the army in decades, yet Westmoreland gave the War College only two and one-half months to complete it. The suspense date he ordered was 1 July 1970. True to its task, the War College completed its assignment and handed in its findings one day ahead of schedule on 30 June.[4] Given the time limitation, the War College did its work well.

The report was entitled the *Study on Military Professionalism*, covered such areas as ethics, morality, and professional competence, and in its conclusions supported Peers's belief that the prevailing attitudes of the officers corps had created serious problems within the army. After studying the materials at hand, Westmoreland seems to have thought so as well. Security classifications were slapped on Peers's memorandum, on the report of the My Lai incident, and on the War College study. The latter, the body of which called for wide dissemination within the officers corps, was circulated, on Westmoreland's orders, only among general officers, an action usually taken only with information of the most sensitive nature.

Since declassified, the *Study on Military Professionalism* is available on request, but most officers within the army remain unaware that such an investigation was ever conducted. This is *prima facie* evidence that the house cleaning called for in the report, and the wide dissemination of its findings, have not been conducted. The suppression of the report over the years since its release seems to indicate that although the army may have taken it seriously, it certainly has not been willing to implement any of its findings. Although the War College is currently engaged in a two- or three-year project studying the ethical, moral, and professional climate within the army today,[5] top military leaders seem more comfortable when mandating studies such as the "Harrison Board," a recently completed year-long mission that reviewed the system of officer education and training in the light of projected requirements on the battlefield of the 1980s.[6]

Westmoreland seems to have called for the original War College study more as a cosmetic measure than as an urgently needed analysis. In his letter to the War College commandant, dated 18 April 1970, he declaimed that "several unfavorable events" had recently occurred within the army that were of "grave concern" to him. Surely this was a strange way to refer to such tragedies as My Lai. He further indicated that he did not take the current focus on "discipline, integrity, morality, ethics, and professionalism" very seriously, for he insisted that "by no means do I believe that the Army as an institution is in a moral crisis."

If there was a moral crisis within the army, why should he insist that none existed? If he was correct in his insistence, then why call for an investigation?

Westmoreland insured that such a review would be a cursory one, despite his call for it to be "conducted with the utmost thoroughness" by allowing only two and one-half months for its completion.[7] It seems evident "that the initiation of the study was never intended by the chief of staff to serve more than a propaganda function (otherwise he would not have suppressed it when the results turned out unfavorably)."[8]

Westmoreland called for the creation of an officer's creed and the War College produced one.

> I will give to the selfless performance of my duty and my mission the best that effort, thought, and dedication can provide.
>
> To this end, I will not only seek continually to improve my knowledge and practice of my profession, but also I will exercise the authority entrusted to me by the President and the Congress with fairness, justice, patience, and restraint, respecting the dignity and human rights of others and devoting myself to the welfare of those placed under my command.
>
> In justifying and fulfilling the trust placed in me, I will conduct my private life as well as my public service so as to be free both from impropriety and the appearance of impropriety, acting with candor and integrity to earn the unquestioning trust of my fellow soldiers—juniors, seniors, and associates—and employing my rank and position not to serve myself but to serve my country and unit.
>
> By practicing physical and moral courage I will endeavor to inspire these qualities in others by my example.
>
> In all my actions I will put loyalty to the highest moral principles and the United States of America above loyalty to organizations, persons, and my personal interest.[9]

It is not a bad creed. It is unfortunate that it was never publicized, never disseminated, never popularized, never held out as a goal worthy of emulation, for the officer corps was in sore need of such a standard.

*   *   *

It has earlier been argued in these pages that after Korea, the army's leaders instituted a new approach within the military. Following the pattern laid out by General Maxwell Taylor as chief of staff, military managers "modernized" the army. They laid emphasis on the army as a corporate structure, as a business conglomerate, to be promoted and expanded in much the same way as General Motors or IBM. So it came to pass that a generation of soldier technicians and bureaucrats, interested and effective in personnel management, were promoted into top slots. "Duty, honor, and country" was replaced by the need to be in the right job at the right time.

The news spread throughout all levels of the army. Careerism, rather than dedication to the welfare of one's men, was the way to get ahead. Such career advancement was best enhanced by "ticket-punching" procedures: be certain to go to jump school so that you could wear airborne wings; pick up Ranger tabs to wear on your uniform sleeve; command a unit as quickly as possible—but not for too long, for that might prevent moving on to the next requirement of staff duty. Secure a coveted assignment in the Pentagon. Seek overseas duty. Remember to enroll in college somewhere and pick up a bachelor's degree and then, if at all possible, a master's degree. Never earn a doctorate—it might indicate that you were an "egghead" out of touch with military reality. Be sure to get on the list of those selected for Command and General Staff College as soon as possible. Pick up the right awards and decorations so that the left hand side of your personnel record jacket contains the correct entries. Get your ticket punched in the right places —and, whatever else, "max" every officer-efficiency report (OER). Do not make mistakes. They hurt. Do nothing rather than commit an error, and at all times "cover your ass."

The system admittedly was not as simplistic or open or brazen as that. Nowhere were these "punches" written down. No list of them existed.[10] No official spokesman ever set them forth as army policy. It was just that officers knew what worked and what did not. They were under real pressure from the time the army adopted the "up or out" policy on promotions. Unless a reserve officer on extended active duty (EAD) had spent extensive time as an enlisted man, it became difficult for him to retire as a senior captain or a major. The army proclaimed that no longer would there be room for those unable or unwilling to progress through officer ranks, so individuals *had* to learn the best ways to reach the next-higher rank in the most efficient way possible.

When junior officers took note of the badges of accomplishment on the tunics of their seniors, they knew what those older officers looked for in younger men. If one's divisional commanding general wore jump wings on his left breast, his subordinates knew he would take note if they earned them also. If the chief of staff had graduated from Ranger School, it did not take young lieutenants long to recognize the utility of wearing shoulder tabs as well.

When lists of below-the-zone promotions came out, containing a significant number of names of men who had earned graduate degrees, army enrollments in colleges near military posts swelled, and thousands of others signed up for university extension courses. It was not usually a case of seeking knowledge for its own sake. It was rather an effort simply to get a degree, any degree, no matter what the course of study might be. (Since it would have to be completed after hours, the easier the work, the better.)

For a time, service with the Special Forces was an important "punch," and it was common to see young officers with little of the training that had originally characterized members of the SF styling around with "green beanies" and bloused boots. Such indicators varied from time to time, depending upon the accomplishments and interests of those in positions of high command. Young officers on the way up, however, were inevitably able to keep up with changes on the invisible roster of punches. These were the sort of punches over which officers had some control.

There were other punches that the army itself insisted upon. One of its most rigorous routines was its requirement of making men into generalists before they ever had time to become really proficient in anything. It made little difference, for example, whether a man had interest in intelligence work. He still had to put in time on someone's staff as an S-2. He might despise operations and training activities, feeling that they only detracted from his own skills in logistics and supply. No matter. He must still serve as an S-3. Even if he had done it for only a few months, it still had to go on his record.

A man utterly skilled in staff work necessarily had to take leave from these duties in which he was proficient and function as a commander of a company or battery so that it could be said of him that he had had "command time." This paved the way for his next promotion, for without service as a commander, one had little opportunity for upward progression. Likewise for those who were gifted leaders, able to inspire others to feats beyond their natural inclination. Even if they had no interest in or skills for other duties, they were still routinely shunted into staff assignments of one variety or another.

This system brought a great deal of experience to young officers on their way up; it also brought grief and caused the loss of thousands of good men who would not or could not put up with such an approach. The *Study on Military Professionalism* pinpointed the problem with this approach. "There is widespread feeling that the Army has generated an environment that rewards relatively insignificant, short-term indicators of success, and disregards or discourages the growth of the long-term qualities of moral and ethical strength on which the future of the Army depends."[11]

One recommendation in the *Study on Military Professionalism* called for "removing from the optimum career patterns for combat arms officers the requirement that to advance rapidly in grade they must command both at battalion and brigade level as well as serve on high level staffs."[12] In stern words that report criticized "the existing climate," which perpetuated the "widespread, officially condoned or institutionalized portion of the performance" of individual officers that varied "significantly" from ideal standards. In such circumstances, officers acted persistently with "selfish behavior that places personal success ahead of the good of the Service," causing them to look upward "to

please superiors instead of looking downward to fulfill the legitimate
needs of subordinates."

Officers were, according to the report, preoccupied "with the at-
tainment of trivial short-term objectives [punches] even through dis-
honest practices that injure the long-term fabric of the organization."[13]

> A scenario that was repeatedly described in seminar sessions and narrative
> responses includes an ambitious, transitory commander—marginally
> skilled in the complexities of his duties—engulfed in producing statistical
> results, fearful of personal failure, too busy to talk with or listen to his
> subordinates, and determined to submit acceptably optimistic reports
> which reflect faultless completion of a variety of tasks at the expense of the
> sweat and frustration of his subordinates. The junior officer . . . is the
> executor of command decisions and bears the brunt of the burden of
> executing simultaneously and flawlessly all the policies conceived by all the
> echelons above him.[14]

A captain complained that "career types are too concerned with
promotions, efficiency reports, and conforming to the wishes of their
commander."[15] Another noted that "too many officers place the value
of a high OER over the welfare of their men."[16] A colonel observed that
"everyone is afraid to make a mistake with someone always looking
over his shoulder. . . . Many, many young officers who realize that
personal ambition and not the long range good of the organization is
the 'why' of certain decisions leave the Army." Those who stay in the
service are those who "are willing to follow that example."[17]

Another colonel stated that "too much attention is being given by
the Army, through its undue emphasis and policies as well as by individuals, on personal advancement or 'ticket punching.' Our professionalism as soldiers has thereby been degraded."[18] A major put the
matter succinctly: "The system forces unethical reporting and practices, and punishes variation."[19] Another major indicated that "commanders more oriented upon 'ticket punching' and not taking any
chances as long as they are in command . . . inhibits what a truly good
unit can accomplish."[20]

A colonel revealed his belief that "too many officers still worry
about accumulating the 'right tickets' rather than performing at their
best in any assignment."[21] Another colonel stated that "the Army has
made it clear that an individual has to have 'certain tickets'—without
these he is in trouble as far as promotions and assignments are concerned. This is short-sighted and does not make use of the talents of the
individual."[22]

One lieutenant colonel mentioned that certain tickets are sought
"not to make a contribution to the Army, not to lead troops and improve their performance, but to fulfill a requirement for the advancement of one's career. Failure of even minor tasks result in elimination

from competition for colonel, war college etc. Hence loyalty to subordinates is given only in furtherance of personal goals, responsibility for failure is avoided and judgment is biased toward 'what effect will this have on me?' "[23] A major agreed with him, feeling that "the tendency in the Officer Corps today is to get 'ticket punched' regardless of the cost . . . the methods used. The attitude of putting forth extra effort to better the organization is sneered at today."[24] A possible solution was indicated by a major who acknowledged that "the Army should redefine officer career patterns in an attempt to allow an officer to attain and maintain high expertise in fewer fields."[25]

Such men indicated "loud and clear" their firm belief that "there is a route you take to the top. If you are going to be a good officer you must compete. . . . You have got to get to school at the right time, you have got to get your master's degree, you've got to get your tour in the Army staff, you've got to get your pertinent overseas tours, you've got to get that command at the right time." They further insisted that the army had "unrealistic requirements" and had to reach the point where it could "recognize the fact that some people are better qualified to do other things than others, that not everyone is a commander, not everyone is an excellent staff officer, but the people that are good at what they are doing ought to be able to stay there and do the job and worry about the performance rather than about the ticket."[26]

Someone else phrased it differently, but his meaning was the same: "Accept the fact that every young man that is given a job to do isn't automatically qualified, just because he's been a platoon leader, to be the S-1 or the S-4."[27] The *Study on Military Professionalism* reiterates the resentment over ticket punching to the point that army managers should have been willing to do something about it shortly after the report was issued: " . . . it wasn't too bad for a guy to be only a commander. Let him be a commander for two or three years if he wants to command a battalion or a company, and do not penalize him because he hasn't got another hole punched in his ticket. On the other hand, if he's not a real good commander, don't force him into commanding. If he's a good staff officer, let him be a good staff officer. And the overall Army, they felt, would be better if we got off of this business of having the requirement to have certain holes punched in the ticket."[28]

There were captains citing "all the tickets you must punch to get to the War College. These are captains! . . . and they were laughing about how can you possibly do all of these things in the few years you have? And they cited it very lucidly. I must do this then I must do the other, but how can I possibly learn any of these things properly in that short a time, but I must serve time in order to advance properly in that short a time. I must go out and punch those tickets in that short a time in order to survive. . . ."[29]

By the fall of 1970 every general in the army who was interested in doing so had the opportunity to benefit from the above quotations. Even if the *Study on Military Professionalism* had been restricted by Westmoreland to circulation only among generals, at least they could read those devastating comments and act on them. Had they wished, they could have conducted their own surveys to amplify the one carried out by the Army War College. They could have submitted such results and their own recommendations to the chief of staff.

Although a document may exist somewhere indicating that one or another general actually did so, to date there is no evidence whatsoever that any high-ranking officer took any action of any kind. The recommendations in the *Study on Military Professionalism* died aborning. Nor is there any documentation or testimony showing that the army places less emphasis upon ticket punching now than it did in 1970.

In 1973, Stuart Loory could still report that "if ticket punching is going to be ended, and there are few left in the military these days who speak well of the system, the services must consider some drastic alternatives . . . in the entire system of career management."[30] Ward Just, another author, could determine no slackening of the army's emphasis upon ticket punching. "The theory is that a man cannot know one job without knowing the other, cannot understand 'line' without knowing 'staff' and vice versa. The officer will proceed as prescribed, skipping when he can but being careful not to skip too often; the process is known as 'getting your ticket punched,' and it means you must get off at all the stops. There has never been a Clausewitz in the American Army because the writing of *Vom Kriege* took time and serious thought. An Army officer has no time to think, and imaginative reflection is discouraged. Tours of duty are rapid, and designed to thrust a man into as many different situations as can be managed. The emphasis is on procedure, detail, fact, nut and bolt."[31]

In June 1971, Colonel David H. Hackworth, a brilliant and much decorated officer on the way to his first star, resigned from the army and told reporters that he had become fed up with the corruption in the officers corps, its ticket-punching approach to careerism. "One cannot blame the officer corps for this system, for they were just awash in the tide of the system; to fight it meant banishment to Fort Nowhere and the guaranteed end of a career."[32]

Lieutenant Colonel [now Colonel] William L. Hauser, in his book *America's Army in Crisis*, wrote that "widespread allegations of manipulation of statistical indicators, unseemly pursuit of rank and decorations, and 'ticket-punching' careerism—even if some of the critics appear to have come into court with unclean hands—are too damning to be ignored."[33] It is important to remember that Hauser was a *defender* of the military system, not a critic, yet the evidence was so strong that there was no way for him to close his eyes to it.

In 1974, Maureen Mylander asserted that "time and ticket-punching have increased the difficulty of differentiating among water walk-ers. Not even subjective judgments come easily when Ph.D.s, Purple Hearts, combat tours, Ranger tabs, parachute wings, commands and key assignments pop up among the records like mushrooms in a rain forest."[34] Author after author has spoken of, and condemned, the sys-tem of ticket punching, with no apparent effect. Officers on active duty today are still careful to meet the undiminished demands of those who check the tickets for appropriate notches. And they remember very well their own, and others', stories.

"I knew one officer well, a captain in the signal corps, and Special Forces qualified. He was a disagreeable individual. No matter what anyone of a more exalted rank asked him to do, he would get it done no matter what it cost his own men. I know that he was taken as a straphanger out on an operation from my camp for the express purpose of winning him a CIB [combat infantryman's badge—a coveted award]. He needed a CIB for promotion to major. After slowing down the operation for four days because he was so out of shape he could not walk, the sergeant in charge sent his point element out to fire four or five rounds. Then he had this captain air evac-ed. He was then put in for the CIB because he had been 'in combat.' "[35]

An artillery captain put it like this:

Vietnam was the only war we had. Career-development purposes were served by it; ticket punching helped. You needed a combat tour, you got one. The main thing was to have (at the time I was there) the right ribbons on your chest when the war ended. The fallacy, though, was that if you were really effective as a combat leader, you got six months. If you were the village idiot and couldn't do anything except to fly around in a helicop-ter and ask the troops if they were getting their mail, you still got six months. The justification for the six-month command had, in reality, noth-ing to do with 'burn-out' but was followed in order to get as many people rotated through the command slots as possible, so after the war the army would have a lot of people for a long time who had 'commanded' in combat.[36]

A National Guard officer, one of the very few who were activated for service in Vietnam, recalled that the "regular-army officers I knew were always very career conscious, often constrained. By and large, I was very disappointed in the caliber of those active army officers be-cause so many gave the impression of being far more concerned with their careers than they did with doing what needed to be done from the standpoint of their troops."[37] It would not be difficult to continue to multiply such comments, but the point has been made.

From the highest levels of army bureaucracy to the lowest levels of second-lieutenant platoon leaders, officers within the military com-plained for years about the debilitating effects of the ticket-punching routine. They were ignored and the system continued unchanged.

*   *   *

To judge the upward progress of officers as they move from one job to the next, from one place to another, the army has devised DA Form, Series 67, the officer-efficiency report (OER). In an effort to create a "report card" on which could be entered a fair, objective, and reliable description of a man and his performance of duty, the Department of the Army has gone through seven such forms in recent years, DA 67-1 through DA 67-7. The latter has been in use since 1 January 1973. DA 67-6 appeared on 1 January 1968, DA 67-5 came into use on 1 August 1963, and so forth. Each has been hailed, at its inception, as superior to its predecessor and not subject to the ills that beset those that had gone before. None have, however, proven to be wholly satisfactory, and with each new revision, observers have soon appeared to point out difficulties and to recommend either the abolition of OERs or the creation of still another form. Thus the army is about ready to begin use of DA 67-8, phasing out the once promising DA 67-7.

The task of rating an officer is probably both necessary and important, and it is certainly not a new duty for supervisors. Standardized rating forms have been around since the 1920s, and more informal reports were included in officers' personnel files for decades prior to that. In the smaller army of yesteryear, efficiency reports did not have the importance they later assumed, for members of the officer corps regularly knew one another, either through personal acquaintance or through reputation. Save for a very few individuals, that is no longer possible.

Thus the army relies upon officers' OERs to guide it in assignment and promotion policies every step of the way. Since OERs are such a key indicator, every officer knows that his chances for promotion or a good assignment hinge on the scores he achieves. When the institution itself mandates that all officers will be managed in an "up or out" program, individuals who have chosen the military for a career cannot help being largely motivated by efforts to secure the best possible rating, for to be "passed over" for promotion twice spells the end of an officer's career.

OERs are filled out on every officer in the army (except lieutenant generals and full generals) on an annual basis, or even more often, if an officer or his immediate supervisor ("rater") is transferred. The rater, and his supervisor, known on the report as the "endorser," assess an officer in such areas as personal qualities, potential for promotion and military schools, and the value they believe the officer has to the army. A third individual, the "reviewer," peruses the completed form, examining it for inconsistencies or errors. Within the military hierarchy of being, it is better to be rated by a full colonel than by a captain, better by a general than by a colonel, for such signatures automatically carry more weight when an OER is considered by a promotion board.

Although there are many parts to an OER, an individual, when he receives his latest "report card," quickly looks at the two crucial areas: has he received a maximum or near-maximum numerical score of between 194 and 200, and have the blocks "promote immediately" or "promote ahead of contemporaries" been checked? If so, then he can rest content until the next time.

Rapid-promotion possibilities during the Vietnam conflict made the necessity for "max" OERs even more important. King reports that in 1960 it took an average of thirty-three years, two months, for a man to move from second lieutenant to colonel; by 1970, it could be done in only thirteen years, four months.[38] For this to occur, however, no adverse OER could appear anywhere along the way. If a negative rating did occur, the unfortunate individual usually simply accepted it and gave up his ambitions of ever achieving high rank, for it was virtually impossible to get an adverse rating changed.

One who did not give up was Lieutenant Colonel Anthony Herbert. Herbert had been quite a soldier. He had experienced combat both in Korea and in Vietnam, first as an enlisted man and then as an officer. Trained as a parachutist and at Ranger School, he also worked toward a doctoral degree in psychology. The area above his left-hand pocket was emblazoned with awards and decorations. He was tough, hardened, proficient in leadership, and not particularly tactful, but he functioned with gusto and skill in whatever assignment he was given. Finally, in 1969, he received appointment as a battalion commander, a job for which he had long hankered.

Under Herbert's leadership, that battalion, which had been a lackluster outfit, did a turnaround and began to establish an excellent combat record. Yet after only fifty-eight days in command of the 173d ABN BN, Herbert was relieved from his assignment, having fallen afoul of Colonel Ross Franklin, the deputy brigade commander, and Major General John W. Barnes, the division commander. Worse, Herbert received an unfavorable OER for the period of his assignment as battalion commander.

Herbert decided to fight the issue. He claimed that he had affronted the two men by his reports of observed war crimes that he had reported to them, which they did not wish to hear, and which they chose not to investigate. In Herbert's opinion, they had covered up atrocities to the eventual and ultimate detriment of the army. He suffered for publicizing this view. His assignment to command and General Staff College was cancelled, and he was rerouted into a dead-end job at Third Army Headquarters in Ft. MacPherson, Georgia. Worse, he was passed over for promotion to permanent (regular army) major.

Despite his appeal within military channels to have his OER expunged from his records, nothing was done until he went public with his case. Angry over the delays, Herbert appeared on the Dick Cavett TV show and was featured in articles in *Life* and other publications, ferociously attacking the army for its sloth in his own case and charging the leadership with covering up Vietnamese war crimes because of its sensitivity about its public image. He spoke of corruption, of rear-area commandoes living in luxury, of the military's inefficiency in prosecuting the war in any appropriate way.

It was only after Herbert became a *cause célèbre* that the Third Army adjutant general recommended favorably on his case, followed by the secretary of the army's review. Their actions culminated in an order for the unfavorable OER to be removed from Herbert's record. By that time his career lay in ruins, and Herbert was so soured that in 1971 he resigned from the army.[39] The army denied the bulk of Herbert's charges and, for a time, circulated several "fact sheets" that claimed to tell the real story about Herbert and his allegations. The whole Herbert episode has become so controversial that it may be years, if ever, before a clearer picture emerges. Undeniably, Herbert enlarged upon some of his own past exploits, had a faulty memory regarding some others, and may well have exaggerated some of the faults of Franklin and Barnes. It is equally undeniable that Herbert had been a well-thought-of, promising officer prior to the onslaught of charges and that *something* caused a man whose whole life was wrapped up in the service to blow the whistle on it. In any case, if securing a ruling expunging an unfavorable OER was that difficult for the strong-minded Herbert, who for a time was backed by favorable press and television coverage, one can imagine the monumental difficulties a friendless second lieutenant or captain would have facing the same task.

OERs have, unfortunately, been traditionally abused in one of two ways, either through downgrading or by inflation. The rebel, the independent thinker, the "boat rocker," can all be sidetracked by an OER rater or endorser capable of writing neutral or carefully phrased negative comments who remembers a real or imagined mistake committed by the officer in question since his last rating period. Such power is bitterly resented by those who have suffered from it. The *Study on Military Professionalism* contained many comments alluding to such fears.

"Commanders must realize," said a captain, "that mistakes are human . . . they should be used as lessons learned and not vehicles for destroying an individual."[40] Another captain admitted that there was too much fear among subordinates of receiving bad OERs if they admitted that their units were less than perfect or if they tried to present a discussion point their superior did not want to hear.[41] Other captains used phrases like "haunted forever by one bad OER," "zapped by the OER," "go to any means to receive a high OER," valuing a "high OER over the welfare of their men,"[42] "the most disturbing administrative farce in the Army," "a measure of following rather than leading," "no one will take a chance lest his OER be lowered and his opportunity for advancement threatened," "innovation is stifled and conformity promoted," "initiative is stifled."[43] Lest these comments be dismissed as simply the grumbling of losers, other grades surveyed for that *Study* included ranks up through full colonel, and those of every category condemned the uses to which OERs have been and are being put.

Not only can OERs be used to condemn; so also can they be used to pave the way for "comers," "hard chargers," and "water walkers." The man who stroked his superior's ego, who covered up his mistakes, who disguised problems as achievements, who manipulated statistics until they indicated "zero defects,"—such a man could inevitably count on receiving "max" OERs. Let the dimensions of the problem not be exaggerated. The military—at all ranks—has extremely competent, thoroughly proficient, wholly devoted, terribly hardworking and obviously talented men. When such individuals perform their duties, they usually do so with exemplary facility. Such dedication is inevitably rewarded at OER time with high grades—as it should be.

Yet recognition of outstanding performance has itself produced problems. If a report recently given me by a senior chaplain within First Army is correct, and I have no reason to doubt it, two years ago some 65 percent of all active-duty chaplains received maximum OERs, that is, their raters and endorsers graded them as perfect. Either the U.S. Army has an unusually high number of perfect chaplains or their commanders are grading them too easily out of fear of otherwise hurting their careers.[44] Another observer has seen the same thing. Colonel J. T. Miller writes that "the degeneration of our officer evaluation system, centered about an inflated evaluation report, has reached such depths that it can no longer be viewed merely as mismanagement; rather it should be called an indictment of the integrity of our officer corps."[45]

There is obvious evidence for his charge. One officer told me that "whenever I filled out an OER, I gave the man the benefit of every possible doubt. Unless I really believed he would be a detriment to the service, I inevitably gave him optimum marks."[46] Another laughingly recalled that "I can't remember the number of second lieutenants, first lieutenants, and captains whom I have described as the best representative of that rank I had ever known. Who ever checks on *me* to see how many times I have said that?"[47] Such attitudes create problems for promotion boards.

One field-grade officer described some of the problems facing those boards. "I recently got promoted below the zone. Part of the reason for that *has* to be Vietnam, for look at the kind of person who sits on promotion boards. Let's say they could have promoted five in my branch—the chaplaincy—below the zone. (They actually promoted only four.) Probably three dozen chaplains in the running, and I just made it below the zone by two to three weeks. The board looked at all our records. All three dozen were about the same in many ways. Combat records made the difference. Someone on the board might have said, 'This guy was wounded two times while this other chaplain seems to have been assigned to a service battalion in Saigon.' The supply and service chaplain just won't get the same consideration as one who had been wounded. For, you see, promotion boards don't look for reasons to promote but for reasons not to do so. And in all of the two or three minutes they spend on a person's record, that's the kind of determination they make."[48]

That officer underestimated the time that many promotion boards spend considering the case of individual officers, but not by much. Two men who were students at the Army War College spoke of a practical exercise in which they had participated. Both men, full colonels, served on a "practice" promotion board. They indicated that there were so many cases to consider and so little time available that on the average, only about five minutes could be devoted to a man's file in order to determine whether he should be promoted from lieutenant colonel to full colonel. They had no time to read narrative comments on past OERs in the file. They could only glance at the records to learn how many punches the man had on his ticket. They felt it was no wonder that officers needed command of a battalion, a staff assignment, a combat infantryman's badge, jump wings, Ranger School, and all the other punches. A man on the way up could not afford to be different unless he could not only meet but also exceed expectations about his ticket. Both colonels indicated that the rapid pace of judgment on their "promotion board" seemed not to upset regular-army classmates as much as it did those students who were Army Reserve or National Guard and who wanted more time to study the records, to read pertinent narratives, and to think about what it all meant. Five minutes to sum up and to judge a man's career seemed insufficient.[49]

The OER system impinges on the integrity of all raters and endorsers who, knowing about the limited time available to promotion boards, feel compelled to use words and numbers that have little or no meaning left to them because they have become so inflated. As more scores float toward the top of the scale, those left in the middle—which should denote average performance—tend to be regarded as negative. A discriminating rater or endorser thus penalizes the officer he evaluates if he fills out an OER honestly. That this is a real peril can be seen in articles that have appeared claiming that even one bad OER can assign an officer to a bleak future.[50] "The results of all this are apparent. There is now a total disbelief in the system and a concomitant question regarding the integrity of all of us who continue its use."[51]

Officers during the Vietnam era thus had two serious constraints under which they operated at all times: 1) the ticket-punching progression of assignments through which they were rotated so rapidly that they gained neither experience nor significant insights into any of the jobs they held, and 2) the necessity officers felt for achieving a maximum score on their OERs for all assigned duties if they expected to remain competitive with their fellows for future jobs, schools, and promotions.

* * *

A corollary of maximum OERs was an official policy fostered by the Department of the Army. This was the military climate of opinion during the Vietnam era that was typified by its insistence on always maintaining an optimistic "damn-the-torpedoes-full-speed-ahead-we-can-accomplish-anything-asked-of-us" attitude. Public advertising of itself to the American public plus internal army sloganeering intended for the troops emphasized such "buzz" phrases as "no problem," "can do," and "zero defects."

From every wall hung posters calling for the impossible goal of zero defects. Seemingly, the army had forgotten that it was peopled by humans, entities who were, by definition, imperfect. It was "no problem" to achieve zero defects, you see, for we "can do" whatever is required. That spirit reigned from Westmoreland down. Westy was quoted as saying, "The armed services were not about to go to the Commander-in-Chief and say that we were not up to carrying out his instructions—as a matter of service pride."[52] That "can do" spirit, demanded regularly of subordinates all the way down to the lowest private, cost wastage in both men and materials. Clearly there were some things that could not be done.

An administrator at the Army War College analyzed the "can do" attitude. "Should the 'can do' spirit be replaced by a 'Sorry, sir, can't do' one? Or perhaps a 'shouldn't do' approach? It was one of our big problems. The military would be given a mission about which they had not been consulted. Only after the decision had been made were they notified, and still they said 'can do.' If they had understood the war, they would have realized the chances of winning were nil and might have said so. Hopefully would have said so. Ought to have said so. The cost to them would be great. Someone should have stood up and said 'We can't do this.' "

When asked whether he would have been willing to risk his career by making such a stand, he replied, "Yes, I would do it. I would have done so as a second lieutenant. Unfortunately, we don't have enough men able to say 'Sorry sir, can't do.' We thought once we got into Vietnam with firepower, mobility, technology, that we could do it. We were filled with that wrongheaded 'can do' spirit."[53]

An instructor at Command and General Staff College put his feelings this way: "The system demands perfection at every level—from potatoes to strategy. It whittles away at one's ethics. There are never supposed to be any deficiencies, any shortfalls. Take the matter of hand receipts. A second lieutenant hand receipts 250 boxes of ammo brass, certifying that all of it has been expended. Does he know? Has he checked? Of course not. It would be physically impossible for him to actually count each piece of brass, given all the other assignments he is also responsible for. So he simply asserts that it has been expended, and signs his name. He knows it's a lie and the person who keeps the signed receipt knows so also. This is true for most property receipts. They are only occasionally checked by a signing officer and when found to be in error are rewritten or juggled so the previous officer can escape a penalty for having lost property (which he probably never had in any case). It all causes an erosion of ethics."[54]

The *Study on Military Professionalism* gave a clear indictment of the demand for perfection. "For those who deal with complex organizations, changing missions, and people of various aptitudes, perfection or 'zero defects' is an impossibility." The *Study* enlarged on its conviction. "It is a simplistic approach that appeals to few people on the working end of the organization. It is especially unappealing to those who take things seriously, who want to accomplish their mission, and who are prone to report the truth. It is antithetical to the Army's proclamation that it is people-oriented. Pressures to achieve unrealistic goals, whether imposed by design or generated through incompetence, soon strain the ethical fiber of the organization."[55]

General DeWitt C. Smith, commandant of the War College, clearly pointed out the difficulties of such demands when he said: "The concept of 'zero defects'—can it lead people to cut corners and fudge? 'Can do' —does it lead people to do things without thinking? The code word 'bottom line'—is it totally stripped of ethical implications?"[56] The attitude did not serve the army well.

*   *   *

A war was on. The army rapidly expanded to meet military needs in Vietnam. Promotions were fairly easy in any case and could be achieved even more quickly if a man was stationed in the war zone. As Halberstam noted: "The war was big enough to satisfy the ambitions of most of those persons who saw in it a way to enhance their own careers. . . . The subtleties and nuances of the Vietnam War [were] displaced by the emotional requirement to 'get my command—be it a company, battalion, regiment, or division.' "[57] There had been no combat commands since the end of the Korean conflict. Those who had fought there as captains, majors, and lieutenant colonels saw in Vietnam an opportunity to reinvigorate their careers and welcomed this new opportunity for promotion to general.

Vietnam gave them what they wanted. Over 99 percent of second lieutenants who remained in the system became first lieutenants. The rate was nearly as good for the next jump, as some 95 percent of first lieutenants were selected for promotion to captain. In the next category, 93 percent of qualified captains were selected for major, and, unbelievably, 77 percent of qualified Majors became Lieutenant Colonels and one out of every two Lieutenant Colonels reached the rank of Colonel.[58]

There is every reason to believe, despite periodic protests by the Department of the Army to Congress as it asked for still more high-ranking slots to fill, that the officer corps was grossly and unnecessarily swollen during the Vietnam conflict. King's figures are revealing: "In 1969 with a total armed force of 3.5 million men there were 1,338 generals and admirals on active duty"—more than during the height of World War II when twelve million Americans were under arms. The same was true of army colonels and navy captains. "In June 1969 there were 18,277 colonels or captains on duty in the armed forces," which again was more than held that rank at the end of the Second World War. Last, "In 1969 there were 407,951 officers of all ranks in the armed forces—a ratio of an officer for every eight servicemen."[59] Hauser put the same issue in a different perspective. In 1971,

> in House hearings on military manpower policy, Representative Otis Pike noted that although the services had 315,000 fewer men than they had had in 1946 [at a time when the United States was rapidly discharging as many men from its World War II Army as it could], they had 26,000 more captains, 21,000 more majors, 15,000 more lieutenant colonels, and 4,000 more colonels. Combat troops comprised only 14 percent of military manpower, compared with 24.1 percent in 1946. . . . The House Appropriations Committee also noted that the Armed Services had more three-star and four-star generals and admirals than at the height of World War II.[60]

It is no wonder the army had to devise a system of combat-command rotation so that its captains, lieutenant colonels, colonels, and generals could have a go at troop command at one level or another. There were simply too many officers of high rank on active duty.

Mylander indicates that by 1973 there were approximately 2,500 lieutenant colonels competing for command of only one hundred battalions. Army brigades are normally commanded by colonels, and at that time, there were some 75 brigade-equivalent commands and nearly 6,000 colonels, of whom nearly 2,000 were in serious competition for the 75 jobs. And there were some 200 major generals—normally division commanders—although only thirteen such positions existed within the army.[61]

That such a proliferation of rank and commands raised the morale of generals and their staffs cannot be doubted. Many career officers who otherwise would have retired as lieutenant colonels now saw at least the possibility of having stars pinned on their shoulders before it was necessary for them to 'fade away.' There is serious doubt, however, that it raised the morale of anyone else, least of all those faced with combat. Far too few heard shots fired either in anger or earnest; too many held down support jobs of various kinds.

Otis Pike had declaimed that in 1971, "Combat troops comprised only 14 percent of military manpower, compared with 24.1 percent in 1946."[62] If his figures were correct, they would indicate that the army had assigned an incredible 86 percent of its available manpower and effort in Vietnam to noncombat troops and units. One wonders why. The army had an answer.

Within combat-service-support branches, technocrat and bureaucrat officers of high rank insisted that American troops should not be sent to fight in Southeast Asia unless they could be supplied at the same time with many of the "comforts of home." General DeWitt Smith describes that practice as "putting them in a climate where, while dying horrible deaths, we [had] a giant PX importing French perfume and nylons right behind them."[63] Howze speaks of our mistakes in Vietnam, among which "was the practice of providing too many luxuries in base camps, including barracks and clubs. We fought World War II without these and they were not necessary in the soldier's short twelve-month tour in Vietnam. Our base camps became too elaborate, soaked up too much manpower, diverted our attention from the basic mission and lessened our operational flexibility."[64]

If Representative Pike's figures for the year 1971 were even close to the average for other years as well, then the army's record for fielding combat troops was not a sterling one. He had claimed that in 1946 some 24.1% of the army's strength was combat ready. Perhaps, in some years, the army surpassed its own record for 1946 and had 25 percent of its soldiers in combat assignments in Vietnam, our only available war zone.

What that meant in terms of combat capability was that the army assigned some 3,285 soldiers for combat-service-support activities for every 1,000 men in the field. (The Soviets currently allot only 580 men per 1,000 for such activities as distributing "beans, bullets, and band-aids.")[65] In 1968, when the U.S. had 543,000 troops in Vietnam, only some 80,000 combat soldiers were among them. The rest were occupied in supply and service tasks.

The number of support troops needed to keep combat soldiers in fighting shape is known in army parlance as "the tooth-to-tail ratio," and one can see that America's dragon had a monstrous tail and very tiny teeth. The technocrats did not mind, however, for the Vietnam "tooth to tail" balance created a "need" for numerous additional logistical commands, each to be headed by a general or two who would have to have high-ranking staffs to aid each of them. It is no wonder that at one point there were over sixty-four army generals serving simultaneously in the tiny country of Vietnam.

*　　*　　*

It was obvious to any observant GI that even in Vietnam there were many places to be that were safe and that more than three-fourths of their fellows were almost as secure as they would have been in a stateside billet. It took a while, however, before that fact sank in. One man put it this way: "It's difficult to explain this to anyone who wasn't there. When a man arrived he thought at first that he was going to a war. He feared that the airplane he rode in would be shot at as it came in for a landing at Tan Son Nhut, or that as soon as it landed he would be thrust into the heart of a firefight. As men arrived (and I know *I* felt that way), they were quite nervous getting off the plane because they had no steel pots, no weapons, no way to go to war.

"All the time they kept looking over their shoulders and would tense up every time a Vietnamese national would come near them. Many then spent the next two or three days at Long Binh in a processing compound expecting the VC to come climbing over the walls any minute. I sat there in that compound, completely helpless. I had that attitude for several weeks until, one day, I finally realized that the war was a very occasional thing. Ninety percent of the time it was like being on a peacetime assignment in garrison back home. The war itself was a very remote thing occurring only in isolated instances for some troops —caught in an ambush or assigned to search-and-destroy missions, jobs like that. We finally realized that, but it took several weeks.

"Then came our turn. Now we could be amused at new guys still arriving, for, like us, they were expecting to be shot at as they walked off the plane. That was everyone's initial impression, expecting to go into a hostile fire zone, suddenly to be at war, and yet not having it happen. Every morning we'd hear reports of what went on around the area to which we were assigned. Some times it would be quiet, some days there would be heavy activity. Yet for the most part, it didn't touch many of us directly."[66] This statement came from a man assigned to a combat unit. (Infantry, armor, and artillery are the three main combat-arms corps. Engineers make up the fourth.)

If life was generally quiet for an artillery officer, how bucolic must it have been for those in combat-service-support units? Even after assignment as an S-4, a service-battery commander, the artillery officer quoted above, could still escape from the rigors and horrors of war when time permitted.

"My fire base was at Qui Nhon, only some twenty miles from 'Red Beach' on the South China Sea. We could go to the beach and swim whenever we could get away from work. We would put on our steel pots and our flak vests and ride in a jeep with a machine gun on it and drive to the beach. It was a large compound, surrounded by concertina wire, had guards there, and was secure. The guards would have been able to repel most anything that might happen short of an all-out attack, and at the worst, they could give those of us on the beach time to get our clothes and weapons and defend ourselves. No firefight activity I know of ever occurred there.

"Special Services had two motor boats there and plenty of water skis. So we'd turn in our weapons, lock up our machine gun, and go water skiing or swim in the South China Sea, or just lie on the beach and soak in the sun. And when we were done, we'd put our pots and vests back on, jump in our jeep, and drive the twenty miles back to our unit with the possibility of an ambush along the way.

"We knew about several little villages that could give us trouble, that were considered unfriendly. We were aware that we should not stop in them but should go through as fast as possible, so we did. I personally never experienced any trouble in those villages although I learned later that at the province level they were considered to be real hot spots. In a sense, it was like a Sunday afternoon in the United States, the main difference being that back home you fought twenty miles of heavy traffic to get to the beach rather than watching for sudden ambush and death. You see, the war was not a World War II–type activity but in many ways was a farce."[67]

There should be no misunderstanding of the man's meaning. He used "farce" not in the sense of broad humor or exaggerated comedy, but in its equally applicable meaning of something strange, absurd, or ridiculous. For it would be strange to go to war expecting to be plunged directly into the worst of circumstances and instead go swimming off a luxurious beach. One might well feel ridiculous after expecting to encounter an armed enemy at any moment only to have weeks go by with never the sound of a shot fired. There would be a kind of absurdity in preparing for the rigors of war while waiting in line at a PX that stocked French perfume and nylons. Men who were not in Vietnam tended to have the idea that it was equally dangerous no matter where one was. Those who were there knew better.

Army-wise enlisted men learned that even in a combat zone, they could work deals for jobs that would keep them out of harm's way. Anything that would keep them within the confines of the relatively safe fire bases or base camps was cherished.

Officers who wished to do so could also secure safe billets. "If you were an infantry officer and needed command of an outfit, it was easy to get assigned to one that traditionally played the role of a palace guard in Saigon, Da Nang, Tay Ninh, or any of the other base areas—which were, of course, still classified as combat commands. Playing palace guard meant that one generally had troops on the perimeter of that base area with an occasional patrol, as deep as 10 or 15 Ks ["K" was the abbreviation for "click" or kilometer], into the interior. Very seldom did they stay out even overnight. Generally out, search and destroy, and then back within the perimeter. For a commander, that wasn't too dangerous of an assignment."[68]

Those assigned to combat positions—officer and enlisted—saw the bulk of their fellows working at safe jobs in secure locations under relatively comfortable circumstances. Swarming base camps were filled with officers functioning in staff jobs or service-support activities who were never in danger of being sent into combat despite the fact that they served in a "war zone."

Assigned to those same locations were combat forces that would periodically move out to sweep areas for VC or NVA troops and then return to camp. The circular, rather than linear, "front line" had frustrations built into it. "No infantrymen moved forward in waves to capture terrain from a visible enemy and secure it. The infantry didn't advance. The artillery never moved. We neither, for the most part, advanced nor retreated. We just remained in the same area, grinding over the same old things, day after day. Our infantry would go out one day, look through a valley, and come home. The next day or next week, they'd do the same thing again. They were in danger on the move to contact and during contact and withdrawal. They were quite safe while back in their base camps."[69]

Such men were the ones who suffered the casualties. After spending a week on an area sweep, sodden from rain, filthy from the muck through which they had straggled, constantly alert to a point far beyond exhaustion from fear of ambush, continually exposed to the danger of injury or death, a unit would limp back to base camp. Returning, they encountered soldiers of all ranks—enlisted men, noncommissioned officers, warrants, and officers—wearing clean clothes and smelling of after-shave lotion, men who were secure in mind and body from the dangers of war.

It was easy for combat troopers to see that a large number of army officers and enlisted men were free from the hazards of combat. Morale plummeted as they asked themselves why they should have to risk life and limb repeatedly while others did not face any particular sacrifice.

Every war has had, necessarily, men working in support activities, far from danger in rear-echelon assignments. And it has been human nature for such individuals to secure for themselves the best equipment and the latest-issue clothing and to "style around" trying to project an image of being experienced and seasoned combat soldiers. During World War II, such men were dismissed by those at the front as "reppledepple commandoes."[70] The saving grace, if any, in earlier conflicts was that such commandoes were far from the front and thus out of sight of those forced to bear the brunt of fighting. They knew they were there —the generals and their staffs, the truckers, the warehouse clerks, the

supply sergeants, the PIO officers, the first lieutenant in charge of personnel records, the finance clerks—but at least it was a case of "out of
sight, out of mind." There was no constant reminder that some men
during wartime are privileged while others are burdened with tasks
fraught with danger.

In the circular warfare in Vietnam, such people were all too visible
too much of the time to combat troops who were unable to share in the
easy lives of the "base-camp commandoes." It is little wonder that
resentment against them set in among combat troopers.

Some chose another route to escape either combat or other onerous
tasks to which they had been assigned. In 1967, throughout the army,
27,000 soldiers deserted their units. By 1968 the number had increased
to 39,234. The figures for 1969 totaled 56,608, while 65,643 deserted
during 1970.[71] These numbers do not include the additional thousands
who went AWOL but who returned before they were reclassified as
deserters. LBJ—Long Binh Jail—was full of those who had been caught.
Nor do they take into account those who chose the route of malingering
—repeatedly going on sick call with pretended illnesses in attempts to
avoid duty.

Morale among combat troopers sank even lower when they
learned of the extent to which corruption permeated all ranks within
the army. Former Deputy Chief of Staff for Personnel and Administration of the Army in Vietnam Brigadier General Earl Cole was questioned about his knowledge of irregularities in the operations of enlisted
men's and noncommissioned officers' clubs (where slot machines alone
raised some $27 million annually). Major General Carl C. Turner, for-
mer provost marshal general of the army, was indicted by a federal
grand jury for obtaining guns under false pretenses. He was sentenced
to three years in prison. A former staff judge advocate for Vietnam
admitted to having accepted illegal favors.

A protégé of Lieutenant General William Depuy, Sergeant Major
of the Army William O. Wooldridge, was accused of taking illicit profits
from the military noncommissioned-officer-club system, of threatening
an officer with physical violence, and of using General Creighton
Abrams's personal airplane to carry crates of whiskey in and out of
Vietnam. Four other sergeants were indicted along with Wooldridge,
including Master Sergeant William W. Higdon, manager of one of
'Nam's largest club systems. Higdon received a dishonorable discharge
and a $25,000 fine. Throughout the "sergeants" scandal,' there were
revelations of widespread bribes, kickbacks, irregularities, extortion,
and negligence of duty at many levels of rank.

Brigadier General John W. Donaldson, commander of the Americal
Division's 11th Brigade, was accused (and cleared) of hunting down
civilians from his command-and-control chopper. Major General Samuel Koster, commander of that division, was accused of covering up the

evidence on My Lai, reduced in rank, and soon retired.

If such men, who had done well in the armed services and who had gained honor and prestige in the service of their nation, did not feel bound by such constraints as honesty or honor, if some could use the military for personal profit, why should an enlisted man drafted for two years feel it necessary to sacrifice life or limb for his country?

The war was torture for those who fought it, yet they saw others using that conflict for personal gain. They saw American contractors enriching themselves through multimillion-dollar building projects. Everyone seemed hell-bent to squirrel away tailored suits while on R and R in Hong Kong, to manipulate currency, to deal in whiskey trades, to hoard a little gold or a few diamonds. They saw themselves ripped off in their own clubs by their own superiors. They were often forced to live in flimsy tents and ramshackle quarters while their more fortunate noncombat brethren were housed in concrete-block, air-conditioned buildings. They swatted mosquitoes and despised the leeches they pulled from their crotches while others picked up fresh laundry from government-provided base facilities.

They never really met any Vietnamese but saw only merchants and bar girls, "artificial people" responding to the American presence: sidewalk businessmen greedy for their scrip, and bar girls in low-cut costumes and lace stockings who would promise anything for a price. The only other Vietnamese they saw were silent, wide-eyed villagers through whose streets they moved during missions. They knew of cynical ARVN and GVN officials willing to barter their own birthrights for a mess of dollars or piasters.

If the great and near-great were questionable, the not great at all were easily despised by combat troopers, particularly if they came to believe that an officer was using them to promote his own career. They had little use for the officer who wanted to make his mark in the short time available to him and in order to do so was willing to cut corners with the safety and well-being of his men.

One of the best young NCOs I have known recalled for me his days in Vietnam, where he served as a radio operator with the Special Forces. "I have probably the average enlisted man's disdain for some of our officer 'leaders.' Too often they made decisions when simply not aware of what was involved—they hadn't been there long enough or were too stupid to know better—yet they had the power to enforce their decisions no matter what it cost those who had to carry them out.

"I am vindicated in my personal hatred of one such officer because he was finally removed by our colonel as an incompetent. I could go on forever about him. One time he put on a .45 automatic in a quick-draw holster and in a room full of men shot three rounds through the top of our team house trying to impress us with his speed. You can bet your ass he impressed us. He got up at ten in the morning; I got up at five.

He held team meetings at 1800 hours to find out what we'd done all day. If he had really been interested, he could have gotten off his dead ass and walked around to find out. He was a coward. He went to 'Nam as a captain; he had to have command time. They gave him the unit I was in. He had no desire whatsoever to be there, never knew what was going on, did no work while he was there, but he had to have command. He was so incompetent that even his making captain could only be attributed to inflated OERs of the Vietnam era."[72] The behavior of such officers was openly destructive of morale, helping to create a rising tide of resentment among those they commanded.

Grunts saw very few officers sharing their dangers with them. Many of those were second and first lieutenants who often were ex-enlisted men who had gone to OCS for a commission, or they were ex-college men who had stayed out of the service for as long as possible through the aegis of ROTC. Such men were young and shared many perceptions with their own enlisted men. They tended to be scared and inexperienced. Many were as fervently devoted as were their grunts in marking off one more day on their calendars. They had no plans for a military career; they simply wanted to put in their time and get out of the army.

These same things held true for younger captains. These were the ones who bore the brunt of combat. Senior captains, majors, and above were more likely to be career-oriented "lifers," doing their fighting from their "eye in the sky" command and control helicopters. From 2,000 feet up they could direct their units in relative safety, rather than having their "ass in the grass" with their troops.

A Vietnam-era sergeant tells how it felt to be there on the ground. "I had great respect for the American grunt, even though many of were junkies, potheads, incredibly lazy, and didn't care. The ordinary, average run-of-the-mill grunt, in a situation where he had no option except to function, would do so to the best of his ability. He was a very functional person, a good individual, capable of making very rational decisions.

"And if some officer, sitting 1,000 feet above him in a helicopter, told him to charge, and if he knew he was going to get wasted if he followed orders, he wouldn't go. He would say, 'I'm sorry, but that's dumb. We won't do it.' Such air operations didn't really cut it. Those up there had to rely on their radios to know what was going on down on the ground. Over those sets commanders heard a great deal of erroneous information, outright lies, mistakes, and panic. I'm not sure I would want to make tactical decisions based upon all that stuff coming over a set while I was that high in the air, but it never seemed to bother too many officers."[73]

More and more American troops, and even their junior-level officers, when sent out on a patrol or sweep or search-and-destroy or clearing mission, came to turn their duties into the sort of thing for which they had laughed at ARVN soldiers on earlier occasions. They developed their own search-and-avoid tactics. They would leave a base camp, strike off into the jungle, find a secure area, and hole up for the duration of the time allotted for their mission. After establishing their own perimeter-defense security, the rest of the men would sleep, write letters, smoke (some even used cigarettes), eat their rations, and wait for the hours to tick away. At the appropriate point, they would pack up and return to base. Some groups even took enemy weapons with them when they went out on such search-and-avoid missions so that upon their return they could report a firefight and demonstrate evidence of enemy casualties for the body-count figures required by higher headquarters.

Even though there were always a few younger officers upon whom grunts could rely, they tended to distrust and detest most of the officers they encountered. The difference between the life of the combat soldier and the safe, pleasant lives of many officers they saw made an unfortunate contrast. And there seemed always to be many officers everywhere. There were.

During World War II the percentage of officers to troops had been 7 percent, or a ratio of roughly one to fourteen. By the time of Korea, officers of the American army comprised 9 percent of the force, or about one in eleven. During the Vietnam era the percentage increased to 15 percent, so that there was one officer for every six-plus enlisted men.[74] As there came to be greater numbers of officers, however, they projected an image to their troops that fewer of them stood in any danger of death. It is little wonder that grunts began to ask why *they* should run risks when their own officers so seldom had to do so.

Statistics seemed to bear out the GIs' suspicions. In a decade of battle, only four generals died in Vietnam. Only one of those, Brigadier General William Bond, was killed by hostile fire, when he was caught by a sniper's round. Three others died during bad weather in helicopter crashes. Only eight full colonels died from enemy fire. It was clear that the more rank a soldier held, the less likely it was that anything would happen to him. Gabriel and Savage stated the problem clearly: "In Vietnam the record is absolutely clear on this point: the officer corps simply did not die in sufficient numbers or in the presence of their men often enough."[75] Seeing few casualties among their own officers, grunts perceived that they were led by men who lacked dedication.

Low morale among American soldiers in Vietnam quickly expressed itself in several ways. Drug usage rose to epidemic proportions. The AWOL and desertion rate skyrocketed. Race riots became an army-wide scandal. The word "fragging" had to be coined to describe attacks by GIs on their own officers and noncommissioned officers.[76] The air force and the navy had to contend with "fodding," that is, foreign-object damage, to highly technical and complicated machinery. Mutiny became so common that the army was forced to disguise its frequency by talking instead of "combat refusals." Officers left the system in droves as soon as they had fulfilled their legal obligations to the army. Draftees bragged that they would "rather throw up than re-up." Lifer and draftee alike became fixated on their own DEROS (Date Estimated Return from Overseas).

The army's explanation for all this was simply that it was faced with the same problems as was the civilian sector; it was a mirror of society as a whole. Its soldiers were drawn from all social strata within the United States. It was a difficult time for the nation, overwhelmed by internal disorder. Consequently, many of the same problems were bound to surface within the military. "A high desertion rate might be explainable, perhaps even a mutiny or two. But when desertion, fragging, mutiny, and drug addiction converge toward something of a sociopathological riptide effect in a period as short as four or five years, explanations based on references to permissive societies and national 'fragmentation' due to unpopular wars simply are not credible."[77]

Credible or not, it was a frequent army explanation of its ills and one that still surfaces from time to time. Not particularly given to instrospection and usually unwilling to admit publicly to any significant failings, the army has fallen back on the description of itself as a mirror of society rather than face the fact that it was beset with serious problems of its own making. Those pressures literally caused the army to disintegrate during the Vietnam War under minimal-stress combat conditions. Fortunately, a few officers are willing to face such unpleasant facts.

One administrator at the Army War College admitted that "the army has been ducking its responsibilities. . . . I think that because of Vietnam, our longest and most traumatic war, and one we can truly say we lost, we've got to look inside—not for scapegoats, not for witch hunts, but in an objective, responsible way, without biases."[78] His strategic location in the army's ultimate school does not, however, insure that any real introspection will ever occur. "I've been around a long time and I've only got a year to go before I retire." He is only a colonel rather than a general. Even the best-intentioned colonels often have a difficult time insuring that they are heard by generals. There still remains much truth in the adage "Generals propose, colonels dispose."[79]

There were still other factors during the Vietnam era that were indications that all was not well within the army. One of the more important signs was the strange rotation policy ordered by Westmoreland. It was the cause of much destruction in unit cohesion and brought about a lack of trust up and down the ladder of command. It also became a further indication to GIs that officers were more interested in pursuing their own careers than in being good commanders and watching out for the welfare of their men.

In the early stages of American involvement in Vietnam, Westmoreland was faced with an officer corps a large part of which had never been "blooded" in combat. Convinced that the American expeditionary force would not be needed very long, Westmoreland set command tours at six months. This would afford many officers the chance to command a unit in combat and would add to the pool of experienced men available within the army.

As it worked out, commanders often held their positions for far less than six months. Such factors as relief, promotion, death, or injury regularly occasioned command replacement more frequently than every six months.[80] Units saw officers come through almost as if they were riding a merry-go-round, and the policy came to be known as the "revolving door" approach to command.

Its effect on units and men was disastrous, for it hurt morale, eroded discipline, and gave officers little opportunity to develop the qualities of leadership so desperately needed in Vietnam. Personnel "turbulence," that is, the turnover in units caused by such rotation, became so great that Westmoreland and the Department of the Army had to disguise the original reason for adopting the six-month policy if it was to be continued in the face of criticism both within and without the military.

Now it was defended on the basis of the tension in which a commander constantly worked, which caused him to "burn out" after but a short time, about six months, in his assignment.[81] Responsibilities were too great, hazards were too dangerous, pressures were too high for a man to continue indefinitely in command. Were he to remain, he might well crumble psychologically in the face of it all. In this way, the earlier decision continued to be defended by military managers as they held to an unwise policy laid down by the febrile Westmoreland.

In 1976, at the army's Command and General Staff College, two students surveyed a sampling of their fellows to determine how many Vietnam-era officers believed the six-month tour to have been necessary to save commanders from "burn-out." The respondents had Vietnam experience at command levels and by 1976 were predominantly majors, sprinkled with a few early promotions to lieutenant colonel. "Interestingly enough, the majority of respondents felt that officers did not 'burn out' after approximately six months in command and that frequent changes did have an adverse effect on morale and discipline. If this was so, why then did we remove such officers from their command position? It certainly lends credence to the argument that we simply played the six month game; six months in command and six months in staff duty."

Some 61 percent disagreed with the "burn-out" theory while only 8 percent were willing to subscribe to it. The authors of that survey noted that "the major deterrent to true professionalism was that an officer did not stay in the same job in the same place long enough to become knowledgeable in the specifics of their situation."[82]

Nor was the *Study on Military Professionalism* silent on the ill effects of the short tour. "A number of officers commented on the staff officer, or the officer from the Pentagon, who has spent years away from troops, getting his ticket punched by getting a command assignment for six months, and on his young staff officer trying to keep him out of trouble and to educate him. By the time they have accomplished it either they were moving on or a new commander was coming in and then they had to go over the same routine again." Elsewhere in the *Study* is the comment that "I think overall that [many officers who served in Vietnam still] have a feeling that they got battalion commanders that they didn't think should even wear the uniform let alone be battalion commanders." One major was quoted in the *Study* as saying that "the short periods of command enhance passing the buck, by a commander, for failures of the unit."[83]

Those feelings, expressed in 1970, seem not to have dimmed with the passage of years. Gabriel and Savage describe the policy of six-month-command tours as "brutally disruptive," particularly at the crucial squad, platoon, and company levels.[84] Since most combat soldiers seldom see their battalion commander and in many cases do not even know who he is, changes at that level were more destructive upon the officers of the units within a battalion than upon common soldiers.

It is at the small-unit (company and below) levels that combat troops have most contact with officers. In military jargon that is where "the rubber meets the road." One of the enlisted men interviewed during preparation of this work recalled bitterly that "at least we were assigned to a unit long enough to know the other guys and how to work with them—who we could rely on and who we had to watch out for. The NCOs in my outfit had their heads together and knew what they were doing. Yet we suffered from a series of inexperienced officers being assigned to us. During my year in-country I had *five* second-lieutenant platoon leaders and *four* company commanders. One CO was pretty good. He had been in 'Nam once before. All the rest were stupid, knew absolutely nothing about what they were supposed to do. We were more experienced than any of them. Yet they acted like little gods. Wanted to do things differently than the guys they replaced no matter whether their ideas were any good or not. And, of course, if you argued with them they'd threaten to write you up on an Article 15, and if you tried to refuse to do what they ordered you'd find yourself in LBJ."[85]

No matter how offensive to common sense or dangerous to life and limb the orders of such young and inexperienced officers might be to their men, the troopers were still supposed "to move out smartly" and carry out all orders in their entirety—"the whole nine yards." Arguments, insubordination, or refusals only brought a man face to face with the UCMJ—the Uniform Code of Military Justice.[86] Yet the men in the ranks were right to feel bitterness over the rapid-rotation policy. Not only did it contradict all the principles of leadership taught by the army in its schools, but it also made it almost impossible for the army to build units that had a sense of *esprit de corps,* with high morale, real personal identity with the institution, and a ready sense of men as comrades in arms who had trained, worked, and fought together.

During Vietnam, the military managers of the army forced the officer corps to turn its back on the need for continuity and experience in combat-command leadership. "Westmoreland couldn't have found a better way, if he had tried, of guaranteeing that our troops would be led by a bunch of amateurs, than to yank officers out of command every six months."[87] Lieutenant Colonel David Holmes agreed. Writing in *Military Review*, he stated that "extended practical experience and rapport . . . is required to develop an understanding [of what is going on], to maintain the quality of leadership required . . . and to acquire the particular . . . tactical skills. . . . The short-tour policy, which often produced commands as brief as six months, undoubtedly contributed to the instances of mutiny, corruption, drug abuse and fragging. It also probably reinforced the ticket punching careerist syndrome still visible in today's officer corps."[88]

John Paul Vann, an early critic of the military approach in Vietnam, and one who was later killed there, likened the army's rotation policy to one that would forever keep America innocent of the realities of Indochina. The United States, he said, had not been in Vietnam for nine years, but for one year nine times. It was a recipe for disaster, not only because it precluded creation of institutional experience from which the army might benefit, but because of its debilitating effect on the officer corps and upon combat soldiers.

Those soldiers were required to serve twelve-month tours while others with more rank could get by with only six months of danger. "Why should I have had to serve twelve months when someone else, not one whit better than me, could get out in half that time?"[89] Soldier after soldier interviewed for this study believed that their duties in combat were far more difficult and onerous than were those of officers, particularly those who commanded at levels higher than company-sized units. Whether or not it was actually more difficult is immaterial; GIs perceived it to be so and for them that was reality.

Many officers were not without sympathy for the position of enlisted men. In the Daxe-Stemberger survey at Fort Leavenworth in 1976, 45 percent of those they questioned subscribed to the statement that "it was unethical for enlisted troops to have to spend twelve months in combat while many officers spent only six months in combat."[90] The army's "Green Machine" moved on its course throughout the Vietnam conflict, heedless of its critics.

*   *   *

Another indication that the Vietnam-era army had difficulties can be seen in its willingness to present awards and decorations to men for doing no more than what they were being paid to do. Presentation of awards for routine activities became so prevalent that the recipients began sneeringly referring to them as "gongs." By early February 1971, the American army in Vietnam had given out a total of 1,273,987 medals for bravery.[91] How many more were given out there prior to the army's withdrawal is not known.[92] By contrast, during the conflict in Korea, only 50,258 medals were awarded, and in all of World War II only 1,766,546 were presented, at a time when there were nearly ten million men under arms.

As the war drew to a close the number of medals awarded skyrocketed. Decorations of all kinds in 1968 totaled 416,693. That year 14,592 soldiers of the U.S. Army died in combat. Two years later, in 1970, when only 3,946 combat deaths were recorded, the number of awards handed out was almost 523,000.[93]

Almost every man who served in Vietnam received an award of one kind or another. It came to the point where medals were issued almost automatically. Army regulations provide strict guidance on qualifications for awards and decorations. They were ignored. Many army units had individuals permanently assigned to the task of writing up citations on individuals so that they could be presented with decorations.

Units even competed with one another to see which could achieve the greatest number of awards. One general, Julian J. Ewell, "the Delta Butcher," kept track of awards received by men of his 9th Division to determine whether they were braver this month than last. It is not surprising that in the eyes of its men, army awards—including even the once coveted Combat Infantryman's Badge—came to have little value.

In this as in many other things, the military brass made invidious distinctions between officers and enlisted men. Enlisted men received an Army Commendation Medal for simply having served in 'Nam; junior officers received the Bronze Star. It was regarded as lèse majesté for an enlisted man to wear a Bronze Star unless he had greatly distinguished himself, for that "gong" was an officer award.

It is routine today to see officers, now captains or majors, who served in Vietnam wearing a Bronze Star. If they experienced any extended amount of combat, they wear it with a "V" device—for valor —affixed. Higher up the ladder of rank were the lieutenant colonels and full bulls. It was common for them to be rewarded for Vietnam service with a Bronze Star, an Air Medal, and very often a Silver Star. If they also served in a staff job, as most did, they received additionally an Army Commendation Medal and a Joint Services Commendation Medal.

Generals received still higher awards for the time they spent in Vietnam: Silver Stars, Distinguished Flying Crosses, Bronze Stars for Valor, and Distinguished Service Medals. The latter was often referred to as "the generals' Good Conduct Medal." Such awards often were handed out for a second or third time as a general moved from one assignment to the next. Those who served in 'Nam came to call such awards "package A" and "package B."

One Vietnam veteran, a chaplain, had this to say about awards. "It's an interesting thing about hero medals. With a chest full of them and twenty-one cents you can get a cup of coffee. But when a man doesn't have them, then it's a different story, for he envies those who do and acquisition of them becomes very important. If I had been a general officer in Vietnam, I would have been sort of dubious about the way they proliferated, but there is a mentality in the army that allows for it. At base it's an ethical problem."[94]

He went on to describe the lowering of standards in awarding of medals and the real competition at various levels of rank to secure such "gongs." "A lot depended on the individual. I had one commander who wanted to get a medal for giving a pint of blood. He was hard-core! And," he said, "think of Air Medals."

The Air Medal was once a respected award, signifying that an individual had performed extremely hazardous service as a member of an air crew. Very occasionally a man might wear not only the medal itself but one—and very rarely—two Oak Leaf Clusters (today called "rat turds") affixed to it, signifying an additional award of the Air Medal for each cluster on it. Of the 1,273,987 awards for bravery referred to above, roughly 800,000 of them were Air Medals. They were handed out so often they came to be perhaps the least respected of the various Vietnam-era decorations. So frequently did individuals receive additional awards of the Air Medal that the army had to substitute numerical devices for Oak Leaf Clusters. Men laughed about receiving their "twenty-seventh Air Medal," a bit of hyperbole that pointed out the commonplace nature of the decoration. It was awarded for the accumulation of a preset number of flights within a combat zone, and to anyone —not just to aircrewmen—who could verify that he had amassed the requisite number. Since Vietnam was a war zone, nearly any flight, no matter how routine or mundane, counted toward the total.

"Think of Air Medals," the chaplain said. "A guy goes up for a five-minute flight in a perfectly peaceful area, and that counted toward an Air Medal. He does everything he can so he can get up in the air and get another Air Medal. It was easy and it was cheap. It was a kind of war-type mentality in Vietnam where some acted as if it was a play war —but elsewhere people were dying."

Another man continued the theme of "play war." An artillery officer, whose first tour in Vietnam ran from March 1968 to late June 1970 and who returned in March 1971 for another year's service, recalled that "at the time I was there the main thing for an officer was to have as many ribbons on his chest as he could by the time the war ended. He never knew when another chance might come, so he tried to get while the getting was good."[95] If such ambitions were banal for junior officers, they were pathetic in more senior ranks.

"The really inappropriate stuff was where a lot of high-ranking officers got hero medals for dipping their helicopters down toward the ground so they could shoot out the window at someone they thought might be VC."[96] At least those individuals had the fortitude to dip their choppers. Others received Silver Stars, Distinguished Flying Crosses, or Distinguished Service Medals for "valorous acts" performed while they hovered two thousand feet above the action. It is no wonder that one major could say: "The only current decorations I admire are the Distinguished Service Cross and the Medal of Honor. All others are tainted by too often being awarded to people who do not deserve them."[97]

He knew what he was talking about. King writes that during 1969, fifty-seven generals returned on rotation from Vietnam.[98] Twenty-six of them—nearly half—came back wearing an award for valor, and not just the Bronze Star with "V" device, but Silver Stars and Distinguished Flying Crosses. Given the nature of their duties, the locations in which they performed them, and the minuscule number of wounds or deaths suffered by generals, it is incomprehensible that in one year 50 percent of the generals in Vietnam could perform acts of valor.

In reality, they wore those decorations for the most commonplace of acts, deeds that if done by lower-ranking men would not even have merited a comment in an officer-efficiency report. Hauser tells of a full colonel who was awarded a Silver Star for flying frozen Thanksgiving turkeys into a "besieged" Special Forces camp.[99]

In such ways could men who had never actually seen battle return from the wars festooned with brightly colored bits of cloth above their left pockets. Sporting them ostentatiously, if not proudly, they could impress the uninitiated (there were still a few around). Nor did there seem to be much rhythm in the award of medals. Hauser tells of one captain who received a Bronze Star for meritorious achievement for the same period of time in which he had received an unsatisfactory rating on his officer-efficiency report.[100] Perhaps such anomalies were simply a case of the right hand not knowing what the left was doing.

One high-ranking officer, however, knew precisely where both his hands were at all times. He was Brigadier General Eugene P. Forrester, for a time the assistant division commander (ADC) of the 1st Cavalry Division. At a ceremony marking his departure for a new assignment he was presented with a Silver Star, always awarded for bravery in combat. He stood there at the ceremony and listened to the citation being read, which detailed the actions he had done that merited award of America's third-highest decoration (only the Distinguished Service Cross and the Medal of Honor outrank it).

One can only wonder what Forrester must have thought as he heard the words of the citation read to those assembled for the ceremony. Surely it must have crossed his mind that he had not done the things being attributed to him. It would be nice to think that some men would have interrupted the ceremony and apologized that an obvious mistake had been made, that awarding the ribbon would be incorrect. Forrester did not do so. He accepted and wore the decoration.

Three enlisted clerks in the division's awards department later contacted a United States congressman, charging that they had been ordered by Major (later Colonel) George E. Newman, the unit's assistant adjutant general, to write up a false citation so that Forrester might be duly honored upon his departure. They did so using words and phrases borrowed from an earlier citation written for another general. Their efforts were then validated by junior officers who certified that they had been eyewitnesses to the general's actions. Making such certifications could only have contributed to the corrupting of those young officers.

Faced with this disclosure the army had no choice but to strip Forrester of his unearned Silver Star. The division's chief of staff defended what had been done, however, because Forrester had a reputation for bravery, so the award of the Silver Star was a fitting one. He branded the men who had "blown the whistle" as "sanctimonious." A later army investigation concluded that Forrester himself was blameless, that he had had no part in securing the award; and in 1972, he was selected to be elevated to major general by an army promotion board.[101]

Given such procedures it is no wonder that high-ranking officers were regularly cited for combat bravery while only something like one-tenth of the enlisted men who saw service in Vietnam received similar awards. It is indisputable that such methods cheapened the whole awards system to the point that entire battalions, including cooks, were assembled in formation so that everyone there might receive the Bronze Star.[102] Nor is it surprising that one who was there could remember how "giving of medals became so commonplace that the names of those to get them sometimes even came out on unit rosters."[103]

The cure for such proliferation of meaningless and even fraudulent awards must come from the top. If such "gongs" did not weigh so heavily in promotion, and if there was a rigid and workable code for controlling and reviewing them, it would not happen. The cheapening of awards during the Vietnam era became so prevalent that perhaps the

army should scrap all existing awards and think up new ones for present
and future use and make them damned hard to come by.

*   *   *

In the Daxe and Stemberger report, many of the students at the
Command and General Staff College spoke their minds freely. One
army officer charged that "generalship of the Vietnam War era must be
considered the dark ages in the army's history." Another concluded
that "opportunism appeared to be the accepted rule," while a major
asserted that "the professional officer went into the war to get what he
could out of it," and another man reported that "many of us (me included) used the war as a vehicle for enjoying the only war we had."

Elsewhere in the pages of that report, someone stated that "it was
the opportunity for everyone to do well and enhance promotion—
particularly 0–6s and 0–7s." A colleague agreed, suggesting that "the
0–6 level seemed to have the most careerists and fewest professionals."
There was an ethical quality to it all, one officer believed, for "ethical
conduct must be put into practice by all levels of command and staff;
not just verbalized." Junior officers, in many ways, were more responsible than senior commanders, for "the closer you were to actual combat
the less concerned you were with your career." One man summed it
up well. "The heart of many of our problems of leadership, integrity,
and professionalism is quite simply that . . . we lowered our standards
and deserved the mess we wound up with."[104]

It hurt. "The U.S. Army was in bad—in horrible—shape in '73. My
God, man, it was almost unusable because of the Vietnamese experience. You had a fantastic breakdown in cohesion; discipline was absolutely shot; there were internal doubts, self-doubts, doubts about the
guy next to you. We didn't have a unit in the U.S. Army in '73 that really
was usable at all in my view, except perhaps for technical units."[105] So
spoke an analyst at Fort Leavenworth's Command and General Staff
College who had spent years thinking about the problems that beset the
army during the Vietnam era.

Official spokesmen for the military managers have denied much of
this, or blamed the results on factors over which the army had no
control. They have redefined the situation so that loss became victory.
"Let me tell you the war was *won*, and then the government made a
political decision to withdraw and leave it for the Vietnamese. By 1969,
the land was as close to being pacified as anyone could have desired.
Everything the French failed to do in Vietnam, we did. People who
weren't there can't imagine the strength of U.S. forces. Immense. More
airplanes, God knows, in our weakest corps area than the French had
in all Indochina. We *won* the war."[106]

Perhaps that is one way to look at what occurred. More often,
however, the generals have admitted that the army suffered a "set-

back" in Vietnam but have then gone on to blame it on the government or society. "Impossible to fight with imposed constraints." "Too much civilian interference and restraints." "The reason we failed was too much civilian interference in military matters—too many constraints. We were in essence handcuffed and not allowed to win."[107] Or "Social changes at home hampered the war more than anything else."[108]

None of it will wash. Enough has been said in this study to demonstrate that it was the army's own approach in Vietnam and the milieu it created for itself there that were responsible for the Vietnam debacle, rather than outside forces working against its success. These were the things that hamstrung it, hastened its professional decay, and brought it to the knife edge of disaster.

It is not enough to suggest, as General Fred Weyand has done, that the entire approach and effort were impossible. He has written, "How do we get democracy in Vietnam? Declare a Magna Carta and wait seven hundred years."[109] That is admittedly clever, but irrelevant. If the cause was hopeless, then he—and others before him—should have clearly pointed that fact out to the American government and then resigned in protest if the president decided to go ahead despite such advice. Nothing of the sort was done.

Look at the "laundry list" of problems that beset the army in Vietnam. It was a climate of misinformation and deceit, of scheming, of disintegration and decay of officer professionalism, of internal doubts and disorder, of misused officer-efficiency reports, of faltering trust of superiors toward their subordinates and suspicion of higher-ranking officers by those below them. It was a time of safety for some contrasted with danger for others, of drugs and desertions and fraggings and combat refusals. Ticket-punching procedures, zero defects, and a "can do" spirit became more important than duty and honor.

There were repple-depple commandoes and corruption and profiteering. One set of rules covered those of high rank while a completely different set held for junior officers. Deliberate deceptions and misleading statistics and attempted cover-ups became commonplace and ordinary. Those without power served twelve months in combat units while the privileged were moved to safety after only six. Those in command demonstrated repeated and flagrant disregard for regulations while awarding themselves and almost everyone else with colored bits of cloth. "All this was, to boil it down to the simplest part, dumb and self-defeating."[110]

Our options are few. We can ignore what happened then and hope that it has gone away by now. We can recognize that there are grave deficiencies within the army but learn to live with them unexamined. We can face the troubles that arose then, identify and catalog them, and improve on the military system in order to minimize the possibility that in the next conflict they will once more paralyze our force structure. We cannot afford to choose the first three, for to do so risks our very national survival.

Despite opportunities to do so, there is precious little evidence that the army has seriously considered the last option. This was predicted. The *Study on Military Professionalism* warned that

> measures can and must be found to ensure that a climate of professionalism exists in the army. The attainment of such a climate is the essential prerequisite for genuine effectiveness. . . . There was no significant evidence that contemporary sociological pressures—which are everpresent—were primary causes of the differences between the ideal and the actual professional climate in the army; the problems are for the most part internally generated; they will not vanish automatically as the war in Vietnam winds down and the size of the army decreases. . . . The present climate is not self-correcting, and because of the nature and extent of the problem, changes must be credibly instituted and enforced by the army's top leadership. Correcting the climate will require more than superficial, transitory measures. The climate cannot be corrected by admonitions.
>
> Concrete modification of the systems of reward and punishment to support adherence to the time-honored principles of an army officer is required.[111]

The *Study* further insisted that "corrective measures must be so clearly stated that they cannot be misinterpreted. . . ."[112] No corrective measures of any significant nature were instituted or enforced by the army's top leadership. No clarion call for reform came. The problems of Vietnam, to one degree or another, remain to plague today's army. That is the "whole nine yards," the entire "ball of wax," "the bottom line."

Six

Emery Upton, a strikingly gifted military man, graduated from West Point in 1861. A month later he was plunged into the fury of the Civil War in action at Bull Run. Throughout the war, he displayed incredible gallantry and courage, an uncommon concern for his men, sharp intelligence, and a willingness to try tactical innovation. When the war ended, he was twenty-six years old and a brevet major general.

In the years that followed, Upton became increasingly hostile to civilian supremacy over the military and toward democracy itself. General William ("Uncle Billy") Tecumseh Sherman, commanding general of the army, assigned Upton as commandant of cadets at West Point and later sent him on a trip around the world to seek out military lessons from other nations. Upton's travels convinced him of the supremacy of the Prussian military system and of its independent position within that society. In his most important book, *A Military Policy for the United States,* published posthumuously in 1904, he condemned America's government for its ineffectual military policies, and for the fact that most lawmakers were abysmally ignorant of military affairs.

Since that time, the term used to designate moods within the army that might possibly lead to military takeover has been Uptonianism or Neo-Uptonianism. There was some talk about such an eventuality toward the end of the Vietnam conflict. In an uncommonly good essay, Lieutenant Colonel John H. Moellering, a Corps of Engineering student at Ft. Leavenworth, studied the disenchanted army officer corps to determine the extent of Neo-Uptonianism within it. Although he found alienation and inward turning, he concluded there was little basis for fears that the army might become a political threat to America's democratic institutions.[1]

Another author, Michael T. Klare, in 1972, published *War without End: American Planning for the Next Vietnams.*[2] Klare was concerned that current military planning threatened to keep the United States involved in a succession of Vietnams. He charged that beginning with President Kennedy's globalistic policies, a new and covertly imperialistic ideology shaped the future of the army's planning, preparing it technically and tactically to interfere again and again in counterinsurgent efforts around the world. Whether or not Klare is correct, it has been demonstrated earlier in this study that the military brass has phased out most of its counterinsurgency training hours[3] and has refocused on the European plains as the preferred area in which it wishes to prepare to fight. In short, the Vietnam experience has been put out of mind.

Such a result is unfortunate but makes it improbable that the army will search for a cure for the illnesses that weakened its performance during Vietnam and that still, like some cancers, grow quietly within its structure. The Army War College *Study on Military Professionalism* called for official action.

> The strong desire expressed almost unanimously by officers to make the operative system more nearly perfect represents a healthy reservoir of energetic idealism. But the individual officer is greatly hampered in any local crusade for adherence to ideal methods by the need to produce results in order to remain competitive for future advancement. Change, therefore, must be instituted from the top of the Army. Admonition is not enough.[4]

It recommended prompt dissemination of the findings of the *Study,* the addition of a course in professional ethics to service-school curricula, and removal from combat-arms officers of the requirement that they must command both at battalion and brigade levels as well as serve on staffs if they were to move up to high rank, taking immediate disciplinary action against officers who violated ethical standards. Other recommendations were included as well.[5]

As earlier noted, the reaction of Westmoreland as chief of staff was to slap a security classification on the *Study,* restricting its circulation to other generals. At a time when the army was in near collapse from many factors pinpointed by the *Study,* nothing positive was undertaken. That first detailed study of army morals, morale, and values disappeared into limbo. Career-management pressures endure that would limit the effectiveness of the army should it again face combat.

Because the *Study* had surveyed only 450 officers (a cross-section of students and faculty drawn from the Army Chaplains School; advanced courses at Forts Benning, Eustis, Knox, and Sill; the Command and General Staff College at Fort Leavenworth; and the 1970 class at the Army War College and certain of its faculty),[6] the Army War College turned its attention again to the same topic the following year. Would the same findings hold true if a larger data base were used? The new survey used 1,800 persons: 721 enlisted men, 46 generals and 874 other officers, 100 West Point cadets, and 43 civilians working for the Department of the Army. Seventeen military bases were involved. The final product, completed in October 1971, was issued under the title *Comprehensive Report: Leadership for the 1970s, USAWC Study of Leadership for the Professional Soldier.*[7]

Once again, as in the earlier *Study,* there were findings that pointed to the existence of real difficulties: transitory commanders, ambitious officers who sacrificed the welfare of their men to further their own careers, entrenched individuals owning but marginal skills, a continuing concern over zero defects and "can do" attitudes, superiors fearing failure willing to blame mistakes on subordinates, leaders unwilling or unable to talk with or listen to subordinates.[8] Obviously no improvement had occurred in the year since the original *Study* had been issued.

Both documents have remained relegated to obscurity in the years since their publication. The *Study* has since been declassified, and the *Comprehensive Report* never bore a security classification, yet neither has been widely examined nor even made generally available to civilian scholars or concerned military officers.

* * *

Many older military professionals—those who have climbed to senior colonel or into the ranks of general—still insist that the army lost Vietnam because outside forces (the press, or government, or society) constrained it from fighting that conflict properly. It could have been won, they claim, with more of the same: more bombers, more divisions of troops, more firepower.[9]

Middle-ranged ranks—senior captains, majors, and lieutenant colonels who fought as younger men in Vietnam—tend not to agree with the assessment of their superiors. They believe that the war should have been conducted with less emphasis upon firepower and more upon nation building and pacification. Their villains were not the villains of their seniors but the seniors themselves, rigid and hidebound, adhering with unrelenting rigor to wrong doctrines and tactics at the wrong time and in the wrong place. Those middle-grade officers lean toward the consensus that the war might have been won had it been focused on the phenomena rather than the epiphenomena of Vietnam—the societal ills that produced guerrillas rather than upon the guerrillas and their NVA allies. Both groups agree on only one point. The war was unwinnable given the way it was fought.

Licking its Vietnam wounds, the army in the years since has continued to function as a separate organism, responding to its own perceptions of priorities and institutional needs. Hostile criticism during the Vietnam era has patterned it to react defensively and with hostility when challenged. It seems to make little difference whether critiques have come from civilians or military men. It is not that the army is opposed to change; it thrives on it. Witness its constant efforts to procure new hardware for its forces and its variations in uniforms over the years: in dress, duty, work, and combat fashions. It has liberalized haircut policies and introduced four-man rooms to replace the old open-bay barracks and cancelled its prohibition of beer inside enlisted quarters. Surface change within the army is kaleidoscopic.

To vary fundamental attitudes and approaches, however, is quite another matter. Recommendations for restructuring the army began soon after the close of World War II, when a group, established by the army, known as the "Doolittle Board" made its report. Named after its chairman, Lieutenant General James ("Jimmy") H. Doolittle (of 1942-raid-over-Tokyo fame), the committee had examined officer–enlisted relationships. Among its several findings, the group urged abolition of many standing distinctions between officer and enlisted personnel, better training for officers, assignments that would allow more effective utilization of officers, promotion policies to be based solely on merit, and harsh crackdowns on abuses of privilege, including stricter punishments to be meted out to those of higher rank. It even suggested that the hand salute could be eliminated. The proposed reforms of the Doolittle Board were quietly laid to rest, never to be seriously considered or enacted.[10] Other reform measures in the years since have met a like fate.

In the last decade there have appeared a pride of authors who have commented, some with clarity, on problems within the army. Some have been knowledgeable civilians; others have had an extensive investment in military careers. Instead of acknowledging what validity there might be to those reports, the army's most visible response has been a quiet yawn.

In the case of critic Anthony Herbert, it did not yawn but rather produced "fact sheets" that focused on the unworthiness of the author rather than upon the issues at stake. Then there were longtime, and supposedly valuable, career officers who resigned in dismay but who chose to keep their own counsel. Brigadier General S.L.A. Marshall (Ret.), military analyst and commentator, described one such man who had been his friend as "overlong in battle and emotionally imbalanced."[11] Once a person became a critic, no matter what value he may have had or credentials he may have held, the army tried to find a way to dismiss him as a "hostile" assailant. It was a difficult battle for any evaluater to win.[12]

* * *

Despite this unexceptional record, it would be fainthearted to stop at this point. Some observations and recommendations are in order and must be made. "The first step in any appraisal . . . is to admit some possibility of being at fault—some degree of blame for the defeat. Just as the alcoholic must admit daily to his alcoholism, the military . . . must admit to . . . failure, corporately and personally."[13] The army need not fear that criticism will lead to excoriation, for although defeat in vital endeavors is always to be avoided, if defeat occurs, good can sometimes be sifted from its ashes.

Historical precedent shows that armies have often profited when they have held post-mortems on their own defeats. (Victors, on the other hand, often grow slothful in their successes, ready to march forth on a new campaign while prepared to refight the last war once again.) Appropriate examples may be seen in the actions of the French and German staffs following World War I. The French lacked the impetus of failure and consequently did not analyze the problems they experienced during the four-year-long stalemate. The Germans, however, analyzed their defeat on the western front and changed organization and doctrine in order to produce their "blitzkrieg" victories of 1939 and 1940.

A massive effort should be launched to assemble, to study, to extrapolate from, and to codify the lessons available to us from army activities of the past—going all the way back to colonial times if necessary. In an earlier portion of this book the point was made that the so-called lessons learned from Vietnam were all too often shoddy ones: e.g., extended, long-range patrolling wears soldiers out; mosquito bars effectively keep insects away if properly emplaced; batteries and equipment should be kept dry if at all possible; two canteens are better than one when men are thirsty. Abraham and his family of herders knew such things as they entered the hill country of Canaan millennia ago.

At least two worthwhile results would issue from such a study.

1)Volumes of contingency background could be developed and computerized, available on printouts on short notice, to aid planners faced with working up operation plans when the army has been called upon to go into action in a particular area. At a minimum, such background material should examine earlier military actions in light of their missions, the enemy, the terrain, the tactics used, and weather conditions at the time. There is much that can be learned from the past that would be helpful to modern commanders responsible for leading troops into battle.

The comment of Santayana was not an idle one when he stated that "those who are ignorant of the past will be condemned to repeat it." Certainly that was the case in Vietnam. Policies were adopted, experiments launched, battles fought—many times in ways nearly identical to earlier French efforts that had failed, as they failed again when tried by United States forces, with the notable exception of Khe Sanh. (Reportedly, as the battle of Khe Sanh began in 1968, the air force requested all French generals who had had any part in the earlier siege of Dienbienphu—including one man well into his eighties—to come to Saigon and share their experiences. Several did so and supplied advice based on their first-hand knowledge of earlier tactics, mistakes, and accomplishments. Of how much value this was is not known, but Khe Sanh was won.)

Throughout the years it spent in Vietnam the army should have spent more time studying the French experience there. Cycles and patterns of fighting were the same in both wars. Physical locations were often identical. The enemy was still the enemy, yet no one correlated such information for use by officers and troops at the operational level. Upon occasion, American officers were surprised to learn that they were engaged in actions upon the very same plot of ground where French troops had fought a decade earlier. Such ignorance is inexcusable. Consequently lives, money, and time were lost because information regarding past French endeavors was unavailable to commanders.

There are many within the army who still claim that there is little to be learned from either the French or American efforts in Vietnam because the situation there was unique. At one level, of course, that is true, for all historical events are never-to-be-repeated ones. Yet similarities exist. In order for study of the past to have real military utility, officers will have to be coached into a willingness to forego their common attitude that no one has ever experienced difficulties quite like the ones they face, that the dead past—with its mistakes—is best left forgotten, and that one's challenges are inevitably *de novo*.

Lieutenant Colonel Vought has asked whether it is "possible that the trauma of having been found fighting the wrong kind of war has so deeply disturbed the Army's leadership that they . . . actually have 'erased the tapes,' expunged the unpleasant memory and are resuming the conventional deterrent role they played in the late 1950s?"[14] His argument is that the army is losing its limited capability for fighting low-intensity, unconventional wars and that this is a mistake as great as its continuing insistence that the only major conflict it will fight will be against the USSR on the plains of Europe. Perhaps it is for that reason that he comments that it is too bad "the United States does not have military malpractice suits."[15]

If computer-stored lessons could be summoned when needed there might be less call for such lawsuits, for surely Jenkins was correct when he charged that one of the army's most serious deficiencies was its "lack of an organizational memory" and could be compared to a recording tape that was periodically erased only to have similar material rerecorded upon it.[16]

Such background computer printouts should obviously not become absolute guides but could be employed by a commander as but one of several valuable resources available to him as he develops his operation plans. Given the fact that the army has long been interested in detailed chronicling of its exploits, it is strange that nothing of this sort has been developed. Untold thousands of books are available that treat earlier battles in minute particularity. Computerizing their lessons would simply be a logical extension of existing material, allowing for its effective utilization by those unable to spend the time necessary to study carefully all the available writings on a given battle area.

With present technology it would still be difficult even to discover all that has been written about a given area or battle, much less assemble that material for study. Computerizing it would prove invaluable. It would allow military professionals to know in detail what they would have to deal with in given situations. In this way army managers would be in better shape to carry out General Fred Weyand's advice.

> As military professionals we must speak out, we must counsel our political leaders and alert the American public that there is no such thing as a "splendid little war." There is no such thing as a war fought on the cheap. . . . The Army must make the price of involvement clear *before* we get involved. . . .[17]

The army could hardly make the price of involvement clear to politicians unless it knew itself what that price amounted to. Computerized knowledge could give it that capability.

2)Computer-enhanced compilations of this kind would also insure better training of recruits. No longer would troops in battle need to learn for themselves through bitter experience things that their professional ancestors had already known. They could go into combat aware of what they needed to do for battlefield survival rather than gaining such knowledge at the expense of perished comrades.

No one should ever again have to find out that local and magnetic conditions can reduce the effectiveness of an AN/PRC-25 radio backpack set or that an AN/PRC-10 can overcome these difficulties. It should never again have to surprise anyone that an overladen soldier is prone to overheating and tends to remain in one spot under enemy fire; or that contact with an enemy in a jungle environment usually occurs at point-blank range; or that overloaded and poorly protected rifle magazines invite stoppages; or that cigarette packages carried in helmet bands violate good camouflage discipline.[18] Such simple wisdom must not be learned again on the battlefield but must be inculcated in soldiers during their training. Printouts detailing such minutiae for a variety of combat circumstances would be of inestimable utility to training cadres. They could be used as checklists to insure that they did not overlook significant factors during their instruction of recruits.

Anyone who has ever made use of computer terminals tied in to the Defense Documentation Center, Defense Logistics Agency, Cameron Station, Alexandria, Virginia, is aware of the fantastic capabilities of that computer to call up available data within programmed categories. Other Defense and army computers have, of course, even greater capacities. Past battlefield lessons would be easy to include in the military's computerized memory banks.

*   *   *

In the first years of the 1970s, the long-festering racial strife within society and within the military caused the Department of Defense to recognize that unless something was done to alleviate racial and ethnic tensions, they would tear apart what little cohesion remained within the armed forces. Resentment, hatred, and violence had already immobilized more than one combat organization. In an effort to remedy that ugly situation, the Secretary of Defense issued Department of Defense Directive 1322.11 (24 June 1971), which prohibited overt displays of prejudice within the military and established the Race Relations Institute at Patrick Air Force Base in Florida.[19]

Every service was ordered to send representatives on a regular basis to the institute for several weeks of temporary duty, during which time they would be exposed to informational lectures about ethnic and racial minorities, small-group "rap" sessions, talks by invited guests, field trips, the opportunity to live for some days in the Miami ghetto area, informal counseling sessions, and psychological "games" that artificially created in participants the attitudes and fears of ghetto dwellers. The entire enterprise was an effort to allow mainstream Americans the opportunity to develop sensitivity toward their fellow citizens who suffered from either overt or covert forms of prejudice and racism.

Those first days at the Race Relations Institute were rowdy ones. A pilot class was quickly rammed through, the curriculum revised, a second "pilot" class taught, and the curriculum revised again before regular classes finally began. No one knew what to do or what to expect. Students enthusiastically greeted every effort at informality, every revelation that the military was racist. Some called for discarding their uniforms in favor of civilian garb. Others wanted to discontinue the practice of saluting. One enlisted man actually assaulted an unfortunate lieutenant colonel, who mildly suggested that it might be wise to retain some modicum of military courtesy. Faculty cliques divided the instructors. Suspicion felt by enlisted men and junior officers for students with field-grade rank hampered development of a smooth operation.

The first commandant of the school, a colonel in the Medical Service Corps, faced with such problems, remained largely invisible. One day, in the men's room where the commandant stood facing a urinal, he was asked by a student standing beside him whether he always "hung out" in there. That was about the extent of student contact with the commandant. He was replaced in a matter of months.

The surprise at the Race Relations Institute was not that minority angers, fears, charges of racism, and suspicions regarding the motives of others surfaced so quickly after the program began. It was not even a source of wonder that nearly insoluble problems faced those assigned to the institute as faculty or students. The surprise was that the school did not quickly sink into oblivion but instead faced its difficulties, over-came many of them, and endured to perform an invaluable function for the armed forces. Its impact upon the several services has been a weighty one. The tensions it was created to address have been exam-ined, confronted, and ameliorated.

A standing lesson is contained therein. Institutions by their very structure tend to resist innovation and change even when the changes have been mandated from the very top. In this case at least, a solution to the problems caused by racial controversy was perceived as impera-tive, and so the secretary of defense ordered a solution of sorts that he imposed upon the military structure despite real resistance. The same thing can be done in other problem areas. The need is clear. Only the army can answer as to whether its determination to correct internal abuses is sufficiently strong for it to act.

This study has focused upon a number of problems faced by the Vietnam-era army that were revealed and aggravated by involvement in Southeast Asia and that endure today either in actuality or in legacy. Those that have been discussed herein include

1. unwillingness of military leaders to dissent from policies of which they disapproved;

2. disinclination of high-ranking officers to resign rather than to go along with tactics and programs that they later claimed they believed to have been detrimental to the army;

3. use of inappropriate tactics in Vietnam including free-fire zones, harassing and interdiction fires, defoliation, search and de-stroy (reconnaissance in force), indiscriminate use of firepower in civilian areas, regular harassment of noncombatants, bombing of the north (and south, down to and including such strategic targets as barnyards), and general tactics of attrition;

4. misunderstanding the nature and needs of counterguerrilla/-counterinsurgent wars of national liberation, and simple refusal to correct such incorrect attitudes;

5. reliance upon and abuse of short-term statistical indicators of progress, such as Hamlet Evaluation Survey figures, body counts, reports of army casualty figures, and others—all of which were regularly and systematically rigged to provide the statistics wanted rather than those that reflected the true course of the war (which probably could not be reflected by statistics alone in any case);

6.   a reluctance to punish overt racist attitudes of GIs toward Vietnamese allies, which promoted brutalization of the attitudes of American soldiers, culminating in the massacre at My Lai as well as in other incidents of torture, murder, and assorted similar acts of counterproductive brutality;

7.   attempted cover-ups by the army—from low-ranking individuals to military managers—of such acts of illegal violence and reluctance to punish those involved;

8.   repeated recurrence of scandals and corruption such as that of the army sergeants, and others;

9.   appearance of pointed indicators of disintegration of morale such as fraggings, AWOLs, desertions, malingering, drug usage, combat avoidance, and combat refusals (mutinies);

10.   misuse of officer-efficiency reports;

11.   careerism that produced such phenomena as "can do" attitudes, zero-defects requirements, assignment turbulence, ticket punching, destruction of trust for one another among officers, superiors willing to sacrifice interests and well-being of subordinates, six-month command and six-month staff assignments in Vietnam, decorations as "gongs" and the improprieties involved in awarding them;

12.   burdening some 14 percent of the soldiers in Vietnam with combat assignments while approximately 86 percent remained in support capacities safely out of danger;

13.   failure to ask for and study objectively reports from the field that suggested alternate approaches;

14.   suppression of reports and recommendations that did not support existing policy, strategy, or tactics;

15.   persecution of those who reported unpleasant truths.

This list is not complete, but it at least covers certain of the main difficulties faced by the Vietnam-era army. All the problems mentioned have at least one factor in common: they were inextricably tied to ethical issues. It is assumed that the army is aware of that fact and recognizes the need for an ethical base for its policies, for it has instituted a few changes.

One progressive step taken by the army has been its assignment of chaplains to the faculties of most of its service schools, taking those men out of their traditional roles as chapel preachers and field counselors and allowing them to teach a broad spectrum of officer students in curriculum areas that fall within their area of specialization. This accomplishes several things. It affords the army an opportunity to make use of the talents of a body of highly trained officers. It gives chaplains a greater opportunity to serve in their chosen profession. It reminds officer students—whenever they see an instructor wearing the cross or tablet insignia—that the one before them can do more than simply "punch the TS card" (not to be confused with ticket punching for officers) of any disgruntled trooper who has a gripe to air. It is a constant reminder that the army and all its officers have a responsibility to consider ethical issues in chosen courses of action.[20]

A second worthwhile step forward has been the army's introduction of classes on ethics in the curricula of its service schools. Ft. Leavenworth has recently incorporated course P913-2, "Military Ethics," into its overall coverage. Handouts are varied. One includes reproductions of various professional creeds, ranging from the one produced by the Army War College's *Study* and a code of ethics used by the air force for its officers to the code of ethics for the National Society of Public Accountants and the Physicians' Code.

Another CGSC student handout incorporates LTG W. R. Peers's memorandum of 18 March 1970 to General Westmoreland (including his statement of leadership requirements in a counterinsurgency environment); an article by Major Richard F. Garvin that appeared in Army in 1977, calling for a recognized ethical code that could help an officer cope with the uncertainties of military life; a reproduction of an officer's oath of office; and reproduction of certain articles describing punitive measures abstracted from the Uniform Code of Military Justice.

A third "tissue issue" at CGSC consists of a selected group of readings on various aspects of leadership, problems of the officer corps, and ethics. Student reaction ranges from "something we've needed for a long time" to "not a subject a combat-arms officer needs to concern himself with," from the "easiest class we have—all a man needs to do is rap—no study needed" to "hard work, for it deals with fundamental issues."[21]

Articles detailing the need for a more ethical climate within the army are gaining currency. Major Allan Futernick, writing in a recent issue of *Military Review*, warns of the "perceived loss of public trust and confidence [in the American military] as a result of Vietnam" and asserts that "since the military is an organization in which the public places a high degree of trust, the public also expects adherence to the absolute ethic." The lower level of military commitment to ethical standards has arisen, Futernick believes, because of "the shift . . . away from [member devotion to the army] as a 'calling' or a 'profession' and movement toward a format increasingly resembling that of an 'occupation.' " The result of such a movement "is that we appear to be heading down a doomsday track at breakneck speed toward an 'ethical Armageddon.' Whether or not the American military survives this ethical conflict, those of us on active duty during these years will always remember it and bear some psychological scars." It is utterly imperative, states Futernick, that "action must be taken within the military to restore the trust and confidence vested in each commissioned officer by his or her commission."[22]

A chaplain who recently discussed the need for rededication to ethical concepts with some of his fellow line officers summed up their attitude as follows: "The consensus among them was that careful study of ethical issues had to start at OBC [Officer Basic Course]—hopefully also at West Point, and in all the ROTC programs at colleges throughout the country—and then consistently at periodic intervals as individuals moved up through the ranks. There was," he warned, however, "much cynicism about anyone's ability to come up with a program that would be taken seriously."[23]

The Army War College has been in the forefront of military schools adding to their curricula classes that deal with ethical considerations. "A small part of the curriculum is devoted to it with the real blessing of General Smith, the commandant. It's something he has been interested in and has pushed ever since he got here. It's not a department but rather is a part of our command and management structure. They're working out the ethics involved in war."[24]

The War College is doing something else. "I have a study project here that's just getting under way to examine the role of the army in Vietnam and to try to find from it lessons we need to learn. The study hasn't really gotten started yet [1977]. But I've done some thinking about it. Perhaps we're still too close to it or too emotionally involved to study it, but I don't think so. The matter is, of course, complex and sensitive, with a voluminous amount of wheat and chaff to separate. . . . Some of the things we will have to consider include 'good' versus 'bad' wars, short wars versus longer ones, cheap versus expensive wars in terms both of dollars and people, total versus limited wars, 'necessary' versus 'unnecessary' conflicts, wars close at hand versus those which will require long and extensive logistic lines, clear-cut results as opposed to conflicts or police actions resulting only in indecisive results, use of the regular forces versus use of 'our boys.'

"We will have to consider the usefulness of military force—is it worth what it will cost? Other things too, such as what is and should be the role of the U.S.A. in the world? What kind of credibility should we strive for? Why, when, where, and how should forces be inserted into action? What the military *must* do is understand what kind of war it is fighting and the people who will be involved therein, on both sides— something we didn't do in Vietnam. We will have to consider the immorality of war and determine whether there are other things so much more immoral that it is acceptable to resort to war.

"This study committee will be about a two-year effort, and the individuals on it will be broken into teams to address various aspects. Each team chairman will have his own cadre and will bring in advisers as he sees fit. We tend to isolate in this study the army from its sister services. And we'll have some students who will volunteer to do pieces of the work. We'll have workshops, symposia, multiple-input sorts of things, with sixty categories or subtopics to cover. It's unofficial, it's unblessed, but it's an open-book approach."

All those words were cheering ones, except those that he used to close the conversation: "We'll try, except where we have to prove a point, to stay out of the tactical area, trying to keep the study on a higher level of grand strategy, national strategy, as it involves the army."[25] A reiterated theme within these pages has been the folly of many of the tactics used by the army in Vietnam. For such a high-level study as that of the War College to ignore this aspect of the American experience in Indochina is both disheartening and short-sighted.

Then there has been the "Harrison Board," recently at work. Although at this writing its findings have not yet been released, this group, operating under the direction of Brigadier General B. L. Harrison, past deputy commander of the Command and General Staff College, has been studying how "individuals and units at all levels can fight and win on the battlefield in the 1980s" in an effort to produce new "soldiers manuals, revised school curriculums and teaching methods, integrated technical documentation and training, war games and simulations."[26] As one would imagine, the board's focus has been on the various aspects of officer education, and one can hope that it will set forth clear recommendations resulting in improvements in the careerism syndrome spoken of earlier.[27]

A recent newsletter has noted the current army emphasis on including classes on ethics in the curricula of its service schools and the appointment of chaplains to those faculties.

The evidence is ample—the "in" subject right now is ethics. . . . moving out of the religion and philosophy departments into the mainstream of functional subjects. . . . The trend is especially evident in the armed forces. New courses in the service academies and professional military schools are now the rule, rather than the exception. Discussion, conferences and seminars on ethical issues and principles are tending to develop more from command interest than the more expected push from chaplains. Whether the revival of attention comes from post-Watergate sensitivities or something more complex, no one is questioning the need. The Air Force Academy's Col. Maltham Waken puts it before the March convention of the Military Chaplains Association in sober terms: "The line between incompetence and immorality is a thinner line in the military vocation than in almost any other profession.[28]

Frank Kowalski, a graduate of the United States Military Academy and a career army officer who retired as a full colonel prior to entering politics and serving as a congressman from 1958 to 1962, wrote as follows:

> The Secretary of Defense should direct the services to incorporate in their school systems—from the military academies through the National War College—and in their various training programs, courses of instruction designed to indoctrinate men and officers at all levels regarding their human responsibilities as soldiers of a great democracy and the overriding obligations of command towards civilian populations in war.[29]

From that suggestion came the memories of the Defense Race Relations Institute that flooded through my mind. If establishment of such an institute could alleviate the gravest of racial and ethnic pressures besetting the military, why could not a Defense Ethics Institute do the same for the ills arising from our Vietnam experience? For let there be no doubt about it, the basic problem from which all else arose was an ethical one.

"There was an obvious inflation of the body count caused by lying. Consequently there was a great deal of dishonesty allowed for within the army."[30] The man who said that had a view of ethics. "One of our Cobra operators had had four years in Vietnam. He'd flown Cobras for two. He stayed not because someone forced or threatened him but because he enjoyed shooting people dead. That's how he defined himself."[31] Such perceptions should be examined and analyzed from an ethical point of view.

A National Guard artillery officer, one of the approximately 25,000 guardsmen called to active duty during the Vietnam conflict, stated that "we were sent to Vietnam by competent authority to do something, to follow orders and to carry out what we were assigned to do. And our troops did that magnificently in spite of all the garbage they faced."[32] That view arises from a specific ethical persuasion.

"The Vietnam lexicon of officialese allowed for a lot of dual meanings for words, so that you could say something without actually having to spell it out. Some of it led to misunderstandings as to what was expected. I believe in My Lai, for example, the instructions given there were to 'take care of people.' That leaves a lot to interpretation. Do you give them flowers and fruit baskets or drop an atomic bomb on them?"[33] One hopes that such a comment indicates that its author has had to come to grips with the ethical implications of language.

"We are good guys and we wear white hats. We play by rules which a lot of armies wouldn't even consider."[34] By such a statement the speaker indicated his belief that Americans have different values, and higher ones, from many other peoples'. It is an ethical view.

"There's a lot that happens in combat. You feel like guys you've known for only a month are closer to you and that you know them better than friends back home you've known for five years. Combat creates a very close relationship among the men of a unit: facing a common threat in strange surroundings is what does it. That's worthwhile to have as an experience."[35] That officer described a human relationship built upon a concept of ethics.

"One of the things that impressed me most would be the first day I arrived in Vietnam. The whole atmosphere at Tan Son Nhut was rather ludicrous. Here there was a war going on in a country which, as you flew over it, was obviously pockmarked by bombs and destruction of all types. We'd return to our base at the end of a flight and there would be rock bands and go-go dancers and clubs and PXs loaded with all the finery of home. The local Hop Tacs were around everywhere. The swimming pools on Sunday afternoons were full of people. Yet the war was very real as the sun would go down. Even at Tan Son Nhut one could look out around the perimeter and see flares popped every few minutes. We could see gunfire off in the distance. Or we could feel the tremendous rumbling of the B-52s on carpet-bombing raids not too far from Saigon. It was a very, very strange contrast that many of us never quite got used to. We had all the comforts of home while the hardships of war were so vividly and so painfully seen in the faces of the Vietnamese people, especially those of the refugees I saw. It was an impression I will long remember."[36] The air-force major who said those things to me in the living room of his home one beautiful summer evening was wrestling with ethical problems.

"Refugees were flown into Tan Son Nhut, people who had just lost everything. They sat with painful expressions and attitudes of desolation, waiting to be taken to temporary living quarters. I do not think I will be able to forget them. Once you have seen a thing like that it stays with you. I saw loads of ARVN troops flown on C-123s up to fight against NVA troops moving south. Their families would see them off right at the aircraft, and would camp at the edge of the runway until it was time for their husbands or brothers or sons to be loaded up. The look of complete terror on the faces of those South Vietnamese troops as they went north was a thing to behold. Again, it was an impression I won't forget. Upon returning to the States I found I was confronted with friends who immediately wanted to know what had happened to me in Vietnam and what I thought about the war there. That agitated and irritated me. I finally came up with a pat comment. I had been too close to the war for too long to be able to reflect upon it."[37] Those comments spring from an ethical concern.

The *Study on Military Professionalism* spoke of double standards, of expectations that leaders should set examples of moral behavior, of prevalent attitudes willing to accept mediocrity, of "freeloaders," of tainted decorations, of "hangers-on," of the erosion of adherence to duty, honor, and country and the substitution of false principles, of moral laxness, of the degrading of professionalism. The very categories under which anecdotes in the *Study* were classified bespoke ethical considerations: standards, integrity, self-interest, loyalty, justice.[38]

A distinction should be made clear. These remarks deal not with "ideal" but with "positive" ethics. Ideal morality, often believed to be the special province of religion and philosophy, deduces principles of right action from an *a priori* view of the good life. Positive ethics consist of codifications of moral principles and rules that are actually observed and/or respected within a particular cultural group or society.

Whether ideal or positive, all moral theory derives from reflection upon what individuals already accept or believe. The purpose of such reflection remains today what it was for the Greeks who first systematically adopted it—to study forms of human behavior in order to discover their worth as means to a better life. Ethics, at base, then, is the study of standards; comparison of what *is* with what *ought* to be.[39] As a professor of philosophy once remarked to me: "There is no built-in guarantee with the study of ethics. Reflection upon it may make one more educated; it does not necessarily make one better."

Despite the lack of guarantees in the study of ethics, a command-level emphasis upon it within the army would be useful. There were no guarantees that the situation would improve when the Race Relations Institute was established. The first few months of its existence seemed to validate the concerns of its opponents rather than the hopes of its supporters. Yet over the course of several years, the institute has demonstrated itself to be one of the more valuable projects begun by the military within recent decades. Setting up a defense-ethics institute might produce similar results of lasting value. This should be a product of the Department of Defense rather than of the Department of the Army, for although this study has concentrated on the problems of the Vietnam-era army, it has done so for purposes of illustration rather than from any belief that the army alone made mistakes. The air force and the navy struggled with "fodding" (foreign-object damage) and other difficulties. Marines set fire to the thatched huts of Cam Ne (4), using their cigarette lighters, so that newsmen might capture the episode on film for American viewers of evening TV.[40] The members of every one of the military services since their inception have had to struggle with ethical problems, although the struggle in Vietnam brought them to a surface-froth of agitation revealing how deep and swift the undercurrent of ethical stresses really were.[41]

A defense-ethics institute could provide a steady leavening of attitudes within the services, as selected individuals attended the institute as students and returned to their own military branch with new concepts. Within their own wings and bases and forts they could act as facilitaters in group study of ethical problems, following a format similar to the one used to bring service people together for sessions devoted to discussion and study of racial/ethnic problems. For that matter (despite current military objections to anything smacking of traditional lecturing), classroom presentations by recognized experts on various aspects of ethics could be used to acquaint large groups in rapid fashion as to issues involved in major areas of the field.

All service schools, beginning with West Point and continuing through officer-candidate school, officer basic courses, branch career courses, Ft. Leavenworth's Command and General Staff College, Ft. McNair's National Defense University, and Carlisle Barracks' Army War College, should have within their curricula significant blocks of time devoted to the study of military ethical problems.

What are the responsibilities of a commander? When is an order lawful and when is it not? What are the serviceman's duties toward a hostile civilian population within a war zone? How far should loyalty to a colleague, a subordinate, a superior extend? Do the ends ever justify the means? Can a drive for personal success ever take precedence over the longer-range goals of a unit or the welfare of troops? How can a platoon leader best care for the interests of his men? The questions are endless; the need for them to be discussed within a command-level emphasis is great.

An obvious group within the military to entrust with the organization and operation of such a defense-ethics institute is the Chaplain Corps. Not only is the chaplaincy the single branch designated to be responsible for the morals and morale of all segments of the military, but its members—by training and inclination—have also received instruction in the major premises and problems of ethics as the discipline has developed within the Western world. Many chaplains have been philosophy majors as liberal-arts undergraduates and thus will have often received an introduction to ethics at that level. In seminary or rabbinical school, such men have opportunity to study ethical issues in comprehensive fashion as they relate to the topics and issues of life at the deepest areas of human concern. These men may not always know the answers, but they are aware of the questions and are familiar with various approaches to possible solutions.

Giving a task of this magnitude to the Chaplain Corps is not without its own difficulties. The men (and the very few women) who have been commissioned in that branch were not picked from trees minutes prior to their oath of office. They are as human as those who serve in any other branch. They have as many weaknesses, as many frailties, as do many of their fellow officers in other specialties. They are sometimes prone to laziness, jealousy, resentment, careerism—to all the ills of temperament that can afflict other military officers. Yet the corps is still dedicated to concepts that relate more easily to ethical concerns than are, say, Signal branch or Engineers or Transportation or others that come to mind. And within the chaplaincy are individuals with a wealth of ability and experience in administration, teaching, theology, history, philosophy, and who are fundamentally "caring" people.

In addition to chaplains, the army should draw from its ranks—wherever they might be serving—those men and women with talents and abilities that would be helpful in organizing and operating a defense-ethics institute, whether they be officer or enlisted. Such a cadre, sharing a common bond in concern for ethical standards, could do much to lift the army from the doldrums of bureaucracy, careerism, and opportunism that have so long plagued it. The suggestion is well worth careful consideration by those at command levels capable of instituting such an organization.

*   *   *

There is a rule in formal debating that new material may not be introduced during a summation that was not presented in the body of the evidence. One would hope that that requirement does not apply here, for it is time to speak of a subject that has not heretofore been mentioned. An omission occurred during the Vietnam conflict that had a grave effect on the army's ability to function there and an equally serious effect on the attitudes of the American people toward the war in Southeast Asia. That omission was the failure of the army managers to urge more strongly that the president of the United States activate the National Guard and the Army Reserve for service in Vietnam.

The army high command initially recommended that the Guard and the Reserve be called up, and opposed the decision by President Lyndon Johnson and Secretary of Defense Robert McNamara not to do so. Wishing both to increase the army's size by 50 percent while avoiding public notice of the extent of American involvement in Vietnam, those two men determined to rely solely on the draft. Young men of draft age had little political clout, little investment as yet in civilian occupations, little influence anywhere—and those who did could always secure a deferment for themselves.

Defense Secretary McNamara insisted that his bright young aides, skilled in operations research and systems analysis (ORSA [called in some quarters "ORSA's asses"]), had demonstrated to his satisfaction that a call-up of reserve components was unnecessary. Military officials bowed to this decision and did not ask for even a limited call-up until after the *Pueblo* incident in 1968.[42]

So, for the most part, America's reserve forces were not called to active duty. They were needed, but politicians believed the social climate to be opposed to such a move.[43] They believed that in a nation that traditionally was as "unmilitary" as was the United States, activating the reserve components should be done only as a last resort. Once again, professional military men refused to put their careers on the line to oppose something they believed to be wrong. They were the experts and surely had asked themselves the question, in Weigley's words, "how, in an unmilitary nation, to muster adequate numbers of capable soldiers quickly should war occur."[44] War existed, and it was incumbent on the army to have sufficient forces of well-trained units to meet its needs.

Perhaps even America was not as unmilitary as some believed. If its citizenry actually opposed war to the extent usually portrayed, the nation would not have fought nine major wars, countless skirmishes, and innumerable interventions and developed such a reputation for sword brandishing within fewer than two hundred years. Perhaps Americans rejected not war but a standing professional army. There is a great deal of evidence to support just that conclusion. While allowing a skeletonized regular army to exist between conflicts, Americans seemed to insist in times of combat and crisis upon widespread popular participation as a prerequisite for allowing society-wide support for a fight, transforming it into a crusade.

We can hope that as a result of the bitter experience of Vietnam, army officials have learned that they cannot fight any sort of protracted war with the support of the home front's civilian sector without bringing those people themselves into the war through activation of those population segments that make up the National Guard and Army Reserve.[45]

At one time or another most officers and noncoms in the reserve components have served on active duty. Following their release from service, they found that there were elements of military life that had appealed to them—but not sufficiently to make the army a career. So they joined a National Guard or Army-Reserve outfit in their hometown. Over the years they worked their way up through ranks to senior noncom or field-grade officer rank.

Periodic reorganizations of their units ordered by the Department of the Army caused them to face recurrent confusion and to earn broad experience. A light-truck company might be reorganized into a Signal Corps company. A 105mm howitzer (towed) battalion might have its tubes taken from it and replaced with eight-inch howitzers or 155mm self-propelled tracked cannon. A support company might be phased out to reappear as an infantry organization. Officers and men often shouted in dismay at what was expected of them, but they coped.

They operated with radios that no self-respecting army unit would have bothered to repair and that had not seen active service for twenty-five years. Tankers drove trucks three generations behind what their active-duty counterparts rode in. Supplies were inevitably short and equipment was often of the "field utility," that is, homemade, variety. Invariably those dedicated men found a way to make things work or to do without. Despite all the rhetoric about "Total forces" and all the concern about "One army," reality has had a tradition of lagging far behind doctrine so far as the reserve components have been concerned. Yet men stayed with it and units survived. They did not have to. They could have gotten out at almost any time they desired. They remained because they wanted to do so.

They have been an interesting breed of men. In small towns, they have been butchers and bakers, farmers and laborers, truck drivers and postmen. On weekends, the town nearly shut down once a month as they donned their uniforms and headed for the armory for their military duties. In larger towns, professional men—teachers and professors, doctors and ministers, lawyers and college presidents, electric-company managers and opticians, druggists and musicians—joined with others of like interest to man brigade activities during the yearly ANACDUTRA (annual active duty for training; currently called AT, or annual training).

In the mid-sixties, the traditional meeting on a weekday evening was abolished and a weekend assembly inaugurated as UTAs (unit training assemblies) gave way to MUTAs (multiple unit training assemblies). The active army sent more equipment to Army-Reserve and National Guard units, and some of those outfits were given important assignments. Certain organizations were designated as SRF units—Selected Reserve Forces. They were to be elite. They could fill vacant personnel positions previously disallowed. They would train every other weekend or as often as necessary to prepare them for mobilization. Equipment was updated.

The oldtimers were willing to do whatever was necessary. Unfortunately they were faced with an influx of new recruits who had no interest in quality performance. They had been faced with the choice of being drafted or joining a National Guard outfit for six years. Some good men came out of that situation, but all too many were resentful time-servers. Morale in reserve-component outfits throughout the Vietnam conflict was generally low, as they became havens for draft avoiders. Yet units trained to become more prepared for the mobilization they expected to come at any time.

It is not that they wanted to go to war. Rather they were willing and ready to do so. No one wants to go off to fight; but thousands of men of reserve-component units were ready to assent to it, interrupting the tenor of their careers, livelihoods, and civilian occupations because they believed they were needed. What in peacetime was a hobby for them was in time of conflict a means of expressing their devotion to their country.

They had served in World War I. They returned in World War II and, in lesser numbers, for Korea. They were not professional soldiers, nor were they hedged in by military-careerist impulses. If they did not make major or lieutenant colonel it was too bad, but it was not a disaster. If a noncom received a chewing-out, it undoubtedly irked him, but he could take it with a different spirit from that of his active-duty counterpart. Who really cared? They had come to fight a war and to get it over with and to get back to their real lives and their civilian jobs.

In two or three years it would all be over and they could resume their Tuesday-evening meetings and, during quiet times, reminisce about their experiences while "answering the call of their country." But then came Vietnam, and the president of the United States did not wish to bring fully to the attention of the American people how very deeply the nation was becoming involved in Southeast Asia. He could activate the reserve components or leave them, for the most part, untouched. He made the wrong choice, deciding instead to rely on the draft to fill army ranks with young men who as yet had no economic or political power. Their absence, even the death of many, would not have the impact on society that would come if he stripped the heartland's small towns of their men.

America went to Vietnam without its reserve components, relying on a professional officer corps of men with an investment in their military careers. At such a time those individuals needed the leavening that the noncoms and officers of the reserve components could give them. It would have helped those in the regular army keep careerism in perspective. The Army Reserve and National Guard needed the experience and training that only service with the active army could provide and that, after all, was their only *raison d'être*. There was little point in maintaining them at immense cost if they were to be relegated to the sidelines at a time when they could truly have been of use.

Both active-army and reserve components were losers as a result of the presidential decision. This has been clearly noted by army generals. One wrote:

> The decision to rely on draftees or regulars instead of calling up reserve units meant that valuable logistics skills were not put to use. The few National Guard and Reserve units that were used in the Da Nang area during the summer and fall of 1968 were very good. BG James W. Gunn, CG, USA Support Command, Da Nang, remarked that "these units proved to be outstanding in every respect. They were composed of mature officers and men who arrived in-country with 100 percent of their TOE strength and equipment. They were for the most part well educated and highly motivated and skilled. . . ."[46]

Another general indicated:

> The decision not to employ the vast resources of the Army Reserve in the expansion of the active duty Army in 1965 stripped from the active Army engineer structure a source of skilled craftsmen that engineer planners relied upon heavily. Until that decision Engineer Reserve units filled with

civilians skilled in construction crafts had been looked upon as the prime source of engineer troops in the event of a military buildup. Suddenly the Army faced the necessity of training soldiers and officers of its Regular Army engineer units to supervise and build major construction projects far more complex than any they had undertaken in the past.[47]

All that is, of course, now in the past. The reserve components were not called up. But what of the future? The army has continued to create contingency plans calling for great reliance upon the reserve components:

> . . . if war broke out tomorrow, 58% of the Army's field artillery, 65% of its combat engineer battalions, 52% of its infantry and armor battalions, 45% of its aviation forces and 65% of all the Army's tactical support is to come from the National Guard and Army Reserve Units.[48]

For there to have been any profit whatsoever from the mistakes it made in Vietnam, the army must be willing when conflict comes again to stand firmly against political recommendations that mobilization of re-serve-component units would "impact negatively" upon the professional or social or economic or political life of communities in which National Guard and Army-Reserve units are located. It must insist, after study of precisely what mix of forces is needed to tailor the military to meet whatever threatening forces confront it, that those reserve-component outfits that are necessary for its efficient functioning be activated. It will not only help the army better prepare itself to face an opponent. It will make it more difficult for American society—or any segments of it—to castigate the military when sons and husbands and fathers are part and parcel of that force structure.[49]

*   *   *

The army must put to better use the insights and talents of its students in such high-level institutions as the Command and General Staff College and the Army War College. Many who attend such schools have thorough training and constructive insights into problems facing the military, gained through education and experience. At both schools there are students who produce capable, thoroughly researched essays and theses dealing with a variety of current problems. Many of those studies have been cited during the course of these pages. Had anyone in command-level positions read them, far different courses of action might have been chosen. Instead, for the most part, such student efforts seem to have been filed in the libraries at Fort Leavenworth and Carlisle Barracks and seldom aired. Compendia of papers, or abstracts, seem not to be made, yet they might prove to be of value to various command-level staffs as they probe the problems of assignments they face. It is a sad waste for such a broad range of training and experience to be ignored.[50]

*　　*　　*

The army has a responsibility to tell the truth. It must eliminate the climate in which grow such common practices as creating three vague categories of casualty figures—light, medium, and heavy—rather than using specific numbers. Reporting "light" casualties when according to its own criteria they were "medium," or reporting "medium" when "heavy" casualties had been suffered, was an obfuscation that did not long fool anyone. It simply lowered the army's credibility. No more acceptable was the practice of listing only men who had actually died in battle as Killed in Action, and classifying those who died during treatment in hospitals as a result of combat wounds as "nonbattle casualties." The result of such statistical juggling was to convince a number of news correspondents and concerned Americans that the army was deliberately hiding the extent of its losses.

The army should release either no figures at all or else accurate ones. Credibility is difficult to regain once it has been lost. Other wartime public-information phrases that came under suspicion were "collateral damage," "suspected enemy structures," "protective-reaction strikes," and all the verbal gymnastics that served only to cast doubt on all army-issue information. They brought skepticism to the American public and total disbelief to the members of the press corps in Vietnam. It was a sure method of losing, once again, the battle for people's "hearts and minds." The army had already failed in that struggle with the Vietnamese people. It failed a second time with its citizenry at home. (Perhaps the worst result of all was that the army high command eventually fell under the sway of its own propaganda, believing its own press releases, finally convinced that all was well despite a plethora of evidence to the contrary.)

*　　*　　*

The Doolittle Board once urged abolition of many traditional distinctions between officer and enlisted personnel, cancelling the requirement for the hand salute, regulating promotions more carefully, providing better officer training, meting out stricter punishments to those of higher rank than those given to lower ranks when privileges were abused, and so forth. The recommendations of the Doolittle Board need to be taken down from whatever dusty shelf they have been relegated to since the report was issued in 1946. The pages of the *Study on Military Professionalism* need to be retrieved from the files. Clerks in some inner Pentagon office need to search for and locate the 1971 *Comprehensive Report: Leadership for the 1970s, USAWC Study of Leadership for the Professional Soldier.* All three—and every other relevant and available staff study—need to be laid out on some executive-length conference table in a Pentagon council room and carefully

studied. Suggestions contained in those reports that can be implemented without damage to the army's fighting capabilities should be
put into effect without further delay. Having never had it before, it is
now time that they be given sober consideration.

*   *   *

The army should continue its study of officer-efficiency-report
forms and derive or develop an evaluation that will lend itself to an
honest description of a man's activities. Such a form should not be
readily susceptible of inflation *or* deflation. Officers should have the
opportunity to learn, to demonstrate initiative, to offer critiques, to
acquire lessons from their mistakes—all without fear that one bad efficiency rating will destroy their careers. What a refreshing change that
would be from the present system, where, according to an Army War
College staff member, "if you are rated above 75 percent of all other
officers in the corps, your career is ruined. You've been damned with
faint praise."[51]
At least the army is trying to improve in this area. The current
efficiency report, DA Form 67-7, is in the process of being phased out,
to be replaced by DA Form 67-8, which will no longer have space for
a numerical rating of an individual's performance. DA Form 67-8 will
emphasize, rather, a narrative paragraph by an officer's rater, which
will consist of an appraisal of an individual's performance.

*   *   *

The very psychological basis of the army system must be altered.
At present, war or preparation for war is the principal means for insuring its own continuity and for career advancement among individuals
within it in the officer corps. The army, of course, must continue to be
ready to face foreign threats dangerous to the security of the United
States. For that reason combat-arms branches must concentrate on
improving their fighting efficiency. Combat-support and combat-service-support units, however, might consider the possibility of working
at home and overseas on efforts supporting various kinds of community
activity.
It would not only be of use to the civilian sector; it would give
additional experience to forces that might face the challenge of advising
foreign governments on effective methods of "internal defense and
development." Perhaps such prior experience would allow for a higher
level of advice than the army was able to offer in Vietnam.

*   *   *

The army must recognize the limits of its power. It must come to
understand and finally come to grips with how it was possible for un-
kempt, ragged jungle fighters headed by dedicated leaders to bring it

to its knees. To learn that lesson will be worthwhile. Once digested, it will enable the army to act with more perceptiveness should it be faced with a similar situation again.

There are those who, on the basis of the Vietnam experience, have concluded that insurgents cannot be beaten. In light of guerrilla movements in Colombia and Venezuela in recent days, in Malaya and Greece of the post-World War II era, that conclusion is insupportable. We made mistakes in Vietnam that, with study, are recognizable and correctable. Approached in appropriate fashion, insurgent efforts can be not only contained but destroyed root and branch.

The other conclusion some have reached is that the fighting spirit and ability of men in the army is low.[52] They contend that it has been too long since the army has been victorious in conflict and that thus its members have no tradition of success, no experience in conquest, and little sense of valor. Again, this is a fellacious notion.

Despite incorrect strategies in Vietnam dictated by the limited imagination and insight of those who were then the army's military managers, "we won all the big battles, even most of the small ones. We emphasized the physical aspects of strategy and tactics and didn't fully understand the psychological aspects which applied in Vietnam, because we were fighting the wrong kind of war. Yet we won the vast majority of battles."[53]

The men who did that job do not need to have their due given to them. They know without being told that they did their duties well. In jungle and rice-paddy firefights, on patrols, during search-and-destroy sweeps, and in technical tasks, American-army GIs fought and performed in a highly competent manner. In bravery, in selflessness, in sacrifice, they achieved a superb rating. Those men did not enter Vietnam with the belief that they were on a fool's errand—that their efforts were doomed to ultimate failure. They went in with the attitude that victory was possible and all that was needed was to find the proper strategic and tactical combinations to ensure success. It was not due to any lack in their fighting capabilities that they were programmed by army managers into tactics and strategies so wrong that they would eventually spell defeat for the cause for which they fought.

The wonder is not that the Vietnam effort of the army failed. Rather, given the difficulties under which its men operated, the surprise is that they did as well as they did, giving a performance that will long be a tribute to their indomitable spirit. Perhaps it is a lesson from which the army leadership can learn.

Appendices

APPENDIX A

Declaration of Independence
of the Democratic Republic
of Vietnam   (Excerpts)

All men are created equal. They are endowed by their Creator with certain inalienable rights, among these are Life, Liberty and the pursuit of Happiness.

This immortal statement was made in the Declaration of Independence of the United States of America in 1776. In a broader sense, this means: All the peoples on the earth are equal from birth; all the peoples have a right to live, to be happy and free.

The Declaration of the French Revolution made in 1791 on the Rights of Man and the Citizen also states: "All men are born free and with equal rights, and must always remain free and have equal rights."

Those are undeniable truths.

Nevertheless, for more than eighty years, the French imperialists, abusing the standard of Liberty, Equality and Fraternity, have violated our Fatherland and oppressed our fellow-citizens. They have acted contrary to the ideals of humanity and justice.

In the field of politics, they have deprived our people of every democratic liberty.

They have enforced inhuman laws; they have set up three distinct political regimes in the North, the Centre and the South of Viet Nam in order to wreck our national unity and prevent our people from being united.

They have built more prisons than schools. They have mercilessly slain our patriots; they have drowned our uprisings in rivers of blood.

They have fettered public opinion; they have practised obscurantism against our people.

To weaken our race they have forced us to use opium and alcohol.

In the field of economics, they have fleeced us to the backbone, impoverished our people and devastated our land.

They have robbed us of our rice fields, our mines, our forests and our raw materials. They have monopolized the issuing of banknotes and the export trade.

They have invented numerous unjustifiable taxes and reduced our people, especially our peasantry, to a state of extreme poverty.

They have hampered the prospering of our national bourgeoisie; they have mercilessly exploited our workers. . . .

The truth is that we have wrested our independence from the Japanese and not from the French.

The French have fled, the Japanese have capitulated, Emperor Bao Dai has abdicated. Our people have broken the chains which for nearly a century have fettered them and have won independence for the Fatherland. Our people at the same time have overthrown the monarchic regime that has reigned supreme for dozens of centuries. In its place has been established the present Democratic Republic.

For these reasons, we, members of the Provisional Government, representing the whole Vietnamese people, declare that from now on we break off all relations of a colonial character with France; we repeal all the international obligation that France has so far subscribed to on behalf of Viet Nam and we abolish all the special rights the French have unlawfully acquired in our Fatherland.

The whole Vietnamese people, animated by a common purpose, are determined to fight to the bitter end against any attempt by the French colonialists to reconquer their country.

We are convinced that the Allied nations which at Teheran and San Francisco have acknowledged the principles of self-determination and equality of nations, will not refuse to acknowledge the independence of Viet Nam.

A people who have courageously opposed French domination for more than eighty years, a people who have fought side by side with the Allies against the fascists during these last years, such a people must be free and independent.

For these reasons, we, members of the Provisional Government of the Democratic Republic of Viet Nam, solemnly declare to the world that Viet Nam has the right to be a free and independent country—and in fact it is so already. The entire Vietnamese people are determined to mobilize all their physical and mental strength, to sacrifice their lives and property in order to safeguard their independence and liberty.

2 September 1945

SOURCE: Ho Chi Minh, *Selected Works* (Hanoi: Foreign Languages Publishing House, 1961), Vol. III.

APPENDIX B

(The following statement was made during research for this work by an American-army officer, at the time a lieutenant colonel, who had vast experience in Vietnam. He arrived in-country in mid-1964, became fascinated with what was happening there, and volunteered for repeated extensions of his tour. He came to speak Vietnamese nearly as well as those born to the language, traveled extensively throughout the country, married a Vietnamese national, and for some years thereafter was regularly called upon by various agencies because of his thorough knowledge of that far-off land.)

"From my own perspective, it is unrealistic and therefore analytically unfeasible to look at anything that occurred in Vietnam from strictly a military point of view, despite the proclivity of the army to do so. Of course, when you are trying to separate something out for the purpose of analysis, you do have to break it into its discrete parts. The army structure did not do that. It could never accept the fact that there could be any point of view other than its own solution of firepower and destruction.

"When I first came into Vietnam I was assigned as an adviser to a Vietnamese district chief. At that time I would go out on operations with PF and RF forces, and, very occasionally, with the ARVN 7th Division. I remember how many of my U.S. officer friends who were captains, majors, and lieutenant colonels would often look at ARVN tactical operations with great reservation, disgusted at what they saw as sloppy tactics. They said ARVN wasn't doing the job properly, according to the best of what was then taught at service schools in the United States Army.

"They claimed to see poor infantry tactics, poor coordination of infantry and artillery, lack of aggressiveness in certain situations where aggressiveness was called for; and they observed repeated failures of ARVN to take up the chase in pursuit operations. Most of all they decried the ARVN tendency to rely on artillery to take over the infantry's role. ARVN seemed unwilling to press infantry assaults, hoping that artillery could do the job and obviate the need for the use of foot soldiers. 'Poor tactics generally,' our advisers said.

"I remember so many of those American advisers saying: 'Oh, if we could only have a few American units here. Just give me an American battalion and

I'll turn this province around' so that it will be somewhere to the right of Ivan the Terrible. Such officers, talking that way, never realized at the time that it wouldn't be long until Lyndon B. Johnson would indeed send American units over there. Suddenly those officer friends of mine had company and battalion commands to lead.

"Strangely enough, I would suggest that one of the most grievous errors many of the newly arrived American units made was the one—the same one —for which we had so often criticized ARVN. Nor was the mistake self-correcting as time went on, but rather became ever more compounded.

"We tried to bring overbearing firepower on target to replace the expenditure of human beings, infantrymen. Americans did that for the same reason ARVN had done so. When ARVN did so it was a cowardly act. When we did so it was to save the lives of soldiers. Now of course it is doctrine taught and studied at Ft. Benning, Georgia, in the infantry school and other places, that such an approach may not be the best way to save lives. While a unit may lose more soldiers right at the time that it is aggressively pressing an assault, in the long run it may actually save lives because aggressive assault will be effective in vitiating enemy units and attenuating their strength. That would be in accord with sound military doctrine as taught at the time. Thus, over a shorter period, the army would mount significant combat operations and thus emerge from the war as victors. In such a way the army would end up saving lives as opposed to being engaged in an endless stalemate or alternatively losing and having an enemy mop *us* up. And such Ft. Benning tactics would probably have worked anyplace and at any time where we could tell the enemy troops from the civilian population; where we could *find* the enemy and destroy him.

"In any case, many American commanders (my old critical friends and the thousands who arrived later), like their Vietnamese counterparts whom they had in the past criticized so vociferously, were not able for many reasons to take the long-range view and implement the doctrine that they, and I, had learned and espoused. So they soon fell into the same practices they had earlier so despised. They did not wish to suffer too many casualties among the men of their units. It was not only a humanistic tension such as we all feel (which is laudable and understandable), but there was also a pressure from above on commanders to keep injuries and casualties down.

"Further, those commanders could call on such a wealth of firepower, air strikes, artillery, so they used those in lieu of sending American boys out to attack the enemy wherever he might have been found. And still the commanders worried about casualty figures. We all remember the Pentagon description of casualties from an operation as being "light" or "moderate." And the commentator on CBS, NBC, or ABC would have to translate that bureaucratic euphemism into something more intelligible for the American people. The army would claim that casualties were "light," and Walter would say that really means "moderate." The army would say casualties were "moderate," and David and Chet would say that really means "heavy." It just became a kind of routine translation. All this generated a lot of pressure on officers not to be a unit commander with an inordinate number of casualties, and so some came to specialize in 'search-and-avoid' missions.

"It not only generated pressure not to use infantry assaults but to substitute firepower for men and to halt operations when night came. Now we had said in earlier years to our Vietnamese counterparts: 'Take the night away from the VC. You've got to be aggressive at nighttime.' You know that at Ft. Benning, Georgia, and at Ft. Leavenworth, Kansas, we *love* night operations. But I submit to you that when we were in Vietnam we did *not* love night operations any more than ARVN did. When I visited American battalions, I found that at nightfall they ceased operations and buttoned up very carefully. Or some commanders would write up patrol plans for night activities but would not actually implement them any more than ARVN did theirs. Our units which *did* go out at night patrolled much shorter distances than they were supposed to, then stopped, dug in, and slept all night. There was a lot of that sort of avoidance, and there is little use in anyone denying it.

"It may perhaps seem strange to say, but the American army would have been better off (indeed, it could hardly have been worse off no matter what it might have done) if it had simply implemented its own doctrine, in the same way that we used to tell ARVN it would be better off if it implemented our way of doing things.

"Another thing. I would suggest that we would have been much better off if many of our military operations had resembled a scalpel rather than a sledge hammer; if we had, for example, made wider use of the marine CAP program. I have to concede to Bill Corson that what his marines were doing was far, far better than what most other American units in Vietnam were doing, such as the 9th US Division down in the Delta, which did horrible things to the people living there. There was absolutely no comparison between CAP and what most army units were doing. For example, if CAP killed fifteen enemy soldiers, they usually had fifteen weapons to swho for it. At the same time, large and small army units were killing fifteen or five or fifty enemies and might not have a single weapon to show for it at the end when the firing stopped—not one! In other words, in plain English, they were killing noncombatants and claiming them as dead enemy soldiers.

"Now I know that CAP teams did not address some of the sophisiticated psychological variables or political factors that probably would have been necessary to address more efficaciously if we had wanted to win the war, but at least they did make their presence in the villages count for something positive. That's more than most any army unit could claim.

"To sum up? Well, perhaps I can say simply that we fought the wrong people in the wrong way. And thus we lost."

APPENDIX C

Memorandum from Lieutenant General William R. Peers, investigative officer for the Son My (My Lai) incident, to General William C. Westmoreland, army chief of staff, 18 March 1970, and accompanying enclosure.

DEPARTMENT OF THE ARMY
WASHINGTON, D.C. 20310

CS (Peers Inquiry)   18 March 1970

MEMORANDUM FOR: CHIEF OF STAFF, US ARMY

SUBJECT: The Son My Incident

1. The recently completed Inquiry of the Son My incident has served to reinforce several of my views regarding the moral and ethical standards required of US Army officers and noncommissioned officers. Accordingly, I feel it appropriate to provide you with a summary of such views while they are still fresh in my mind and before they become diffused in the aftermath of the formal findings previously forwarded to you. The summary of such views is inclosed herewith.

2. In stating these views, it is not my intent to prescribe the overall character and qualities required of an officer or noncommissioned officer. Rather it is to focus on some of the unique requirements placed upon an individual chosen to serve in a position of responsibility in a counter-insurgency environment such as existed in South Vietnam at the time of the Son My incident.

3. I have no doubt that these views influenced the judgments, findings and the recommendations contained in the formal report of investigation. They are provided to you for whatever use you may deem appropriate.

1 Incl
as

W. R. PEERS
Lieutenant General, USA

Leadership Requirements
in a Counterinsurgency Environment

1. Throughout the Vietnam war, Headquarters MACV has consistently placed great emphasis on the other side of the war—the Pacification Program —the battle for the hearts and minds of the people. In addition to the directives on this broad subject and the discussions at the various senior commanders' conferences, the matters of soldierly conduct and the proper treatment of Vietnamese civilians have been topics continually emphasized by senior military and civilian officials during their visits to the forces in the field. This guidance has provided direction to the actions of all US subordinate commands and agencies within South Vietnam and is of sufficient clarity, quality, and strength as to preclude any doubt as to what was and is intended of our conduct toward the Vietnamese people.

2. The application of this guidance may have been more forceful and direct on the part of some commanders than in the case of others. Based on my knowledge of the war in South Vietnam, however, most senior combat commanders have adopted extremely high standards and criteria in transmitting such guidance to their subordinate commanders and in overseeing the results of that guidance.

3. My interpretation of the guidance noted above, my views concerning the attitudes and moral standards required of personnel in the US Army, and my exposure to the events of Son My, have all served to temper the feelings expressed below:

   a. Commanders at all echelons are responsible for the actions and the welfare of all of the men under them. A commander cannot delegate such responsibility to his subordinates nor can he shrug it off by indicating a lack of knowledge. It is his duty to ferret out potential and actual trouble areas and to be on the spot to take corrective action. Obviously, he cannot do this alone. Instead, he must have an effective system of command and control so that his desires and concerns are communicated and reflected throughout his command.

   b. There can be no vacillation with the truth. Statements and reports, whether in combat or garrison, must be precise, factual, and complete, with no shading of the unpleasant or unflattering aspects of such reports. Officers who fail to adhere to this practice violate their commission.

   c. All officers, irrespective of their position, are responsible for taking corrective action on the spot when they see something wrong. Whether the officer is a commander or a staff officer, and whether the violator belongs to his unit or another makes no difference. If the officer does not take corrective action at once, he fails completely in his responsibilities.

   d. Because men's lives are at stake in combat, there can be no acceptance of mediocre leadership nor mediocrity in performance of other duties relating to the support of combat. Failures in leadership or in the performance of duty in combat are due cause for and should demand the removal or reassignment of the officer concerned to positions of lesser responsibility.

e. Directives and regulations, no matter how well prepared and intended, are only pieces of paper unless they are enforced aggressively and firmly throughout the chain of command. To be effective, a commander must make his presence felt by insuring that the information and guidance contained in directives are communicated to the appropriate unit level and members of his command.

f. The Army General and Special Staff System is designed to assist commanders in the conduct and administration of their operations. On the one hand, a commander who fails to effectively utilize the talents and experience of his staff will not be able to achieve the full potential of his command. On the other hand, assignment to a staff position carries with it the responsibility to assist and advise the commander in the planning and execution of functions affecting the entire command. Hence, within his area of interest, a staff officer shares part of the responsibilities with those of the commander.

g. Leadership is most effective when it is conducted on a person-to-person, face-to-face basis; it cannot effectively be exercised over a telephone, radio, or any other form of electronic communication. To be effective a combat leader frequently must be on the ground with his men to know firsthand the situation that exists.

h. Senior noncommissioned officers provide the link between the commander and the enlisted personnel of a unit. They serve as a sounding board, and an informal but highly effective communications means for providing information and suggestions to the commander. They are the prime means for determining the condition and well-being of the men, and to alert him to any trouble spots which may arise. To be effective, commanders must utilize their capabilities to the fullest.

i. A commander must be constantly alert to changes in the attitude and temperament of his men and the units to which they belong. Ground combat in a counterinsurgency environment may develop frustrations and bitterness which manifest themselves in acts quite apart from that which would normally be expected. Accordingly, commanders must be quick to spot such changes and to take appropriate corrective action. Any indications of an attitudinal change from one of physical toughness in combat to senseless brutality requires immediate remedial action by the commander concerned.

j. An effective combat commander must from time to time require troops to do things which at the moment may be against their will. For example, after a full day's operation, to dig in at night and build overhead cover can be sheer drudgery. Popularity of the leader does not necessarily accrue from requiring troops in the jungle to properly care for themselves and their equipment, or continually maintain their security. Forcing unpleasant duties on men, in thier own and their unit's best interest, is an accepted part of combat leadership. It is a difficult and encompassing job, requiring discrimination between what is necessary and right and that which is patently illegal.

k. In the heat of battle, some officers and men tend to lose sight of the more fundamental issues upon which the war is being waged. Along with the attitudinal changes described above, this can lead to winning a battle or

two but losing a war. It is an inherent and paramount responsibility of
the commander to insure that his officers and men understand, are
constantly reminded of, and put into practice the principles of discriminate and tightly controlled application of firepower; genuine and practical concern for private property no matter how valueless or insignificant
it may appear; humane treament and care of refugees, noncombatants,
and wounded (whether friendly or enemy); and the judicious safeguard-
ing and processing of suspects and prisoners of war.

l. An officer's highest loyalty is to the Army and the nation. On those rare
occasions when people around him engage in activities clearly wrong
and immoral, he is required by virtue of his being an officer to take
whatever remedial action is required, regardless of the personal consequences.

4. The combat commander at any level who fails to keep these considerations uppermost in his mind and in the minds of the men who serve under him,
invites disaster. In my view, the validity of thes considerations and their importance to us, as soldiers, are borne out in a review of the events of Son My.

APPENDIX D

The following analysis of the goals and methods of insurgent forces in South Vietnam is set forth so that the interested reader may determine the procedures by which "people's revolutionary warfare" moves toward its objectives. The United States Army chose to meet the threat of Vietnamese insurgency with overwhelming firepower and reliance upon technological devices, ignorant of the fact that adverse effects often accrue from using excessive force in a "people's war."

The names sound strange to our ears: Binh Long, Xinh Dinh, Cap Lao, Kinh Duc, An Khe, Viet An and Phu My; to the Viet Cong, those communities and hundreds of others were targets for action. Communist cadres returned repeatedly to such sites to terrorize government sympathizers, assassinate prominent collaborators, and lecture villagers and indoctrinate them in slogans of the revolution. It was customary among the Viet Cong, or more properly, members of the People's Revolutionary Party, to develop simple slogans *(khau hieu)* encompassing the goals of their struggle, thus making it easy for both cadre and peasants to keep doctrines and missions clearly in mind.[1]

The basic and longstanding objective of the PRP was independence. In one sense, the PRP did not consider itself an insurgent movement at all, for "insurgency" connotes an uprising against some "established" government. Members of the PRP never believed in the legitimacy of southern governments. They saw only a succession of titular regimes based in Saigon. Such administrations had offices and operations in larger towns and cities, in province or district capitals; they commanded an army and enjoyed aid from the United States. Yet, es-

---

[1]This discussion is based on three kinds of sources: a number of lengthy interviews with involved principals, familiarity with many of the requisite primary documents, and wide reading in secondary studies. Interested readers should consult such works as Jeffrey Race, *War Comes to Long An: Revolutionary Conflict in a Vietnamese Province* (Berkeley: University of California Press, 1972); Gerald Hickey, *Village in Vietnam* (New Haven: Yale University Press, 1964); Taber, *The War of the Flea*; and a thirty-two page study by the then chief of the Strategic Research Group, National War College, produced in accordance with that institution's mission of "conducting research and study in the field of national security": John M. Collins, *The Vietnam War in Perspective* (Washington: National War College, 10 May 1972).

tranged from their own subjects, insensitive and hardened to the sufferings of their own people, habituated to callousness as to their own wrongdoings and corruption, never able to command the respect or allegiance of any significant proportion of the population in the South—such regimes were easily dismissed by the PRP as illegitimate. It could thus consistently work toward its basic goal of independence no matter which government sat in Saigon, from Diem through Thieu.

The PRP could point with pride to the long years during which it had held to its objective of independence, first against the French, then the Japanese, then the French again, and finally, against all the successive United States-backed regimes. The PRP taught that Vietnam must be free from both puppet governments and foreign control. It was a policy with which people could identify—a combination of nationalism and patriotism. Cadremen could inevitably whip up renewed enthusiasm for this goal whenever they desired by pointing out recent instances of Saigon's misrule (those were always easy to find), ranging from official misuse of government funds to misappropriation of commodities allocated for countryside peasants, extortion, false imprisonment and torture and execution, theft from private individuals by government officials, sham elections, and the continued ravaging of the people and their country by the long war. The PRP occasionally summed up their objective in the slogan "peace, independence, and national reunification" *(hoa binh thong nhut)*.

It had strong appeal, for Vietnamese have a significant and abiding sense of national heritage developed as a result of a thousand-year struggle for identity against the Chinese, and a similar hundred-year period of conflict with the French. So Vietnamese in the villages listened when a Viet Cong cadreman told how consummation of this objective could accomplish such great things as ending ruinous inflation, lowering bankruptcy rates, alleviating unemployment, and putting a stop to political instability. Furthermore, people were taught, *hoa binh thong nhut* would lessen such societal evils as youth's growing disrespect for their elders and for traditional ways of doing things; it would retard robbery and murder rates; and it would end the deflowering and degradation of Vietnamese women by American imperialist interventionists.

Success in the revolution would not only restore independence, unification, ethnic solidarity, and other such virtues; it would, the PRP proclaimed, produce "freedom and democracy" *(tu do dan chu)*. This second objective focused upon the increasingly burdensome governmental regulations emanating from the autocrats in Saigon: travel restrictions, constantly changing identification cards, ever higher taxes, unnecessary expenses piled upon those least able to pay, and the inability of the poor to procure justice in the face of appointed or "elected" officials, A province chief for Long An Province, Mai Ngoc Duoc, put it well: ". . . the very best fertilizer for the communist apparatus is [governmental] injustice and corruption. If a country can eliminate injustice and stamp out corruption—if it can clean out its government—then the communists cannot develop,"[2] Saigon would not, or could not, do this. Consequently, the PRP flourished as more and more of the populace came to believe it had their real interests at heart.

---

[2]Quoted in Race, *Long An*, p. 46.

A third goal of the PRP emphasized economic issues under the slogan "popular livelihood" *(dan sinh)*. Here their cadremen were all things to all people. To workers in the cities the VC concentrated on such ills as runaway inflation and high unemployment; when talking with farmers, they averred that land problems were uppermost.

PRP cadre knew that in order for their revolutionary warfare to succeed, the movement they espoused did not need to be better or more effective on any absolute scale than that of the Saigon government; it had only to be measurably better than what people currently enjoyed—and that was not difficult.

The PRP also recognized that in order to keep their followers loyal and to attract new recruits, all revolutionary leaders within the party's Central Office for South Vietnam (COSVN), or among the hard inner-pyramidal core of the PRP, or within the broad-based National Liberation Front must give indication of great dedication far beyond simple personal ambition. Leaders must at all times hold high their ideology—their "cause"—to explain the reasons behind the insurgency. They were careful never to appear as mere opportunists and thus had to be able to explain the often confused nature of the conflict they waged.

It was crucial for leaders to establish that revolutionary violence was a natural and moral way to achieve the goals of the party. This, after all, was "total war," and cruelty, indifference, and high casualties were justified. Mao had said it: in a social revolution there should be little regard for "stupid scruples about benevolence, righteousness and morality." In this way, any violent acts committed out of necessity could be seen by the populace to be neither chaotic nor meaningless, but as acts crucial to further the great "cause." Through such means PRP cadremen aroused the expectations of those with whom they worked, miring them ever deeper in their cause, and allowing fewer and fewer to stand apart from the great work at hand.

Since many revolutionary cadremen were themselves of peasant origins, they had little trouble understanding and supporting the needs of those in agricultural hamlets and villages. Farmers wanted land of their own. They wanted to be free from landlords and tax collectors. They wanted peace so that they could live in safety and without oppression. These things the guerrillas promised them. The PRP preached that the revolution, when successful, would end exploitation and bring justice to all; everyone would be taxed fairly. Once again, peasants would have a voice in their own governance as village administrations returned to their traditional form. Landlords would be cast out and the land redistributed. But these were only promises and by themselves would not be sufficient to enlist the enduring sympathies of cynical and skeptical peasants.

So the Viet Cong acted. In areas that they controlled, they did precisely what they promised to do everywhere one day in the future. Since government tax collectors feared to enter the area, the VC themselves levied and collected fair taxes from the citizenry. They redistributed land. People were given a voice in village councils. Canals and dikes were rebuilt, hedges replanted. And the supporters of the PRP became legion. In this way the PRP succeeded in arousing the people. Its secret weapon was its ability to inspire others to share its own burdens, all the while working together toward a better future. Thus VC guerrillas came to have secure bases from which to operate, and from which they could not easily be dislodged. Government police or soldiers, usually moving about the countryside only during daylight hours, found a stony wall of silence when they questioned villagers about the whereabouts of guerrillas. Saigon's sources of information dried up as the populace found the courage to remain silent in the face of official questioning. Those who did talk—for whatever reason—were first warned against repeating their error. If they did so the VC executed them, often publicly, as a grim reminder to others not to cooperate with the government.[3] Without meeting much real opposition, guerrillas using such tactics took over ever larger portions of the countryside, further restricting operations of Saigon governments to cities and urban areas. Despite its use of terror, the PRP was an excellent persuader of the uncommitted through its championing of the people.

As soon as guerrillas controlled any area sufficiently for it to be regarded as a safe and secure base of operations, they launched irregular-warfare operations from it. The initiative for conflict lay with them. They began the insurgency in South Vietnam. They were the ones who decided when and where to strike. The Saigon government and its army, "guardian" of public and private property in the south, found itself constantly on the defensive. Everywhere it had vast and expensive properties to protect: communities large and small, from the tiniest hamlet to metropolitan Saigon; roads, bridges, culverts, rail beds, trestles, signals, switches, rolling stock; warehouses, wharfs, drydocks, and ships; microwave relay stations, wires, telephone cables, radio stations, and fences; agricultural lands stretching from the Ca Mau Peninsula in the south to the Song Ben Ha River north of Quang Tri.

Valuable properties of the Army of the Republic of Vietnam (ARVN), designed to defend the government, were in themselves tempting and attractive targets for insurgents: soldiers, tentage, field rations, pistols, rifles, automatic weapons, mines, radios, hand grenades, barracks and headquarters buildings, armored personnel carriers, trucks and convoys, air bases—with all their sophisticated electronic gear. Thus both government and army had an abundance of costly holdings that were vulnerable to guerrilla attack.

The Viet Cong, in their poverty, had a certain freedom of action. They had nothing to defend but their own lives. They owned nothing but their clothes and their weapons (which usually had been captured from their enemies). They defended no territory, but moved freely from one location to another as the need arose. As Taber phrases it, they had no "establishment to maintain, no

---

[3]See Denis Warner, *The Last Confucian* (New York: MacMillan and Company, 1953). Warner makes a pungent observation, on page 89, when he states: "Summary Viet Cong justice for a village chief guilty of corruption or brutality did not offend the peasants. On the contrary, it tended to endow the Viet Cong with some of the characteristics of Robin Hood and his band of merry men." Also consult George K. Tanham, *Communist Revolutionary Warfare* (New York: F. A. Praeger, 1962). Although this focuses primarily on the organization and tactics of the Viet Minh, it has information of interest regarding later years. For a procommunist view of insurgency, see Wilfred G. Burchett, *Vietnam: Inside Story of the Guerrilla War* (New York: International Publishers, 1965). Another interesting account is that of the RAND Corporation, *Origins of the Insurgency in South Vietnam, 1954–1960: The Role of the Southern Vietminh Cadres* (Santa Monica: RAND Corporation, 1967). A good analysis of "revolutionary warfare" and the way it has differed from country to country may be found in Douglas S. Blaufarb, *The Counter-insurgency Era: U.S. Doctrine and Performance, 1950 to the Present* (New York: Macmillan Free Press, 1977), particularly Chapters One and Two.

tanks to risk in battle, no garrisons subject to siege, no transport vulnerable to air attack nor aircraft to be shot down."[4]

If tracked by superior forces, guerrillas could bury their weapons in hidden caches and blend into the peasant population of the countryside, people whose allegiance would eventually provide one side or the other with victory. Had the Viet Cong not had the loyalty of those within whose villages, hamlets, and farms they hid, they could not have endured. Their tactics would have cast them in the role of bandits and warlords, and they would have been cut down, root and branch, by the Saigon government. But because they fought for a cause with which people could identify, men and women gave them active aid, consented to their activities, and supported them in their revolution.

Saigon, and its American ally, made the fatal mistake of perceiving the Viet Cong as conspirators from the north who, through terror tactics, were making political robots of the South Vietnamese country folk. They regarded the VC as outside the social environment of the south, manipulating their minions in obscure ways for sinister purposes. They were, of course, wrong. Taber phrases it succinctly.

> When we speak of the guerrilla fighter we are speaking of the political partisan, an armed civilian whose principal weapon is not his rifle or his machete but his relationship to the community, the nation, in and for which he fights. . . . It would be an error to consider him as a being apart from the seed bed of revolution. He himself is created by the political climate in which revolution becomes possible, and is himself as much an expression as he is a catalyst of the popular will towards such change.[5]

Saigon's task was plain. Faced with a revolution, it had to combat it by destroying the promises held out to the populace by the Viet Cong. It had to demonstrate amply that the insurgents could not and would not succeed. The government failed in its task. It chose to ignore real social problems that cried out for redress. It tightened political control, heightening the repression of the people. It assumed that the insurgents were little more than bandits and terrorists who could be rooted out through conventional military means.[6]

While the PRP understood the revolution in South Vietnam to be a phase-by-phase socio/politico/military process (and consequently acted multidimensionally), the Saigon government saw the problem as merely an action to be met militarily (hence it reacted in a one-dimensional manner). Sophistication lay on the side of the PRP. Even high-ranking South Vietnamese army officers failed to perceive the nature of the conflict they faced. One man, Colonel Nguyen van Nguu, presumably should have known better. A graduate of the Military Cadet School in Vung Tau, and a province chief from 1966 to 1969, he expressed his attitudes toward the Viet Cong in ways that revealed the paucity of his own (and by implication, his government's) understanding of revolutionary warfare. "The reason that the Vietcong use guerrillas," he said, "is because they are weak and do not have enough strength to attack us directly. Thus they must use guerrillas to wear us down."[7] Race, who conducted the interview, mused on the

[4]Taber, *The War of the Flea*, p. 22.
[5]Taber, *The War of the Flea*, pp. 21, 19.
[6]Robert H. Williams, *A Construct of Insurgency-Counterinsurgency in Vietnam* (McLean, VA: Research Analysis Corporation, 1966).
[7]Race, *Long An*, p. 241.

meaning of those words. "This view, that guerrilla techniques are 'the weapon of the weak,' and thus presumably are inappropriate once one is 'strong,'" was a fallacous notion not only held by the South Vietnamese but also "fundamental in current American military doctrine."[8]

Even had the government of South Vietnam sought to adopt guerrilla tactics as a means of counterinsurgency warfare, it would have been unavailing.

> The guerrilla can afford to run and hide. The counter-insurgent gains nothing by doing so; he surrenders everything. The guerrilla can disguise himself as—in fact he can be—a peaceful agrarian worker, and still spread his message. In a similar role, the counter-insurgent would be merely a police spy. The guerrilla can run and hit. The counter-insurgent gains nothing by such tactics—even if similar targets were available to him, and they are not.[9]

Consequently, in counterinsurgency activities, the Saigon government relied heavily on military solutions. A reasonably strong army allowed it to command most of the important roads, at least during daylight hours. Unfortunately, it was fighting an enemy that had no need of roads, for it was without transport or heavy artillery. Guerrillas avoided government-controlled roads, passing unseen on either side of them at a distance of, perhaps, one hundred yards, moving in safety through jungle and rice paddies. The government seized and held strong points that commanded nothing, since its enemy was not interested in stationary defenses and seldom contested for either strong points or territory. The ARVN fought "to occupy territory, roads, strategic heights, vital areas; the guerrilla fought to control people, without whose cooperation the land was useless to its possessor." Consequently the government's actions were doomed to failure, for Vietnam was too large, its population was too great, the landscape provided too much natural cover within which guerrillas could hide, and army forces were too small.[10]

President Diem found himself facing a nasty, festering wound that he was unable to disinfect. While, during the early stages of insurgency, the Viet Cong had operated in scattered bands of company or even platoon strength, they later fought with forces as large as battalions. What had once been scattered guerrilla raids then became major assaults by mobile strike columns. Pursued by the ARVN, guerrillas dispersed, later to resume small-unit harassment. Conventionally trained troops found such warfare more and more difficult to combat. Strikes against cities forced Diem to pull in ARVN reinforcements from the countryside, leaving guerrillas clearly in control of rural areas.

Every foray of ARVN into the back country, every battle with insurgents, every civilian casualty produced further attrition of governmental strength and new recruits for the Viet Cong, as previously uncommitted Vietnamese decided to spurn allegiance to the Saigon government that caused them so much pain and terror and death. When ARVN won battles, it created additional bitterness and despair in those who saw their kin and friends slaughtered. That such deaths might even have often been accidental did not lessen the bitterness of those affected. When they knew such killings were deliberate, peasants readily volunteered for service with the Viet Cong. (Nor did this change with the entry

[8]*Ibid.*
[9]Taber, *The War of the Flea*, p. 24.
[10]Taber, *The War of the Flea*, p. 63.

of the American army into the fray. One officer who served in Vietnam commented that he was certain that village sweeps inevitably did more harm than good. A village that was "only" 80 percent VC could usually be counted upon to be a solid 95 percent in favor of the insurgents after an American troop unit had combed through its huts and people.[11]

When ARVN lost firefights, erstwhile supporters and collaborators lost confidence in the government and defected to the Viet Cong. "The greater the violence, the wider and more severe the negative results. Yet, on the other hand, to wage less vigorous campaigns was to permit the VC to throw wider their net, with the same results: increasing defections, widening alienation."[12] For country people, contacts with the government were inevitably unpleasant: tax collectors, police officials, ARVN troops (who brought artillery fires, automatic weapons, napalm, and death). Peasants could hardly be expected to show —or feel—enthusiasm for such a government. For these reasons, even the reluctant eventually came to feel sympathetic toward the Viet Cong, who often came from their own hamlets and who shared their danger and their burdens and afflictions.[13] They too joined their voices in the words of a Viet Cong song:

WE ARE PEASANTS IN SOLDIER'S CLOTHING
WAGING A STRUGGLE FOR A CLASS OPPRESSED FOR A THOUSAND YEARS.
OUR SUFFERING IS THE SUFFERING OF THE PEOPLE.

The lyrics might leave something to be desired, but their sentiments made very effective propaganda.

What was the government to do? It lost ground to the VC when it fought; not to do so was to give up the land without contest. Diem considered military force to be the most efficient way to wipe out the guerrillas, but this was as difficult as untying the Gordian knot, because he could neither separate them from nor identify them within the populace. Even Diem was aware that it would solve nothing to destroy the entire population. And so the Viet Cong continued to wear down its military opponent. It fed and fanned the fires of revolution by enlisting ever larger segments of the people against Saigon. It strove to discredit the government in all its acts and to isolate it even from its supporters. The VC sought to wreck the credit of the government of South Vietnam, to undermine its economy, to overextend its resources. The Viet Cong believed that if it could accomplish these things then ultimately the Saigon government would disintegrate.

Colonel Nguyên Be, longtime commandant of South Vietnam's National Training Center for Rural Construction Cadre at Vung Tau, once commented on the results of the PRP insurgency. "It caused my country to mobilize, to raise a huge army. It created financial chaos. For several years, the expenditure of Vietnam's army was annually five times the size of the national budget and the national budget was three times the size of our gross national product."[14] Had

[11]Subject interview.
[12]Taber, *The War of the Flea*, p. 88.
[13]The interested reader may wish to consult Truong Chinh, *Primer for Revolt: The Communist Takeover in Vietnam* (New York: F. A. Praeger, 1963).
[14]Interview with Colonel Nguyên Be, Washington, D.C., 23 June 1977. At that time Be was working with the Department of Health, Education, and Welfare as an advisor on Vietnamese refugee resettlement. I have no idea whether his views on Vietnamese

it not been for massive and unstinting American aid, neither Diem nor any of his successors could long have maintained the south as a separate geopolitical entity.

The PRP never lost sight of the fact that their struggle was both political and social. Even when its actions focused on military operations, its goals remained essentially political. The façade was insurgency; the structure was built of radical social and political change. In the face of all this, the task of the government of South Vietnam was primarily to resist PRP/VC inroads—and ultimately to destroy them—through a self-proclaimed counterrevolution. In this it failed utterly.

For Diem (and his successors)—and for Vietnam's American ally—"nation building" seemed to have but one meaning: consolidation of political power in Saigon through a powerful unitary state. They pursued this goal despite the fact that it flew directly in the face of Vietnam's long history, which had emphasized political decentralization and village autonomy.

There were many other, more productive efforts that the government of South Vietnam might have made. It could have become more involved in agricultural assistance to the peasantry: selling fertilizer and pumps at cost, disseminating technical information on planting and harvesting techniques. It could have distributed improved and low-cost—or free—seed. It could have offered unsecured loans to tenant farmers who traditionally could not get loans except at exorbitant interest. It could have pushed redistribution of land and restricted the prices extracted by absentee landlords through rack rents from unfortunate renters.

The government should have declared a social revolution of its own to convince the nation that its goal was real independence, real nationalism, real dedication to improving the lot of the peasantry. It should have avoided corruption and favoritism. It should have repudiated and banned governmental imprisonment of those who disagreed with it. It should have instituted tax reforms. It did none of these things.[15]

Most heads of the South Vietnamese government could not countenance the thought of any conceivable rival occupying a position from which he might launch a *coup d'etat.* They seldom felt secure except when they could terrorize all possible opponents, and regularly they tried to neutralize or destroy the power of those who disagreed with them. Their recourse, when faced with insurgency, was a "knee-jerk" reliance upon force. They gave little consideration to possible political and social alternatives that might have turned the

---

finances were correct, but even if they are in error they still indicate that Diem's expenditures were out of kilter with the resources of his own nation.

[15]James B. Henry, *The Small World of Khanh Hau* (Chicago: Aldine Publishers, 1964) is a good portrayal of the economic life and limited opportunities for development in a Vietnamese agricultural settlement during the Diem years. Other works of interest on these points include Edward G. Lansdale, "Vietnam: Do We Understand Revolution?" *Foreign Affairs* XLIII (1964): 75–86; Wilfrid G. Burchett, *Vietnam: Inside Story of the Guerrilla War* (New York: International Publishers, 1965); J. A. Pustay, *Counterinsurgency Warfare* (Glencoe: The Free Press, 1965); and Doughlas E. Pike, *Notes from the Underground: The Mystique of a Viet Cong* (Saigon: February 1962). Pustay was an air-force major, Pike served as special-projects officer for the United States Information Agency (USIA), and Lansdale continued to work for the CIA. By the time he wrote this work he was a major general.

people toward support of the government rather than toward the Viet Cong. Indeed, many government policies seemed bent on doing the very things that would inevitably turn people against it and cause an opposition army to spring up like blades of grass in a field.

Such leaders were able to affect only Vietnam's political superstructure— the national army, the skeletal nationwide administrative hierarchy, and the populated cities—but they never created a system that would reach the foundations of Vietnamese society—the village. They allowed no mass political parties. They nurtured no local institutions. Uninterested in and perhaps incapable of real social change, such administrations never put down deep roots in the soil of Vietnamese culture.[16]

Even when men such as Ngo Dinh Diem could be roused into trying new programs, such operations tended to be faulty in conception and ineffectual in execution.[17] He seemed oblivious to the value systems of his own native culture, as evidenced by his acceptance of various suggestions that culminated in his adoption of the "strategic hamlet" movement of 1962. Diem knew that many villages were under constant threat from the Viet Cong, and also that many districts did not have sufficient "supporters" of the government living in them. He thought he could remedy both ills in one stroke. He would move peasants from threatened villages to new ones in former Viet Minh strongholds. The United States cooperated in this project, known as the Staley Plan—Operation Sunrise—which began with the razing of existing villages and the regrouping of entire communities into newly built settlements.[18] These were constructed at specifically determined sites, fortified and protected by rings of concertina wire, punji (bamboo) stakes implanted in the ground with their sharpened edges pointing outward to impale unwary attackers, mud walls, ditches, and moats.

The attitudes of those forced to move to such communities were not happy ones. The reason may be found in a popular Vietnamese tune of the time, sung when young people moved into an ancestral home:

This house, this house is ours now,
Our ancestors have built it with so much hardship
That we must take care of it and keep it safe
For ten thousand years, along with our country.[19]

Their new houses had certainly not been built by their ancestors but were rather newly erected in unfamiliar locations.

---

[16]See, for example, the limited view of William A. Nighswonger, *Rural Pacification in Viet Nam: 1962–1965* (Washington: Advanced Research Project Agency, 1966).

[17]See Robert Scigliano, *South Vietnam: Nation under Stress* (Boston: Houghton Mifflin, 1963). For a study by one who was a close associate of Diem prior to breaking with him in 1962, see Nguyên Thai, *Is South Vietnam Viable?* (Manila: Carmelo and Bauermann, Inc., 1962). For a view of Diem's half-hearted efforts at creating a "revolutionary ideology," see John C. Donnell, "National Renovation Campaigns in Vietnam," *Pacific Affairs* XXXII, 1 (April, 1959): 73–88.

[18]Named after Dr. Eugene Staley, a Stanford Research Institute economist, the program was called "Sunrise." Whereas the VC had heretofore ruled the night hours, these new hamlets would protect the people from them. Thus the "dawn" would come when they would be safe. See Gabriel Kolko, *The Roots of American Foreign Policy* (Boston: Beacon Press, 1969), pp. 120–121.

[19]A very similar version appears in Lederer, *Our Own Worst Enemy*, pp. 178–179n.

The government hoped the program would help villagers defend themselves against marauding bands of VC until government troops could be contacted by radio and brought in to rout the enemy. Governmental cadres were trained to move in to each village scheduled for relocation in order to prepare its people for the move. They would follow such villagers to their new settlement and orient them to life there. Cadres would provide simple governmental services, dig wells, survey fields, offer medical care. A school would be built and staffed with a teacher. Younger peasants would be provided with minimal small-arms training, given weapons, and entrusted with defense of the settlement, acting as a village militia. Police forces were to work with the inhabitants, gaining their trust, so that they would be willing to identify Viet Cong members to the government.

Some villages would not have to be relocated but simply consolidated. Many Vietnamese hamlets were clusters of homes, although some—scattered out from the main group at distances from one hundred yards to a mile—were outlying ones. These would have to be destroyed or dismantled and the people moved inside the newly erected defensive perimeter.

People would be issued new plastic identification cards. Curfews would be established. Those out after curfew would be, *ipso facto,* Viet Cong bandits. Provincial police and soldiers would set up checkpoints to control population movements and set ambushes to trap unwary guerrillas. Security zones would be marked off in widening circles around such settlements as pacification spread through the countryside. Establishing such a settlement would require time, patience, and an understanding of villagers."

As Hilsman has reported: "It was to be a program, for one lone strategic hamlet could not effectively defend itself. It would be an oil blot, spreading upon the water from sea to mountains and jungle."[20] The project did not work. Whether they were called agrovilles or strategic hamlets or new-life villages, they were bitterly resented by those forced to live in them. Pleasant recalcitrance at moving should should have been expected, for often they resisted moving even a few hundred yards away from their traditional home sites, their family graves, their ancestral fields. The whole effort did little more than keep the countryside seething with discontent against the Diem regime.[21]

In addition to those of Staley, the ideas of Sir Robert Thompson of Great Britain played an important part in the formulation of those strategic-hamlet efforts. Regarded by both South Vietnamese and Americans as a foremost ana-

---

[20]Roger Hilsman, *To Move a Nation: The Politics of Foreign Policy in the Administration of John F. Kennedy* (Garden City: Doubleday, 1967), p. 431. Hilsman, who had seen Southeast Asia at first hand with the OSS during World War II, served as head of intelligence in the State Department and then as assistant secretary of state for the Far East under John Kennedy.

[21]*An Examination of the Viet Cong Reaction to the Vietnamese Strategic Hamlet Operation* (Santa Monica: The RAND Corporation, July 1964); Military Assistance Advisory Group, Vietnam, *Village Early Warning System: Reports Covering Current Status of System in Dar Lac and Phu Yen Provinces* (2 October 1962); Lê Châu, *La Révolution paysanne du Sud Viet-Nam* (Paris, 1966), pp. 16–24, 54–79; Nguyên Kien, *Le Sud-Vietnam Depuis Dien-Bien-Phu* (Paris, 1963), pp. 122–130; W. P. Davison, *Some Observations on Viet Cong Operations in the Villages* (Santa Monica: The RAND Corporation, May 1968); and Chalmers Johnson, "Civilian Loyalties and Guerrilla Conflict," *World Politics,* XIV, 4 (July, 1962): 646–661.

lyst and expert on guerrilla warfare, Thompson came by his reputation honestly. He had been the principal architect of Britain's victory over Chinese
insurgents in Malaya in the late 1950s. His strategy there had secured victory
when a British defeat seemed inevitable. Later, Thompson headed the British
Advisory Mission to South Vietnam from 1961 to 1965, then he became a
consultant to the RAND Corporation think tank in California.

Thompson knew insurgent movements at first hand. "Where a guerrilla
force enjoys support from the people, whether willing or forced, it can never
be defeated by military means, however much it is harassed and attacked,
shelled, mortared, and bombed by superior forces of infantry and artillery, air
and sea power." He further contended that "it is the essence of the guerrilla
force that it avoids combat, except in conditions of its own choosing. It retains
the initiative and selects its own targets. The only way to defeat [such a force]
is to cut it off from its true base of support—the people."[22]

Thompson had gone into Malaya at a time when Malayans faced a threat
from Chinese insurgents. Through his persuasiveness," effective tactics were
employed against the guerrillas. To protect the Malayans, he had them moved
from their homes and settlements in unsecured areas into fortified villages.
They were trained in self-defense to fight off attacks of foraging guerrillas.
Thompson learned that there were roughly eight thousand insurgents. Inasmuch as they were Chinese, differing in appearance from indigenous Malays,
he was able to keep track of the number captured and killed. Dealing as he was
with a definite figure, it was simple for him to determine how the struggle was
progressing by subtracting prisoners and dead from the total number of guerrillas who had originally mounted the threat in Malaya. British and native troops
went on missions deep into the jungle looking for insurgents, flushing them
from their hiding places, killing or capturing them. Eventually Thompson and
his forces destroyed the insurgent threat in Malaya.

Thompson also understood something about the insurgent mentality. He
knew that nation building was a more important war measure than defeating
guerrillas in battle. He recognized that if peasants in protected settlements
could understand that they were better off under the existing government than
they would be under the guerrilla-proposed one, if they could be kept safe from
attack and retaliation by insurgents, in time they would commit themselves to
support of the existing government. They would have the courage to deny
rebels supplies and shelter and food. They would be a people armed for their
own protection, with government military and paramilitary troops to reinforce
them.[23]

Flushed with success, hailed as the savior of Malaya, Thompson found
himself called upon by other nations as an advisor on counterinsurgency techniques. He continued to argue that the idea that government existed for the

[22]Quoted in Hilsman, *To Move a Nation*, p. 430. Also see United States Information Agency, *The Viet Cong: Patterns of Communist Subversion* (Washington: Government Printing Office, Research Report R-8-66, January 1966).

[23]Sir Robert Thompson, *No Exit from Vietnam* (New York: David McKay Company,
Inc., 1969), and *Defeating Communist Insurgency: The Lessons of Malaya and Vietnam*
(New York: F. A. Praeger, 1966), by the same author. Also see the excellent study by
Lucien Pye, *Guerrilla Communism in Malaya* (Princeton: Princeton University Press,
1965).

benefit of its people was a revolutionary one. He insisted that peasant recognition of the fact that governments could really care about their welfare was as important and earth shaking and revolutionary as any program that Communists anywhere could offer. He counseled that in all situations of revolutionary warfare, central emphasis should be given to political and civic action. Orthodox military priorities and tendencies must be subjugated to efforts at "nation building." He warned that indiscriminate firefights in populated areas—or any military actions that wantonly allowed killing of civilians—would inevitably push the population away from support of existing governments and toward active enthusiasm for the insurgents. And in all these things he was right.

Experienced and wise as he was, he could also be very wrong. When called upon for advice in South Vietnam, he repeated there his earlier program for Malaya.[24] As an expert, he was respected and listened to and his counsel was followed, but this time with disastrous results. Strategic hamlets in Malaya were fine. People there did not have deep attachments to a particular plot of soil as did the Vietnamese. Malays were glad to move into a fortified settlement that would afford them protection. Vietnamese did so only under duress, and they despised the government that forced them away from ancestral homes.

In Malaya, insurgents were of a different national stock. Few basic sympathies united guerrillas and people, so it was easy to separate the interests of the two groups. In Vietnam, guerrillas in many cases *were* the people. They came from them, fought for them, and were succored by them. The more the government pursued the revolutionary warriors, the more the people themselves felt persecuted. The more civilians that were killed in battle, the more recruits turned up at VC camps to offer their services.

Insurgents and local people were of the same racial and national stock. There was no way to distinguish among them, as there had been in Malaya. Nor was there any way for the government to know the total number of those involved in revolutionary warfare. Thus, unlike in Malaya, body counts were meaningless. Yet American advisors in Vietnam embraced the brilliant tactics of the British counterinsurgency expert and encouraged Diem in his program of strategic hamlets, spoke of the practice of body counts as a superb innovation, and suggested continuation of field tactics that would one day become known as "search and destroy" operations. They were either ignorant of, or callous toward, the fact that the situation in Vietnam was different from what it had been in Malaya. They seemed collectively unaware that tactics that had worked in Malaya had already been tried by the French in Vietnam and had failed.

No one seemed aware of the simple truth that Roger Hilsman later verbalized and that should be memorized by every soldier who must serve in counterinsurgent operations: the very best weapon for fighting a guerrilla is a knife; the very worst is a bomber. The second-best weapon is a rifle; the second-worst is artillery.[25] And Americans, their government becoming increasingly involved in Southeast Asia, were told that "every quantitative measurement we

---

[24]The very different situations in Malaya and Vietnam are carefully pointed out in Milton Osborne, *Strategic Hamlets in South Vietnam* (Ithaca: Cornell Southeast Asia Program, 1965).

[25]Hilsman, *To Move a Nation*, p. 433.

have shows we're winning this war."[26] The slogans and buzzwords would soon fill the air: "We have turned the corner." "Victory is in sight." "Peace is at hand." "We can see the light at the end of the tunnel." "We had to destroy the village to save it." All of them would be both wrong and self-defeating.

An outgrowth of the strategic-hamlet plan was Operation Oil Spot, begun by the government of South Vietnam in 1964. Its central idea was that pacification would start from a secure base and expand slowly outward by means of clear-and-hold military operations. These would be followed by hamlet cadres that would consolidate cleared areas through economic, sociological, political, and psychological means in hopes of getting the population to support the government. If successful, Oil Spot would also embolden rural inhabitants to ferret out the Viet Cong understructure among them and denounce such individuals to the government. It would allow security forces of local males to be organized in sufficient strength to guarantee security after larger ARVN forces moved on to clear and hold other territories. Saigon hoped that this plan would work more effectively than did the strategic-hamlet program, since working from a secure base outward appreciably reduced the number of separated localities that had to be defended. This would supposedly give the government an advantage in positioning its heavy reaction forces.

Nevertheless, Oil Spot faltered, mainly for the same reasons that caused the strategic-hamlet experiment to fail. Military forces, in an essentially defensive stance, were unable to protect from Viet Cong attack and subversion the fruits of months of painstaking, costly pacification efforts. Thus "Operation Oil Spot" came a cropper as had others before it and as others still to come would also inevitably fail—for they all stemmed from the mistaken conviction of the military-force-first school that once the VC were defeated or driven from an area, *then* pacification could begin.[27]

This fixation on the use of military force was not a peculiarity of Diem alone. It was reinforced time and again by United States advisors up to the highest levels. One-time Chairman of the Joint Chiefs of Staff General Earle G. Wheeler was fond of saying, "It is fashionable in some quarters to say that the problems in Southeast Asia are primarily political and economic rather than military. I do not agree. The essence of the problem in Vietnam is military."[28] Wheeler made this comment in a speech at Fordham University, 7 November 1962. That was the caliber of understanding of the man who would, under Lyndon Johnson, serve as army chief of staff. He certainly was not alone in his attitudes.

Newsweek reported on 21 August 1961 that "military sources were downright enthusiastic about the gains being made in Vietnam. 'We're really making

---

[26]This statement, sent out on a wire-service report, was made on 16 May 1962 by Robert S. McNamara only some *forty-eight hours after he had arrived in Vietnam.* Nowhere is there greater evidence for his capacity for self-deception.

[27]An example of that kind of reasoning may be found in an interesting essay that is very "hawk"-like indeed: James M. Lee, *Which Strategy for Advanced Insurgency: Pacification or Combat?* (USAWC student essay, 13 January 1967). Lee, a lieutenant colonel of infantry, believed that combat alone was sufficient to destroy any insurgent movement.

[28]Quoted in Harry Brandon, *Anatomy of Error* (Boston: Gambit Publishers, 1969), p. 23.

hay for the first time in a hell of a long while,' one veteran officer said confidently." A few weeks later, General Maxwell D. Taylor gave the ultimate answer of a military man as to what to do with captured Viet Cong infiltrators: "Why not shoot them?"[29]

The *Christian Science Monitor* put it another way.

> Since the [South Vietnamese] army finds sullen villagers and does not know which are pro-Communist and which are merely dissatisfied with Saigon, and since the army must do its job, it shoots anyone seen running or looking dangerous. It often shoots the wrong peasants. They are in the records of battle listed as Communists. Anyone killed is automatically a Vietcong.[30]

Things had not changed much from the days of French intervention in Vietnam, when they had freely admitted that the way to find a Viet Minh casualty was simply to look for the body of any dead Vietnamese.[31]

The navy did not wish to be left out of the pattern of comment. Admiral Harry D. Felt believed that "if our present military successes continue, we can win this war in three years."[32] And Brigadier General Frank A. Osmanski, an army logistics officer in South Vietnam, estimated that Diem's government forces "are still outkilling the Viet Cong 4 to 1."[33]

These attitudes, of course, filtered downward. A young infantry lieutenant colonel parroted such views when he wrote that the doctrine was unsupportable that declared that "guerrilla war, regardless of stage, is essentially a political one and should be waged more on the political than the military front."[34] It is not surprising that even on the economic level, American aid was oriented toward paying for Diem's ever growing army.

Were there suitable alternatives open to South Vietnamese governments and their American advisers? Of course, Colonel Nguyên Be had regularly suggested one of them. Born in 1929 in central Vietnam's Thua Thien province. Be had seen both sides of the conflict. During Viet Minh days, he had been a battalion commander for the army of that organization. In 1954, at the time of the Geneva Convention, he was a lieutenant colonel up for promotion. When ARVN was formed, the highest rank open for him was that of a first lieutenant. Corson described Be as an honest man among the thieves of the government and military in Vietnam, an ascetic among whores, who practiced an austerity in his own life that was unusual in Vietnam. He was a man who refused to participate in the readily available practices of corruption that were a continuing factor in the life of his nation.[35] Be was highly—and sometimes visibly—critical of the Saigon administrations and consequently received few favors from them.

Under Ngo Dinh Diem, however, Be became commandant of the National Training Center for Rural Construction Cadre at Vung Tau and as such was intimately involved in efforts at "nation building." Training given individuals

---

[29]Quoted by *U.S. News and World Report*, 6 November 1961.
[30]*Christian Science Monitor*, 8 March 1963.
[31]*Supra*, pp. 10–11.
[32]Quoted by *Newsweek*, 15 July 1963.
[33]Quoted in *Time*, 1 November 1963.
[34]Lee, *Which Strategy for Advanced Insurgency?*, p. 11.
[35]Corson, *The Betrayal*, p. 279.

at NTC was intense and rigorous, and incorporated certain "Communist" techniques of communal living, self-criticism sessions, and memorizing of simple and easily expressed principles. The course was a thirteen-week one, and when NTC operated at full capacity, it was capable of graduating about five thousand cadremen every five weeks. Be was determined that those who left NTC to return to their own villages did so with a sense of service, sacrifice, and reform. His goals were two: to cleanse local governments of corruption, substituting for it renewed self-governing villages, and to produce individuals capable of countering VC inroads into the culture.

Be recognized early that the only real solution to the struggle facing South Vietnam was for the government to meet the needs of its own people. This could not be done, he saw, through using military force as a first line of defense. Rather, the government *had* to send its roots down among the "earth" of the people. Despite his best efforts, the Saigon government never came to understand appropriate priorities because of its primary reliance upon military force to combat the insurrection.

In talking with him now, one finds him able to be a great deal more forward and open than he was able to be in earlier years while he was still an officer in the Vietnamese army. Diem, he recalls, "was the leader of a marginal group of individuals who had already been westernized, who lived in cities, who had received intensive Western education." Such people, he states, "had views which were much different than the great mass of the Vietnamese people." Their westernization and European educations gave them more opportunities, and so "during the French occupation they helped the French in every way they could." Be recalls that the French "trained the Vietnamese in their own ways to be such things as civil servants, and never let the Vietnamese run anything for themselves or never gave them managerial skills. Political leaders who had ability were often exiled, and in reality, it could be said that we did not have any political leaders who were not servants of the French. People were trained to be loyal to their boss. Only by acting in that way," states Be, "could people be successful in working for their own careers. They became powerful families in Vietnam, in the Annam government under the control of France. Very powerful. Many of them were Catholic, but whether so or not, they were westernized."

Be reflects that "those were the only capable people in Vietnam, for they had received training. And when the French left, you see, those were the ones who became political leaders. It was out of this group that Diem emerged. And after the French period, when American advisers came, the purpose of such men was to continue French policy.[36] And this French-educated elite was not able to compete effectively with Communist political movement."

Colonel Be insists that "the main reason for the fall of Vietnam was not because Westmoreland or Abrams fired too many bullets, or because of the decline in American military aid in later years, but because *from the beginning*, the buildup of leadership in Vietnam came from a marginal group of people like

---

[36]Not everyone would have agreed with Be on this point. Indeed, one study that attempted to show the distinctive differences between the policies of the United States and the earlier ones of France is Richard E. McConnell, *Franco-American Policy Divergence in Vietnam* (USAWC student thesis, 3 May 1965).

Diem. Always against the *real* people."

Another man present during that conversation asked, "Do you know what Be means when he says the *real* people? He is talking in terms of a majority, or at least a great number, of the rural population—the peasants. These were the ones who had no way to articulate to Westerners the way they felt and believed. They spoke no French, no English, only their own native tongue. Outsiders could not understand them, and the French-educated and - influenced Vietnamese elite had either forgotten or repudiated their traditional ways of thinking."

"In other words," I suggested, "they had no way to articulate their needs to those in a position to do something about them, and further," those in power had no particular interest or desire in learning what those needs were."

"Precisely," replied Be. "Like myself, I am exceptional case. I have a French education and I have tried to practice my French and my English, but my English is very broken because I am self-taught. But I have tried always to remain in touch with feelings of real people. For instance, many Americans wanted to go to Vietnam to set up educational systems and teach people there to read and write and do mathematics. Yet, if you are talking to a real peasant, the concept about education is traditional. First of all he wants to educate his children to be polite and to learn the ways of the ancestors, not to read, write, and do mathematics. Do you see? That would only be of second importance.

"So if you talk to real people through an intellectual Vietnamese inter- preter," the intellectual has been educated in a Western way so even he cannot conceive what the peasant really wants to do and is thus unable to explain that man's wants to you. And the intellectual expects the peasant to explain his ideas in a Western way and becomes disgusted when he cannot; he is angry with his countryman for being ignorant and stupid. But the real person is not those things; he is just acting in real Vietnamese way."

Colonel Be, sitting in that little office where our interview took place, began to warm to his subject. He had, undoubtedly, said these things many times before to other interviewers, but the thoughts were close to his heart and he had failed to convince others when to have done so might have made a difference. "So I told these things to President Diem. I even told them to President Thieu and to many other people, and all of them are very sad of me [angry with me], but it is true. President Diem, for instance, didn't like to listen, for he was like an emperor of Vietnam, but at least he was from a powerful Mandarin family of Hué, and he had a sense of national pride. But he was too severe towards the Vietnamese and was criticized by lots of real people. His generals were civil servants, as in every country, and worked for the army system." They were people who have to be loyal, who have to execute policy, but who never have the creative ideas. And when the generals were in power," they didn't want to stop the war because without war a general has no profit and no pride. And we listened to them when they said 'Fight more, kill more VC.' "

Indignation flickered across Be's usually passive face, "And we always lis- tened to foreign advisers. For in our country we always considered that any Westerner would be an adviser, much more clever and much more ex- perienced," and know much better than our own people. So when Sir Robert Thompson suggested the idea of strategic hamlets, Diem listened because

Thompson was considered an expert on anticommunism. So my government try to move our people from the rural endangered areas—away from their rice fields to a slum agglomeration. And in that slum agglomeration, they are exposed to the worst aspects of Western society. Also they are exposed to many consumer goods which before they didn't know about but now must have for themselves, yet without enough money to buy them.

"Such a slum agglomeration caused trouble, because once you concentrate people in one specific area where they do not belong, they have to abandon their traditional ways and traditional leadership. They don't respect their traditional leaders anymore as they would in a normal village. In old village people respect their elders, who are leaders. But now, in a new agglomeration, a girl who is working for a GI advisor, uneducated girl, working hard for American GI, she can get three, four, five times more money than tradition. So the values have been changed."[37]

And finally, Be arrived at his point—a discussion of the proposals he had made years earlier to the leaders of his country. "We had to have our own people's army, people's militia, living in traditional villages and hamlets, not in new agglomerations everyone hated." I told leaders that the problem was not 'How do we get the people on our side?' but rather 'How do we get on the people's side?'

"It was really impossible for the government to adapt the real people's attitudes and institutions in the villages in such a way that they would support President Diem's rule. Instead, the government should have tried to restructure itself around the interests of the peasants. Since basic social unit was traditional village, defense should come from 'People's Self-Defense Forces' recruited from village people. They would not try to combat VC units but would strengthen village so that VC could not move about in such secret. Properly run, PSDF would isolate enemy from people in same way VC worked to isolate people from government. Yet people would not be fighting for 'nation' or 'President Diem' or 'President Thieu.' They would fight for themselves."

Be had wanted to see military service reformed. The Saigon government had drafted or recruited young men, sending them out of their home districts and provinces to serve anywhere in the country where the army might need them. Be believed this to be wrong. Given the strong localistic feelings of the Vietnamese, he urged that these men serve in their home communities unless they actually volunteered for duty elsewhere. He also criticized the governmental practice of hiring hamlet youths, giving them intensive military training in basics so that they might then be assigned to protect their homes against marauding VC units. In doing this, Be has stated, "they were now trained in conventional warfare and so became ineffective in fighting guerrilla war."

---

[37]For two different Western views on resettlement see Joseph J. Zasloff, "Rural Resettlement in South Viet Nam: The Agroville Program," *Pacific Affairs* XXXV, 4 (Winter, 1962–1963): 327–340; and Milton Osborne, *Strategic Hamlets in South Viet-Nam* (Data Paper #55, Ithaca: Cornell Southeast Asia Program, 1965). Osborne would agree with Be's view regarding the unsuitability of instituting Thompson's Malaya reforms in Vietnam, for he gives a searching assessment of this unsuccessful program, pointing out the very different circumstances prevailing in Vietnam from the ones at the time of the earlier resettlement program in Malaya.

In sum, Be hoped to steal the thunder from the Marxist Viet Cong by creating a government-sponsored social revolution, including new political organizations, different ways of serving in the military, greater emphasis upon education, and realistic approaches to land reform. These programs would not have been aimed at either the middle or upper classes but at the peasantry. The new social revolution would have centered on the village and its tradition of independent self-rule. Once again, in modern times, as in ancient ones, it would have been a case of the "emperor's" authority ending at the village gate. In this way, peasants would have come to feel that what they did was in their own best interests rather than for the profit of some far-off central government.

In all this, the role of the professional military would have been minimal, for "it is always difficult for generals to forsake the things they have learned and which have worked for them and try something new. They don't like to try new things. Still, just as the government must ask how it can get on the real people's side, so the army leaders should have tried to assimilate the military into the people rather than training the people in the way of the army. This is why clear-and-hold operations did not work. We can clear with our military troops. But who will hold? The people have to do so. And when the army is separate from the people, we get no cooperation from them, even those populace who were not really Communist or pro-Communist. They didn't like us because we had no people's organization on our side."[38]

Would Be's proposals have worked? At this late date there is, of course, no way of knowing. One can be certain, however, that they could not have failed any more completely than did those efforts that Diem and his successors insisted upon that relied primarily upon military force to save South Vietnam. Obviously there were options other than those that Diem was able to see. Be's was but one of them.

Sadly, however, the American army did no better. Having forgotten lessons learned from conflicts with guerrilla forces over two centuries; refusing to read available accounts of the doctrine of revolutionary warfare recounted by theorist/practitioners of the twentieth century, such as Mao Tse Tung or Che Guevara or Ho Chi Minh, or anyone else; failing to study analyses of such revolutionaries by writers like Taber; unwilling to listen to its own officers who were capable of offering it sensible counsel—the American army blindly plunged ahead in Vietnam on a heedless course toward self-destruction.

---

[38]All comments reproduced from tapes made during an interview with Nguyên Be, Washington, D.C., 23 June 1977.

APPENDIX E

U.S. Army and Total U.S. Military Personnel
in South Vietnam through 1968

	Army Personnel	*Total Military Personnel*
31 December 1960	800	900
31 December 1961	2,100	3,200
31 December 1962	7,900	11,300
31 December 1963	10,100	16,300
31 December 1964	14,700	23,300
31 March 1965	15,600	29,100
30 June 1965	27,300	59,900
30 September 1965	76,200	132,300
31 December 1965	116,800	184,300
31 March 1966	137,400	231,200
30 June 1966	160,000	267,500
30 September 1966	189,200	313,100
31 December 1966	239,400	485,300
31 March 1967	264,600	420,900
30 June 1967	285,700	448,800
30 September 1967	296,100	459,700
31 December 1967	319,500	485,600
31 March 1968	337,300	515,200
30 June 1968	354,300	534,700
30 September 1968	354,200	537,800
31 December 1968	359,800	536,100

APPENDIX F

Major U.S. Army Unit Arrival Dates
(* = formed in Vietnam)

Unit	*Date of Arrival*
Military Assistance Advisory Group	August 1950
Military Assistance Command, Vietnam	February 1962*
U.S. Army Support Command, Vietnam	March 1964*
5th Special Forces Group	October 1964
1st Logistical Command	April 1965*
173d Airborne Brigade	May 1965
U.S. Army, Vietnam	July 1965*
2d Brigade, 1st Infantry Division	July 1965
1st Brigade, 101st Airborne Division	July 1965
Field Force, Vietnam	September 1965*
1st Cavalry Division (Airmobile)	September 1965
18th Engineer Brigade	September 1965
1st Infantry Division (-)	October 1965
3d Brigade, 4th Infantry Division	December 1965
2d Brigade, 25th Infantry Division	January 1966
II Field Force, Vietnam	March 1966*
HQ and 1st Brigade, 25th Infantry Division	April 1966
1st Signal Brigade	April 1966
44th Medical Brigade	April 1966
1st Aviation Brigade	May 1966
HQ and 2d Brigade, 4th Infantry Division	August 1966
196th Light Infantry Brigade	August 1966
11th Armored Cavalry Regiment	September 1966
18th Military Police Brigade	September 1966
1st Brigade, 4th Infantry Division	October 1966
3d Brigade, 25th Infantry Division	October 1966
199th Light Infantry Brigade	November 1966
HQ, 1st and 3d Brigades, 9th Infantry Division	December 1966

2d Brigade, 9th Infantry Division	January 1967
20th Engineer Brigade	August 1967
23d Infantry Division (Americal)	September 1967*
198th Light Infantry Brigade	October 1967
3/17 Cavalry Squadron (Airmobile)	October 1967
7/17 Cavalry Squadron (Airmobile)	October 1967
11th Light Infantry Brigade	December 1967
HQ, 2d and 3d Brigades, 101st Airborne (Airmobile) Division	December 1967
3d Infantry Brigade Task Force, 82d Airborne Division	February 1968
7/1 Cavalry Squadron (Airmobile)	February 1968
Provisional Corps, Vietnam (later redesignated XXIV Corps)	March 1968*

APPENDIX G

Chart Showing Political and Military Leaders of the United States and Political Leaders of South Vietnam from the Beginning to the End of American Involvement

On the following page is a graphic presentation of political and military leaders of the United States and South Vietnam and the years during which they held office. The legend for the graph is as follows:

United States presidents

American secretaries of state

American secretaries of defense

United States ambassadors to Vietnam

Commander, United States Military Assistance Advisory Group, Vietnam (USMAAGV) [This command was absorbed into United States Military Assistance Command, Vietnam (USMACV) during 1964.]

Commander, USMACV

South Vietnamese premiers

Years

Chart of American and South Vietnamese leadership, 1949–1975

① U.S. Presidents
- Harry TRUMAN ('49–'53)
- Dwight EISENHOWER ('53–'61)
- John KENNEDY ('61–'63)
- Lyndon JOHNSON ('63–'69)
- Richard NIXON ('69–'74)
- Gerald FORD ('74–'75)

② Secretaries of State
- Dean ACHESON
- John DULLES
- Christian HERTER
- Dean RUSK
- William ROGERS
- Henry KISSINGER

③ Secretaries of Defense
- Louis JOHNSON
- George MARSHALL
- Robert LOVETT
- Charles WILSON
- Neil McELROY
- Thomas GATES
- Robert McNAMARA
- Clark CLIFFORD
- Melvin LAIRD
- Elliot RICHARDSON
- James SCHLESINGER

④ Ambassadors
- Donald HEATH
- REINHARDT
- Eldridge DURBROW
- Frederick NOLTING
- Henry LODGE
- Maxwell TAYLOR
- Henry LODGE
- Ellsworth BUNKER

⑤ ⑥ Military Commanders
- John ("Iron Mike") O'DANIEL
- Samuel WILLIAMS
- Lionel McGARR
- Charles TIMMES
- Paul HARKINS
- William WESTMORELAND
- Creighton ABRAMS
- Fred WEYAND

⑦ South Vietnamese Leaders
- BAO DAI
- NGO DINH DIEM
- MINH
- KHANH
- HUONG
- QUAT
- Nguyem Cap KY
- Nguyem THIEU

Years: '49 '50 '51 '52 '53 '54 '55 '56 '57 '58 '59 '60 '61 '62 '63 '64 '65 '66 '67 '68 '69 '70 '71 '72 '73 '74 '75

Notes

Chapter One

[1] These views were offered to the student audience in an address made by GEN William C. Westmoreland on 11 April 1978 at the United States Command and General Staff College, Ft. Leavenworth, Kansas. A condensed version of his remarks was published as "Vietnam in Perspective," *Military Review* LIX, 1 (January 1979): 34–43.

[2] Available literature on Vietnam, its history and culture, is extensive. Readers interested in additional information might consult such works as Keith Buchanan, *The Southeast Asian World* (New York: Doubleday Anchor, 1968); Dick Wilson, *Asia Awakes: A Continent in Transition* (New York: New American Library Mentor, 1970); Ellen Hammer, *Vietnam Yesterday and Today* (New York: Holt, Rinehart and Winston, 1966); Robbins Burling, *Hill Farms and Padi Fields: Life in Mainland Southeast Asia* (Englewood Cliffs: Prentice-Hall, 1965); or Banning Garrett and Katherine Barkley, *Two, Three . . . Many Vietnams* (San Francisco: Harper and Row's Canfield Press, 1971).

[3] This tradition endured. Thus the generals from Big Minh to Kanh, Ky, and Thieu who held power in South Vietnam had neither social respect nor the trust of their people.

[4] A soldier student at the Army War College clearly knew the reality of life in Vietnam when he wrote: "The only governmental structure that consistently has claimed the loyalty and support of the people in Vietnam is the village. [It] is the central fact in the life of every Vietnamese, and, even today, Vietnamese are expected to make annual pilgrimages to their native villages." See LTC Maurice D. Roush, *Strategy for Vietnam: Pacification or Combat?* (U.S. Army War College, student paper, 9 October 1967), p. 3. Unfortunately for the American war effort, his insights failed to achieve notable distribution into higher ranks. An excellent source on this subject is Gerald Hickey, *Village in Vietnam* (New Haven: Yale University Press, 1964).

[5] An acceptable biography of the North Vietnamese leader is that by Jean Lacouture, *Ho Chi Minh: A Political Biography* (New York: Vintage Books, 1968). A good treatment of nineteenth-century occupation of Vietnam is J. F. Cairns, *The Eagle and the Lotus: Western Intervention in Vietnam, 1847–1968* (Mystic, CT: Lawrence Verry, Inc., 1969). See also Arthur M. Schlesinger, Jr., *The Bitter Heritage: Vietnam and American Democracy, 1941–1966* (New York: Fawcett World Library, 1966); Edgar Snow, *The Other Side of the River* (New York: Random House, 1961); Allen B. Cole, ed., *Conflict in Indo China and International Repercussions: A Documentary History, 1945–1955* (Ithaca: Cornell University Press, 1956); and Marvin Gettleman, ed., *Vietnam: History, Documents, and Opinions* (New York: New American Library Mentor, 1970).

[6] For an excerpted text of the Vietnamese Declaration of Independence, see Appendix A.

[7] For a discussion of this point, see Ronald Steel, *Pax Americana* (New York: Viking

Press, 1967). See also Russell H. Fifield, *Southeast Asia in United States Policy* (New York: Praeger, 1963). President Roosevelt had, during the Second World War, shown some resistance to a reimposition of French rule in Indochina when peace should come, but had died before any hopes he might have had could be effected. President Truman's attention lay elsewhere, despite the fact that American observers in the field submitted to the State Department's good analyses of the Indochinese political situation based on contacts with leading participants. See, for example, "The Interest of the United States in Nationalist Opposition to Restoration of French Rule in Indochina," *Foreign Relations of the United States*, 1946, VIII, *The Far East*, U.S. Department of State Publication 8554 (Washington: Government Printing Office, 1971).

Few Americans were proficient in the use of the Vietnamese language despite occasional classes of instruction. An OWI school near Washington, D.C., had taught Southeast Asian languages during the war, and one observer has pointed out that Vietnamese was taught at the University of California at Berkeley when he was on duty there from 1951 to 1954 with the ROTC unit.

[8]John T. McAlister, Jr., *Vietnam: The Origins of Revolution* (New York: Alfred A. Knopf, 1970), vii. See also Robert Scheer, *How the United States Got Involved in Vietnam* (Santa Barbara: Center for the Study of Democratic Institutions, 1965).

[9]See *Department of State Bulletin* (Washington: Government Printing Office, 12 June 1950): 977–78. For the extent of French-held territory as of May 1953, see the map on the following page.

[10]Alexander Kendrick, *The Wound Within: America in the Vietnam Years, 1945–1974* (Boston: Little, Brown and Co., 1974), pp. 57–8.

[11]Lansdale was one of the most interesting of the colorful characters who moved in and out of Indochina. For a fascinating story well worth reading, see his *In the Midst of Wars* (New York: Harper and Row, 1972).

[12]*U.S. News and World Report*, 19 February 1954.

[13]Quoted by *Time*, 28 September 1953.

[14]See Russell H. Betts, *Viet Cong Village Control: Some Observations on the Origin and Dynamics of Modern Revolutionary War* (Cambridge: Massachusetts Institute of Technology Center for International Studies, 1969).

[15]For additional reading on the early developments in Vietnam after the rise of Diem, consult Franklin B. Weinstein, *Vietnam's Unheld Elections* (Ithaca: Cornell Southeast Asia Program, 1966); Ellen J. Hammer, *The Struggle for Indochina* (Stanford: Stanford University Press, 1954); Brian Crozier, "The Diem Regime in Southern Vietnam," *Far Eastern Survey* XXIV, 4 (April 1955); Robert Scigliano, *South Vietnam: Nation Under Stress* (Boston: Houghton-Mifflin, 1963); Jean Lacouture, *Vietnam: Between Two Truces* (New York: Random House, 1966); B.S.N. Murti, *Vietnam Divided* (New York: Asia Publishing House, 1964); Donald Lancaster, *The Emancipation of French Indochina* (London: Oxford University Press, 1961); Robert Shaplen, *The Lost Revolution: The U.S. in Vietnam, 1946–1966* (New York: Harper and Row Colophon, 1966); The Rand Corporation, *Negotiations and Vietnam: A Case Study of the 1954 Geneva Conference* (Santa Monica: The RAND Corporation, 1968); Jules Roy, *The Battle of Dienbienphu* (New York: Harper and Row, 1965); Jean Lacouture and Philippe Devillers, *La Fin D'une Guerre, Indochine 1954* (Paris: Editions du Seuil, 1960).

For other views of early developments in Vietnam, consult Elie Abel and Marvin Kalb, *The Roots of Involvement: The U.S. in Asia, 1784–1971* (New York: W. W. Norton & Co., 1971); Franz Schurmann, Peter Dale Scott, and Reginald Zelnik, *The Politics of Escalation in Vietnam* (Greenwich, CT: Fawcett, 1966); and Hilaire du Berrier, *Background to Betrayal: The Tragedy of Vietnam* (Boston: Western Islands Press, 1965).

For early military views, see Joseph F. H. Cutrona, *Peace in Vietnam: An Acceptable Solution* (Carlisle Barracks: USAWC student essay, 22 April 1966); Richard J. Hesse, *Negotiations on Vietnam, 1954–1966* (Carlisle Barracks: USAWC student essay, 22 April 1966); Joe M. Palmer, *Factors Which will Influence Political Negotiations in Vietnam* (Carlisle Barracks: USAWC student essay, 15 December 1965); and an assessment of the use of American forces by Y. Y. Phillips, *An Appraisal of the Employment of U.S. Ground Troops in South Vietnam* (Carlisle Barracks: USAWC student paper, April 1967). Another approach to that topic is James G. Boatner, *American Tactical Units in Revolutionary Development Operations* (Air War College Research Report Number 3570, Maxwell AFB, Alabama, April 1968).

For some differences between the earlier approach taken by France and that of the United States, see Richard E. McConnell, *Franco-American Policy Divergence in Vietnam* (Carlisle Barracks, USAWC student essay, 3 May 1965).

[16]Edward G. Lansdale, "Viet Nam: Do We Understand Revolution?" *Foreign Affairs* XLIII (October 1964): 76. Lansdale had, by this time, been promoted from colonel to major general. His comments, appropriate in 1964, were easily as applicable throughout the period of American intervention in Vietnam.

The American military needed more study of the doctrine of revolutionary warfare. It is a part of that body of theory that guerrillas must eventually move through successive stages of development until they become strong enough to act as a regular army; at that point they pit themselves against the constituted military of the government they hope to topple. Castro did so in Cuba. Mao did so in China. The United States did so during the Revolutionary War against Britain. In the long run, if insurgents are to win through to their goal of toppling a government, they will have to raise and equip a standing army and win some battles.

So long as guerrillas remain irregular warriors, they will not destroy an existing government nor take over a nation. They will simply remain scabs on the face of the body politic, but that body will spend most of its time scratching those scabs, which will become very raw indeed. At that stage, however, guerrilla forces can be found and destroyed.

Mao, for all the talk, was run all over China until he built up a regular army. Aguinaldo failed in his insurrectionist efforts in the Philippines. Giap's victory at Dien Bien Phu was not a guerrilla effort, nor was Tet 1968 an insurgent operation. In none of those cases, and in others that could be endlessly cited, did guerrillas bring down a *de jure* government.

A nation that enjoys the support of its own people will almost inevitably win such battles. In the past and in many places, governments have gone about cleaning out nests of guerrillas by first gaining the support of their own people and by demonstrating that the insurgents have no real grievances, no legitimate calls for reform. They are no more than bandits, to be despised by decent folk.

In such a situation a government has a legitimate claim on the loyalties of its people. The populace remains supportive of its rulers. The army continues to function efficiently and with dedication. For all segments of the population there are goals to work toward and guidelines to adhere to. Under such circumstances, when a government shows itself truly interested in the welfare of its society, guerrilla forces can only be delaying factors against the operations of a conventional army.

Where a government remains intransigent, when it is more interested in self-aggrandizement than in reform, when it stifles all opposition, when it supports only privilege and vested interests, when it regularly increases the burdens borne by those least able to carry them, then that government can be destroyed by guerrillas, as South Vietnam was to find out clearly and dramatically. Under those conditions, the people will become ever more alienated from their own government and increasingly sympathetic toward the aims and aspirations of an insurgency. "Where a guerrilla force enjoys support from the people, whether willing or forced, it *can never be defeated by military means,* however much it is harassed and attacked, shelled, mortared, and bombed by superior forces of infantry and artillery, air and sea power" (Sir Robert Thompson, quoted in Hilsman, *To Move a Nation,* p. 430; italics added.)

South Vietnam and the United States military endeavored to do precisely those things to the VC and their NVA allies. As we know, the effort failed.

[17]Masai's story itself is an interesting one. Sometime earlier, he had been rounded up with others of his tribe and put on board a prison train destined for Ft. Marion (St. Augustine), Florida. Somewhere in Alabama, Masai managed to escape from the train. Alone, unaided, in completely unfamiliar territory, ignorant of his own location, bereft of both weapons and tools, he made his way back to the sanctuary of his own Southwest mountain fastness—*without once being seen by another human being during the entire trek.*

[18]LTG Julian J. Ewell and MG Ira A. Hunt, Jr., *Sharpening the Combat Edge: The*

Use of Analysis to Reinforce Military Judgment (Washington: Government Printing Office, 1974). 13.

¹⁹Douglas Kinnard, *The War Managers* (Hanover: University Press of New England, 1977).

²⁰Robert Taber, *The War of the Flea: A Study of Guerrilla Warfare, Theory and Practice* (New York: Citadel Press, 1965), p. 11.

²¹Examples of these men's writings would include such works as Mao Tse-tung, *Selected Military Writings* (Peking: Foreign Languages Press, 1963); Régis Debray, *Revolution in the Revolution?* (New York: MR Press, 1967); Che Guevera, *Guerrilla Warfare* (New York: F. A. Praeger, 1961); Mao Tse-tung, *Basic Tactics* ([translated by S. R. Schram] New York: F. A. Praeger, 1966); Ho Chi Minh, *On Revolution* (New York: F. A. Praeger, 1967); Vo Nguyên Giap, *People's War, People's Army* (New York: F. A. Praeger, 1962); Cf. Bernard B. Fall, *Ho Chi Minh on Revolution* (New York: F. A. Praeger, 1967); Andrew Sinclair, *Che Guevera* (New York: Viking, 1970); and Jay Mallin, ed., *"Che" Guevera on Revolution* (New York: Delta, 1969). Sun Tzu, *The Art of War* (London: Oxford University Press, 1977). Sun Tzu, *The Art of War* ([translated by Sam Griffiths] London: Oxford University Press, 1977).

²²Taber, *War of the Flea*, pp. 131–32.

²³Just a very few of the sources then readily available that could have been consulted would include David Galula, *Counterinsurgency Warfare: Theory and Practice* (New York: F. A. Praeger, 1964); Otto Heilbrunn, *Partisan Warfare* (New York: F. A. Praeger, 1962); General Harold K. Johnson, "Subversion and Insurgency: Search for a Doctrine," *Army XV* (November 1965); J. Farmer, *Counterinsurgency: Principles and Practices in Viet-Nam* (Santa Monica: RAND Corporation, 1964), and his *Counterinsurgency: Vietnam, 1962–1963* (Santa Monica: RAND Corporation, 1963); and Paul A. Jureidini *et al.*, *Casebook on Insurgency and Revolutionary Warfare: 23 Summary Accounts* (Washington: American University Press, 1962 [Special Operations Research Office, American University]). Despite the fact that some of these studies were funded by the Central Intelligence Agency—and many Praeger books during the Vietnam era were simply printed outlets for CIA views—some of these writings were actually quite good.

²⁴Jeffrey Race, *War Comes to Long An; Revolutionary Conflict in a Vietnamese Province* (Berkeley: University of California Press, 1972), pp. ix–x. Also consult Bill G. Smith, *Revolution and Rebellion in Vietnam* (United States Army War College student thesis, 3 May 1965).

²⁵Race, *War Comes to Long An*, p. x.

²⁶"Staffing" is a military term meaning study of a topic or document by one or more components of a commander's staff.

²⁷Subject interview.

²⁸Ted Robert Gurr created a theoretical model of the conditions necessary for civil violence. For Gurr, there was no one thing that, when present, would produce in men a state of mind favorable toward the use of violence. Rather, he posited the premise that "the necessary preconditions for violent civil conflict is relative deprivation," that is, a perceived "discrepancy between people's value expectations and their environment's value capabilities." Gurr's views are valuable in explaining not only the revolutionary process generally but the Vietnamese experience in particular. See Ted Robert Gurr with Charles Ruttenberg, *The Conditions of Civil Violence: First Tests of a Casual Model* (Princeton, NJ: Center of International Studies, Research Monograph No. 28, April 1967).

²⁹William Corson, a retired marine lieutenant colonel, was in charge of that force's Combined Action Program (CAP) in the I Corps area of Vietnam. That assignment gave him opportunity to observe at first hand the effects of the war on the people there. Regarding pacification activities in a DMZ village complex, he later said: "We had conspired with the government of South Vietnam to literally destroy the hopes, aspirations and emotional stability of thirteen thousand human beings. . . . This was not and is not war, it is genocide." See his book *The Betrayal* (New York: W. W. Norton and Company, 1968).

³⁰See LTC George S. Patton, *Portrait of an Insurgent: A Study of the Motivation*

of the Main Force Vietnamese Communist Fighting Man (Carlisle Barracks, PA: United States Army War College thesis, 25 April 1965). Hereafter abbreviated as USAWC. This work remains classified.

[31]John T. McAlister, Jr., *Vietnam: The Origins of Revolution* (New York: Alfred A. Knopf, 1970), p. vii.

[32]William J. Lederer, *Our Own Worst Enemy* (New York: W. W. Norton and Company, 1968), p. 20 and 20n.

[33]So suggested Gavin in his speech to the student body at the Command and General Staff College, 3 March 1976. See also his writings, such as *Crisis Now* (New York: Random House, 1968), especially Chapter III.

[34]These thoughts were delivered by Timmes in his speech to the student body, Command and General Staff College, 9 April 1976.

[35]An analysis of the theory and practice of guerrilla warfare is included as Appendix D.

[36]Ward Just, *Military Men* (New York: Alfred A. Knopf, 1970), p. 230.

[37]Lederer, *Our Own Worst Enemy,* pp. 23–4.

[38]Some of the official literature dealing with terrorism includes United States Operating Mission to Vietnam, *Vietcong Use of Terror: A Study* (Saigon, May 1966); RAND Corporation, *Origins of the Insurgency in South Vietnam, 1954–1960: The Role of the Southern Vietminh Cadres* (Santa Monica: RAND Corporation, 1967); Douglas E. Pike, *Notes From the Underground: The Mystique of a Viet Cong* (Saigon, February 1962). As America became increasingly involved in Vietnam, various governmental agencies cranked out large numbers of studies on various aspects of the war and on the life and culture of Vietnam. A sampling of such titles would include Department of the Army, *A Pocket Guide to Vietnam* (DA Pamphlet 360–411, Washington: Government Printing Office, 5 April 1966); United States Information Agency, *The Viet Cong: Communist Party and Cadre* (Research Report R-74-66, Washington, Government Printing Office, April 1966); United States Military Assistance Command, Vietnam (Command Information Pamphlet 11-67, Saigon, April 1967); *USMACV, GVN National Police Fact Sheet* (Saigon, 6 June 1967); *USMACV, Types of Cadres in GVN* (Fact Sheet, Saigon, 8 December 1967); *USMACV, Revolutionary Development Cadre* (Fact Sheet, Saigon, 5 March 1967); *USMACV, Village and Hamlet Elections* (Command Information Pamphlet 14-67, Saigon, April 1967); *USMACV, Revolutionary Development* (Command Information Pamphlet 4-67, Saigon, February 1967); United States Agency for International Development, *The 1967 Revolutionary Development Program* (Office of Field Operations Memorandum Number 200-66, Saigon, 9 December 1966); Office of Civil Operations, United States Embassy, Saigon, *Report on Revolutionary Development* (New Life Development Division Operational Memorandum Number 05-67, Saigon, 16 January 1967), and *OCO/USMACV, Military-Civil Teams* (Saigon, 22 March 1967). Indeed, as the war progressed, official publications attempting to deal with the many facets of Vietnam appeared in a paper cascade that threatened to bury the presses themselves.

[39]For a work with a different attitude toward those "bandit remnants," see the study by the pro-Communist Wilfred G. Burchett, *Inside Story of the Guerrilla War* (New York: International Publishers, 1965).

[40]*New York Times,* 6 December 1962.

[41]*New York Times,* 5 June 1962.

[42]Hal Dareff, *The Story of Vietnam* (New York: Avon Books, 1967), p. 120.

[43]For a view of such developments as seen from Hanoi, consult Tran Van Giau and Le Van Chat, *The South Viet Nam Liberation National Front* (Hanoi: Foreign Languages Publishing House, 1962).

[44]*Time,* 9 August 1963.

[45]Dareff, *Story of Vietnam,* p. 134.

[46]A worthwhile study that covers these early years from 1954 to 1964, with an excellent depiction of the difficulties of the Diem regime, is that by George Chaffard, *Indochine: Dix ans d'Indépendance* (Paris: Calmann-Lévy, 1964). Chaffard, a correspondent for *Le Monde,* served for many years in Southeast Asia. See also Robert Shaplen, *The*

Lost Revolution (New York: Harper and Row, 1965).

⁴⁷Kendrick, *The Wound Within*, p. 146. For the next several years pesticide and defoliant use increased. In 1966 the Department of State reported that "about 20,000 acres of South Vietnamese crops had been destroyed with herbicides to deny food to the guerrillas," a figure that did not include areas denuded for purposes of denying the insurgents jungle cover for their activities. See *New York Times*, 10 March 1966. On 10 September 1966, the same newspaper told how the United States Army was tripling its efforts at defoliation and destruction of crops.

⁴⁸See LTC Maurice D. Routh, *Strategy for Vietnam: Pacification or Combat?* (USAWC student paper, 9 October 1967). Also see John E. McCleary, *Military Factors Contributing to Failure to Contain Insurgency in Vietnam during 1960–1963* (USAWC case study, 8 March 1971). This latter work bears a *confidential* classification.

Chapter Two

¹Subject interview.

²See Brian M. Jenkins, *The Unchangeable War* (Santa Monica: RAND Corporation, November 1967, RM-6278-ARPA), p. 7. This document bears a "For Official Use Only" classification. Another book worth consulting that deals with the impact of imperception is Ralph K. White, *Nobody Wanted War: Misperception in Vietnam and Other Wars* (New York: Doubleday, 1968). Other works of interest include David Halberstam, *The Making of a Quagmire* (New York: Random House, 1965); Henry Brandon, *Anatomy of Error: The Inside Story of the Asian War on the Potomac* (Boston: Gambit Incorporated, 1969); Chester L. Cooper, *The Lost Crusade: America in Vietnam* (New York: Dodd, Mead and Co., 1970); Theodore Draper, *Abuse of Power* (New York: The Viking Press, 1967); Alain C. Enthoven and K. Wayne Smith, *How Much Is Enough? Shaping the Defense Program, 1961–1969* (New York: Harper and Row, 1971); Townshend Hoopes, *The Limits of Intervention* (New York: David McKay Co., Inc., 1969); David Halberstam, *The Best and the Brightest* (New York: Random House, 1972); Henry F. Graff, *The Tuesday Cabinet: Deliberation and Decision on Peace and War Under Lyndon B. Johnson* (Englewood Cliffs: Prentice-Hall, 1970).

Although its title should have been "*Old* Lessons in a *New* War," a paper worth reading is that by 1LT Ross S. Kelly, "New Lessons in an Old War," *Infantry* (January–February 1973): 32–37. See also LTC William H. Miller, *US Army Infantry Tactics in Vietnam* (Air War College report #4045, May 1970), a copy of which is available at the Air University Library, Maxwell Air Force Base, Alabama.

³White, *Nobody Wanted War*, pp. 253–56.

⁴Jenkins, *Unchangeable War*, pp. 6–7. See also Nayan Chanda, "A Permanent State of Misery," *Far Eastern Economic Review* LXXXVI (11 October 1974): 12–14.

⁵LTC Carl F. Bernard, *The War in Vietnam: Observations and Reflections of a Province Senior Advisor* (USACGSC Student Paper, 1969), *passim*. An interesting view of problems facing early American missions in Vietnam may be found in John Mecklin, *Mission in Torment* (Garden City: Doubleday and Company, 1965). The literature is extensive. Items worth consulting include the following: LTC Robert M. Montague, *Advising in Government: An Account of the District Advisory Program in South Vietnam* (USAWC Student essay, 18 February 1966) and *Pacification: The Overall Strategy in South Vietnam* (USAWC Student essay, 22 April 1966); David C. Bowie *et al.*, *Pacification and Long Term Development in Vietnam: Questionnaire Analysis* (McLean, VA: Research Analysis Corp., 1966); Chester L. Cooper *et al.*, *The American Experience with Pacification in Vietnam: An Overview* (Arlington: Institute for Defense Analysis, 1972); Allen E. Goodman, *Government and the Countryside: Political Accommodation and South Vietnam's Communal Groups* (Santa Monica: RAND Corporation, 1970), and by the same author, *Politics in War: The Bases of Political Community in South Vietnam* (Cambridge: Harvard University Press, 1973); Joshua Menkes and Raymond G. Jones, *Pacification in Vietnam: A Survey* (Arlington: Institute for Defense Analysis, 1967); William G. Prince *et al.*, *Analysis of Vietnamization: A Description of the War, 1967–1970*

(Ann Arbor: The Bendix Corporation, 1971); J. L. Penquite, *Hamlet Regression Following the Departure of a Revolutionary Development Team* (Final Report for Research Task #5B, Minneapolis: Central Data Corporation, 1969); James Farmer, *Counterinsurgency: Principles and Practices in Vietnam* (Santa Monica: RAND Corporation, 1964), and by the same author, *Counterinsurgency: Vietnam, 1962–1963* (Santa Monica: RAND Corporation, 1963); *US Combat Forces in Support of Pacification: Lessons Learned #80* (Saigon, USMACV, 1965); Robert H. Williams, *A Construct of Insurgency-Counterinsurgency in Vietnam* (McLean: Research Analysis Corporation, 1966); *Analysis of the Hamlet Evaluation System* (Saigon, USMACV, 1969); Dorothy Clark and Charles R. Wyman, *An Exploration Analysis of the Reporting, Measuring and Evaluating of Revolutionary Development in South Vietnam* (McLean: Research Analysis Corporation, 1968); Dorothy Clark, *The Hamlet Evaluation System in the Republic of Vietnam* (McLean: Research Analysis Corporation, 1968); Department of Defense, *Counterinsurgency Research and Development Symposium Proceedings,* meeting of 15–17 September 1970, Ft. Bliss, TX (Arlington: Advanced Research Projects Agency, 1970); LTC Richard L. Prillaman, *Is History Repeating Itself in Vietnam?* (USAWC student thesis, 1968); LTC Douglas T. Kane, *Coup d'Etat: The Threat to South Vietnam's Search for Stability* (USAWC student thesis, 1968); LTC Boyd T. Bashore, *Diem's Counterinsurgency Strategy for Vietnam: Right or Wrong?* (USAWC student case study, 1968); LTC J. G. Clemons, Jr., *The Dilemma of the Vietnam Enclaves* (USAWC student essay, 1967); Department of the Army, *Field Manual 31-73: Advisor Handbook for Counterinsurgency* (Washington: Government Printing Office, 23 April 1965); US Army War College, *Instructional Bulletin 13: Changes in Counterinsurgency Terminology* (Carlisle Barracks, 26 September 1966).

[6]Bernard, *The War in Vietnam, passim.*

[7]Admiral Ulysses Simpson Grant Sharp and General William C. Westmoreland, *Report on the War in Vietnam (as of 30 June 1968): Report on Air and Naval Campaigns Against North Vietnam and Pacific Command-wide Support of the War (June 1964–July 1968) and Report on Operations in South Vietnam (January 1964–June 1968)* (Washington: Government Printing Office, 1968), p. 85. Hereafter cited as Sharp-Westmoreland, *Report on the War in Vietnam.*

[8]Robert W. Komer, *Bureaucracy Does Its Thing: Institutional Constraints on US-GVN Performance in Vietnam* (Santa Monica: RAND Corporation, August 1972), p. 48.

[9]Quoted in MAJ James H. Chapman, *The US Army and Pacification in Vietnam: An Assessment of the Army's Ability to Cope with an Insurgency* (USACGSC student paper, 1976), p. 25. A survey of the army's efforts may be consulted in Major General George S. Eckhardt, *Vietnam Studies: Command and Control, 1950–1969* (Washington: Government Printing Office), *passim.* See also LTC Bill G. Smith, *Revolution and Rebellion in Vietnam* (USAWC student thesis, 3 May 1965).

[10]See Theodore Draper, *Abuse of Power* (New York: Viking Press, 1967), *passim,* for a description of the machinations used by both military and governmental planners to justify the decision to bomb North Vietnam.

[11]Sharp-Westmoreland, *Report on the War in Vietnam,* pp. 11–48. For a popular account of various aspects of the air war, see Frank Harvey, *Air War—Vietnam* (New York: Bantam, 1967).

[12]Gen. J. P. McConnell, *Air Force Policy Letter for Commanders* (Washington: Government Printing Office, 15 October 1967).

[13]Kendrick, *The Wound Within,* p. 6. How effective the bombing of an underdeveloped, agriculturally based nation might be could have been determined by comparison with the bombing of an advanced, industrial one. "Albert Speer, the Nazis' production chief, writes in his memoirs that the bombing never reduced production significantly, partly because the Germans were able to repair damaged factories faster than the Allies calculated, but primarily because intelligence on what the crucial targets were often was faulty and the bombing was often inaccurate."—James D. Dickenson, "There's a B-1 bomber in your future," *The Washington Star,* 27 June 1977. "Conversations with Speer today indicate that he remains convinced that Allied saturation bombing during World War II was ineffective in lowering production and that its main accomplishment was to raise civilian morale, lengthening the war and making resistance of Germans to advancing Allied armies more tenacious."—Subject interview.

[14]The next day, 5 August, Navy LTJG Everett Alvarez ejected from his battle-damaged A-4 airplane. Captured by the North Vietnamese, he thus became the first American pilot to be made a prisoner of war by the North Vietnamese. For a study of life as a POW, see John A. Dramesi, *Code of Honor* (New York: W. W. Norton and Co., 1975).

[15]LTC William R. Corson, *The Betrayal* (New York: W. W. Norton and Co., 1968), p. 80.

[16]Two officers who argued strongly on behalf of greater use of air power set forth their views at the Army War College. See LTC Douglas S. Weart, USAF, *Limited Surprise in Limited War* (USAWC student essay, 13 November 1967), and LTC Howard F. O'Neal, USAF, *Bomb North Vietnam—The Answer or a Searching Question* (USAWC student essay, 13 November 1967). General John P. McConnell, chief of staff of the air force, claimed that "I believe that if we had gone in 1965 and pounded them when they didn't have any defenses, we would have been better off today," quoted in the *New York Times*, 5 October 1967, under a headline stating "Air Chief Says Bomb Curbs Led to a Rise in Casualties."

See also such contemporary literature as "Pilot Loss Linked to Bombing Curbs," *New York Times*, 24 October 1967; "Peace Through Bombing," *New York Times*, 17 September 1967; "Shackled Air Power," *Washington Post*, 2 September 1967; "U.S. Aides Say Raids Slow Flow of Supplies to Hanoi," *New York Times*, 3 October 1967; "Vietnam Air War Objectives 'Soundly Conceived': Sec Def.," *Commanders Digest* III, 3 (August 1967): 1; the article by General Maxwell Taylor, "The Case for Continued Bombing of North Vietnam," *The Washington Star*, 22 October 1967.

Other pertinent literature includes an article by Joseph C. Harsch, "Truck Versus Dam," *Christian Science Monitor*, 6 September 1967; William V. Kennedy, "Who Are the Peacemakers," *Air Force and Space Digest*, 3 (July 1967): 50–53; John F. Loosbrock, "North of the Border," *Air Force and Space Digest* XLIX, 3 (March 1966). 8–9; Louis Stockstill, "Truth in Packaging," *Journal of the Armed Forces* CV (9 September 1967); 13.

Just a few of the books written on this subject include Eugene M. Emme, *The Impact of Air Power* (Princeton: D. Van Nostrand Company, Inc., 1959); Amos A. Jordan, Jr., *Issues of National Security in the 1970s* (New York: Frederick A. Praeger, 1967); William W. Kaufman, *The McNamara Strategy* (New York: Harper and Row, 1964); Raymond G. O'Connor, *American Defense Policy in Perspective* (New York: John Wiley and Sons, Inc., 1965); Franz Schurmann, Peter Dale, and Reginald Zelnik, *The Politics of Escalation in Vietnam* (Greenwich: Fawcett Publications, Inc., 1966).

[17]See "Dangerous Air War Becomes Deadly," *U.S. News and World Report*, 18 September 1967: 41; and an article by Ted Sell, "Air Loss Costs 3 Times More than Damage," *Philadelphia Inquirer*, 11 October 1967.

[18]Maxwell D. Taylor, *Swords and Plowshares* (New York: W. W. Norton and Company, 1972), p. 404.

[19]James Cameron, *Here Is Your Enemy* (New York: Holt, Rinehart, and Winston, 1966), p. 66.

[20]Corson, *The Betrayal*, p. 67.

[21]On enclaves, see James M. Gavin, "A Communication on Vietnam," *Harper's Magazine* CCXXXII (February 1966): 16–21. For other views see LTC Joseph F. H. Cutrona, *Peace in Vietnam: An Acceptable Solution* (USAWC student essay, 22 April 1966); LTC Joseph G. Clemons, Jr., *The Dilemma of the Vietnam Enclaves* (USAWC student essay, 13 January 1967); "General Wheeler's Reply to the Enclave Theory," *U.S. News and World Report*, 7 February 1966; MG Max S. Johnson, USA (Ret.), "General Gavin's Enclave Theory," *U.S. News and World Report*, 7 February 1966.

[22]For these figures, see Corson, *The Betrayal*, p. 63, and Kendrick, *The Wound Within*, p. 183.

[23]See Corson, *The Betrayal*, p. 63.

[24]Specifically, they were organized under ROAD Tables of Organization and Equipment (TOEs) of the F and G series. See LTC Y. Y. Phillipps, "The ROAD Battalion in Vietnam," *Army* XVI (September 1966), wherein the author reports on the suitability of

ROAD infantry battalion organization for operations in Vietnam, based upon his observations while he was a battalion commander there with the First Infantry Division. See also Jac Weller, "The U.S. Army in Vietnam: A Survey of Aims, Operations, and Weapons, Particularly of Small Infantry Units," *Army Quarterly and Defense Review* LXXXV, 1 (October 1967), based on personal observations by the author, who is a noted military journalist and historian. Weller concentrates on small-unit weapons and tactics as they affect organization.

Other comments of some worth include those by COL. Lawrence L. Mowery, "Vietnam Report," *Infantry* (January–February 1971), in which the author, senior member of a U.S. Continental Army Command (CONARC) liaison team, specifies his observations of infantry-unit organization and tactics while visiting infantry units in 'Nam in the fall of 1970, and *Maj.* J. Avera, "Return of the Combat Support Company," *Infantry* (September–October 1970), wherein Avera describes the organization of and the need for the combat-support company.

[25]Philipps, "The ROAD Battalion in Vietnam," p. 54.

[26]Phillips, "The ROAD Battalion in Vietnam," p. 54.

[27]Weller, "The U.S. Army in Vietnam," p. 49. See also the U.S. Army Combat Developments Command Liaison Detachment, *Trip Report*, Americal Division, 20–21 January 1968 (22 January 1968), pp. 3–4.

[28]Philipps, "The ROAD Battalion in Vietnam," p. 56; Weller, "The U.S. Army in Vietnam," p. 50; 196th Light Infantry Brigade (Separate), *Operations Report—Lessons Learned*, 1 February 1967 to 30 April 1967 (undated report), p. 12.

[29]3d Brigade, 82d Airborne Division, *Operations Report—Lessons Learned*, period ending 31 October 1969 (19 March 1970). See also U.S. Army Combat Developments Command Liaison Detachment, *Trip Report*, 4th Infantry Division, 15–16 January 1968 (19 January 1968), pp. 1–3; and U.S. Army Combat Developments Command Liaison Detachment, *Trip Report*, 25th Infantry Division, 8 January 1968 (10 January 1968), p. 3.

[30]Avera, "Return of the Combat Support Company," pp. 44–5. Obviously, the air-defense section of combat support companies was not activated in situations in Vietnam.

[31]See 196th Light Infantry Brigade (Separate), *Operations Report—Lessons Learned*, *loc. cit.*, 3d Brigade, 82d Airborne Division, *Operations Report—Lessons Learned*, Period ending 30 April 1968 (4 September 1968), p. 4; 1st Brigade, 5th Infantry Division (Mechanized), *Operations Report—Lessons Learned*, Period ending 31 October 1968 (7 March 1969), p. 11. This last ORLL is the only one of several examined in which there is reference to submission of a request for MTOE action.

[32]GEN Hamilton H. Howze, U.S.A. (Ret.), "Vietnam: an Epilogue," *Army* (July 1975): 13–14.

[33]Quoted in Ward Just, *Military Men* (New York: Alfred A. Knopf, Publishers, 1970), p. 187.

[34]Quoted in Just, *Military Men*, p. 185.

[35]William C. Westmoreland, *A Soldier Reports* (Garden City: Doubleday and Company, Inc., 1976).

[36]It may be that such high-ranking officers tended to concentrate on the first of MacArthur's triad, rather than on the entirety of his emphasis upon "duty, honor, country."

[37]Kinnard, *The War Managers*, p. 116.

[38]Maureen Mylander, *The Generals: Making It, Military Style* (New York: The Dial Press, 1974), p. 211.

[39]Kinnard, *The War Managers*, pp. 25, 154, 164.

[40]King, *Death of the Army*, pp. 107–08.

[41]Kendrick, *The Wound Within*, p. 127.

[42]King, *Death of the Army*, p. 59.

[43]Townshend Hoopes, *The Limits of Intervention* (New York: David McKay Company, Inc., 1969), p. 62.

44*Ibid.*, p. 63.

45His reward for the debacle in Vietnam that occurred under his leadership was promotion to the position of army chief of staff. Similar promotion came to his two successors, General Creighton Abrams and General Fred C. Weyand.

46Figures are drawn from Charles B. MacDonald and Charles V. P. von Luttichau, *The United States Army in Vietnam* (Washington: Government Printing Office, n.d.), pp. 625–26. This pamphlet was written as a supplement to and for inclusion in recent editions of Maurice Matlow, ed., *American Military History* (Washington: Government Printing Office, 1969).

47Westmoreland had opportunity to learn that there was more to defeat of the enemy than pouring devastating amounts of firepower upon them. Of many possible illustrations of that fact, one of the best occurred more than ten years prior to the American buildup in Vietnam, during early 1953 in the Republic of Korea. A Chinese-held hill, "Spud" Hill, was selected by the American command as a site for a test of the efficacy of firepower combined with infantry as a means of capturing terrain during combat. The test was to be known as Operation Smack. The operation began on 12 January 1953, when American artillery began dropping rounds on Spud Hill. In all, some twenty-two thousand rounds of artillery shells landed on the target. Planes dropped some 360,000 pounds of bombs and twenty-two napalm tanks on the hill.

As D-Day, 25 January, came closer, use of lethal shelling continued. Four thousand five hundred rounds of mortar shells, 100,000 rounds of 40mm and 50-caliber ammunition, 125,000 rounds of 30-caliber ammunition, and two thousand rounds of 90mm tank shells churned the earth of Spud Hill. On D-Day, soldiers of the 7th Infantry Division moved forward onto the slopes of the hill. In addition to their small-arms rifle fire, they used six hundred and fifty hand grenades in their assault.

The Chinese used perhaps one-tenth of the ammunition spent by the 7th Division and suffered fewer than sixty casualties in *retaining* the hill. "All in all, Operation Smack was a fiasco." See Walter G. Hermes, *United States Army in the Korean War: Truce Tent and Fighting Front* (Washington: Government Printing Office, 1966), pp. 386–88.

48General Charles Timmes, address to the student body, Command and General Staff College, Ft. Leavenworth, Kansas, 9 April 1976.

49LTC James M. Lee, *Which Strategy for Advanced Insurgency: Pacification or Combat?* (Carlisle Barracks: USAWC student essay, 13 January 1967), p. 13.

Chapter Three

1Subject interview.

2*Time* magazine, 15 September 1967.

3LTC Wilman D. Barnes, *The Vietnam Barrier: Maginot Mentality or Imaginative Strategy?* (USAWC student essay, 27 October 1967), p. 18. One of the worst puns of all time must have been that created by a writer discussing the electronic barrier. See Gene Famiglietti, "Can De Fence Be Ignored?" *Army Times* (27 September 1967).

4Lederer, *Our Own Worst Enemy*, p. 199. If ARVN generals were corrupted by money, American flag officers were twisted through their devotion to statistics. Kinnard indicates much the same thing. He asks, "What precisely did it mean that 37% of the base camps were neutralized at any one time? Could not the enemy subsequently return or build new ones in the endless jungles? [Nor were] quality or costs usually shown along with results. For example, to say that a certain highway was cleared for use did not indicate the quantity, quality, or frequency of traffic that could move on a road. Nor did it give the cost in resources to keep the road open. In other words, if a particular road was open, how important was it . . . ? . . . in aggregate [the indicators] did not really tell how the war was going." See Kinnard, *War Managers*, p. 72.

The war corrupted more than our military leaders. Polnar writes that "the war itself is corrupting. . . . Air Force guys can make lots of loot, extra Vietnam pay, all untaxed. Flight crews fight each other for Vietnam duty. Guys make one over-flight a month from

Laos, Thailand, or a carrier and get extra pay. Loadmasters, who are absolutely crucial, balk at going to Germany because there's more in it for them personally in Asia." See *No Victory Parades*, p. 155.

[5]Jonathan Schell, as quoted in Erwin Knoll and Judith N. McFadden, *War Crimes and the American Conscience* (New York: Holt, Rinehart and Winston, 1970), pp. 62–3. Halberstam makes a significant point in his work *Best and Brightest*, p. 667: "When Neil Sheehan traveled with Westmoreland on his plane in the summer of 1966 he asked if Westmoreland was not worried by the enormity of civilian casualties which the bombing and shelling were causing in the South. 'Yes,' said Westmoreland, 'but it does deprive the enemy of the population, doesn't it?' It was a significant comment; it meant that for all the Army's distaste for the war, the fire power loosed on both enemy and population, the American command was aware of what it was doing and sanctioned it; messy, yes, but the only way to separate the Vietcong from his strategic base."

What it did, of course, was create refugees. Taber reports that prior to Tet 1968, there were some 800,000 homeless people in South Vietnam. That offensive, and the reactive strikes of the American armed forces, caused the creation of another 700,000 refugees. In May 1968 alone, shelling and bombing and the consequent fires that resulted destroyed more than 10,000 homes in Saigon suburbs, adding another 102,000 refugees to the total. "Each new chapter in the struggle illustrated the nature of the U.S. dilemma created by guerrilla tactics: to oppose the guerrilla forces, the Americans were compelled to destroy the very country they were fighting for, yet not to fight was also to lose it." See Taber, *War of the Flea*, p. 87. Logically, the horns of a dilemma may be attacked frontally or by going between or around them. Perhaps those in charge might have considered attacking the *problems* on which the guerrillas fed rather than attacking the people.

[6]A study dealing with morale problems of race and drugs in the army is that by Haynes Johnson and George C. Wilson, *Army in Anguish*: A Washington Post NATIONAL REPORT (New York: Pocket Books, 1972).

[7]Kinnard, *War Managers*, p. 46.

[8]Quoted in Boyle, *Flower of the Dragon*, pp. 186–87.

[9]Bernard Fall, "Viet Nam in the Balance," *Foreign Affairs* XLV, 1 (October 1966): 10.

[10]Subject interview.

[11]Johnson and Wilson, *Army in Anguish*, p. 76.

[12]Johnson and Wilson, *Army in Anguish*, p. 78.

[13]Subject interview.

[14]Georgie Anne Geyer, "Military Soul-Searching," *Washington Post*, 20 June 1977.

[15]Subject interview. While Gavin's enclave strategy had as its goal the object of denying the enemy victory, Westmoreland's search-and-destroy tactic would, it was hoped, bring about the total defeat of the VC and NVA effort. See Kinnard, *War Managers*, p. 39. Kinnard claims that 58 percent of the generals he interviewed, at some point or other, believed such a tactic to be unsuitable (p. 45), while 86 percent believed its execution left a great deal to be desired or else was only barely adequate. Some 42 percent thought large-scale search-and-destroy operations, such as Cedar Falls, were "overdone from the beginning." Kinnard points out that "these replies show a noticeable lack of enthusiasm, to put it mildly, for [Westmoreland's] tactics and by implication for his strategy in the war." (p. 45)

In the face of such statistics, one can today only wonder where the voices of those dissident generals was when it might have counted for something.

[16]Subject interview.

[17]*Pentagon Papers,* Gravel Edition, III, p. 397.

[18]Komer, *Bureaucracy Does Its Thing*, p. vii.

[19]Thompson, *No Exit from Vietnam*, p. 135.

[20]Norman Hannah, "Vietnam: Now We Know," *National Review* (11 June 1976); 613.

[21]Dave Richard Palmer, *Readings in Current Military History* (West Point: Department of Military Art and Engineering, 1969), p. 94.

[22]Kinnard, *War Managers*, p. 40.

[23]*Conversations with Enemy Soldiers in Late 1968/Early 1969: A Study of Motivation and Morale* (Santa Monica: The RAND Corporation, 1970).

[24]LTC Zeb B. Bradford, Jr., "US Tactics in Vietnam," *Military Review*, LII, 2 (February 1972): 74.

[25]*Ibid.*, 72.

[26]See LTG Harry W. O. Kinnard, "Victory in the Ia Drang: The Triumph of a Concept," *Army* XVII, 9 (September 1967); 73.

[27]See MAJ Frank E. Allgood, USMC, "Progress and Prep Fires," *Marine Corps Gazette* LI, 9 (September 1967); 29–31. He discusses the pros and cons of using preparatory fires on LZs.

[28]One man interviewed for this study told of his own experience with an unsuccessful search-and-destroy mission. "We helicoptered into an area, landing on the edge of a little Vietnamese cemetery. I was on the next-to-last chopper. We did not know it, but literally living underground at the cemetery was a whole battalion of enemy troops, and we landed right on top of them at a time when they were staging some sort of assembly there. All hell just broke loose.

"I got hit leaving my chopper, not very seriously. Luckily I got out on the left side, as did the radio operator. Most of the others got out on the right side and were really hit bad. There was chaos there for a while and no one could tell what was going on. I got on the radio, for I knew we were in trouble, and in just a few minutes the sky was full of gunships. They were too late for most of the boys, for in my platoon everyone was killed but me and my radio operator, and both of us were wounded. Yet there was no way the NVA could have gotten to us, for the gunships laid down a wall between us and them. The ships stayed up there all night, occasionally dropping flares so they could see to keep the NVA troops away until they could get us out. We had landed about five in the afternoon and weren't extracted until about eight the next morning. We didn't accomplish much."

Yet not all search-and-destroy missions ended badly. Another officer recalled that "on an island south of Danang we found a major enemy hospital that had been functioning for at least three or four years. It had been built up over perhaps ten to twelve years, with a triple subterranean tunnel network in an area where the water tables were generally no more than six to eight feet below ground. Yet they had managed to shore the place up and go subterranean with pumps and bilges to keep the place pumped out. Quite an engineering feat. They had fairly modern operating tables, collapsible modules that could be reassembled, generators to give the tunnels good ventilation. It was quite an operation in an area not even suspected to house VC activity. Needless to say, it was no longer usable when we finished with it."

[29]*Time*, 25 August 1967, p. 22.

[30]*New York Times*, 21 November 1966.

[31]*Washington Post*, 22 November 1966.

[32]*New York Times*, 22 November 1966.

[33]LTC James R. Lay, *Search and Destroy Operations* (USAWC student essay, 13 November 1967), p. 11. See also LTC William H. Miller, *US Army Infantry Tactics in Vietnam* (Air War College Report 4045, Maxwell AFB, Alabama, 1970).

[34]Thompson, *No Exit from Vietnam*, p. 136.

[35]Various analyses worth consulting on the doctrine of search and destroy and the army's experiences with it may be found in Boyd T. Bashore, "The Name of the Game is 'Search and Destroy,' " *Army* XVII, 2 (February 1967): 56–62; Bryce F. Denno, "Military Prospects in Vietnam," *Orbis* IX, 2 (Summer 1965): 411–417; George E. Dexter, "Search and Destroy in Vietnam," *Infantry* LVI, 4 (July–August 1966): 36–42; David H. Hackworth, "No Magic Formula," *Infantry* LVII, 1 (January–February 1967): 32–37; Edgar O'Ballance, "Strategy in Vietnam," *Army Quarterly and Defense Journal* XCIII, 2 (January 1967): 166–67; Willard Pearson, "Find 'em, Fix 'em, Finish 'em," *Army Digest*, XXI, 12 (December 1966): 14–21; and "Report on Vietnam," *Army Green Book* 1967 (October 1967); 105–125.

[36]Subject interview. Another individual interviewed for this study summed up the situation very succinctly. "A platoon leader down on the ground would get in a serious firefight. Hovering above him would be his company commander, his battalion commander, his brigade commander, and still higher might be the divisional commander if it was something really exceptional going on, all asking him for SITREPS [situation reports]. *The platoon commander should probably have told them all to go to hell.*" Still another man commented: "We *did* have the 'eye in the sky' crap with high-level commanders trying to direct the actions of a company on the ground. My battalion commander once told me that 'I had more real independent command authority as a 2 LT platoon leader than I have as an 05 Battalion Commander here'—because of the air-mobile capabilities which made it possible for division, corps, and even USARV commanders to fly safely over units engaged in combat."

[37]Subject interview.

[38]Subject interview.

[39]Subject interview.

[40]Subject interview.

[41]Subject interview.

[42]Subject interview.

[43]Mylander, *The Generals*, p. 194.

[44]Subject interview. An interested reader may wish to consult Zeb Bradford, Jr., and Frederic J. Brown, *The United States Army in Transition* (Beverly Hills: Sage Publications, 1973), which touches on several of the problems mentioned here.

[45]Kinnard, *War Managers*, p. 46.

[46]Just, *Military Men*, p. 230.

[47]Kinnard, *War Managers*, p. 47.

[48]Kinnard, *War Managers*, p. 47.

[49]Subject interview.

[50]Subject interview.

[51]Subject interview. For the army's own view of artillery in Vietnam, see MG David E. Ott, *Vietnam Studies: Field Artillery, 1954–1973* (Washington: Government Printing Office, 1975). The main difficulty with this work, as with all the volumes in the *Vietnam Studies* series, is that after reading it one has the impression that the United States emerged victorious from Vietnam.

[52]Kinnard, *War Managers*, p. 67.

[53]One among countless available examples is Jeffrey S. Milstein, *Dynamics of the Vietnam War: A Quantitative Analysis and Predictive Computer Simulation* (Columbus: Ohio State University Press, 1974).

[54]Quoted in Roger Hilsman, *To Move a Nation*, p. 523.

[55]Kinnard, *War Managers*, p. 71.

[56]Murray Polner, *No Victory Parades: The Return of the Vietnam Veteran* (New York: Holt, Rinehart and Winston, 1971), p. 56.

[57]MAJ William I. Lowry, *Strategic Assessment of the War in Vietnam: Truman through Kennedy* (USACGSC student paper, 1976), p. 22.

[58]LTC Richard A. McMahon, *Let's Bury the Body Count* (USAWC student essay, 13 December 1968), p. 1. Kinnard reports that only 2 percent of his generals thought the body count was a valid way of measuring progress in the war and but 4 percent believed that a "kill ratio" was a valuable indicator. Conversely, some 61 percent stated they thought body counts to be inflated. Those generals offered such comments as "The immensity of the false reporting is a blot on the honor of the army." "The bane of my existence and just about got me fired as a division commander. They were grossly exaggerated by many units primarily because of the incredible interest shown by people like McNamara and Westmoreland. I shudder to think how many of our soldiers were killed on a body-counting mission—what a waste." "A fake—totally worthless." "Often blatant lies." See Kinnard, *War Managers, passim.*

[59]Judges 15: 15.

[60]*Newsweek*, 12 February 1968.

[61]The *New Yorker*, 2 March 1968.

[62]*Newsweek*, 29 July 1968.

[63]*New York Times*, 28 August 1968. Polnar writes of a dust-off pilot who lamented that "what I couldn't explain away, however, then or now, were the fake casualty rates our side kept announcing. They were lies. I once read a *Stars and Stripes* article about VC dead and American and ARVN casualties in a particular action. I myself had carried a minimum of fifty Americans, dead or nearly dead, they were so badly destroyed, back to Nha Trang. When I multiplied this figure with the number of aircraft in my unit, plus similar units of this type operating in the vicinity, I knew it was a lousy distortion. If we weren't getting the figures straight on the spot, then how accurate could they be, I thought, in the newspapers across the country?" See *No Victory Parades*, p. 55.

[64]*Life*, 5 April 1968.

[65]See, for example, *Time*, 30 June 1967.

[66]See Bernard Weinraub, "76 Americans Die in Ambush on Vietnam Ridge," *New York Times*, 25 June 1967, and Tom Buckley, "Foe Toll at 106 in Vietnam Clash," *New York Times*, 26 June 1967.

[67]"The aspect of the body count that bothered me was that it was done in a time when the army certainly needed the support of U.S. public opinion, and that didn't help to get it, to have reports sent home of people running through the jungles gleefully counting bodies. Second, I lost men and other commanders lost men while they were engaged in the dubious art of body counting—killed by ambushes, by snipers, by booby traps. We didn't need to lose people in such a way simply to create a statistical chart somewhere."—Subject interview.

[68]McMahon, *Let's Bury the Body Count*, p. 6.

[69]Subject interview.

[70]Daly, *Hero's Welcome*, p. 63.

[71]*Study on Military Professionalism* (Carlisle Barracks, Pennsylvania: USAWC, 30 June 1970), pp. B-1–10.

[72]McMahon, *Let's Bury the Body Count*, p. 8.

[73]*Ibid.*

[74]The preceding instances have been drawn from McMahon, *Let's Bury the Body Count*, pp. 8–10.

[75]Phil G. Goulding, "Ten Problems of Ho Chi Minh," *Army Digest* (August 1968): 6.

[76]*New York Times Magazine*, 9 June 1968.

[77]"War Termination—A Synopsis," *Selected Readings: Military Strategy Seminar*, Vol. I, USAWC, pp. 2–1.

The so-called Lopez War, although little-known, was one of the bloodiest in history. Francisco Solano Lopez became president of Paraguay when he was thirty-five and ruled from 1862 to 1870. The war began in the last days of 1864 and continued without real let-up until 1870. Lopez had managed to alienate Uraguay, Argentina, and Brazil, all three of which joined in a powerful coalition against Paraguay. Undaunted, Lopez managed to resist for over five years by imposition of ruthless rule at home and stubborn military resistance to his enemies. Young and old alike were dragooned into military service. Boys of twelve found themselves fighting alongside their grandfathers, and those who tried to avoid Paraguayan military service were given cruel and lingering deaths.

By 1870, the population of Paraguay had been reduced from 525,000 to 221,000. Only some 28,000 males remained in the entire population. For more on the Lopez War, see Hubert Herring, *A History of Latin America* (New York: Alfred A. Knopf Publishers, 1972), pp. 815ff.

[78]Daly, *Hero's Welcome*, p. 22.

[79]*Ibid.*, pp. 54–55.

[80]*Ibid.*, p. 62. For anecdotes of combat and troop life in Vietnam told from a very

positive viewpoint, see Jim G. Lucas, *Dateline: Vietnam* (New York: Award Books, 1967), and, for a more skeptical attitude, see Richard Tregaskis, *Vietnam Diary* (New York: Holt, Rinehart and Winston, 1963).

[81]Murray Polner, *No Victory Parades: The Return of the Vietnam Veteran* (New York: Holt, Rinehart and Winston, 1971), p. 55.

[82]*Ibid.*, p. 24.

[83]*Ibid.*, p. 102.

[84]Subject interview. At the time, this individual was assigned to the staff of the Combined Arms Training and Doctrine Activity (CATRADA), Ft. Leavenworth, Kansas.

[85]Polner, *No Victory Parades*, p. 71.

[86]*Ibid.*, p. 38.

[87]Herbert, *Soldier*, p. 238.

[88]*Ibid.*, pp. 246-47.

[89]Subject interview.

[90]The testimony given there was printed and published by the VVAW under the title *The Winter Soldier Investigation: An Inquiry into American War Crimes* (Boston: Beacon Press, 1972).

[91]*Winter Soldier*, p. 164.

[92]For an excellent and full account, see the recent book by William R. Peers, *The My Lai Inquiry* (New York: W. W. Norton and Co., 1979). A view that surveys the entire problem of the lawful conduct of combat is that by Peter D. Trooboff, ed., *Law and Responsibility in Warfare: The Vietnam Experience* (Chapel Hill: University of North Carolina Press, 1975).

My Lai, of course, was not the first recorded incident where an American military unit committed an atrocity. Sixty-odd years earlier, during America's involvement in the Philippine Insurrection, other such actions occurred.

When the U.S. took over the Philippine Islands from Spain during the Spanish-American War, the insurrectionists initially welcomed our forces, grateful for the aid we rendered in freeing the islands of Spanish colonial rule. When it shortly became apparent that we did not intend to leave, their attitude changed and the insurrection continued.

Emilio Aguinaldo became leader of the Philippine guerilla forces, and their ambushes and hit-and-run tactics proved difficult for the U.S. Army to handle. The military, however, swore to "civilize the Filipinos with a Krag," if necessary. (The Krag-Jorgenson was the standard military rifle of that era.) Filipinos, on the other hand, believed they were already civilized and that the issue was, rather, home rule.

In its efforts to control the insurrection, the American army found itself doing things in the Philippines—including the use of concentration camps and "water cure" tortures—for which the Spanish had been condemned when they used them in Cuba.

Reaction finally came in the United States as prominent citizens in many walks of life joined together to publicize what we were doing in those Pacific islands and to call for an end to it. Education was represented by President Eliot of Harvard. Samuel Gompers of the American labor movement, and Andrew Carnegie, the business magnate, cooperated for perhaps the only time in their lives. Jane Addams of Chicago's Hull House and Mark Twain also joined the movement, as did dozens of others. Twain remarked that if the atrocities continued, the red, white, and blue bunting of the American flag should be hauled down in the archipelago and replaced with the skull and crossbones.

It is always difficult to discriminate among an enemy populace during military actions—particularly when guerilla soldiers are involved. Such difficulty, however, does not mean that it then becomes acceptable to act indiscriminately.

[93]This chart accompanied *News Release*, Office of the Assistant Secretary of Defense (Public Affairs), Washington: 13 November 1974.

[94]Herbert C. Kelman, "The Military Establishment," *Society* (May/June 1975): 18-22.

[95]King, *Death of the Army*, p. 122.

[96]*Study on Military Professionalism* (Carlisle Barracks: USAWC, 30 June 1970), p. B-1-28.

[97]Kinnard, *War Managers*, p. 51.

[98]Kinnard, *War Managers*, pp. 51, 52, 53. See also Peter D. Trooboff, ed.. *Law and Responsibility in Warfare: The Vietnam Experience* (Chapel Hill: University of North Carolina Press, 1975).

[99]Subject interview.

[100]Gabriel Kolko, *The Roots of American Foreign Policy* (Boston: Beacon Press, 1969), p. 131.

[101]Kendrick, *The Wound Within*, p. 29. As readers know, the traumas were not restricted to Southeast Asia. For a clear picture by two of President Ford's clemency-board senior officials of how millions in America responded to the war in Vietnam, see Lawrence M. Baskir and William A. Strauss, *Chance and Circumstance: The Draft, the War and the Vietnam Generation* (New York: Vintage, 1978).

Chapter Four

[1]Genesis 4: 8–9.

[2]The nation-building efforts cited in the text refer to situations that had one major difference from circumstances faced by the American army in Vietnam. In Cuba, in the Philippines, in Germany and Japan, the army was assigned such tasks *after* military victory had been achieved. Difficult as its duties were, they were easier than they would have been if it had been ordered to accomplish them prior to pacification and defeat of the enemy.

Marine Corps activities in the I Corps area, however, are but one example of the fact that nation-building efforts could be carried on in an alien land amidst an alien culture while faced with an alien enemy. Results there were graphic and concrete. Some army activities likewise brought promising results, but as an entity, the army concentrated on firepower against an elusive enemy in tactics that seldom brought it any nearer "the light at the end of the tunnel."

[3]Subject interview.

[4]Subject interview.

[5]Maurice D. Roush, *Strategy for Vietnam: Pacification or Combat?* (USAWC student essay, 9 October 1967), pp. 16, 1. For the emphasis upon pacification stressed by the U.S. Army see the various publications of the United States Military Assistance Command, Vietnam, *Command History*, 1965, 1966, 1967, 1968, 1969, 1970, 1971, 1972–March 1973, 1973, 1974. Some are still classified "top secret."

[7]Quoted from M. W. Browne, *The New Face of War* (New York: Bobbs-Merrill Company, Inc., 1965), pp. 121–22.

[8]Robert E. Huber, *How to Win in Vietnam* (USAWC student essay, 13 November 1967), pp. 11, 9, 4, 7, 8. See also Charles R. Ray, *Strategic Assessment of the War in Vietnam: The Johnson Years* (USACGSC student paper, 1976).

[9]James H. Chapman, *The US Army and Pacification in Vietnam: An Assessment of the Army's Ability to Cope with an Insurgency* (USACGSC student paper, 1976).

[10]Brian M. Jenkins, *The Unchangeable War* (Santa Monica: RAND Corporation, 1970).

[10]Richard A. McMahon, *Let's Bury the Body Count* (USAWC student essay, 13 December 1968).

[11]V. H. Lipsey, *Vietnamization or Victimization?* (United States Air Force Air University, Air War College, Maxwell Air Force Base, Alabama, Study Number 4985, April 1973).

[12]Lieutenant Colonel Charles R. Smith, *Repetitive Tours in Vietnam for Infantry Captains* (USAWC staff study, 10 February 1969), an essay that bears a "confidential" classification. See also Major Armando Lujan, Major David Menig, and Captain Dwight Beck, *The U.S. Army Force in Vietnam, 1969–1975: A Study in Macro Force Development* (USACGSC student paper, 1976), which also bears a "confidential" classification. See

Louis Walt, *Strange War, Strange Victory* (New York: Ace Books, 1968).

[13]LTC James C. Barnes, Jr., *The Battle of Khe Sahn: Sound Strategy or Costly Miscalculation* (USAWC case study, 5 February 1969), which bears a "secret" classification.

[14]See, for example, the fiscal year-end reports published annually by the United States Army Combat Developments Command, Ft. Belvoir, Virginia, which are known as *Combat Operations Loss and Expenditure Data Reports—Vietnam*.

[15]To use these reports, one must either have the proper security clearance or receive special permission from the Secretary of the Air Force (SAFOIP), Washington, D.C. 20330, from whose office emanates the proper authorization. The center at Maxwell is a rich lode for researchers, containing something like 33,000,000 pages of historical material on the air force from its beginnings to the present, with another 2,000,000 added yearly.

[16]An example of the manner in which they are filed can be given by considering the case of Fred C. Weyand. As a lieutenant general, he was in command of II Field Force, Vietnam. His report is thus filed as *Senior Officer Debriefing Report, LTG Fred C. Weyand, CG, IIFFV, 29 March 1966 to 1 August 1968*, and bears a "secret" classification.

[17]Some of these *Senior Officer Debriefing Reports* (SODR) are available in the classified section of the CGSC library; others may be consulted at the Center for Military History (CMH) in Washington, D.C.; still additional ones are currently "lost" in the unmanageable mass of uncatalogued Vietnam materials stacked in boxes at the Federal Records Center, Suitland, Maryland.

[18]LTG Fred C. Weyand, CG, IIFFV, March 1966 to August 1968, *Senior Officer Debriefing Report*.

[19]BG Carleton Peer, Jr., DSA, III Corps and III CTZ, May to November 1969, SODR.

[20]BG D. P. McAuliffe, DSA, MR3, December 1969 to November 1970, SODR.

[21]BG S. A. Matheson, CG, 1st BDE, 101st AM DIV, 2 March 1968, SODR. For comparison, see such other SODRs as LTG Charles A. Corcoran, CG, IFFV, May 1968 to February 1970; LTG Melvin Zais, CG, XXIV Corps, June 1969 to June 1970; MG Donn R. Pepke, CG, 4th INF DIV, November 1968 to November 1969; MG John J. Tolson, CG, 1st CAV, April 1967 to July 1968; MG O. M. Barsanti, CG, 101st Air CAV DIV, July 1968 to July 1969; MG Charles P. Stone, CG, 4th INF DIV, August 1970 to January 1971; BG E. R. Ochs, CG, 173d ABN BDE, August 1970 to January 1971; BG George W. Dickerson, CG, 3d BDE, 82d ABN DIV, December 1968 to December 1969; COL George B. Carrinton, SA, Capital Military District, MACV, March 1968 to October 1968; COL Travis Stephens, PSA, II CTZ (period not stated, report dated 12 March 1970); LTC John L. Bringham, DSA, Tuyen Duc Province, May 1971 to December 1972; LTC Robert E. Smith, SA, Pleiku Province, May 1971 to December 1972; LTC Robert E. Wagner, SA, Quang Tin Province, December 1970 to July 1972.

[22]Halberstam, *Best and Brightest*, p. 657.

[23]General Vo Nguyen Giap as quoted in Bernard, *Observations and Reflections of a Province Senior Adviser*, p. 7. See also James H. Chapman, *The U.S. Army and Pacification in Vietam: An Assessment of the Army's Ability to Cope with an Insurgency* (USACGSC student report, 1976).

[24]Kinnard, *War Managers*, p. 25.

[25]*Ibid.*, p. 28.

[26]*Ibid.*, p. 45. Some of those operations were vast. OPERATION CEDAR FALLS, named after the hometown of a Medal of Honor recipient, occurred in January 1967 in the Iron Triangle base area. Some thirty thousand soldiers had as their objective the destruction of all villages in an area forty miles square. The troops moved in, evacuated all inhabitants, and burned houses and crops. All males were treated as if they were VC, and even women and children were regarded as "hostile civilians" and were relocated to new settlements elsewhere.

OPERATION JUNCTION CITY occurred north of Tay Ninh City in War Zone C from February to May 1967. Anyone desiring to read further on such large-scale search-and-destroy operations should consult the work by Jonathan Schell dealing with CEDAR FALLS, entitled *The Village of Ben Suc.* (New York: Alfred Knopf, 1967). One of the government's *Vietnam Studies* series also deals with such operations and is written by LTG Bernard W. Rogers, CEDAR FALLS—JUNCTION CITY: *A Turning Point* (Washington: Government Printing Office, 1974).

[27] *Ibid.*, p. 47.

[28] *Ibid.*, p. 48.

[29] *Ibid.*, p. 50.

[30] *Ibid.*, p. 58.

[31] *Ibid.*, p. 74.

[32] Kinnard, *War Managers*, p. 75.

[33] *Ibid.*, p. 110.

[34] *Ibid.*, p. 112.

[35] *Ibid.*, p. 144.

[36] *Ibid.*, p. 153.

[37] *Ibid.*, p. 154.

[38] Subject interview.

[39] Further comments on such matters may be found in MAJ William R. Nolen, *Vietnam Assessment: Base Camp, Night Defensive Positions and Fire Support Base Defense* (USACGSC student essay, 1976); LTG John H. Hay, Jr., *Tactical and Materiel Innovations: Vietnam Studies* (Washington, Government Printing Office, 1974); Headquarters, XXIV Corps, *Defense Against Sapper Attacks* (14 March 1969, USACGSC number 12975.6); Headquarters, USMACV, *Counter Measures against Standoff Attacks*, Lessons Learned Number 71 (13 March 1969, USACGSC number 12975.6); 1st Infantry Division, *Tactical Lessons of the Vietnam War* (USACGSC Library); 1st Brigade, 101st Airborne Division, *Tactical Lessons of the Vietnam War* (USACGSC library); Army Concept Team in Vietnam, *Fire Support Base Defense, Final Report* (Project Number ACG-80f, Department of Army, 6 April 1972, USACGSC Library Number 5849.237).

[40] Taken from a typescript prepared for an unnamed, undated briefing. The manuscript is filed in the classified section of the USACGSC library. Italics added.

[41] Subject interview. Readers might wish to compare the observations from after-action reports set forth herein with a book by W. Scott Thompson and Donaldson D. Frizzell, *The Lessons of Vietnam* (New York: Crane, Russak and Co., 1977). A strange book, it contains selected proceedings from two conferences held at the Fletcher School of Law and Diplomacy in 1973 and 1974. Participants at those meetings included such important men as Robert Komer, Major General Edward Lansdale, Ambassador Henry Cabot Lodge, Brigadier General S. L. A. Marshall, Sir Robert Thompson, and General William C. Westmoreland—many of the very same men who led the United States and its military into such drastic mistakes in Vietnam.

They do not appear, in this book, to be much wiser than were the lower-level leaders within the army who fought in Vietnam. Their lessons learned include such obvious ones as that (1) it is important to have indigenous political systems that can attract sustained popular support; (2) the United States is apparently unable to engage in prolonged overseas military adventures when its national interests are not directly involved; (3) there was a cultural clash between the Americans and the Vietnamese; (4) a graduated military response seldom achieves its objectives; (5) the United States lacked clearly defined goals in Vietnam; (6) the United States disregarded the lessons of history—particularly those of the French in Indochina—during its intervention in Vietnam.

While addressing themselves to issues that were totally obvious on the face of them, the distinguished participants failed to consider such important factors as the effect of the United States defeat in Vietnam on current and future American soldiers serving in an army that has not really won a conflict since 1945.

Far more realistic were the observations of Roger A. Beaumont, "A Challenge to Professionalism: Leadership Selection," *Military Review* LVIII, 3 (March 1978): 77–87. He noted that among the important lessons of Vietnam were the following: (1) an enemy should not be fought on ground that cannot be blockaded. It did not, he noted, work in 1812–1814, in Korea, or in Vietnam. (2) 'Surprise' should not be dropped from the list of principles of war "without expecting a logarithmic increase in costs," (3) No one should expect officers trained in a previous war to think more rapidly than two and one-half miles an hour while fighting a current conflict. (4) Unit morale will not go up while a short-tour system is in use. (5) Capital-intensive tactical technologies such as stand-off missiles cannot be canceled without a concommitant loss of skilled military technicians. (6) The military must never lose clear sight of the past or it will continue to be embarrassed (as for instance when the air force ignored the Strategic Bombing Survey's findings that bombing does not break civilian morale; Albert Speer could have stated the same thing without the necessity for a new survey). Beaumont concludes with the observation that "it is little comfort to rationalists to consider that Winfield Scott or David Farragut might have designed a strategy for Vietnam as effective as anything that came out of think tanks and puzzle palaces."

[42]Kinnard, *War Managers*, p. 67.

[43]Subject interview.

[44]Komer, *Bureaucracy Does Its Thing*, p. viii.

[45]*Ibid.*, p. 8.

[46]*Ibid.*, p. 48.

[47]*Army Times*, 8 May 1978.

[48]Komer, *Bureaucracy Does Its Thing*, p. 7.

[49]General Paul D. Harkins, quoted in *Newsweek*, 29 June 1964.

[50]General Maxwell W. Taylor, "*Meet the Press*," NBC, 8 August 1965.

[51]General Earle G. Wheeler, "*Issues and Answers*," ABC, 15 August 1965.

[52]Admiral U.S. Grant Sharp, Commander in Chief, Pacific, quoted in *New York Times*, 21 October 1965.

[53]Major General Harry W. O. Kinnard, quoted in *U.S. News and World Report*, 18 July 1966.

[54]Brigadier General (Ret.) S. L. A. Marshall, quoted in *Newsweek*, 12 September 1966.

[55]General William C. Westmoreland, *Life*, 11 November 1966.

[56]Lieutenant General Jonathan O. Seaman, quoted by *Time*, 3 March 1967.

[57]General Harold K. Johnson, *U. S. News and World Report*, 11 September 1967.

[58]Admiral U.S. Grant Sharp, *New York Times*, 13 October 1967.

[59]Robert Komer, *Newsweek*, 1 January 1968.

[60]General William C. Westmoreland, *New York Times*, 7 April 1968. The Tet Offensive of the North Vietnamese Liberation Front began on 30 January 1968. Troops of General Giap bombed and invaded thirty-six of the south's forty-four provincial capitals and sixty-four of its 292 district capitals. They did well in some cases, reaching the main runway of Ton Son Nhut's vast air base and taking the old Vietnamese capital city of Hue. Nor was even Saigon safe. Early in the morning of 31 January, the United States Embassy compound was attacked in a six-hour battle, at the end of which all attackers were either dead or captured.

Nearly everywhere, the enemy achieved tactical advantage with the suddenness and surprise of its attacks. The enemy caused extensive damage, many casualties, a real loss of morale among both ARVN and U.S. forces, and considerable confusion everywhere. The Tet offensive did not wane until 4 February, although it continued after that in such areas as Saigon, Hue, Da Lat and Phan Thiet. Hue was not recaptured until 23 February. Thereafter, enemy pressure continued only at Khe Sanh, and even there the enemy withdrew in mid-March. Interested researchers may wish to consult the Vietnamese-language publication by LTC Pham Van Son, Chief, Military History Division, J5, Joint General Staff, RVNAF: *The Viet Cong "TET" Offensive (1968)*, and Peter Braestrup, *Big Story: How the American Press and Television Reported and Interpreted the Crisis of TET 1968 in Vietnam and Washington* (2 vols., Boulder: Westview Press, 1973).

[61]Admiral John S. McCain, Jr., interview in *Reader's Digest*, February 1969.

[62]Colonel William Pietsch, Chief Military Aide, United States Diplomatic Mission, Phnom-Penh, Cambodia, quoted in *Newsweek*, 29 June 1970.

[63]General William C. Westmoreland, Washington *Sunday Star*, 16 April 1972.

[64]*Study on Military Professionalism* (Carlisle Barracks: USAWC, 30 June 1970), p. B-1-6.

[65]*Study on Military Professionalism*, p. B-1-6.

[66]*Ibid.*

[67]*Ibid.*, p. B-1-13.

[68]Commander Robert E. Mumford, Jr., suggests that the war produced these problems within the navy also. They thus were not a phenomenon solely of the army. See "Get Off My Back, Sir!" *United States Naval Institute Proceedings* (August, 1977).

[69]During several interviews with staff officers and school instructors of upper field-grade rank, they repeatedly made comments such as "Virtually nothing has come out of Vietnam in terms of lessons learned." One lieutenant colonel affirmed that "I talked with at least two generals and an entire string of colonels on the issue, and found every one of them to have impermeable minds." Another man remarked that "the only military lesson learned is that an army doesn't fight a war without popular support. But other than that—which we should have known as a matter of course even before Vietnam—in terms of how to fight a war better; how to function in fact in an internal conflict and to do so successfully, the lessons learned are very scattered and rarely put together in the proper form where they were really absorbed by people who could internalize those lessons. And it will only be another couple of years before anybody with experience at all, in this business, is out of the army."

Many such officers seem to have tried to convince their superiors of certain facts regarding "low-intensity conflicts," i.e., counterinsurgency warfare. "I had a discussion with one of our local generals, and another with one in Washington within the last three weeks on this project. I don't know what, if anything, will come of the talks."

One lieutenant colonel, interviewed at USACGSC just prior to his retirement, spoke of a "briefing I attended at DCSOPS [Deputy Chief of Staff for Operations], where one of the generals brought up the fact that we were teaching jungle warfare in Panama. But he didn't seem to know that what we were teaching there was simply jungle warfare against an enemy just as if we were still fighting Japan in the Pacific in World War II. The training in Panama has nothing to do with low intensity, or 'counterguerrilla' warfare. But that was not the time to give him a lecture. His comments typify the type of problem the army faces. Everybody goes for the thing they know about. I asked him, 'Well, what happens when you have low-intensity warfare in Norway? Principle learned at Ft. Sherman in Panama won't be particularly applicable there, will they?' He thought I was a smart-ass, but I was really dealing with a basic problem which he didn't seem to understand."

Still another individual, an instructor at the Army War College, told how he felt the need "to iron out all my moral problems before I retire, since I'm not going to get another promotion. So, having thought about some of these issues for a long time, I put my suggestions into a letter to the DCSPER [Deputy Chief of Staff for Personnel] a couple of days ago. That's all I can do—tell them what I know—what they make or refuse to make of it, is their problem."

One staff officer, decrying the fixation of the army on conflict in Europe, commented that "I'm getting nervous over the fact that we are failing to recognize—and have failed to recognize—the realities of the world around us. Everyone wants to stand at the Fulda Gap and shake their genitalia at the Russians. This is idiotic. It's not likely to be the place where we'll have to fight." [The secretary who transcribed tapes of my interviews initially rendered "Fulda Gap" as "folded gap"!]

An officer whose current duty assignment is at the Pentagon insisted that the basic problem is that senior officers never really listen to anyone. A graduate of the Military Academy, he recalled when General of the Army Omar Bradley made a speech there and pointed out how important it was for army officers to know how to listen. He told how Bradley said, "If one man tells you you are a jackass, it doesn't mean too much. If five men tell you you are a jackass, it is time to go out and buy yourself some hay." (With some differences, the same story is told by Joseph Ellis and Robert Moore, *School for Soldiers: West Point and the Profession of Arms* [New York: Oxford University Press, 1974], p. 47.) This officer concluded, "If it's important for West Point cadets, it's even more important for general officers."

[70]The quotes are taken from Kinnard, *War Managers*, pp. 29, 31.

[71]The series of Vietnam Studies that had been completed at the time of this writing include the following titles: LTG Bernard W. Rogers, *CEDAR FALLS—JUNCTION CITY: A Turning Point* (Washington: Government Printing Office, 1974); COL Francis J. Kelly, *U.S. Army Special Forces*, 1961–1971 (Washington: Government Printing Office, 1973); MG George S. Eckhardt, *Command and Control*, 1950–1969 (Washington: Government Printing Office, 1974); LTG Willard R. Pearson, *War in the Northern Provinces* (Washington: Government Printing Office, 1975); MG William B. Fulton, *Riverine Operations*, 1966–1969 (Washington: Government Printing Office, 1973); LTG John H. Hay, Jr., *Tactical and Materiel Innovations* (Washington: Government Printing Office, 1974); LTG Joseph M. Heiser, Jr., *Logistical Support* (Washington: Government Printing Office, 1974); LTG Julian Ewell, *Sharpening the Combat Edge* (Washington: Government Printing Office, 1974).

Other titles in preparation and their authors include LTG John J. Tolson, *Airmobility*, 1961–1971; MG Joseph A. McChristian, *The Role of Military Intelligence*, 1965–1967; LYG Carroll H. Dunn, *Base Development in South Vietnam*, 1965–1970; LTG Stanley R. Larsen and BG James L. Collins, Jr., *Allied Participation*; MG Thomas M. Rienzi, *Communications-Electronics*, 1962–1970; BG James L. Collins, Jr., *Training and Buildup of ARVN*; MG Spurgeon Neel, *Medical Support*, 1965–1970; MG Leonard B. Taylor, *Financial Management of the Vietnam Conflict*, 1962–1972; MG George S. Prugh, *Law at War —Vietnam*, 1964–1973; MG Donn A. Starry, *Armor in Vietnam*; MG David E. Ott, *Artillery in Vietnam*; MG Charles R. Myer, *Division-Level Communications*.

[72]Ploger, *U.S. Army Engineers*, 1965–1970, p. 179.

[73]*Ibid.*, p. 197.

[74]Heiser, *Logistic Support*, p. 4.

[75]Heiser, *Logistic Support*, p. 255 and *passim*.

[76]Pearson, *The War in the Northern Provinces*, 1966–1968, p. 107.

[77]Quoted from USMACV, *US Combat Forces in Support of Pacification: Lessons Learned*, Number 80 (Saigon: USMACV, 29 June 1970), p. i. See also USMACV, *The Concept of Pacification and Certain Definitions and Procedures*, Serial Number 0270 (Saigon: USMACV, 2 March 1965), which still bears a "confidential" stamp.

At the Center for Military History can be found the series *United States Army, Vietnam: Evaluations of U.S. Army Combat Operations in Vietnam* (volumes I through IX), which are variously classified as "secret" or "confidential" or "for official use only." Other sources of interest would include David Jickling, *Improving the Administration of Revolutionary Development* (Saigon: U.S. Agency for International Development Mission to Vietnam, January 1967); Department of the Army, *Internal Defense and Development: U.S. Army Doctrine* (Washington, Government Printing Office, 28 November 1974); Department of Defense, *Reemphasis on Pacification: 1965–1967—United States-Vietnam Relations, 1945–1967* (Washington: Government Printing Office, 20 September 1971); Headquarters, USMACV, *Command Information Pamphlet 4-67: Revolutionary Development* (Saigon: February 1967). There is also Army Field Manual 31-73, *Advisor Handbook for Counterinsurgency*, 23 April 1965, which gives a good view of the early attitude toward nation building.

A few secondary sources include Julian Paget, *Counterinsurgency Operations: Techniques of Guerrilla Warfare* (New York: Walker and Co., 1967); David Galula, *Counterinsurgency Warfare* (New York: Praeger, 1964); Roger Darling, "A New Conceptual Scheme for Analyzing Insurgency," *Military Review* LIV, 2 (February 1974); S. W. Smithers, Jr., "Combat Units in Revolutionary Development," *Military Review* XLVII, 10 (October 1967).

[78]Army Field Manual 100-20, *Internal Defense and Development, U.S. Army Doctrine*, p. 1-1.

[79]*Reemphasis on Pacification*: 1965–1967; *United States-Vietnam Relations*, 1945–1967, Department of Defense, 20 September 1971. See also USAWC Instructional Bulletin Number 13, *Changes in Counterinsurgency Terminology* (Carlisle Barracks, USAWC, 26 September 1966), pp. 1–4.

[80]During the course of research for this study, the single most insightful man with

whom I spoke talked at length about American expectations and American mistakes that began very early when there were only army advisers on the scene in Vietnam, but which continued to mar the performance of the United States Army in all the years thereafter. Interested readers who would like to benefit from his comments are referred to *Appendix* B.

[81]Quoted from Mike Gravel, *The Pentagon Papers* (5 vols., Boston: Beacon Press, 1970), Book 3, IV, B. 3, p. 16.

[82]*Pentagon Papers,* Gravel edition, Book 3, IV. B. 3., pp. 68–9. Some observations by North Vietnamese leader Vo Nguyen Giap, all published in Hanoi, by the Foreign Languages Publication House, include *Initial Failure of the US Limited War (1967); Once again We Will Win (1966); South Vietnam: A Great Victory (1967)*. See also Robert L. Sansom, "Working Paper on Viet Cong Economics," (USAID Economic Division, National Archives, April 1967), an unpublished report that speaks of the VC activities in the economic sector. Two early secondary sources that speak of some difficulties in South Vietnamese and American military efforts are Chester A. Bain, *Vietnam: The Roots of Conflict* (Englewood Cliffs: Prentice-Hall, 1967), and Hugh Deane, *The War in Vietnam* (New York: Monthly Press Review, 1963).

A lieutenant-colonel student at the USAWC came up with the novel thesis that a major cause of the Vietnamese conflict was ARVN, for it failed to show the people that it was their army fighting for their needs and goals, a factor that caused the South Vietnamese people to lose faith in their own fighting force. "Without the acceptance and support of the people, ARVN had little chance to succeed." This lack of support was compounded upon arrival of American units, for officers and advisers of the United States Army, "fresh from experiences against the Communists in Korea, had their own ideas as to how ARVN should be organized and what type of war they should be prepared to fight. Research, as well as history, proves that this approach to the situation was wrong." Even here, however, the author faulted ARVN. "Despite the fact that the Americans had not done their homework . . . there is no excusable reason why ARVN, after years of experience in this type of warfare, did not insist on being organized and prepared for counter-guerrilla warfare." See William R. Madden, Jr., *Did ARVN Invite War?* (USAWC case study, 9 March 1970), pp. 53–55.

[83]See John H. Adkins, *War Type, Population and Security: Keeping the Basics in Mind* (Ann Arbor: The Bendix Corporation, 1972); Booz-Allen Applied Research, Inc., *Program Review and Analysis Improvement System (PRAISE): Lessons Learned in Development, Conduct and Phaseover of Instruction to the Republic of Vietnam Armed Forces* (Washington: Booz-Allen Applied Research, Inc., 1971); Dorothy Clark and Charles R. Wyman, *An Exploration Analysis of the Reporting, Measuring, and Evaluating of Revolutionary Development in South Vietnam* (McLean, Va: Research Analysis Corporation, 1968); Dorothy Clark and Charles R. Wyman, *The Hamlet Evaluation System in the Republic of Vietnam*: TP-308 (McLean, VA: Research Analysis Corporation, 1968); Peter Collins, "South Vietnam: The Battle for Hearts and Minds," *Far Eastern Economic Review* , LXXXV (2 August 1974); Michael Charles Conley, *The Communist Insurgent Infrastructure in South Vietnam: A Study of Organization and Strategy* (Washington: The American University, 1967); David C. Eaton, "Education as an Aspect of Development: South Vietnam," *Southeast Asia* (Summer 1971); W. P. Davison, *Some Observations of Viet Cong Operations in the Villages* (Santa Monica: The RAND Corporation, 1967); Frances FitzGerald, *Fire in the Lake: The Vietnamese and the Americans in Vietnam* (Boston: Little, Brown and Co., 1972); Allan E. Goodman, *Politics in War: The Bases of Political Community in South Vietnam* (Cambridge: Harvard University Press, 1973); *Basic Issues and Potential Lessons of Vietnam* (4 vols., Croton-on-Hudson, NY: The Hudson Institute, Inc., 1970); *A Preliminary Appraisal of People's Self-Defense Forces in South Vietnam* (Croton-on-Hudson, NY: The Hudson Institute, Inc., 1969); *Americans and Vietnamese: A Comparison of Values in Two Cultures* (McLean, VA: Human Sciences Research, Inc., 1968); *Analysis of PSYOP Effectiveness Indicators* (McLean, VA: Human Sciences Research, Inc., 1973); *Military Advising in Vietnam*: 1969–1970 (McLean, VA: Human Sciences Research, Inc., 1973); *Psychological Operations Studies: Vietnam* (McLean, VA: Human Sciences Research, Inc., 1971); *A Study of Mass Population Displacement in the Republic of Vietnam* (2 parts, McLean, VA: Human Sciences Research, Inc., 1969); *A Study of Values, Communication Patterns and Demography of Rural South Vietnam*

(McLean, VA: Human Sciences Research, Inc., 1968); *The Use of Cultural Data in Psychological Operations Programs in Vietnam* (McLean, VA: Human Sciences Research, Inc., 1968).

See also *Preliminary Examination of the Hamlet Evaluation System* (Arlington, VA: Institute for Defense Analyses, 1968); Robert Keatley, "Indochina—What Went Wrong?" *Wall Street Journal,* 11 April 1970; *Psychological Studies of Southeast Asian Populations* (Cambridge, Mass: Massachusetts Institute of Technology, 1969); Joshua Menkes and Raymond Jones, *Pacification in Vietnam: A Survey* (Arlington, VA: Institute for Defense Analyses, 1968); Jeffrey S. Milstein, *Dynamics of the Vietnam War: A Quantitative Analysis and Predictive Computer Simulation* (Columbus, Ohio: Ohio State University Press, 1974); William A. Nighswonger, *Rural Pacification in Vietnam: 1962-1965* (Washington: The American University, 1966); *Accommodation in South Vietnam: The Key to Sociopolitical Solidarity* (Santa Monica: The RAND Corp., 1967); *Impact of Pacification on Insurgency in South Vietnam* (Santa Monica: The RAND Corp., 1970); J. L. Penquite, *Hamlet Regression Following the Departure of a Revolutionary Development Cadre Team* (New York: Control Data Corp., 1969, Final Report for Research Task Number 5B).

Further material includes Douglas Pike, *War, Peace and the Viet Cong* (Cambridge: Massachusetts Institute of Technology Press, 1969); *Measurement of Pacification Progress in Vietnam* (McLean, VA: Research Analysis Corp., 1968); *Improving Effectiveness of the Chieu Hoi* Program (Cambridge: Simulmatics Corp., 1967); *Observations on Psychodynamic Structures in Vietnamese Personality* (Cambridge: Simulmatics Corp., 1966); *A Socio-Psychological Study of Regional/Popular Forces in Vietnam* (Cambridge: Simulmatics Corp., 1967); *Case Studies and Model for Pacification Support Operations* (Washington: Advanced Research Projects Agency, 1968); *Pacification Attitude Analysis System (PAAS)* (Saigon: Military Assistance Command, Vietnam, 1971); *The Rural Development Cadre System Command Manual* (Saigon: Military Assistance Command, Vietnam, 1970); *Terrorist Incident Reporting System* (Saigon: Military Assistance Command, Vietnam, 1971); *The Effectiveness of Intercultural Relations Training for Vietnam Advisors* (San Diego: Naval Personnel and Training Research Laboratory, 1973); Thomas Volgy, *What Have We Done? An Examination of Some Scholarly Literature on the Vietnamese Conflict* (Tucson: Institute of Government Research, University of Arizona, 1973).

See also *Vietnam: Lessons and Mislessons* (Santa Monica: The RAND Corporation, 1969); *User's Guide to the RAND Interviews in Vietnam* (Santa Monica: The RAND Corporation, 1972); and *A Review of Social Science Research in Vietnam with Procedural Recommendations for Future Research in Insurgent Settings* (Arlington, VA: Institute for Defense Analysis, 1968).

[84]See John S. Parsons, Dale K. Brown, and Nancy R. Kingsbury, *Americans and Vietnamese: A Comparison of Values in Two Cultures* (McLean, VA: Human Sciences Research, Inc., 1968); and Martin Sternin, Robert J. Teare, and Peter G. Nordlie, *A Study of Values, Communications Patterns, and Demography of Rural South Vietnam* (McLean: Human Sciences Research, Inc., 1968).

Despite difficulties referred to in the text, the attitude of those early MAAG advisers was an optimistic one. MG Charles Timmes (Ret.) offered a reason for such enthusiasm when he spoke to officer student members of the Vietnam Assessment Study Group at CGSC on 9 April 1976. He described the attitude as "unbridled enthusiasm" among men who refused to consider any negative aspects in their reporting on the situation then as they saw it. The same attitude was shared by higher-level officers in Pacific Command and in the Pentagon.

He believed it unfortunate that U.S. advisers generally equated the ARVN units with which they worked with those American outfits they had known and experienced. They placed too much emphasis upon large-unit operations without first determining the squad and platoon operational efficiency of their assigned ARVN units. MAAG advisers should have been people well versed in unconventional operations, but few men versed in that field were sent to Vietnam. Indeed, the army did not have very many officers knowledgeable or experienced in the subject. Finally, Timmes reported that there was real difficulty in making the Vietnamese hierarchy—military or political—aware of the necessity of integrating security and pacification programs.

Timmes did not mention that the U.S. Army in later years found itself faced with the same difficulty and that its own leadership was at least as recalcitrant in implementing such integration as the Vietnamese had been.

(In addition to MAAG, MACV was formed in February 1962, commanded by General Paul D. Harkins. Although MACV eventually superseded MAAG, the latter was retained as an organizational structure until mid-1964. Timmes was one of its last commanders.)

Interested persons might find William I. Lowry, *Strategic Assessment of the War in Vietnam—Truman through Kennedy* (Ft. Leavenworth: CGSC student paper, 1976) worth consulting. See also Russell H. Fifield, *Americans in Southeast Asia* (New York: Thomas Y. Crowell Co., 1973).

[85]Quoted from the address of MG Charles Timmes (Ret.) at USACGSC, 9 April 1976. See also John H. Damewood and Thompson A. Terrell III, *Neutralization of the Viet Cong Infrastructure by US/GVN, 1960–1970* (USACGSC student paper, 25 May 1976), p. 30 and *passim*.

[87]Ernest Bairdain, *Psychological Operations Studies—Vietnam* (McLean, VA: Human Sciences Research, Inc., 1971) and *Lessons Learned #30—Psychological Warfare/Civil Action* (Saigon: USMAAG, 1963).

[88]The Marine Combined Action Program (CAP) may well have been the only successful American project of any kind in Vietnam. CAP teams were formed in 1965, soon after the marines arrived in 'Nam. They operated only in the northern provinces of South Vietnam, in I Corps, within the Marine TAOR. The CAP program was the only one ever conducted in Vietnam in which ARVN nationals served under United States command. It worked wonders, just as the same policy had done with soldiers of the ROK during the Korean conflict.

At the peak, 114 CAP teams were in operation, each of which was composed of a squad of fourteen marines, one of which was the sergeant in command. There was also a navy corpsman assigned to each team. Integrated with the marines and under their direction was a Popular Force (PF) platoon of thirty-four Vietnamese.

CAP teams were assigned to sites close to some military objective such as a road junction, an important waterway, a base, and so forth. They sought to improve the performance of the PF with which they worked and to protect the people of a hamlet or village and provide them with a degree of law and safety.

The work was unspectacular—patrolling, ambushes, guard mounts, rebuilding dikes, digging wells, repairing hedges—but CAP teams got the job done. They actually produced results. Vietnamese near them came to feel safe from VC depredations. Officials no longer fled to safe hideouts at nightfall but began to spend the hours of darkness in those hamlets and villages where their responsibilities were. VC bands, rejected by the people of such hamlets, actually moved away to other areas. Binh Ngahi, for example, was secured with the expenditure of but *one* round of artillery in an entire year.

William Corson, who for a time headed the CAP program, openly admitted that much of the success came as a result of ignoring governing regulations. He wrote that "the course of action selected was and is contrary to the spirit and intent of every directive, regulation, or order issued by COMUSMACV and the U.S. Embassy in Saigon, all of which require U.S. forces to serve as a forerunner of GVN control. . . . My primary purpose was . . . to enable the people . . . to become strong enough to resist the predatory incursions of both the GVN and the Vietcong."

The program was also inexpensive. Lederer notes that the cost of maintaining the entire marine troop strength of fifteen officers and 1,200 enlisted men (as of 1968) who lived and worked in the five northern provinces, with a Vietnamese population of about 260,000, was only roughly one-fifth of what it would cost to maintain 1,200 army troops engaged in search-and-destroy missions.

Instead of creating additional recruits for the VC, CAP teams actually subtracted from the totality of the guerrilla force facing them. Had the concept been adopted throughout Vietnam by American forces there, it might have meant that the war could have had a very different ending.

Useful sources on the CAP program include Corson, *The Betrayal*, Chapters 6 and 7; Lederer, *Our Own Worst Enemy*, p. 186, 174–205; Bruce C. Allnutt, *Marine Combined Action Capabilities: The Vietnam Experience* (McLean, VA: Human Sciences Research, Inc., 1969); Robert O'Neill, *Military Civic Action: A Unique Approach in Military Assistance* (Maxwell AFB: Air War College, 1967); *The Marines in Vietnam, 1954–1973: An*

Anthology and Annotated Bibliography (Washington: History and Museums Division, HQ, U.S. Marine Corps, 1974); *U.S. Marines in Vietnam: The Advisory and Combat Assistance Era, 1954–1964* (Washington: History and Museums Division, HQ, U.S. Marine Corps, 1977); Charles W. Blyth, "Fuel for the Lamps of Tri Buu," *Marine Corps Gazette* LIII, 2 (February 1969); William D. Parker, *Civil Affairs in I Corps, Republic of South Vietnam, April 1966 to April 1967* (Washington: Historical Branch, G-3 Division, HQ, U.S. Marine Corps, 1970); David A. Clement, "Le My, Study in Counterinsurgency," *Marine Corps Gazette* LI, 7 (July 1967); "The War in Vietnam: Civic Action," *ibid.* XLIX, 10 (October 1965); R. E. Williamson, "A Briefing for Combined Action," *ibid.* LII, 3 (March 1968); Thomas M. Pratt, III, "Population and Resources Control," *ibid.* LIV, 9 (September 1970); William C. Homberg, "Civic Action," *ibid.* L, 6 (June 1966); Jonas M. Platt, "Military Civic Action," *ibid.* LIV, 9 (September 1970); F. J. West, Jr., "Fast Rifles," *ibid.* LI, 10 (October 1967); Norman K. Standord, "Bamboo Brigades," *ibid.* L, 3 (March 1966); Gary E. Todd, "Three Point Program for Vietnam," *ibid.* LIV, 4 (April 1970); and Russel H. Stolfi, *U.S. Marine Corps Civic Action Efforts in Vietnam*, March 1965–March 1966 (Washington: Historical Branch, G-3 Division, HQ, U.S. Marine Corps, 1968).

[89]J. A. Koch, *The Chieu Hoi Program in South Vietnam*, 1963–1971 (Santa Monica: The RAND Corp., 1973).

[90]Koch, *The Chieu Hoi Program*, p. 108.

[91]*Ibid.*, p. 107.

[92]Carl F. Bernard, *The War in Vietnam: Observations and Reflections of a Province Senior Advisor* (Ft. Leavenworth: USACGSC student paper, October 1969), p. 9.

[93]Westmoreland, *Soldier Reports*, p. 429.

[94]See Bernard, *The War in Vietnam*, *passim*. Also see Michael R. Pearce, *Evolution of a Vietnamese Village: Duc Lap since November 1964* (Santa Monica: The RAND Corporation, 1966); Robert L. Gallucci, *Neither Peace nor Honor: The Politics of American Military Policy in Vietnam* (Baltimore: The Johns Hopkins University Press, 1975); Robert William Chandler, "U.S. Psychological Operations in Vietnam, 1965–1972," (Ph.D. dissertation, George Washington University, 1974); and Warren H. Milberg, "The Future Applicability of the Phoenix Program," (Master's thesis, Auburn University/Air University, Maxwell AFB, 1967).

[95]Allen E. Goodman, "The Political Implications of Rural Problems," *Asian Survey* (August 1970), pp. 677–78.

[96]See Douglas S. Blaufarb, *The Counter Insurgency Era: US Doctrine and Performance, 1950 to the Present* (New York: Glencoe Free Press, 1977), *passim*.

[97]See William L. Knapp, *Phoenix/Phuong Hoang and the Future: A Critical Analysis of the US/GVN Program to Neutralize the Viet Cong Infrastructure* (Carlisle Barracks: USAWC student essay, 1971). See also Michael Charles Conley, *The Communist Insurgent Infrastructure in South Vietnam* (Washington: Center for Research in Social Systems, The American University, 1967); W. P. Davison and Joseph J. Zasloff, *A Profile of Viet Cong Cadres* (Santa Monica: The RAND Corp., 1966).

[98]Subject interviews.

[99]Peter Collins, "South Vietnam: The Battle for Hearts and Minds," *Far Eastern Economic Review* LXXXV (2 August 1974): 10–11. See also Donald Bletz, *The Role of the Military in U.S. Foreign Policy* (New York: Praeger, 1972), pp. 278–81.

[100]One wonders, during work on a study such as this, why so few top military men spoke out in disdain or wrath or unbelief at army (and civilian) policies in Vietnam. Why were the gainsayers inevitably of lower rank? Why did no general give voice to the following? Our failures there have been at least 95 percent due to our incomprehension and inability to cope with the political dimensions of the problem. . . . If we had understood these problems, we should certainly not have gone in. . . . Among those errors that were primarily military, I should put at the top the failure to anticipate properly the importance of giving the opponent a sanctuary which comprises his entire homeland. For over three years, it was not a sanctuary against bombing (which also failed to deliver the results expected of it—and let us hear no more from Admiral US Grant Sharp about our not having done enough bombing); but it has always been a complete sanctuary against ground force incursion, which meant that the enemy could . . . take as much or as little

of the war as he wanted and could shift his degree of participation whenever he wanted. . . . But that disaster pales in comparison with the consequences of our wilfull blindness in trying to shore up a corrupt, inefficient and thoroughly unpopular regime. We had no business trying, and we could not succeed. (Bernard Brodie, "Why Were We So [Strategically] Wrong?" *Military Review* LII, 6 [June 1972]: 44.)

[101]Brian M. Jenkins, "The Unchangeable War," RM-6278-1-ARPA (Santa Monica: RAND Corporation, September 1972), p. 5, p. 2.

[102]Sir Robert Thompson, *No Exit from Vietnam* (New York: David McKay, 1969), pp. 129-30.

[103]Kinnard, *War Managers*, p. 4.

[104]Kinnard, *War Managers*, p. 44. See also Amos A. Jordan, *Foreign Aid and the Defense of Southeast Asia* (New York: Praeger, 1963), pp. 41, 57, 84, 94, 95, 98; *An Essay on Vietnamization* (Santa Monica: The RAND Corp., March 1971); *Employment of Airmobile ARVN Forces in Counterinsurgency Operations* (Washington: U.S. Army Concept Team in Vietnam, 1973).

[105]William G. Prince and Raymond Tanter, *The Republic of Vietnam Armed Forces Under Varying Threat Conditions: Implications for a People's Army* (Ann Arbor, The Bendix Corp., 1971).

On the takeover of the south, see Tiziano Terzani, *Giai Phong! The Fall and Liberation of Saigon* (New York: Ballantine Books, 1976), and Defense Attaché Office, *The Final Forty-Five Days in Vietnam* (22 May 1975).

[106]See, for example, *Army Roles, Missions, and Doctrine in Low Intensity Conflict* (Ft. Belvoir, VA: Combat Developments Command Institute of Advanced Studies Report, 1971).

[107]Subject interview.

Chapter Five

[1]LTG William R. Peers, *Report of the Department of the Army Review of the Preliminary Investigations into the My Lai Incident* (2 vols., Washington: Government Printing Office, 14 March 1970).

[2]*News Release*, Office of the Assistant Secretary of Defense (Public Affairs), Washington: 13 November 1974.

[3]Peers's memorandum is reproduced in its entirety in Appendix C.

[4]*The Study on Military Professionalism* (Carlisle Barracks; USAWC, 30 June 1970).

[5]Subject interview.

[6]See *Military Review* LVIII, 7 (July 1978): 39.

[7]*Study on Military Professionalism*, p. 53.

[8]Richard A. Gabriel and Paul L. Savage, *Crisis in Command: Mismanagement in the Army* (New York: Hill and Wang, 1978), p. 165.

[9]*Study on Military Professionalism*, p. 55.

[10]They may not have been written down, but they were so much a part of military life that an air-force major's wife could comment that "by the time my husband was a first lieutenant, I knew exactly what he needed to do for his own career progression; what he would do if he were to be promoted along with his contemporaries; what he would have to do if he wanted to be considered for 'below the zone' promotions. I got my information from the best source in the world—other officers' wives."—Subject interview.

[11]*Study on Military Professionalism*, p. v.

[12]*Ibid.*, p. vii.

[13]*Study on Military Professionalism*, p. 13.

[14]*Ibid.*, pp. 13-14.

[15]*Ibid.*, p. 15.

[16]*Ibid.*

[17]*Ibid.*, p. 16.

[18]*Study on Military Professionalism*, p. B-1-2.

[19]*Ibid.*, p. B-1-3.

[20]*Ibid.*, p. B-1-4.

[21]*Ibid.*

[22]*Ibid.*

[23]*Ibid.*

[24]*Ibid.*

[25]*Study on Military Professionalism*, p. B-1-5.

[26]*Ibid.*, p. B-1-11.

[27]*Ibid.*, p. B-1-12.

[28]*Study on Military Professionalism*, p. B-1-18.

[29]*Ibid.*, p. B-1-24.

[30]Stuart H. Loory, *Defeated: Inside America's Military Machine* (New York: Random House, 1973), p. 64.

[31]Just, *Military Men*, pp. 107–09.

[32]COL David H. Hackworth, "Army Leadership is Ineffective," *Washington Post*, 29 June 1971.

[33]William L. Hauser, *America's Army in Crisis: A Study in Civil-Military Relations* (Baltimore: The Johns Hopkins University Press, 1973), p. 185.

[34]Maureen Mylander, *The Generals: Making It, Military-Style* (New York: The Dial Press, 1974), p. 143.

[35]Subject interview.

[36]Subject interview.

[37]Subject interview.

[38]King, *Death of the Army*, p. 165.

[39]The above synopsis is drawn from the pages of Anthony R. Herbert, *Soldier* (New York: Holt, Rinehart and Winston, 1973). A good survey of the Herbert case is given in Hauser, *Army in Crisis*, pp. 178–79.

[40]*Study on Military Professionalism*, p. 14.

[41]*Ibid.*

[42]*Ibid.*, p. 15.

[43]*Study on Military Professionalism*, p. B-1-4.

[44]Subject interview.

[45]J.T. Miller, "Integrity and Reality and Writing Up OERs," *Army* Magazine (April 1977), reproduced in Military Ethics pamphlet, P913-1, Command and General Staff College student issue.

[46]Subject interview.

[47]Subject interview.

[48]Subject interview.

[49]Subject interviews.

[50]John C. Bahnsen, Jr., and R. William Highlander, "Writing a Readable OER," *Armor* (July–August 1976).

[51]Miller, "Integrity and Reality and Writing Up OERs," CGSC Pamphlet, p. L1-AS-2-5.

[52]Quoted in King, *Death of the Army*, p. 74.

[53]Subject interview.

[54]Subject interview.

[55]*Study on Military Professionalism*, p. 24.

[56]Geyer, "Military Soul-Searching," *Washington Post,* 20 June 1977.

[57]Halberstam, *Best and Brightest,* p. 75.

[58]These figures are given by Mylander, *The Generals,* pp. 75–76.

[59]King, *Death of the Army,* p. 170.

[60]Hauser, *America's Army in Crisis,* pp. 177–78.

[61]The figures are drawn from Mylander, *Generals,* p. 74.

[62]Quoted in Hauser, *America's Army in Crisis,* pp. 177, who draws his information from Dick Seelmeyer, "Trouble with Our Military Brass Is There's Too Much of It," *Philadelphia Inquirer,* 19 October 1971, p. 29.

[63]Geyer, "Military Soul-Searching," *Washington Post,* 20 June 1977.

[64]GEN Hamilton H. Howze (USA, Ret.), "Vietnam . . . an Epilogue," *Army* (July 1975): 15.

[65]These figures are supplied by CPT Ronald J. Brown in *Armor* LXXXV, 6 (November–December 1976).

[66]Subject interview.

[67]Subject interview.

[68]Subject interview.

[69]Subject interview.

[70]One man interviewed on this subject told how "my driver and I went to a meeting at corps headquarters in Danang, driving straight there from a tour of fire bases from Khe Sanh to the Hsi Van Pass. We were dusty, muddy, and otherwise showing signs of having been in some unpleasant places. My jeep even had two bullet holes in it.

"While I went into a building to arrange billets, my driver stood by the jeep. When I came back out, a First Lieutenant in starched jungle fatigues and spit-shined jungle boots was chewing out my driver as a 'disgrace to the uniform' because of his appearance. I gently remonstrated with the young lieutenant by locking his heels and expressing my disgust at his lack of sensitivity and common sense. Unfortunately, this was an all too common occurrence."

[71]These figures are given in King, *Death of the Army,* p. 98, and represent army-wide, not Vietnam-forces, totals. Westmoreland dismissed the figures as "not alarming," when compared to World War II statistics on desertions, ignoring the fact that the army then had almost ten million men while by the Vietnam era it peaked at about three million. In point of fact the figures were alarming indeed and clearly pointed to a dangerous situation within the military.

[72]Subject interview.

[73]Subject interview.

[74]The figures are given in Gabriel and Savage, *Crisis in Command,* p. 31.

[75]*Ibid.,* p. 16. For a broader view of the Vietnam activities of the U.S. military than that given in Gabriel and Savage's excellent work, see Guenter Lewy, *America in Vietnam* (New York: Oxford University Press, 1978). Lewy is requisite reading for anyone interested in understanding the problems faced in Vietnam by the United States Army.

[76]One man commented during an interview that "I don't think fragging was directed as much at people by frustrated individuals as at the army system. When successful, of course, fraggings were just plain murder, but still usually not aimed at a particular man, for victims seemed so often to have been randomly selected. Someone got fragged just because he happened to be in the wrong place at the wrong time. We had one new battalion commander who came in. On his second day they tried to get him. Surely he had done nothing in that short period of time so bad that anyone would want to kill him. He was just there, a target for frustration."

[77]Gabriel and Savage, *Crisis in Command,* p. 59.

[78]Subject interview.

[79]For another view of recent efforts at military introspection, see Sam C. Sarkesian, "An Empirical Reassessment of Military Professionalism," *Military Review* LVII, 8 (August 1977). 3–20. A different approach is given by CPT Philip O. Benham, Jr., USAR,

OPMS: Demise of the Whole Officer Concept?" *Military Review* LVIII, 6 (June 1978): 67–72. Still a third is LTC James B. Channon, "Preparing the Officer Corps for the 1990s," *Military Review* LVIII, 5 (May 1978): 10–23.

⁸⁰See MAJ Thomas V. Draude, *When Should a Commander Be Relieved? A Study of Combat Reliefs of Commanders of Battalions and Lower Units During the Vietnam Era* (USACGSC student paper, 1976). This is available only from the National Technical Information Service of the United States Department of Commerce. NTIS accession number is AD AØ297Ø6.

⁸¹It is not as if there were no data base from which another, more responsible, decision could have been made. Adopted in haste and early demonstrated to be unwise, the six-month-rotation policy seems to have been continued more out of stubbornness and rigidity than for any rational reason. Because of the importance of this irresponsible policy, I append to this note citations for just a fraction of the available material bearing upon this problem.

On the twelve-month in-country tour length, see DCSPER [Deputy Chief of Staff for Personnel], *Study of the Twelve Month Vietnam Tour* (Department of Army: Washington: Government Printing Office, 29 June 1970), and U.S. Army, Vietnam, *Tour 365* (Saigon: 1969).

For individual and unofficial views by men knowledgeable about the subject, consult LTC Norman S. Helms, AG, *Replacement System in Vietnam from Buildup to Mid-1969* (USAWC case study, 8 May 1970); LTC John W. Lundberg, *The Army Oversea Personnel Replacement System in Future War* (USAWC student thesis, 8 March 1963); LTC George R. Sedberry, *Army Replacements* (USAWC student thesis, 25 January 1960).

For official studies, see U.S. Army Adjutant General School, *Memorandum 66-3: Theater Army Replacement System* (Ft. Benjamin Harrison, November 1968); U.S. Army, *Army Regulation 612-2: Personnel Processing—Preparing Individual Replacements for Oversea Movement (POR) and US Army Oversea Replacement Station Processing Procedures* (Washington: 18 August 1969); U.S. Army, *Army Regulation 614-30: Assignments, Details, and Transfers—Oversea Service* (Washington: 22 October 1968); U.S. Army, *US Army Replacement System: DCSPER Staff Study* (Washington: 10 March 1959); U.S. Army, *A Study of Army Manpower and Personnel Management* (Office of the Director of Coordination and Analysis Systems Analysis Division: Washington: May 1965); U.S. Army, *Army Regulation 612-1: Personnel in a Training, Transient, and Patient Status* (Washington, 29 October 1958); and U.S. Army, *Field Manual 12-2: Adjutant General Support in Theaters of Operation* (Washington: 16 January 1968).

Historical analyses include such items as Office of the Chief of Military History, *The Replacement System in the U.S. Army: An Analytical Study of World War II Experience* (Washington: 14 September 1950); U.S. Army, *Replacement System, World-wide, World War II: Report of Replacement Board* (Book One-Four, Washington: 12 December 1947); General Staff, G-1, *Comments on Report of the Replacement Board: Memorandum* (Washington: 15 January 1948); U.S. Army, *DA Pamphlet 20-212: History of Military Mobilization in the United States Army, 1775–1945* (Washington, 1955); and U.S. Army, *DA Pamphlet 20-211: The Personnel Replacement System in the United States Army* (Washington, 1954).

Information detailing actual experience with the six-month policy was documented in such reports as the following: U.S. Army, Vietnam, *Battlefield Reports: A Summary of Lessons Learned* (Vol. I, 30 August 1965 and Vol. II, 30 June 1966, Tan Son Nhut [O USARV BRSL Aug 65 and USARV BRSL Oct/Dec 65]); U.S. Army, Vietnam, *Operational Report on Lessons Learned*, Tan Son Nhut, 1 January to 30 April 1966 [OO USARV LL OR Jan/Apr 66, 1 July 1966], 1 May to 31 July 1966 [O USARV LL OR May/Jul 66, 7 September 1966], 1 August to 31 October 1966 [O USARV LL OR Aug/Oct 66, 27 November 1966], 1 November 1966 to 31 January 1967 [OO USARV LL OR Nov 66/Jan 67, 28 February 1967], 1 February to 30 April 1967 [O USARV LL OR Feb/Apr 67].

U.S. Army, Vietnam, *Operational Report—Lessons Learned*, Long Binh, 1 May to 31 July 1967 [OO USARV LL OR May/Jul 67, 15 August 1967], 1 August to 31 October 1967 [OO USARV LL OR Aug/Oct 67, 20 November 1967], 1 November 1967 to 31 January 1968 [O USARV LL OR Nov 67/Jan 68], 1 February to 30 April 1968 [O USARV LL OR Feb/Apr 68, 20 May 1968], 1 May to 31 July 1968 [O USARV LL OR May/Jul 68, 12

August 1968], 1 August to 31 October 1968 [O USARV LL OR Aug/Oct 68, 15 November 1968], 1 November 1968 to 31 January 1969 [O USARV LL OR Nov 68/Jan 69, 13 February 1969].

Operating at Cam Ranh Bay was the United States Army's 22d Replacement Battalion. See its *Biographical Sketch*—22d REPLACEMENT BATTALION (Cam Ranh Bay, 1969), and its following reports: USARV 22 RPBN OR LL, 1 June 1966 to 31 January 1967. Additional records of the 22 RPBN include: Letter, AVIE-CO, 30 April 1967, Subject: Operational Report for Quarterly Period Ending 30 April 1967, Reports Control Symbol CSFOR-65; Letter, AVIE-CO, 14 November 1967, Subject: Operational Report for Quarterly Period Ending 31 October 1967, Reports Control Symbol CSFOR-65 (W-FQM-HB); Letter, AVIE-CO, 14 February 1968, Subject: Operational Report for Quarterly Period Ending 31 January 1968, Reports Control Symbol CSFOR-65 (W-FQM-HB); Letter, AVIE-CO, 15 August 1968, Subject: Operational Report for Quarterly Period Ending 31 July 1968, Reports Control Symbol CSFOR-65 (WFQMAA); Letter, AVIE-CO, 15 February 1969, Subject: Operational Report for Quarterly Period Ending 31 January 1969, Reports Control Symbol CSFOR-65 (WFQMAA); Letter, AVIE-CO, Subject: Recommendation for Award of Meritorious Unit Commendation, dated 8 August 1968 and another dated 20 July 1969.

At Long Binh the 90th Replacement Battalion held sway. See its *Biographical Sketch —90th Replacement Battalion* (Long Binh: 1969). Its reports, similar in nature to those of the 22d Replacement Battalion, cover its personnel-processing activities from 1966 until its phase-out. Of interest, however, is *Replacement Battalion Workload: Statistical Report of Workload in 22d and 90th Replacement Battalions for Period May 1968 through August 1969* (USARV, 1969).

In all these documents, despite the fact that some are entitled *Lessons Learned*, there is no effort to demonstrate the inadequacies of the six-month tour or its deleterious effect on the army in Vietnam.

[82]MAJ Arnold Daxe, Jr., and CPT Victor J. Stemberger, *Vietnam Assessment: Officer Professionalism* (USACGSC student paper, 1976), pp. 7–8, 11.

A major commented: "All those who have talked with me about the six-month-command, six-month-staff concept agreed that it was crap. They felt, as I did, that a commander never really got a handle on his unit, that by the time he was competent, he was moved or DEROSed [Date of Estimated Return from Overseas]. Often their staff duty came before their command time, thus putting persons without real understanding of the problems of 'Nam into planning and support jobs, making decisions and recommending courses of action that were detrimental, dangerous, and deadly to the grunt on the ground."—Subject interview.

[83]*Study on Military Professionalism*, pp. B-1-11, B-1-20, B-1-5.

[84]Gabriel and Savage, *Crisis in Command*, p. 13.

[85]Subject interview. LBJ was Long Binh Jail, one of the major detention facilities for military offenders in Vietnam.

[86]In the middle sixties, a cover story for a national magazine was entitled "Military Is to Justice What Martial Is to Music."

[87]Subject interview.

[88]David R. Holmes, "Some Tentative Thoughts after Indochina," *Military Review* LVII, 8 (August 1977): 86–7.

[89]Subject interview. A study providing real insight into the attitudes of enlisted men circa 1967–1968 and that enlarges on the above comment is Michael Herr, *Dispatches* (New York: Avon, 1978).

[90]Daxe and Stemberger, *Officer Professionalism*, p. 13.

[91]I first encountered these figures in Hauser, *America's Army in Crisis*, p. 175. He pointed to the original source, an article in the *Washington Post*, 14 February 1971, entitled "Viet Medals Exceed 2 Million."

[92]If it is calculated that some seven years of conflict had passed in Vietnam prior to 1971, then an average of approximately 182,000 had been awarded every year. If that figure is anywhere near correct, then by the time of American withdrawal, some 1,-700,000 awards *for bravery* had been presented.

[93]Hauser, *America's Army in Crisis*, p. 175.

[94]Subject interview.

[95]Subject interview.

[96]Subject interview.

[97]*Study on Military Professionalism*, p. B-1-2.

[98]King, *Death of the Army*, p. 103.

[99]Hauser, *America's Army in Crisis*, p. 174.

[100]Hauser, *America's Army in Crisis*, p. 174.

[101]See Mylander, *Generals*, p. 80; King, *Death of the Army*, p. 42, 104; Hauser, *America's Army in Crisis*, p. 174.

[102]Subject interview.

[103]Subject interview.

[104]Daxe and Stemberger, *Vietnam Assessment*, pp. 11–12.

[105]Subject interview.

[106]Subject interview.

[107]Kinnard, *War Managers*, p. 31.

[108]Daxe and Stemberger, *Vietnam Assessment*, p. 11.

[109]GEN Fred G. Weyand and LTC Harry G. Summers, Jr., *Vietnam Myths and American Military Realities*, a pamphlet without information as to date printed, location produced, or publisher. Page 3. (A copy may be found in the CGSC Library.)

[110]Subject interview.

[111]*Study on Military Professionalism*, pp. ii, 30, 32.

[112]*Ibid.*, p. 34.

Chapter Six

[1]LTC John H. Moellering, *Neo-Uptonianism: A Likely Occurrence in the Army's Professional Officer Corps Today?* (USACGSC student paper, 1972).

[2]Michael T. Klare, *War without End: American Planning for the* Next *Vietnams* (New York: Random House Vintage, 1972).

[3]The best study of this development currently available is LTC Donald B. Vought, "Preparing for the Wrong War," *Military Review* LVII, 5 (May 1977): 16–34.

[4]*Study on Military Professionalism*, p. vi.

[5]*Ibid.*, pp. vi–viii.

[6]*Ibid.*, p. 4.

[7]*Comprehensive Report: Leadership for the 1970s, USA WC Study of Leadership for the Professional Soldier* (Carlisle Barracks, 20 October 1971).

[8]*Ibid., passim.*

[9]For a view of the betrayals and abandonment of those who supported us in our military effort in Vietnam when the end came, see Frank Snepp, *Decent Interval* (New York: Vintage, 1978).

[10]James H. Doolittle, *Officer–Enlisted Man Relationships* (Senate Document 196, Washington: Government Printing Office, 1946).

[11]*Los Angeles Times*, 11 July 1971, as quoted in Hauser, *America's Army in Crisis*, p. 182.

[12]For a time there were rumors within the officer corps that even LTC William L. Hauser's erudite but mild analysis had done his career no good, despite the fact that his book is actually a work of apologetics on behalf of the military establishment inasmuch as he attributes the cause of ills within the army to societal factors, whitewashing any responsibility the army might have had to clean its own house. Despite this, it is a book well worth readingand gives evidence that its author is capable of independent thought

and analysis. As he has since been promoted to full colonel, it is enough to make one hope that someday he may become chief of staff.

[13]MAJ James S. Dickey, *Vietnam Assessment: The American Spirit, the Army Officer, and Vietnam—A Commentary* (USACGSC student paper, 1976), p. 3.

[14]LTC Donald B. Vought, "Preparing for the Wrong War?" *Military Review* LVII, 5 (May 1977): 32. This article is an excellent presentation by a man who was one of the army's most insightful thinkers, and should be mandatory reading for every military policy planner. Vought, unfortunately now retired, should have been selected for early and rapid promotion into the ranks of general so that he could have made the kind of contributions he was so eminently fitted for. It is one of the disasters of military life that this did not occur.

[15]*Ibid.*, p. 28.

[16]Jenkins, *The Unchangeable War*, p. 8.

[17]Weyand and Summers, *Vietnam Myths*, p. 5.

[18]As indicated earlier in this study, such simple and low-level insights were repeatedly entered on after-action reports of combat units in Vietnam as "valuable" lessons learned from contact with the enemy.

[19]The enabling regulation of the Department of the Army for participation in the program is AR 60-21.

[20]How well this approach works will, of course, depend upon the quality of those chaplains selected for such assignments. The tension that must exist in their work, as they try to balance devotion to duty with dedication to the responsibilities of their vocation, is summed up in the motto of the chaplaincy: *pro deo et patria*—for God and country. Some chaplains have been known to act as if they had reversed the order of that slogan, while others have seemed to focus on but one or the other of its halves to the exclusion of the other. An individual assigned to the faculty of a service school must strive to fulfill both portions. Two recent books by chaplains are troubling, for while they depict well the aspects of the chaplaincy that their authors wish to address, neither concentrates on the ethical issues underlying the army's Vietnam venture. See CH (COL) John J. O'Connor, *A Chaplain Looks at Vietnam* (Cleveland, World Publishing Company, 1968) and CH (LTC) Curry N. Vaughan, Jr., with Bob Slosser, *Battleground: A Personal Account of God's Move upon the American Military Forces* (Plainfield, NJ: Logos International, 1978).

[21]Subject interviews.

[22]Allan J. Futernick, "Avoiding an Ethical Armageddon," *Military Review* LIX, 2 (February 1979): 21, 19, 18, 22.

[23]Subject interview.

[24]Subject interview.

[25]Subject interview.

[26]*Military Review* LVIII, 7 (July 1978): 39.

[27]An indication of the army's recent interest in the subject of ethics may be seen in a one-page article that appeared on the inside back cover of *Military Review* LIX, 1 (January 1979): 97. The statement follows:

The US Army school system is revitalizing its formal courses of instruction in professional military ethics. This resurgent, overt interest in ethics, the heart and soul of the military profession, is an encouraging milestone as we prepare for the 1980s. The subject of ethics, however, must not be relegated to the classroom alone or to discussions in the abstract. The blade of military ethics, forged in the service schools, must be honed constantly by the whetstone of day-to-day realities in the field. This demands both a common understanding of what our ethic is and a willingness to discuss this ethic in terms of daily occurrences and challenges.

Differences in the understanding of the military ethic do exist, and the disparity is normally a function of age. This is natural, since we are shaped by our experiences, and the officers commissioned in the 1970s matured in a different milieu than those, for example, who were commissioned in the 1950s. Both groups, however, are equally dedicated to the Army and to the country. Their perceptions, although different, are equally valid and honest. The constant task we face is to reduce these differences in perception and to encourage a common understanding of our ethic throughout the entire officer spectrum, from lieutenant to general.

Understanding, either among different peoples or among different generations, is best engendered by dialogue and discussion. Optimally, such discussion should be spontaneous and frequent. The pressing demands of daily activities, however, often militate against this happening, and it is, therefore, incumbent upon the senior officers to promote these discussions. One technique which works equally well either with a staff section of three officers or a battalion of 30 officers is to provide a point of reference for a discussion and then to assemble the unit officers under relaxed, informal conditions for the discussion.

Reference, or start points, abound in military literature, the best of which may well be *The Armed Forces Officer*. Published by the Department of Defense, Armed Forces Information Service, it is available through normal publication channels. Clearly and concisely written, the book discusses the philosophy of officer responsibilities and ideals, punctuated by pointmaking vignettes and concrete examples. The chapters also average less than 10 pages each, and are thus short enough to be read at a single sitting by even the most harried commander or staff officer. Using Chapter 2, "Forming Military Ideals," as the starting point, require all officers to read the chapter prior to a given date. On the given date, have an officers' call breakfast at the post officers' club. Following a leisurely breakfast, encourage all present to participate in an open discussion of the chapter and its relation to the unit. Such an open discussion will invariably strengthen both the ethic and the unit by developing a greater common understanding within the officer corps.

Regardless of the technique, it is imperative that we keep before us constantly a true and noble ethic to which we all subscribe. And it must be kept alive in the field, for it cannot survive if maintained only in the schools.

[28]"Ethics Is 'In' (Or Is It Ethics *Are* 'In'?), *Chaplaincy Letter: A News Supplement*, No. 78/1 (May 1978): 2–3.

[29] *War Crimes and the American Conscience*, pp. 147–48.

[30]Subject interview.

[31]Subject interview.

[32]Subject interview.

[33]Subject interview.

[34]Subject interview.

[35]Subject interview.

[36]Subject interview.

[37]*Ibid.*

[38]*Study on Military Professionalism*, pp. B-1-1 *et passim*.

[39]A long-established text on this subject is that by Cecil De Boer, *The If's and Ought's of Ethics: A Preface to Moral Philosophy* (Grand Rapids: William B. Eerdmans Publishing Co., 1936).

[40]An article that explains what happened at Cam Ne (4) according to LTC V. E. Ludwig, commander, 1st BN, 9th Marines, at the time of the incident in August of 1965 is that by the editors, "The War in Vietnam: Cam Ne (4)," *Marine Corps Gazette* XLIX, 10 (October 1965): 28–30.

[41]An air-force major recalled recently his service at Cam Ranh Bay in Vietnam. At one point, just prior to the arrival of a high-ranking officer for an inspection visit, a friend said to him, "Another general is flying in tomorrow. You know what that means. There'll be another coverup." Such attitudes seem endemic within all branches of the military.

[42]See Alain C. Enthoven and K. W. Smith, *How Much Is Enough? Shaping the Defense Program*, 1961–1969 (New York: Harper and Row, 1971).

[43]CPT John C. MacKercher, USN, *Personal Perceptions of the Vietnam War* (Wash-

ington: National Defense University, June 1975), p. 5.

[44]Russell F. Weigley, *History of the United States Army* (New York: Macmillan and Co., 1967), p. 496.

[45]A good depiction of current doctrine regarding these units may be found in *DA Pamphlet* 135-3: *A Guide to Reserve Components of the Army* (Washington, HQ, Department of the Army, July 1977).

[46]LTG Joseph M. Heiser, Jr., *Vietnam Studies: Logistic Support* (Washington: Government Printing Office, 1974), p. 256.

[47]MG Robert R. Ploger, *Vietnam Studies: US Army Engineers*, 1965–1970 (Washington: Government Printing Office, 1974), p. 183.

[48]LTC Mel Jones, "The All Volunteer Army: Is It Really Working?" *The National Guardsman* XXXII, 2 (February 1978): 6.

[49]Only sons and husbands and fathers were mentioned. In that regard, COL Jones comments: "As for women in combat, it is an option the sooner discarded the better, unless we find a way to change the world's thinking. Otherwise, we shall learn the hard way, just as the Israelis did, that an enemy army dominated by males will not quit, even when beaten, if it is learned that the opposing force is feminine." *Ibid.,* p. 7.

Both active- and reserve-component forces have viewed the all-volunteer, zero-draft army with suspicion and have made plain their view that they would rather have conscription reinstated. Despite their protestations, the All Volunteer Force Structure (AVFS) has worked thus far. The active forces have drawn sufficient volunteers to meet and exceed their needs; the reserve components have been faced with a personnel shortfall and are crying piteously to Congress that only reinstitution of the draft can save them from disintegration.

In some cases, those who have joined active- and reserve-component forces have been less well educated, less well trained, and less intelligent than had been hoped, inasmuch as the military has so many jobs that necessitate highly skilled men. On the other hand, observation at two Armed Forces Entry and Examining Stations (AFEES) affords ample evidence that many of the personnel assigned to such duty drive potential recruits away by their callous attitudes and treatment of the young men and women who come to an AFEES for preliminary physical examinations and Military Occupation Specialty (MOS) counselling. One young man waited all day, while station personnel lounged around drinking coffee and gossiping, to have a question answered that would have taken five minutes. The horror stories at AFEES stations are legion. The ineptitude and uncaring attitudes of duty personnel extends from station commanders to the lower ranks, and there desperately needs to be a shakeup within recruiting command of such assigned personnel.

One advantage of the AVFS is that it returns America to its traditional posture of reliance upon a small, well-trained force of regulars save during times of national emergency and thus lessens the headlong tumble of America toward a garrison-state mentality. The other major advantage is that for it to work well, the military will have to conduct a drastic internal overhaul, instituting long-needed reforms.

For the military view, see William R. King, "The All-Volunteer Armed Forces: Status, Prospects and Alternatives," *Military Review LII*, 9 (September 1977): 3–15, wherein the author argues that the AVFS reduces our international credibility, lowers our ability to defend ourselves and to meet worldwide commitments, and enables even the peacetime army to cope with significant emergencies only after long delays and at great cost.

[50]A good article discussing possibilities inherent in the AWC is that by BG Edward B. Atkeson, "Military Art and Science: Is There A Place in the Sun for It?" *Military Review* LVII, 1 (January 1977): 71–81.

[51]Subject interview.

[52]See the rebuttal to such positions by LTC David R. Holmes, "Some Tentative Thoughts after Indochina," *Military Review* LVII, 8 (August 1977): 87.

[53]Subject interview.

Select Bibliography

A definitive history of America's military involvement in Vietnam will not be written for a long time. The sources for such a series will not be available for years. The Federal Records Center in Suitland, Maryland, has already acquired over thirty thousand cubic feet of military records from Vietnam and is currently receiving an additional ten thousand cubic feet of such sources from Thailand. *No one* knows what is in those packing cases, and personnel at the Federal Records Center face perhaps a decade of sorting, saving, discarding of trash, and cataloging before those primary materials will become of use to researchers.

In order to tell the Vietnam story carefully, a writer would have to examine the records of many agencies. The Records Management Division, the Adjutant General's Office, United States Army, has already identified some fifteen linear feet of records produced just by the Pacification Studies Group of CORDS (Civil Operations and Revolutionary Development Support). That organization conducted major analyses dealing with the mobilization of the Vietnamese population. The Research and Analysis Directorate of CORDS (which handled "Hamlet Evaluation Surveys" and other matters) has still more documents.

All of the dozens of agencies created an encyclopedic trove of paper files detailing their activities. Pertinent comments, assessments, evaluations, analyses, criticism, and projections spewed forth by the thousands from the Agency for International Development (AID); the Commander in Chief, Pacific (CINC-PAC); the Military Assistance and Advisory Group (MAAG), Military Assistance Command, Vietnam (MACV); and the United States Army, Vietnam (USARV). Within each of the last three commands were dozens of smaller, semiautonomous organizations, each contributing its share to the growing mountain of paper. They include, to name only two, the Mobile Advisory Logistics Team (MALT) and the Mobile Advisory Team (MAT).

Then there were the headquarters: the Joint Chiefs of Staff (JCS), the Joint U.S. Military Advisory and Planning Group (JUSMAG), the Office of the Secretary of Defense (OSD), the Office of the Secretary of State (OSS). And there were the papers produced by such civilian organizations as the Michigan State University Advisory Group (MUSG), the RAND Corporation, and others. There

were the Office of Civil Operations (OCO), the United States Information Agency
(USIA), the Central Intelligence Agency (CIA). Papers flowed into files from the
typewriters of the official groups of other nations as well, including the British
Advisory Mission (BAM) and the Korean Military Advisory Group (KMAG).

Actions at the time they occurred were "interpreted" for the American
people through the work of such agencies as the Joint U.S. Public Affairs Office
(JUSPAO), while certain types of materials were collected by the United States
Army's Center for Military History (CMH). And all that is just the beginning.
Also necessary to consult would be the papers of all American presidents who
served during the years in which America was involved in Indochina, plus the
aides-memoire of their cabinets and chief advisers. To that mountain of Xerox
copies would have to be added files from hundreds of congressional offices in
both the House and the Senate.

In addition to American records, there are those of the French army,
located in Le Service Historique de l'Armée, in the Château de Vincennes, on
the eastern edge of Paris. Already available are more than fifteen thousand
cartons of documents covering the years of French activity in Indochina to late
1954 or early 1955.

For balance, one would then consult television transcripts and run old
television videotapes until the eyes failed, read learned and popular journals of
opinion, and pore over microfilm of long-outdated wire-service reports in newspaper morgues. Last would come the collecting of the multitude of secondary
works on Vietnam that have already been published.

That would be the procedure to follow in writing a definitive history of
America's military involvement in Vietnam. Another approach has been followed by the author of this book.

The method used here has been to scale down the focus of this inquiry to
manageable proportions. No attempt has been made to deal with most facets
of the Vietnamese story, but instead to treat only some of the internal workings
of the American army. A lively curiosity, mastery of certain research skills,
twenty-two years of military service, many friends, hundreds of interviews, and
perusal of documents and published works that shed light on the topic under
study—all seemed sufficient to undergird this monograph with a solid founda-
tion. Some, but not all, of the materials consulted are listed below. Others are
omitted because of their tertiary nature, or because (in the case of some military
documents) their classification was such as to preclude quoting from them or
even summarizing them in a general way.

The pages that follow list those materials which were of aid in the preparation of this study. It is regrettable that by necessity, no listing can be given for
the scores of interviews conducted in the months of preparation for this book.

Articles

Allgood, MAJ Frank E. "Progress and Prep Fires." *Marine Corps Gazette* LI,
    9 (September 1967).
Atkeson, BG Edward B. "Military Art and Science: Is There a Place in the Sun
    for It?" *Military Review* LVII (January 1977).

Avera, MAJ J. "Return of the Combat Support Company." *Infantry* LX, 5 (September–October 1970).

Bahnsen, John C., Jr., and William R. Highlander. "Writing a Readable OER." *Armor* LXXXV, 4 (July–August 1976).

Bashore, LTC Boyd T. "The Name of the Game is 'Search and Destroy.' " *Army* XVII, 2 (February 1967).

Beaumont, Roger A. "A Challenge to Professionalism: Leadership Selection." *Military Review* LVIII, 3 (March 1978).

Benham, CPT Philip O., Jr. "OPMS: Demise of the Whole Officer Concept?" *Military Review* LVIII, 6 (June 1978).

Blyth, Charles W. "Fuel for the Lamps of Tri Buu." *Marine Corps Gazette* LIII, 2 (February 1969).

Bradford, LTC Zeb B. "U.S. Tactics in Vietnam." *Military Review* LII, 2 (February 1972).

Brodie, Bernard, "Why Were We So (Strategically) Wrong?" *Military Review* LII, 6 (June 1972).

Carver, George A., Jr. "The Faceless Viet Cong." *Foreign Affairs* XLIV, 3 (April 1966).

Chanda, Nayan. "A Permanent State of Misery." *Far Eastern Economic Review* LXXXVI (11 October 1974).

Channon, LTC James B. "Preparing the Officer Corps for the 1990s." *Military Review* LVIII, 5 (May 1978).

Clement, David A. "Le My: Study in Counterinsurgency." *Marine Corps Gazette* LI, 7 (July 1967).

Collins, Peter. "South Viet Nam: The Battle for Hearts and Minds." *Far Eastern Economic Review* LXXXV (2 August 1974).

Crozier, Brian. "The Diem Regime in Southern Vietnam." *Far Eastern Survey* XXIV, 4 (April 1955).

Darling, Roger. "A New Conceptual Scheme for Analyzing Insurgency." *Military Review* LIV, 2 (February 1974).

Denno, Bryce F. "Military Prospects in Vietnam." *Orbis* IX, 2 (Summer 1965).

Dexter, George E. "Search and Destroy in Vietnam." *Infantry* LVI, 4 (July–August 1966).

Donnell, John C. "National Renovation Campaigns in Vietnam." *Pacific Affairs* XXXII, 1 (April 1959).

Eaton, David C. "Education as an Aspect of Development: South Vietnam." *Southeast Asia* (Summer 1971).

"Ethics Is 'In' (Or Is It Ethics Are 'In'?)." *Chaplaincy Letter: A News Supplement*, No. 78/1 (May 1978).

Fall Bernard. "Viet Nam in the Balance." *Foreign Affairs* XLV, 1 (October 1966).

Futernick, Allen J. "Avoiding an Ethical Armageddon." *Military Review* LIX, 2 (February 1979).

Gavin, GEN James. "A Communication on Vietnam." *Harper's* CCXXXII (February 1966).

Goodman, Allen E. "The Political Implications of Rural Problems." *Asian Survey* (August 1970).

Gouldnig, Phil G. "Ten Problems of Ho Chi Minh." *Army* XVIII, 8 (August 1968).

Hackworth, COL David H. "No Magic Formula." *Infantry* LVII, 1 (January–February 1967).

Hannah, Norman. "Vietnam: Now We Know." *National Review* (11 June 1976).

Holmes, LTC David R. "Some Tentative Thoughts after Indochina." *Military Review* LVII, 8 (August 1977).

Homberg, William C. "Civic Action." *Marine Corps Gazette* L, 6 (June 1966).

Howze, GEN Hamilton H. "Vietnam . . . an Epilogue." *Army* XXV, 7 (July 1975).

Johnson Chalmers. "Civilian Loyalties and Guerrilla Conflict." *World Politics* XIV, 4 (July 1962).

Johnson, GEN Harold K. "Subversion and Insurgency: Search for a Doctrine." *Army* XV, 11 (November 1965).

Jones, LTC Mel. "The All Volunteer Army: Is It Really Working?" *National Guardsman* XXII, 2 (February 1978).

Kelly, 1LT Ross S. "New Lessons in an Old War." *Infantry* LXIII, 1 (January–February 1973).

Kelman, Herbert C. "The Military Establishment." *Society* (May–June 1975).

Kennedy, William V. "Who Are the Peacemakers?" *Air Force and Space Digest* L, 7 (July 1967).

King William R. "The All-Volunteer Armed Forces: Status, Prospects and Alternatives." *Military Review* LII, 9 (September 1977).

Kinnaird, LTG Harry W. O. "Victory in the Ia Drang: The Triumph of a Concept." *Army* XVII, 9 (September 1967).

Loosbrock, John F. "North of the Border." *Air Force and Space Digest* XLIX, 3 (March 1966).

Mowery, COL Lawrence L. "Vietnam Report." *Infantry* LXI, 1 (January–February 1971).

Mumford, CDR Robert E., Jr. "Get Off My Back, Sir." *United States Naval Institute Proceedings* (August 1977).

O'Ballance, Edgar. "Strategy in Vietnam." *Army Quarterly and Defense Journal* XCIII, 1 (January 1967).

Pearson, LTG Willard. "Find 'em, Fix 'em, Finish 'em." *Army* XVI, 12 (December 1966).

Phillipps, LTC Y. Y. "The ROAD Battalion in Vietnam." *Army* XVI, 9 (September 1966).

Platt, Jonas M. "Military Civic Action." *Marine Corps Gazette* LIV, 9 (September 1970).

Pratt, Thomas M., III. "Population and Resources Control." *Marine Corps Gazette* LIV, 9 (September 1970).

Sarkesian, Sam C. "An Empirical Reassessment of Military Professionalism." *Military Review* LVII, 8 (August 1977).

Smithers, S. W., Jr. "Combat Units in Revolutionary Development." *Military Review* XLVII, 10 (October 1967).

Standord, Norman K. "Bamboo Brigades." *Marine Corps Gazette* L, 3 (March 1966).

Stockstill, Louis. "Truth in Packaging." *Journal of the Armed Forces* CV (9 September 1967).

Todd, Gary E. "Three-Point Program for Vietnam." *Marine Corps Gazette* LIV, 4 (April 1970).

"Vietnam Air War Objectives 'Soundly Conceived': Sec. Def." *Commanders Digest* III, 3 (August 1967).

Vought, LTC Donald B. "Preparing for the Wrong War?" *Military Review* LVII, 5 (May 1977).

"The War in Vietnam: Cam Ne (4)." *Marine Corps Gazette* XLIX, 10 (October 1965).

"War in Vietnam: Civic Action." *Marine Corps Gazette* XLIX, 10 (October 1965).

Weller, Jac. "The U.S. Army in Vietnam: A Survey of Aims, Operations, and Weapons, Particularly Small Infantry Units." *Army Quarterly and Defense Review* LXXXV, 1 (October 1967).

West, F. J., Jr. "Fast Rifles." *Marine Corps Gazette* LI, 10 (October 1967).

Westmoreland, GEN William C. "Vietnam in Perspective." *Military Review* LIX, 1 (January 1979).

Williamson, R. E. "A Briefing for Combined Action." *Marine Corps Gazette* LII, 3 (March 1968).

Zasloff, Joseph J. "Rural Resettlement in South Viet Nam: The Agroville Program." *Pacific Affairs* XXXV, 4 (Winter 1962–1963).

Contract Studies

1. The American University

Case Studies and Model for Pacification Support Operations. Washington: Advanced Research Projects Agency, 1968.

Conley, Michael C. *The Communist Insurgent Infrastructure in South Vietnam: A Study of Organization and Strategy.* Washington: The American University, Center for Research in Social Systems, 1967.

Jureidini, Paul A., et al. *Casebook on Insurgency and Revolutionary Warfare: 23 Summary Accounts.* Washington: The American University, Special Operations Research Office, 1962.

Nighswonger, William A. *Rural Pacification in Vietnam: 1962–1965.* Washington: The American University, Advanced Research Projects Agency, 1966.

2. The Bendix Corporation

Adkins, John H. *War Type, Population and Security: Keeping the Basics in Mind.* Ann Arbor, MI: The Bendix Corporation, 1972.

Prince, William G., et al. *Analysis of Vietnamization: A Description of the War, 1967–1970.* Ann Arbor, MI: The Bendix Corporation, 1971.

Prince, William G., and Tanter, Raymond. *The Republic of Vietnam Armed Forces under Varying Threat Conditions: Implications for a People's Army.* Ann Arbor, MI: The Bendix Corporation, 1971.

3. The Brookings Institute

Major Problems of United States Foreign Policy, 1950–1951. Washington: The Brookings Institute, 1950.

4. Booz-Allen Applied Research, Inc.

Program Review and Analysis Improvement System (PRAISE): Lessons Learned in Development, Conduct, and Phase-Over of Instruction to the Republic of Vietnam Armed Forces. Washington: Booz-Allen Applied Research, Inc., 1971.

5. Center for International Studies

Pike, Douglas E. *War, Peace, and the Viet Cong*. Cambridge: MIT Center for International Studies, 1969.

Psychological Studies of Southeast Asian Populations. Cambridge: MIT Center for International Studies, 1969.

Viet Cong Village Control: Some Observations on the Origin and Dynamics of Modern Revolutionary War. Cambridge: MIT Center for International Studies, 1969.

6. Center of International Studies

Gurr, Ted Robert, with Charles Ruttenberg. *The Conditions of Civil Violence: First Tests of a Causal Model*. Princeton, NJ: Research Monograph Number 28, Center of International Studies, April 1967.

7. Control Data Corporation

Penquite, J. L. *Hamlet Regression following the Departure of a Revolutionary Development Cadre Team*. New York: Final Report for Research Task Number 5B. Control Data Corporation, 1969.

8. The Hudson Institute

Basic Issues and Potential Lessons of Vietnam. 4 volumes. Croton-on-Hudson, NY: The Hudson Institute, Inc., 1970.

Preliminary Appraisal of People's Self-Defense Forces in South Vietnam. Croton-on-Hudson, NY: The Hudson Institute, Inc., 1969.

9. Human Sciences Research, Inc

Allnutt, Bruce C. *Marine Combined Action Capabilities: The Vietnam Experience*. McLean, VA: Human Sciences Research, Inc., 1969.

Analysis of PSYOP Effectiveness Indicators. McLean, VA: Human Sciences Research, Inc., 1973.

A Study of Mass Population Displacement in the Republic of Vietnam. 2 parts. McLean, VA: Human Sciences Research, Inc., 1969.

Bairdain, Ernest. *Psychological Operations Studies—Vietnam*. McLean, VA: Human Sciences Research, Inc., 1971.

Military Advising in Vietnam: 1969–1970. McLean, VA: Human Sciences Research, Inc., 1973.

Parsons, John S.; Brown, Dale K.; and Kingsbury, Nancy R. *Americans and Vietnamese: A Comparison of Values in Two Cultures*. McLean, VA: Human Sciences Research, Inc., 1968.

Sternin, Martin; Teare, Robert J.; and Nordlie, Peter G. *A Study of Values, Communications Patterns, and Demography of Rural South Vietnam*. McLean, VA: Human Sciences Research, Inc., 1968.

The Use of Cultural Data in Psychological Operations Programs in Vietnam. McLean, VA: Human Sciences Research, Inc., 1968.

10. Institute for Defense Analysis

A Review of Social Science Research in Vietnam with Procedural Recommenda-

tions for Future Research in Insurgent Settings. Arlington, VA: Institute for Defense Analysis, 1968.

Cooper, Chester L., *et al. The American Experience with Pacification in Vietnam: An Overview.* Arlington, VA: Institute for Defense Analysis, 1972.

Menkes, Joshua, and Jones, Raymond. *Pacification in Vietnam: A Survey.* Arlington, VA: Institute for Defense Analysis, 1968.

Preliminary Examination of the Hamlet Evaluation System. Arlington, VA: Institute for Defense Analysis, 1968.

11. Institute of Government Research

Volgy, Thomas. *What Have We Done? An Examination of Some Scholarly Literature on the Vietnamese Conflict.* Tucson: Institute of Government Research, University of Arizona, 1973.

12. The RAND Corporation

Accommodation in South Vietnam: The Key to Sociopolitical Solidarity. Santa Monica, CA: The RAND Corporation, 1967.

An Essay on Vietnamization. Santa Monica, CA: The RAND Corporation, March 1971.

An Examination of the Viet Cong Reaction to the Vietnamese Strategic Hamlet Operation. Santa Monica, CA: The RAND Corporation, July 1964.

Conversations with Enemy Soldiers in Late 1968/Early 1969: A Study of Motivation and Morale. Santa Monica, CA: The RAND Corporation, 1970.

Davison, W. P. *Some Observations of Viet Cong Operations in the Villages.* Santa Monica, CA: The RAND Corporation, 1968.

Davison, W. P., and Zasloff, Joseph J. *A Profile of Viet Cong Cadres.* Santa Monica, CA: The RAND Corporation, 1966.

Ely, Paul. *Lessons of the War in Indochina.* 2 volumes. Translated from the French by V. J. Croizat. Santa Monica, CA: The RAND Corporation, 1967.

Farmer, J. *Counterinsurgency: Principles and Practices in Viet-Nam.* Santa Monica, CA: The RAND Corporation, 1964.

Farmer, J. *Counterinsurgency: Vietnam 1962–1963.* Santa Monica, CA: The RAND Corporation, 1963.

Goodman, Allen E. *Government and the Countryside: Political Accommodation and South Vietnam's Communal Groups.* Santa Monica, CA: The RAND Corporation, 1970.

Impact of Pacification on Insurgency in South Vietnam. Santa Monica, CA: The RAND Corporation, 1970.

Jenkins, Brian M. *The Unchangeable War.* Santa Monica, CA: The RAND Corporation, November 1967. This bears a 'for official use only" classification.

Koch, J. A. *The Chieu Hoi Program in South Vietnam, 1963–1971.* Santa Monica, CA: The RAND Corporation, 1973.

Komer, Robert W. *Bureaucracy Does Its Thing: Institutional Constraints on US-GVN Performance in Vietnam.* Santa Monica, CA: The RAND Corporation, August 1972.

Mozingo, D. P., and Robinson, T. W. *Lin Piao on 'People's War': China Takes a Second Look at Vietnam.* Santa Monica, CA: The RAND Corporation, November 1965.

Negotiations and Vietnam: A Case Study of the 1954 Geneva Conference. Santa Monica, CA: The RAND Corporation, 1968.

Origins of the Insurgency in South Vietnam, 1954–1960: The Role of the Southern Vietminh Cadres. Santa Monica, CA: The RAND Corporation, 1967.

Pearce, Michael R. *Evolution of a Vietnamese Village: Duc Lap since November 1964*. Santa Monica, CA: The RAND Corporation, 1966.
User's Guide to the Rand Interviews in Vietnam. Santa Monica, CA: The RAND Corporation, 1972.
Vietnam: Lessons and Mislessons. Santa Monica, CA: The RAND Corporation, 1969.

13. Research Analysis Corporation

Bowie, David C., *et al. Pacification and Long-Term Development in Vietnam: Questionnaire Analysis*. McLean, VA: Research Analysis Corporation, 1966.
Clark, Dorothy, and Wyman Charles R. *An Exploration Analysis of the Reporting, Measuring, and Evaluating of Revolutionary Development in South Vietnam*. McLean, VA: Research Analysis Corporation, 1968.
Clark, Dorothy, Wyman, and Charles R. *The Hamlet Evaluation System in the Republic of Vietnam*. McLean, VA: Research Analysis Corporation, 1968.
Measurement of Pacification Progress in Vietnam. McLean, VA: Research Analysis Corporation, 1966.

14. The Simulmatics Corporation

A Socio-Psychological Study of Regional/Popular Forces in Vietnam. Cambridge, MA: Simulmatics Corporation, 1967.
Improving Effectiveness of the Chieu Hoi Program. Cambridge, MA: Simulmatics Corporation, 1967.
Observations on Psychodynamic Structures in Vietnamese Personality. Cambridge, MA: Simulmatics Corporation, 1966.

15. Southeast Asia Program, Cornell

Osborne, Milton. *Strategic Hamlets in South Viet-Nam*. Data Paper Number 55. Ithaca, NY: Southeast Asia Program, Cornell University, 1965.
Weinstein, Franklin B. *Vietnam's Unheld Elections*. Ithaca, NY: Southeast Asia Program, Cornell University, 1966.

Miscellaneous

Chandler, Robert W. "U.S. Psychological Operations in Vietnam, 1965–1972." Ph.D. dissertation, George Washington University, 1974.
Collins, John M. *The Vietnam War in Perspective*. Washington: National War College, 10 May 1972.
Doolittle, James H. *Officer–Enlisted Man Relationships*. Senate Document 196. Washington: Government Printing Office, 1946.
MacKercher, John C. *Personal Perceptions of the Vietnam War*. Washington: National Defense University, June 1975.
McConnell, J. P. *Air Force Policy Letter for Commanders*. Washington: Government Printing Office, 15 October 1967.
Sharp, ADM Ulysses Simpson Grant, and Westmoreland, GEN William C. Report on the War in Vietnam (as of 30 June 1968): *Report on Air and Naval Campaigns Against North Vietnam and Pacific Command-Wide Support of the WAR (June 1964–July 1968) and Report on Operations in South Vietnam (January 1964–June 1968)*. Washington: Government Printing Office, 1968.

The Effectiveness of Intercultural Relations Training for Vietnam Advisors. San Diego, CA: Naval Personnel and Training Research Laboratory, 1973.

Published Works

Abel, Elie, and Kalb, Marvin. *The Roots of Involvement: The U.S. in Asia, 1784–1971.* New York: W. W. Norton & Co., Inc., 1971.

Bain, Chester A. Vietnam: *The Roots of Conflict.* Englewood Cliffs, NJ: Prentice-Hall, Inc., 1967.

Baskir, Lawrence M., and Strauss, William A. *Change and Circumstance: The Draft, the War and the Vietnam Generation.* New York: Vintage Press, 1978.

Blaufarb, Douglas S. *The Counter Insurgency Era: U.S. Doctrine and Performance, 1950 to the Present.* New York: Glencoe Free Press, 1977.

Bletz, Donald. *The Role of the Military in U.S. Foreign Policy.* New York: Frederick A. Praeger, 1972.

Boyle, Richard. *Flower of the Dragon: The Breakdown of the U.S. Army in Vietnam.* San Francisco: Ramparts Press, 1972.

Bradford, Zeb, Jr., and Brown, Frederic J. *The United States Army in Transition.* Beverly Hills, CA: Sage Publications, 1973.

Braestrup, Peter. *Big Story: How the American Press and Television Reported and Interpreted the Crisis of TET 1968 in Vietnam and Washington.* 2 volumes. Boulder, CO: Westview Press, 1973.

Brandon, Henry. *Anatomy of Error: The Inside Story of the Asian War on the Potomac.* Boston: Gambit, Inc., 1969.

Browne, M. W. *The New Face of War.* New York: Bobbs-Merrill Company, 1965.

Buchanan, Keith. *The Southeast Asian World.* New York: Doubleday Anchor, 1968.

Burchett, Wilfred G. *Vietnam: Inside Story of the Guerrilla War.* New York: International Publishers, 1965.

Burling, Robbins. *Hill Farms and Padi Fields: Life in Mainland Southeast Asia.* Englewood Cliffs, NJ: Prentice-Hall, Inc., 1965.

Buttinger, Joseph. *The Smaller Dragon.* New York: Frederick A. Praeger, 1968.

Buttinger, Joseph. *Vietnam: A Political History.* New York: Frederick A. Praeger, 1968.

Cairns, J. F. *The Eagle and the Lotus: Western Intervention in Vietnam, 1847–1968.* Mystic, CT: Lawrence Verry, Inc., 1969.

Cameron, James. *Here Is Your Enemy.* New York: Holt, Rinehart and Winston, 1966.

Cerf, Jay H., and Posen, Walter, editors. *Strategy for the 60s: A Summary and Analysis of Studies Prepared by 13 Foreign Policy Research Centers for the United States Senate.* New York: Frederick A. Praeger, 1961.

Chaffard, Georges. *Indochine: dix ans d'indépendance.* Paris: Calmann-Levy, 1964.

Chinh, Truong. *Primer for Revolt: The Communist Takeover in Vietnam.* New York: Frederick A. Praeger, 1963.

Clutterbuck, Richard L. *The Long, Long War: Counterinsurgency in Malaya and Vietnam.* New York: Frederick A. Praeger, 1966.

Cole, Allan B., editor. *Conflict in Indochina and International Repercussions: A Documentary History, 1945–1955.* Ithaca, NY: Cornell University Press, 1956.

Cooper, Chester L. *The Lost Crusade: America in Vietnam.* New York: Dodd, Mead and Company, 1970.

Corson, LTC William R. *The Betrayal.* New York: W. W. Norton & Co., Inc., 1968.

Daly, James, and Bergman, Lee. *A Hero's Welcome: The Conscience of Sergeant James Daly vs. the United States Army.* Indianapolis, IN: Bobbs-Merrill Company, 1975.

Deane, Hugh. *The War in Vietnam.* New York: Monthly Press Review, 1963.

DeBoer, Cecil. *The If's and Ought's of Ethics: A Preface to Moral Philosophy.* Grand Rapids, MI: William B. Eerdmans Publishing Company, 1936.

Debray, Regis. *Revolution in the Revolution?* New York: Monthly Review Press, 1967.

Dramesi, LTC John A. *Code of Honor.* New York: W. W. Norton & Co., Inc., 1975.

Du Berrier, Hilaire. *Background to Betrayal: The Tragedy of Vietnam.* Boston: Western Islands Press, 1965.

Dareff, Hal. *The Story of Vietnam.* New York: Avon Books, 1967.

Draper, Theodore. *Abuse of Power.* New York: Viking Press, 1967.

Eden, Anthony. *Full Circle.* London: Cassell Publishers, 1960.

Eisenhower, Dwight D. *Mandate for Change: The White House Years, 1953–1956.* New York: Signet, 1963.

Ellis, Joseph, and Moore, Robert. *School for Soldiers: West Point and the Profession of Arms.* New York: Oxford University Press, 1974.

Emme, Eugene M. *The Impact of Air Power.* Princeton, NJ: D. Van Nostrand Company, 1959.

Enthoven, Alain C., and Smith, K. Wayne. *How Much Is Enough? Shaping the Defense Program, 1961–1969.* New York: Harper and Row, 1971.

Fall, Bernard B. *Ho Chi Minh on Revolution.* New York: Frederick A. Praeger, 1967.

Fall, Bernard B. *The Two Vietnams.* New York: Frederick A. Praeger, 1964.

Fifield, Russell H. *Americans in Southeast Asia.* New York: Thomas Y. Crowell Company, 1973.

Fifield, Russell H. *Southeast Asia in United States Policy.* New York: Frederick A. Praeger, 1963.

FitzGerald, Frances. *Fire in the Lake: The Vietnamese and the Americans in Vietnam.* Boston: Little, Brown and Company, 1972.

Gabriel, Richard A., and Savage, Paul L. *Crisis in Command: Mismanagement in the Army.* New York: Hill and Wang, 1978.

Galula, David. *Counterinsurgency Warfare: Theory and Practice.* New York: Frederick A. Praeger, 1964.

Gallucci, Robert L. *Neither Peace nor Honor: The Politics of American Military Policy in Vietnam.* Baltimore: The Johns Hopkins University Press, 1975.

Garrett, Banning, and Barkley, Katherine. *Two, Three ... Many Vietnams.* San Francisco: Harper and Row's Canfield Press, 1971.

Gavin, LTG James M. *Crisis Now.* New York: Random House, 1968.

Gettleman, Marvin E., editor. *Vietnam: History, Documents, and Opinions.* New York: New American Library Mentor, 1970.

Giap, Vo Nguyen. *Initial Failure of the US Limited War.* Hanoi: Foreign Languages Publication House, 1967.

Giap, Vo Nguyen. *Once Again We Will Win.* Hanoi: Foreign Languages Publication House, 1966.

Giap, Vo Nguyen. *People's War, People's Army.* New York: Frederick A. Praeger, 1962.

Giap, Vo Nguyen. *South Vietnam: A Great Victory.* Hanoi: Foreign Languages Publication House, 1967.

Giau, Tran Van, and Chat, Le Van. *The South Vietnam Liberation National Front.* Hanoi: Foreign Languages Publication House, 1962.

Gigon, Fernand. *Les Américains face au Vietcong.* Paris: Falmarion, 1965.

Goodman, Allen E. *Politics in War: The Bases of Political Community in South Vietnam.* Cambridge: Harvard University Press, 1973.

Gordon, Bernard K. *Toward Disengagement in Asia: A Strategy for American Foreign Policy.* Englewood Cliffs, NJ: Prentice-Hall, Inc., 1969.

Graff, Henry F. *The Tuesday Cabinet: Deliberation and Decision on Peace and War under Lyndon B. Johnson.* Englewood Cliffs, NJ: Prentice-Hall, Inc., 1970.

Gravel, Mike. *The Pentagon Papers.* 5 volumes. Boston: Beacon Press, 1970.

Guevera, Che. *Guerrilla Warfare.* New York: Frederick A. Praeger, 1961.

Halberstam, David. *The Best and the Brightest.* New York: Random House, 1972.

Halberstam, David. *The Making of a Quagmire.* New York: Random House, 1965.

Hammer, Ellen J. *The Struggle for Indochina.* Stanford, CA: Stanford University Press, 1954.

Hammer, Ellen J. *Vietnam Yesterday and Today.* New York: Holt, Rinehart and Winston, 1966.

Harvey, Frank. *Air War—Vietnam.* New York: Bantam Books, 1967.

Hauser, LTC William L. *America's Army in Crisis: A Study in Civil-Military Relations.* Baltimore: The Johns Hopkins University Press, 1973.

Heilbrunn, Otto. *Partisan Warfare.* New York: Frederick A. Praeger, 1962.

Henry, James B. *The Small World of Khanh Hau.* Chicago: Aldine Publishers, 1964.

Herbert, LTC Anthony, B. *Soldier.* New York: Dell Publishing Company, 1973.

Hermes, Walter G. *United States Army in the Korean War: Truce Tent and Fighting Front.* Washington: Government Printing Office, 1966.

Herr, Michael. *Dispatches.* New York: Avon Books, 1978.

Herring, Hubert. *A History of Latin America.* New York: Alfred A. Knopf Publishers, 1972.

Hickey, Gerald. *Village in Vietnam.* New Haven: Yale University Press, 1964.

Hilsman, Roger. *To Move a Nation: The Politics of Foreign Policy in the Administration of John F. Kennedy.* Garden City, NY: Doubleday, 1967.

Honey, P. J., editor. *North Vietnam Today.* New York: Frederick A. Praeger, 1962.

Hoopes, Townshend. *The Limits of Intervention.* New York: David McKay Company, 1969.

Johnson, Haynes, and Wilson, George C. *Army in Anguish: A Washington Post National Report.* New York: Pocket Books, 1972.

Jordan, Amos A. *Foreign Aid and the Defense of Southeast Asia.* New York: Frederick A. Praeger, 1963.

Jordan, Amos A. *Issues of National Security in the 1970s.* New York: Frederick A. Praeger, 1967.

Just, Ward. *Military Men.* New York: Alfred A. Knopf Publishers, 1970.

Kahin, George M., and Lewis, John W. *The United States in Vietnam: An Analysis in Depth of the History of America's Involvement in Vietnam.* New York: Delta Press, 1967.

Kaufman, William W. *The McNamara Strategy.* New York: Harper and Row, 1964.

Kendrick, Alexander. *The Wound Within: America in the Vietnam Years, 1945–1974.* Boston: Little, Brown and Company, 1974.

King, LTC Edward L. *The Death of the Army.* New York: Saturday Review Press, 1972.

Kinnard, Douglas. *The War Managers.* Hanover: University Press of New England, 1977.

Klare, Michael T. *War without End: American Planning for the Next Vietnams.* New York: Random House Vintage, 1972.

Knoll, Erwin, and McFadden, Judith N. *War Crimes and the American Conscience.* New York: Holt, Rinehart and Winston, 1970.

Kolko, Gabriel. *The Roots of American Foreign Policy.* Boston: Beacon Press, 1969.

Lacouture, Jean. *Ho Chi Minh: A Political Biography.* New York: Random House Vintage, 1968.

Lacouture, Jean. *Vietnam: Between Two Truces.* New York: Random House, 1966.

Lacouture, Jean, and Devillers, Philippe. *La Fin d'une Guerre, Indochine, 1954.* Paris: Editions du Seuil, 1960.

Lancaster, Donald. *The Emancipation of French Indochina.* London: Oxford University Press, 1961.

Lansdale, COL Edward. *In the Midst of War.* New York: Harper and Row, 1972.

Lederer, William J. *Our Own Worst Enemy.* New York: W. W. Norton & Co., Inc., 1968.

Lewy, Guenter. *America in Vietnam.* New York: Oxford University Press, 1978.

Loory, Stuart H. *Defeated: Inside America's Military Machine.* New York: Random House, 1973.

Lucas, Jim G. *Dateline: Vietnam.* New York: Award Books, 1967.

MacDonald, Charles B., and von Luttichau, Charles V. P. *The United States Army in Vietnam,* in Matlow, Maurice, editor, *American Military History.* Washington: Government Printing Office, 1969.

McAlister, John T., Jr. *Vietnam: The Origins of Revolution.* New York: Alfred A. Knopf Publishers, 1970.

McCuen, John J. *The Art of Counter-Revolutionary War: The Strategy of Counter-Insurgency.* Harrisburg, PA: Stackpole Press, 1966.

Mallin, Jay, editor. *"Che" Guevara on Revolution.* New York: Delta Press, 1969.

Mao Tse-tung. *Basic Tactics.* Translated by S. R. Schram. New York: Frederick A. Praeger, 1966.

Mao Tse-tung. *Selected Military Writings.* Peking: Foreign Languages Press, 1963.

Mecklin, John. *Mission in Torment.* Garden City, NY: Doubleday, 1965.

Milstein, Jeffrey S. *Dynamics of the Vietnam War: A Quantitative Analysis and Predictive Computer Simulation.* Columbus, OH: Ohio State University Press, 1974.

Minh, Ho Chi. *On Revolution.* New York: Frederick A. Praeger, 1967.

Murti, B.S.N. *Vietnam Divided.* New York: Asia Publishing House, 1964.

Mylander, Maureen. *The Generals: Making It, Military Style.* New York: Dial Press, 1974.

O'Connor, CH (COL) John J. *A Chaplain Looks at Vietnam.* Cleveland, OH: World Publishing Company, 1968.

O'Connor, Raymond G. *American Defense Policy in Perspective.* New York: John Wiley and Sons, 1965.

Osgood, Robert E. *Limited War.* Chicago: University of Chicago Press, 1957.

Paget, Julian. *Counterinsurgency Operations: Techniques of Guerrilla Warfare.* New York: Walker and Company, 1967.

Palmer, Dave Richard. *Readings in Current Military History.* West Point, NY: Department of Military Art and Engineering, USMA, 1969.

Pike, Douglas E. *Notes from the Underground: The Mystique of a Viet Cong.* Saigon: February 1962.

Pike, Douglas E. *Viet Cong: The Organization and Techniques of the National Liberation Front of South Vietnam.* Cambridge: MIT Press, 1966.

Polnar, Murray. *No Victory Parades: The Return of the Vietnam Veteran.* New York: Holt, Rinehart and Winston, 1971.

Pustay, J. A. *Counterinsurgency Warfare.* Glencoe, CA: The Free Press, 1965.

Pye, Lucien. *Guerrilla Communism in Malaya.* Princeton: Princeton University Press, 1965.

Race, Jeffrey. *War Comes to Long An: Revolutionary Conflict in a Vietnamese Province.* Berkeley, CA: University of California Press, 1972.

Roy, Jules. *The Battle of Dienbienphu.* New York: Harper and Row, 1965.

Schell, Jonathan. *The Village of Ben Suc.* New York: Alfred A. Knopf, Publishers, 1967.

Schlesinger, Arthur M., Jr. *The Bitter Heritage: Vietnam and American Democracy, 1941–1966.* New York: Fawcett World Library, 1966.

Schurmann, Franz; Scott, Peter Dale, and Zelnik, Reginald. *The Politics of Escalation in Vietnam.* Greenwich, CT: Fawcett Books, 1966.

Scigliano, Robert. *South Vietnam: Nation under Stress.* Boston: Houghton-Mifflin Publishers, 1963.

Shaplen, Robert. *The Lost Revolution: The U.S. in Vietnam, 1946–1966.* New York: Harper and Row Colophon, 1966.

Sinclair, Andrew. *Che Guevera*. New York: Viking Press, 1970.

Snepp, Frank. *Decent Interval*. New York: Vintage Press, 1978.

Snow, Edgar. *The Other Side of the River: Red China Today*. New York: Random House, 1961.

Steel, Ronald. *Pax Americana*. New York: Viking Press, 1967.

Sun Tzu. *The Art of War*. London: Oxford University Press, 1977.

Vaughan, LTC Curry N., with Bob Slosser. *Battleground: A Personal Account of God's Move upon the American Military Forces*. Plainfield, NJ: Logos International, 1978.

Vietnam Veterans against the War. *The Winter Soldier Investigation: An Inquiry into American War Crimes*. Boston: Beacon Press, 1972.

Taber, Robert. *The War of the Flea: A Study of Guerrilla Warfare, Theory, and Practice*. New York: Citadel Press, 1965.

Tanham, George K. *Communist Revolutionary Warfare*. New York: Frederick A. Praeger, 1962.

Taylor, GEN Maxwell D. *Swords and Plowshares*. New York: W. W. Norton & Co., Inc., 1972.

Terzani, Tiziano. *Giai Phong! The Fall and Liberation of Saigon*. New York: Ballantine Books, 1976.

Thai, Nguyen. *Is South Vietnam Viable?* Manila: Carmelo and Bauermann, Inc., 1962.

Thompson, Sir Robert K. G. *Defeating Communist Insurgency: The Lessons of Malaya and Vietnam*. New York: Frederick A. Praeger, 1966.

Thompson, Sir Robert K. G. *No Exit from Vietnam*. New York: David McKay Company, 1969.

Thompson, W. Scott, and Frizzell, Donaldson D. *The Lessons of Vietnam*. New York: Crane Russak and Company, 1977.

Tregaskis, Richard. *Vietnam Diary*. New York: Holt, Rinehart and Winston, 1963.

Trooboff, Peter D., editor. *Law and Responsibility in Warfare: The Vietnam Experience*. Chapel Hill, NC: University of North Carolina Press, 1975.

Walt, GEN Louis. *Strange War, Strange Victory*. New York: Ace Books, 1968.

Walter, Richard J. *Cold War and Counter-Revolution: The Foreign Policy of John F. Kennedy*. New York: Viking Press, 1972.

Warner, Denis. *The Last Confucian*. New York: Macmillan and Company, 1953.

Weigley, Russell F. *History of the United States Army*. New York: MacMillan and Company, 1967.

Westmoreland, GEN William C. *A Soldier Reports*. Garden City, NJ: Doubleday, 1976.

White, Ralph K. *Nobody Wanted War: Misperception in Vietnam and Other Wars*. Garden City, NJ: Doubleday, 1968.

Wilson, Dick. *Asia Awakes: A Continent in Transition*. New York: New American Library Mentor, 1970.

United States Air Force Air War College
Publications and Documents

Boatner, James G. *American Tactical Units in Revolutionary Development Operations.* Maxwell Air Force Base, Alabama: Air War College Research Report Number 3570, April 1968.

Lipsey, V. H. *Vietnamization or Victimization?* Maxwell Air Force Base, Alabama: United States Air Force Air University Study Number 4985, April 1973.

Milberg, Warren H. *The Future Applicability of the Phoenix Program.* Maxwell Air Force Base, Alabama: Auburn University/United States Air University master's thesis, 1967.

Miller, LTC William H. *US Army Infantry Tactics in Vietnam.* Maxwell Air Force Base, Alabama: Air War College Research Report Number 4045, May 1970.

Military Civic Action: *A Unique Approach in Military Assistance.* Maxwell Air Force Base, Alabama: Air War College, 1967.

United States Army
Army Combat Developments Command

Army Roles, Missions, and Doctrines in Low Intensity Conflict. Ft. Belvoir, VA: USACDC Institute of Advanced Studies Report, 1971.

Combat Operations Loss and Expenditure Data Reports—Vietnam. Ft. Belvoir, VA: USACDC, 1970.

Trip Report, Americal Division, 20–21 January 1968. Ft. Belvoir, VA: USACDC, 22 January 1968. Liaison Detachment.

Trip Report, 4th Infantry Division, 15–16 January 1968. Ft. Belvoir, VA: USACDC, 19 January 1968. Liaison Detachment.

Trip Report, 25th Infantry Division, 8 January 1968. Ft. Belvoir, VA: USACDC, 10 January 1968. Liaison Detachment.

United States Army
Army War College
Publications and Documents

Barnes, LTC James C. *The Battle of Khe Sahn: Sound Strategy or Costly Miscalculation?* Carlisle Barracks: USAWC case study, 5 February 1969. This is classified "secret."

Barnes, LTC Wilman D. *The Vietnam Barrier: Maginot Mentality or Imaginative Strategy?* Carlisle Barracks: USAWC student essay, 27 October 1967.

Bashore, LTC Boyd T. *Diem's Counterinsurgency Strategy for Vietnam:*

Right or Wrong? Carlisle Barracks: USAWC student case study, 20 April 1968.

Clemons, LTC Joseph G. *The Dilemma of the Vietnam Enclaves.* Carlisle Barracks: USAWC student essay, 13 January 1967.

Comprehensive Report: Leadership for the 1970s. United States Army War College Study of Leadership for the Professional Soldier. Carlisle Barracks: 20 October 1971.

Cutrona, LTC Joseph F. H. *Peace in Vietnam: An Acceptable Solution.* Carlisle Barracks: USAWC student essay, 22 April 1966.

Helms, LTC Norman S. *Replacement System in Vietnam from Buildup to Mid–1969.* Carlisle Barracks: USAWC case study, 8 May 1970.

Hesse, LTC Richard J. *Negotiations on Vietnam, 1954–1966.* Carlisle Barracks: USAWC student essay, 22 April 1966.

Huber, LTC Robert E. *How to Win in Vietnam.* Carlisle Barracks: USAWC student essay, 13 November 1967.

Instructional Bulletin 13: *Changes in Counterinsurgency Terminology.* Carlisle Barracks: USAWC student issue, 26 September 1966.

Kane, LTC Douglas T. *Coup d'état: The Threat to South Vietnam's Search for Stability.* Carlisle Barracks: USAWC student thesis, 1968.

Knapp, LTC William L. *Phoenix/Phuong Hoang and the Future: A Critical Analysis of the US/GVN Program to Neutralize the Viet Cong Infrastructure.* Carlisle Barracks: USAWC student essay, 1 July 1971.

Lay, LTC James R. *Search and Destroy Operations.* Carlisle Barracks: USAWC student essay, 13 November 1967.

Lee, LTC James M. *Which Strategy for Advanced Insurgency: Pacification or Combat?* Carlisle Barracks: USAWC student essay, 13 January 1967.

Lundberg, LTC John W. *The Army Oversea Personnel Replacement System in Future Wars.* Carlisle Barracks: USAWC student thesis, 8 March 1963.

Madden, LTC William R., Jr. *Did ARVN Invite War?* Carlisle Barracks: USAWC case study, 9 March 1970.

Montague, LTC Robert M. *Advising in Government: An Account of the District Advisory Program in South Vietnam.* Carlisle Barracks: USAWC student essay, 18 February 1966.

Montague, LTC Robert M. *Pacification: The Overall Strategy in South Vietnam.* Carlisle Barracks: USAWC student essay, 22 April 1966.

McCleary, LTC John E. *Military Factors Contributing to a Failure to Contain Insurgency in Vietnam During 1960–1963.* Carlisle Barracks: USAWC case study, 8 March 1971. This bears a "confidential" classification.

McConnell, LTC Richard E. *Franco-American Policy Divergence in Vietnam.* Carlisle Barracks: USAWC student thesis, 3 May 1965.

McMahon, LTC Richard A. *Let's Bury the Body Count.* Carlisle Barracks: USAWC student essay, 13 December 1968.

O'Neal, LTC Howard F. *Bomb North Vietnam—The Answer or a Searching Question?* Carlisle Barracks: USAWC student essay, 13 November 1967.

Palmer, LTC Joe M. *Factors Which Will Influence Political Negotiations in Vietnam.* Carlisle Barracks: USAWC student paper, 15 December 1965.

Patton, LTC George S. *Portrait of an Insurgent: A Study of the Motivation of the Main Force Vietnamese Communist Fighting Man.* Carlisle Barracks: USAWC student thesis, 25 April 1965. This bears a "secret" classification.

Phillips, LTC Y. Y. *An Appraisal of the Employment of U.S. Ground Troops in South Vietnam.* Carlisle Barracks: USAWC student paper, 14 April 1967.

Prillaman, LTC Richard L. *Is History Repeating Itself in Vietnam?* Carlisle Barracks: USAWC student thesis, 25 May 1968.

Roush, LTC Maurice D. *Strategy for Vietnam: Pacification or Combat?* Carlisle Barracks: USAWC student paper, 9 October 1967.

Sedberry, LTC George R. *Army Replacements.* Carlisle Barracks: USAWC student thesis, 25 January 1960.

Smith, LTC Bill G. *Revolution and Rebellion in Vietnam.* Carlisle Barracks: USAWC student thesis, 3 May 1965.

Smith, LTC Charles R. *Repetitive Tours in Vietnam for Infantry Captains.* Carlisle Barracks: USAWC staff study, 10 February 1969. This bears a "confidential" classification.

Study on Military Professionalism. Carlisle Barracks: USAWC study for the army chief of staff, 30 June 1970.

"War Termination—A Synopsis." *Selected Readings*: Military Strategy Seminar. Carlisle Barracks: USAWC student issue.

Weart, LTC Douglas S. *Limited Surprise in Limited War.* Carlisle Barracks: USAWC student essay, 13 November 1967.

United States Army
Center for Military History
Vietnam Studies

Eckhardt, MG George S. *Command and Control, 1950–1969.* Washington: Government Printing Office, 1974.

Ewell, LTG Julian J., and Hunt, MG Ira A., Jr. *Sharpening the Combat Edge: The Use of Analysis to Reinforce Military Judgment.* Washington: Government Printing Office, 1974.

Fulton, MG William B. *Riverine Operations, 1966–1969.* Washington: Government Printing Office, 1973.

Hay, LTG John H., Jr. *Tactical and Material Innovations.* Washington: Government Printing Office, 1974.

Heiser, LTG Joseph M. *Logistic Support.* Washington: Government Printing Office, 1974.

Kelly, COL Francis J. *Army Special Forces, 1961–1971.* Washington: Government Printing Office, 1973.

Ott, MG David E. *Field Artillery, 1954–1973.* Washington: Government Printing Office, 1975.

Pearson, LTG Willard R. *War in the Northern Provinces.* Washington: Government Printing Office, 1975.

Ploger, MG Robert R. *US Army Engineers, 1965–1970.* Washington: Government Printing Office, 1974.

Rogers, LTG Bernard W. *CEDAR FALLS—JUNCTION CITY: A Turning Point.* Washington: Government Printing Office, 1974.

United States Army
Command and General Staff College
Publications and Documents

Bernard, LTC Carl F. *The War in Vietnam: Observations and Reflections of a Province Senior Advisor.* Ft. Leavenworth: USACGSC student paper, October 1969.

Chapman, MAJ James H. *The US Army and Pacification in Vietnam: An Assessment of the Army's Ability to Cope with an Insurgency.* Ft. Leavenworth: USACGSC student report, 1976.

Damewood, MAJ John H., and Terrell, MAJ Thompson A., III. *Neutralization of the Viet Cong Infrastructure by US/GVN, 1960–1970.* Ft. Leavenworth: USACGSC student paper, 25 May 1976.

Daxe, MAJ Arnold, Jr., and Stemberger, CPT Victor J. *Vietnam Assessment: Officer Professionalism.* Ft. Leavenworth: USACGSC student paper, 1976.

Dickey, MAJ James S. *Vietnam Assessment: The American Spirit, The Army Officer, and Vietnam—A Commentary.* Ft. Leavenworth: USACGSC student paper, 1976.

Draude, MAJ Thomas V. *When Should a Commander Be Relieved? A Study of Combat Reliefs of Commanders of Battalions and Lower Units during the Vietnam Era.* Ft. Leavenworth: USACGSC student paper, 1976.

1st Brigade, 101st Airborne Division. Tactical Lessons of the Vietnam War. Typescript in the USACGSC Library.

1st Infantry Division. Tactical Lessons of the Vietnam War. Typescript in the USACGSC Library.

Gavin, LTG James M. Speech to the USACGSC student body. 3 March 1976.

Headquarters. XXIV Corps. Defense Against Sapper Attacks. 14 March 1969. Typescript in the USACGSC Library.

Lujan, MAJ Armando; Menig, MAJ David; and Beck, CPT Dwight A. *The US Army Force in Vietnam, 1969–1975: A Study in Macro Force Development.* Ft. Leavenworth: USACGSC student paper, 1976. This work bears a "confidential" classification.

Lowry, MAJ William I. *Strategic Assessment of the War in Vietnam: Truman through Kennedy.* Ft. Leavenworth: USACGSC student paper, 1976.

Miller, J. T. "Integrity and Reality and Writing Up OERs." *Army* XXVII, 4 (April 1977), reproduced in Military Ethics pamphlet P913-1. Ft. Leavenworth: USACGSC student issue.

Moellering, LTC John H. *Neo-Uptonianism: A Likely Occurrence in the Army's Professional Officer Corps Today?* Ft. Leavenworth: USACGSC student paper, 1972.

Nolen, MAJ William R. *Vietnam Assessment: Base Camp, Night Defensive Positions and Fire Support Base Defense.* Ft. Leavenworth: USACGSC student essay, 1976.

Sauvageot, LTC Jean A. *Update of the Situation in the Republic of Vietnam.* Ft. Leavenworth: USACGSC report, 18 February 1975. This work bears a "secret" classification.

Timmes, MG Charles J. Speech to the USACGSC student body. 9 April 1975.

Weyand, GEN Fred G., and Summers, LTC Harry G., Jr. *Vietnam Myths and American Military Realities.* N.p., n.n., n.d. Printed copy located in USACGSC Library.

Westmoreland, GEN William C. Speech to the USACGSC student body. 11 April 1978.

United States
Department of the Army

Army Regulation 612-1: *Personnel in a Training, Transient, and Patient Status.* Washington: Government Printing Office, 29 October 1958.

Army Regulation 612-2: *Personnel Processing—Preparing Individual Replacements for Oversea Movement (POR) and US Army Oversea Replacement Station Processing Procedures.* Washington: Government Printing Office, 18 August 1969.

Army Regulation 614-30: *Assignments, Details, and Transfers—Oversea Service.* Washington: Government Printing Office, 22 October 1968.

A Study of Army Manpower and Personnel Management. Office of the Director of Coordination and Analysis Systems Analysis Division. Washington: Government Printing Office, May 1965.

Comments on Report of the Replacement Board: Memorandum. Army General Staff, G-1. Washington: Government Printing Office, 15 January 1948.

DA Pamphlet 20-211: *The Personnel Replacement System in the United States Army.* Washington: Government Printing Office, 1954.

DA Pamphlet 20-212: *History of Military Mobilization in the United States Army, 1775–1945.* Washington: Government Printing Office, 1955.

DA Pamphlet 135-3: *A Guide to Reserve Components of the Army.* Washington: Government Printing Office, July 1977.

DA Pamphlet 360-411: *A Pocket Guide to Vietnam.* Washington: Government Printing Office, 5 April 1966.

Field Manual 12-2: *Adjutant General Support in Theaters of Operation.* Washington: Government Printing Office, 16 January 1968.

Field Manual 31-73: *Advisor Handbook for Counterinsurgency.* Washington: Government Printing Office, 23 April 1965.

Field Manual 100-20: *Internal Defense and Development, U.S. Army Doctrine.* Washington: Government Printing Office, 28 November 1974.

Replacement System, World-Wide, World War II: *Report of the Replacement Board.* Washington: Government Printing Office, 12 December 1947.

Study of the Twelve Month Vietnam Tour. Deputy Chief of Staff for Personnel (DCSPER). Washington: Government Printing Office, 29 June 1970.

Theater Army Replacement System: Memorandum 66-3. Ft. Benjamin Harrison: Adjutant General School, November 1968.

The Replacement System in the U.S. Army: An Analytical Study of World War II Experience. Washington: Government Printing Office, 14 September 1950.

US Army Replacement System: Staff Study. Deputy Chief of Staff for Personnel (DCSPER). Washington: Government Printing Office, 10 March 1959.

United States
Military Assistance Advisory Group
(USMAAG)

Lessons Learned Number 30: Psychological Warfare/Civil Action. Saigon: US-MAAG, 1963.

Village Early Warning System: Reports Covering Current Status of System in Dar Lac and Phu Yen Provinces. Saigon: USMAAG, 1962.

United States
Military Assistance Command, Vietnam
(USMACV)

Analysis of the Hamlet Evaluation System. Saigon: USMACV, 1969.

Command Information Pamphlet 4-67: Revolutionary Development. Saigon: USMACV, February 1967.

Command Information Pamphlet 11-67: The Religions of Vietnam. Saigon: USMACV, April 1967.

Counter Measures against Standoff Attacks: Lessons Learned Number 71. Saigon: USMACV, 13 March 1969.

GVN National Police Fact Sheet. Saigon: USMACV, 6 June 1967.

Pacification Attitude Analysis System (PAAS). Saigon: USMACV, 1971.

Revolutionary Development Cadre Fact Sheet. Saigon: USMACV, 5 March 1967.

Terrorist Incident Reporting System. Saigon: USMACV, 1971.

The Concept of Pacification and Certain Definitions and Procedures. Serial Number 0270. Saigon: USMACV, 2 March 1965. This bears a "confidential" classification.

The Rural Development Cadre System Command Manual. Saigon: USMACV, 1970.

Types of Cadres in GVN Fact Sheet. Saigon: USMACV, 8 December 1967.

U.S. Combat Forces in Support of Pacification: Lessons Learned Number 80. Saigon: USMACV, 1965.

Village and Hamlet Elections. Saigon: USMACV, April 1967.

United States Army
Senior Officer Debriefing Reports
(SODR)

Barsanti, MG O.M. Commanding General. 101st Air Cavalry Division, July 1968 to July 1969.

Bringham, LTC John L. District Senior Adviser. Tuyen Duc Province, May 1971 to December 1972.

Carrinton, COL George B. Senior Adviser. Capital Military District, MACV, March 1968 to October 1968.

Corcoran, LTG Charles A. Commanding General. First Field Force, Vietnam (IFFV), May 1968 to February 1970.

Dickerson, BG George W. Commanding General. 3d Brigade, 82d Airborne Division, December 1968 to December 1969.

Matheson, BG S. A. Commanding General. 1st Brigade, 101st Air Mobile Division, 2 March 1968.

McAuliffe, BG D. P. District Senior Adviser. MR3. December 1969 to November 1970.

Ochs, BG E. R. Commanding General. 173d Airborne Brigade, August 1970 to January 1971.

Peer, BG Carleton, Jr. District Senior Adviser, III Corps and III CTZ, May 1969 to November 1969.

Pepke, MG Donn R. Commanding General. 4th Infantry Division, November 1968 to November 1969.

Smith, LTC Robert E. Senior Adviser. Pleiku Province, May 1971 to December 1972.

Stephens, COL Travis. Province Senior Adviser, II CTZ. 12 March 1970.

Stone, MG Charles P. Commanding General, 4th Infantry Division, August 1970 to January 1971.

Tolson, MG John J. Commanding General. 1st Cavalry, April 1967 to July 1968.

Wagner, LTC Robert E. Senior Adviser. Quang Tin Province, December 1970 to July 1972.

Weyand, LTG Fred C. Commanding General. II Field Force, Vietnam (IIFFV), 29 March 1966 to 1 August 1968. "Secret" classification.

Zais, LTG Melvin. Commanding General. XXIV Corps, June 1969 to June 1970.

United States
United States Army, Vietnam
(USARV)

Battlefield Reports: A Summary of Lessons Learned. Volume I, 30 August 1965 and Volume II, 30 June 1966. Tan Son Nhut: USARV, 1966.

Biographical Sketch—90th Replacement Battalion. Long Binh: USARV, 1969.

Biographical Sketch—22d Replacement Battalion. Cam Ranh Bay: USARV, 1969.

Employment of Airmobile ARVN Forces in Counterinsurgency Operations. Washington: U.S. Army Concept Team in Viet Nam, 1973.

Fire Support Base Defense, Final Report. Project Number ACG-80f. Washington: USARV, 6 April 1972.

1st Brigade, 5th Infantry Division (Mechanized). Operations Report—Lessons Learned, period ending 31 October 1968. USARV, 7 March 1969.

196th Light Infantry Brigade (Separate). Operations Report—Lessons Learned, 1 February 1967 to 30 April 1967. USARV, [n.d.].

3d Brigade, 82d Airborne Division. Operations Report—Lessons Learned, period ending 30 April 1968. USARV, 4 September 1968.

3d Brigade, 82d Airborne Division. Operations Report—Lessons Learned, period ending 31 October 1969. USARV, 19 March 1970.

22d Replacement Battalion. Operations Report—Lessons Learned, 1 June 1966 to 31 January 1967. USARV, [n.d.]

Replacement Battalion Workload; Statistical Report of Workload in 22d and 90th Replacement Battalions for Period May 1968 through August 1969. Saigon: USARV, 1969.

Tour 365. Saigon: USARV, 1969.

United States
Agency for International Development
(USAID)

Jickling, David. Improving the Administration of Revolutionary Development. Saigon: USAID, January 1967.

Sansom, Robert L. "Working Paper on Viet Cong Economics." Washington: USAID Economic Division, April 1967.

The 1967 Revolutionary Development Program. Office of Field Operations Memorandum Number 200-66. Saigon: USAID, 9 December 1966.

United States Congress

U. S. Congress. Alleged Assassination Plots Involving Foreign Leaders: An Interim Report of the Select Committee to Study Governmental Operations with Respect to Intelligence Activities: United States Senate. Washington: Government Printing Office, November 1975.

U. S. Congress. Congressional Record, C, 1037. Washington: Government Printing Office, 9 July 1954.

United States Department of Defense

Counterinsurgency Research and Development Symposium Proceedings. Meeting of 15–17 September 1970 at Ft. Bliss, TX. Arlington: Advanced Research Projects Agency, 1970.

News Release. Office of the Assistant Secretary of Defense for Public Affairs. Washington: 13 November 1974.

Reemphasis on Pacification: 1965–1967: United States—Vietnam Relations, 1945–1967. Washington: Government Printing Office, 20 September 1971.

The Final Forty-Five Days in Viet Nam. Defense Attaché Office, 22 May 1975.

United States Department of State

Bulletin. Department of State. Washington: Government Printing Office, 12 June 1950.

Bulletin. Department of State. Washington: Government Printing Office, 3 July 1950.

We Will Stand in Vietnam. Washington: Government Printing Office, 1970.

United States Information Agency (USIA)

The Viet Cong: Community, Party, and Cadre (Research Report R-74-66). USIA. Washington: Government Printing Office, April 1966.

The Viet Cong: Patterns of Communist Subversion (Research Report R-8-66). USIA. Washington: Government Printing Office, January 1966.

United States Marine Corps

Parker, William D. *Civil Affairs in I Corps, Republic of South Vietnam, April 1966 to April 1967.* Historical Branch, G-3 Division, USMC. Washington: Government Printing Office, 1970.

Stolfi, Russel H. *U.S. Marine Corps Civic Action Efforts in Vietnam, March 1965–March 1966.* Historical Branch, G-3 Division, USMC. Washington: Government Printing Office, 1968.

The Marines in Vietnam, 1954–1973: An Anthology and Annotated Bibliography. History and Museums Division, USMC. Washington: Government Printing Office, 1974.

The Marines in Vietnam: The Advisory and Combat Assistance Era, 1954–1964. History and Museums Division, USMC. Washington: Government Printing Office, 1974.

United States Office of Civil Operations (OCO)

Military-Civil Teams. Saigon: OCO, 22 March 1967.

Report on Revolutionary Development (New Life Development Division

Operational Memorandum Number 05-67). Saigon: OCO, 16 January 1967.

United States Operating Mission, Vietnam

Vietcong Use of Terror: A Study. Saigon: USOM, V. May 1966.

Index